Aboriginal Art and Australian Society

Aboriginal Art and Australian Society
Society

Hope and Disenchantment

Laura Fisher

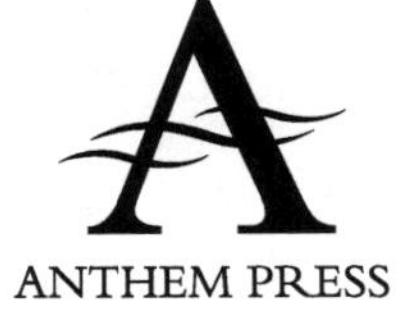

ANTHEM PRESS

Anthem Press
An imprint of Wimbledon Publishing Company
www.anthempress.com

This edition first published in UK and USA 2019
by ANTHEM PRESS
75–76 Blackfriars Road, London SE1 8HA, UK
or PO Box 9779, London SW19 7ZG, UK
and
244 Madison Ave #116, New York, NY 10016, USA

First published in the UK and USA by Anthem Press 2016

British Library Cataloguing-in-Publication Data
A catalogue record for this book is available from the British Library.

ISBN-13: 978-1-78527-182-3 (Pbk)
ISBN-10: 1-78527-182-2 (Pbk)

This title is also available as an e-book.

For David Fisher

CONTENTS

Preface and Acknowledgements — xi

Introduction — 1

Part I.   **Governance, Nationhood and Civil Society** — **15**

Chapter 1.   New Intercultural Relationships in the Post-Assimilation Era — 17

     1.1   Cultural Trauma in Australian Public Culture — 17

     1.2   The End of Assimilation and the Rise of Aboriginal Culture — 18

     1.3   Paul Keating, Indigenised Settler Nationalism and Reconciliation — 27

Chapter 2.   Aboriginal People Mobilising Aboriginal Art — 31

     2.1   Aboriginal Art Mobilised in Political and Legal Domains — 31

     2.2   Aboriginal Art, Activism and Pan-Aboriginal Identity — 33

     2.3   Urban Indigenous Aesthetic Public Spheres — 38

Chapter 3.   Understanding Aboriginal Art Subsidy — 41

     3.1   'Meaningful Work': Making Sense of Aboriginal Art Subsidy — 41

     3.2   The Ambiguity of Aboriginal Art Sector Policy — 46

Chapter 4.   The State Mobilising Aboriginal Art — 49

     4.1   The Acquisition, Endorsement and Appropriation of Aboriginal Art and the Growth of Aboriginal Public Culture — 49

Chapter 5.   'Aboriginal Culture' at the Nexus of Justice, Recognition and Redemption — 57

     5.1   Cultural Loss, Cultural Rights and Keeping Culture Strong — 57

| | 5.2 | Aboriginal Art as Metonymic for Aboriginal Culture | 64 |
| | 5.3 | Conclusion to Part I | 68 |

Part II.   **Contemporary Aboriginal Art in the 1980s**   **71**

Chapter 6.   The Emergence of Aboriginal Art in the 1980s   75
- 6.1   The Cultural Cringe and Provincialism   76
- 6.2   The Emergence of Contemporary Aboriginal Art   77
- 6.3   Artistic and Critical Approaches to Aboriginal Art   79
  - 6.3.1   Cultural convergence and rapprochement   79
  - 6.3.2   'Killing me softly': cultural colonialism and ethnocide   81
  - 6.3.3   Landscape and tribalism   83
  - 6.3.4   Appropriation   83
  - 6.3.5   Postmodernism and conceptualism   86
  - 6.3.6   Social justice   88
- 6.4   The Overseas Reception of Aboriginal Art   89
- 6.5   Postcolonial Critique and Urban Aboriginal Voices   93
- 6.6   The Bicentenary   96
- 6.7   Conclusion to Part II   97

Part III.   **Negotiating Difference**   **103**

Chapter 7.   Negotiating Aboriginal Difference   105
- 7.1   Four Facets of Difference   105
- 7.2   The Cosmopolitan and the Tourist: Being an Outsider with Aboriginal Art   111
- 7.3   Authenticity and 'The Story'   113

Chapter 8.   The Art/Anthropology Binary   117
- 8.1   The Disciplinary Relationship between Art and Anthropology   121
- 8.2   Western Secularisation and the Differentiation of Primitive Art   125
- 8.3   Anthropology, Colonialism and the Urban Aboriginal Art Movement   126
- 8.4   Conclusion to Part III   129

Part IV.   **Aboriginal Art, Money and the Market**   **133**

Chapter 9.   Ethics and Exploitation in the Aboriginal Art Market   139
- 9.1   The Bifurcation of the Aboriginal Art Market   143
- 9.2   Where Does the Value of Aboriginal Fine Art Reside?   145
- 9.3   Morality and Money in the Aboriginal Art Arena   149

Chapter 10.   'Aboriginal Mass Culture' and the Cultural Industries   155
          10.1   A Critical History of 'Aboriginal Mass Culture'
                 and Visual Culture   155
          10.2   Aboriginal Art and Culture and the Cultural
                 Industries   160
          10.3   What Do 'Aboriginal Mass Culture' and the
                 Cultural Industries Do to Aboriginal Fine Art?   164
          10.4   Aboriginal Artistic Labour, the Economic
                 Imperative and the Crisis of Aboriginal
                 Art's Value   166
          10.5   Conclusion to Part IV   170

Conclusion   173

Notes   185

References   199

Index   235

PREFACE AND ACKNOWLEDGEMENTS

This book has taken shape over ten years, with the majority of the research undertaken between 2007 and 2012 when I completed my doctorate at the University of New South Wales. It seems a good idea to recall the atmosphere in which I began. At that time there was a sense of extraordinary momentum surrounding the Aboriginal art movement. The first National Indigenous Art Triennial, *Culture Warriors*, was staged at the National Gallery of Australia in 2007, and the gallery was preparing its expansive Indigenous art wing, which was launched in 2010. Significant exhibitions of John Mawurndjul (Basel, Switzerland and Hannover, Germany) in 2006, and Emily Kame Kngwarreye (Osaka and Tokyo, Japan) in 2008, and the varied architectural commissions for the Musée du quai Branly in Paris seemed to signal that Aboriginal artists were reaching audiences offshore in a way that few Australian artists had in the country's history. Both the primary and secondary market in Aboriginal art had become intensely competitive as Aboriginal art experienced a speculative boom befitting the years immediately prior to the global financial crisis. Many people were wondering whether Aboriginal artists themselves were benefiting from this boom.

This was surely a significant moment in Australian cultural history, and my aim when I began my PhD was to draw together the many threads of artistic and social change that had led to this moment. But more than this, I wanted to understand how Indigenous people's pursuit of justice in the settler state had shaped Aboriginal art's trajectory and inflected its meanings. This line of questioning remains at the heart of this book.

Despite the reworkings that have occurred in subsequent years, the book retains something of the outlook of my younger self, and is still in some ways moored to the climate of acceleration, expansion and controversy in which I was immersed. It focuses largely on the years between the election of Prime Minister Gough Whitlam and the global financial crisis. While it does touch on some events and debates of the very recent past, the present circumstances of Indigenous affairs, for example, are for the most part beyond its scope. I became less insecure about this retrospectivity while listening to the public commentary following the deaths of Gough Whitlam in 2014 and his successor Malcolm Fraser in 2015. I hope that the book's value lies in the story it tells about two significant trajectories of social change that were galvanized by Whitlam's reforms: the transformation of Australian artistic culture and the transformation of the political relationship between Indigenous and non-Indigenous Australians. The book traces the activities in the arts and culture, in activism, in civil society and in governance that reveal how these trajectories were not just concurrent, but evolved in dynamic relation with each other.

There are many people who have helped me to write this book. My doctoral candidature was supported by the inaugural Petre Foundation Scholarship at UNSW. I wish more people were aware of Daniel Petre's dedication to fostering a stronger philanthropic culture in Australia, and I thank him for selecting what was really a left-field project, and for his kind and personable support. I also extend heartfelt thanks to my supervisor Paul Jones for making my PhD journey – drawn out as it was – calm and fulfilling. Paul's generosity, pragmatism and humour gave me the confidence to think meta and find a language with which to explore the vexed questions that underlie this project. His approach to social and cultural research remains a touchstone of my own research ethos. I also feel very fortunate to have had Claudia Tazreiter as my cosupervisor, and thank her for her warmth and encouragement. Tim Rowse and Fred Myers examined my doctoral thesis, and this book has benefited greatly from their scrutiny of my research as examiners, and the ideas we've shared in subsequent discussions. I admire both immensely as scholars who work across disciplines and unfailingly bring analytical depth to the problems they study, and I learn something new each time I revisit their work.

In 2008 and 2009 I was employed as a research assistant on the Storylines Project, writing Indigenous artists' biographies for *Design and Art Australian Online* (DAAO). During this time I worked closely with co-researchers Vivien Johnson and Tess Allas, as well as DAAO 'boss' Olivia Bolton. The Storylines Project greatly enriched the research process I undertook for this book, as I had the privilege of interviewing many Indigenous artists who taught me about the art that falls in the cracks between the so-called urban and remote. Shirley Angus is one such artist who has shared her life with me and is now a friend, and others from whom I learnt a great deal were Janine McAullay Bott and Lucy Williams Connelly. More than this, I have been personally enriched by the friendships of Vivien, Tess and Olivia, who have each in different ways contributed to my understanding of not only Aboriginal art but also why art matters.

This book has been informed by interviews I conducted during my PhD with art collectors, gallerists, dealers, curators, auction house professionals, artists, scholars and others both in Australia and Europe. These interviews challenged my assumptions in surprising ways, and this book would have turned out very differently had I not left the library and had these conversations. There were also numerous informal conversations which fuelled my thinking. I thus owe a great debt to the following people for sharing their reflections and observations with me: Merryn Schriever, Charlie Cooper, Wally Caruana, Michael Hill, Helen Tilbury, Elizabeth Death, Stefano Spaccapietra, Jennifer Biddle, David Throsby, Richard Moore, Jilda Simpson, Nardi Simpson, R E A, Gerd Plewig, Ann Snell, Adam Knight, Michael Reid, Bertrand Estrangin, Brenda L. Croft, Tim Acker, Brian Tucker, David Smith, Alastair Stevenson, Howard Morphy, George Petitjean, Djon Mundine, Neil Murphy, Bernice Murphy, Christopher Hodges, Dana Kornhauser, Laurentia Leon, Christine Godden, Chris Reid, Alison Kelly, Tim Klingender, Josh Lilly, Will Owen, Robert Norris, Beverly Knight, Margo Neale, Luc Berthier, Theresa and Gérard Burkhardt, Catherine Crawford, Euan Hills, Anne De Waal, Mary Durack, Graeme Galt, Bill Gregory and Bruce Latimer.

There are certain people who I wish to thank particularly for their generosity and comradeship as fellow researchers, and for providing feedback on drafts and ideas at turning points in the development of this book. They are Jon Altman, Chrischona Schmidt, Lisa Stefanoff, Michael Symonds and Vivien Johnson. Tony Bennett and Veronica Tello provided indispensable advice as I prepared to reconstruct the thesis into a manuscript that a publisher might take seriously. John Gardiner-Garden at the Australian Parliamentary Library was kind enough to look over my accounts of the policy changes mapped in this book, and I thank him for his very helpful comments. In recent years I have worked collaboratively with Gay McDonald on writing projects that treat certain ideas and histories that are also explored in this book. I know the rewriting process has benefited from the open exchange of ideas that has underpinned this collaboration, and I look forward to its next phase.

In 2015 I began a post-doctoral fellowship at Sydney College of the Arts, University of Sydney. After several years of unpredictable casual work, I was able to complete the final editing stages of this book in a quiet office in the peaceful surrounds of this beautiful campus. In these leaner times when opportunities for younger researchers are thinning, the privilege of these circumstances is not lost on me. Thanks to Jacqueline Milner, Ann Elias, Bianca Hester, Colin Rhodes, Saskia Beudel, Oliver Watts, Robyn Backen and Mikhaela Rothwell for their welcome.

I am indebted to the three anonymous reviewers for their insightful and considered feedback, which helped me refine the manuscript and think more carefully about its scope. Thanks also to Reko Rennie for graciously granting me permission to use an image of his artwork on the cover, and photographer Paul Patterson and the City of Sydney for providing the image. And thanks to the editorial and copyediting team at Anthem Press and Mark for help with the indexing task.

Parts of this book have appeared previously in article or book chapter form, and I thank the respective publishers for allowing them to be reproduced in modified form here. Chapter 8 is derived in part from the article 'The Art/ Ethnography Binary: Post-colonial Tensions within the Field of Australian Aboriginal Art' published in *Cultural Sociology* 6(2) in 2012, http://cus.sage-pub.com/content/6/2/251.abstract, doi: 10.1177/1749975512440224. I am grateful to the peer reviewers and editor David Inglis for their very helpful feedback, which assisted me in clarifying the arguments presented in that chapter as a whole. Chapter 10 is derived in part from the article 'Aboriginal Mass Culture: A Critical History' published in *Visual Studies* 29(3) in 2014, copyright Taylor and Francis, available online http://www.tandfonline.com/ doi:10.1080/1472586X.2014.941556. This article also benefited greatly from the critical feedback of reviewers. Finally, sections of Part IV were published as the chapter 'Some Reflections on Aboriginal Art's Relationship with Money' in the collection *Art and Money* (2015), edited by Peter Stupples. These are published with the permission of Cambridge Scholars Publishing. I extend thanks to Peter Stupples and the audience to whom I delivered the paper at the *Art and Money* Symposium in Dunedin, New Zealand, in 2013.

My son Max was born in October 2009, when I was halfway through the PhD, and I have been hugely fortunate to have had the support of family members and friends both when completing the thesis and the book. My mother, Wendy, and mother-in-law, Gillian, met the challenge as grandmothers; I couldn't have done it without them. I am also grateful to Tom and Andy for their ongoing support, as well as to Michael and Suzie, Sally and Steve, Cherry, Roger, Wendy, Chris and Sarah. Max himself makes the academic life seem more bizarre by the minute, and a life of art seem hugely more sensible. My final thanks are extended to my husband, Jamie, for casting his sharp editorial eye over this manuscript in its early and later phases and deliberating over every problem with me. Your passion for the creative life and pursuit of the true and the good always uplifts and inspires me.

INTRODUCTION

In the 1960s and 1970s, Australian governments relinquished the idea that Aboriginal society and culture would inevitably diminish and began dismantling the segregationist and assimilationist paradigms of Indigenous policy that had prevailed for the previous century. Not only were governments now obliged to address the obstacles that prevented Aboriginal people from participating in mainstream Australian society, Aboriginal citizens were recognised as constituting a distinct people who had retained unique traditions and values in spite of colonisation. The corollaries of this acknowledgement were policies and civic discourses of atonement, and interventions designed to forestall further cultural loss and to empower Aboriginal people to determine their own cultural futures. In subsequent decades the implications of this transition were negotiated in the theatres of land rights and native title, the National Inquiry into the Separation of Aboriginal and Torres Strait Islander Children from their Families, Reconciliation, the History Wars, the rise and fall of the Indigenous governance organisation ATSIC[1] and many others. They have also been negotiated through the flourishing of Aboriginal cultural forms in the arts and popular culture, particularly, as I will explore in this book, through the medium of Aboriginal art.[2]

The many strands of the contemporary Aboriginal art movement – though continuous with older, precolonial traditions – can be mapped closely against the political changes that have taken place since the 1960s. Indeed in some ways the story of Aboriginal art can be read as the poetic manifestation of two interrelated projects of the post-assimilation era: on the one hand, a dispossessed people's struggle for emancipation and recognition, and on the other, a redemptive programme pursued by governments and members of civil society to embrace Indigenous people's difference and establish a positive space for this difference within the nation. Aboriginal art has amplified Indigenous demands for justice and recognition and confronted contemporary forms of racism and discrimination. It has also been a vital forum for asserting Indigenous land custodianship and picturing the aftermath of dispossession and colonisation. Yet as much as it has been a platform for Indigenous cultural expression, it has been a medium through which non-Indigenous Australians have encountered this amorphous thing called "Aboriginal culture", contemplated the miracle of its survival and regeneration, and contended with the question of how they themselves are implicated in the ethical problems that sit at the heart of the settler state condition.

This book is a historical study of Aboriginal art, but one that diverges somewhat in intent and approach from the art historical tradition. The reader will find that, with few exceptions, I engage only cursorily with specific artists and their artworks. Instead, I pursue a kind of macroanalysis of Aboriginal art's presence and mutability across different social, political and cultural domains. The book thus takes a step back from the experiences, the political and social concerns, the heritage and the place-specific meaning of Aboriginal art, about which there is now so much excellent literature. It aims to encourage an understanding of the other forces that have galvanised Aboriginal art and made it meaningful in Australian society – forces that often exceed the very premises of fine art discourses or are only presented in a superficial way.

In essence this book explores how Aboriginal art has been entangled with Australian society's negotiation of Indigenous people's status within the nation. As James Clifford argues, when we study Indigenous movements we need to locate them in 'shifting power relations, particular histories of conquest, hegemony, and inventive survival that interact with new regimes of freedom and control' (2013, 14–15). Aboriginal art's many idioms materialise the way Indigenous people as individuals and as a collectivity have negotiated these intercultural fields of power relations. Clifford's words underline the need for scrutiny of Aboriginal art's traverse of the fields of Indigenous social justice movements and Indigenous affairs governance – as art, as symbolic visual culture, as a vehicle for Indigenous agency and a vehicle for Indigenous policy. With this in mind, my hope is that the book achieves two things. First, I hope it contributes to the development of a more nuanced understanding of Aboriginal art's reception in Australian society. Second, I hope it illuminates the aesthetic dimensions of a range of governmental, intellectual, activist and civil society projects that have negotiated Australian histories of loss and profound inequality and the continued presence of Indigenous ways of being. In other words, I hope people recognise that the Aboriginal art movement provides a valuable vantage point from which to better understand recent Australian cultural and political history.

Aboriginal art has both problematised Western aesthetic values and reached far beyond the aesthetic sphere to inhabit national public culture in complicated ways. In view of this I have approached the Aboriginal art phenomenon sociologically, which entails looking at art as a forum of meaning making that arises through social relationships and recognising that it is a repository of cultural information that exceeds the intentions of the artist (Shiner 2001; Wolff 1981; 1983; Bourdieu 1993; Eyerman 2006). Reading Aboriginal art *with* the artist and articulating the biographical, poetic and conceptual dimensions of their work – a project that has in itself been immensely challenging in many circumstances – only gets us so far. As Alfred Gell writes, 'Art objects are characteristically "difficult". They are difficult to make, difficult to "think", difficult to transact. They fascinate, compel, and entrap as well as delight the spectator. Their peculiarity, intransigence, and oddness is a key factor in their efficacy as social instruments' (1998, 23). Gell's take on art as 'enmeshed in a texture of social relationships' points to why we need to draw on a range of historical and critical resources to properly locate the Aboriginal art movement in the intercultural spaces of the post-assimilation era. We also need to be prepared to demystify art's conventions in the areas of curatorship, art criticism, the art market and so on. Some of the greatest tensions around Aboriginal art's meaning and value have arisen when these conventions have been unable to assimilate aspects of Aboriginal art, and ultimately it is through close examination of these tensions that we can elicit the most important truths. I am by no means the first to take this approach: Fred Myers's thorough and persistently astute *Painting Culture* (2002) brings ethnographic and sociological insights to bear on the movement of Papunya painting into the high-art sphere between the 1970s and the end of the millennium. Vivien Johnson's biographies of Michael Nelson Jagamarra (1997) and Clifford Possum Tjapaltjarri (2003), accounts of the Papunya movement (e.g., 2007, 2015) and consideration of Aboriginal art's commercial appropriation (1996) are similarly enlightening in a sociological sense. Jon Altman has consistently provided vital economic and policy analysis of the movement, in the 1989 Review of the Aboriginal Arts and Crafts Industry (Altman et al. 1989) and numerous other publications (e.g., Altman 1988, 2005a, Altman et al. 2002). And Nicholas Thomas's *Possessions: Indigenous Art/Colonial Culture* (1999), Howard Morphy's *Becoming Art* (2008) and Ian McLean's *White Aborigines* (1998) and compilation *How Aborigines Invented the Idea of Contemporary Art* (2011) are also far-reaching investigations of the place of Aboriginal art in Australian culture and the challenge it poses to fine art traditions to which I've often returned while writing this book.

In drawing out the points at which cultural, social, political and economic dimensions of Aboriginal art's story interconnect, it has been necessary to prioritise thematic continuities over temporal continuities. This means that the book examines the Aboriginal art phenomenon prismatically rather than chronologically, and historical context is woven through each chapter. I hope the reader will forgive the redundancies and overlaps that could not be avoided with this approach. For the most part, the book focuses on the years leading up to the 2006–2007 Inquiry into Australia's Indigenous visual arts and craft sector.

The chapters are organised into four parts. Part I examines the governance paradigms, political movements and public discourses that together established a place for affirmative formulations of Aboriginal culture in Australian public life. It revolves around a fact that is regularly acknowledged in Aboriginal art scholarship but is not so frequently substantiated in great depth: Aboriginal art has mediated the redemptive political and civil society project that followed from the decline of the assimilation paradigm. Rather than reviewing the way this project has provided the context for the flourishing of the Aboriginal art movement, I treat the two as evolving symbiotically. On the one hand, we see how the prerogatives of restoring Aboriginal people's dignity, improving their social and economic well-being and renovating the national image shaped the way Aboriginal art was subsidised and came to prominence in Australian visual culture. On the other, we see how the aesthetic power of Aboriginal art has been harnessed to serve a range of agendas in Indigenous and national affairs.

Part II focuses on a particularly dynamic period in Aboriginal art's history: the 1980s. During this decade Aboriginal art was embraced as a somewhat iconoclastic contemporary art movement at a time when the Australian art world was in a state of upheaval. The unprecedented vitality and critical tendencies of Australian art practitioners, writers and curators gave rise to a range of complex dialogues between non-Indigenous and Indigenous cultural expressions. Concurrently, Indigenous social justice concerns were brought to bear on the institutional, professional and funding frameworks of the Australian art world.

Part III examines the way Aboriginal difference is negotiated in the Aboriginal art arena. It explores the way art norms and ascriptions of value are complicated by the ethnic specificity of Aboriginal art, and interact with the wider social, political and moral questions that attend to Aboriginal identity in Australian society. This is illustrated by the contested status of anthropological expertise, which I explore in detail.

Part IV explores the way Aboriginal art and culture was rapidly commercialised and accrued value in the fine arts market in parallel with the aesthetic, intellectual and governance trajectories discussed in earlier sections of the book. Here the discourses around ethics and exploitation in the Aboriginal art market are the focus, and I argue that they reflect the high stakes involved in sustaining particular models of consecration that mask and distort many of the social and economic realities underpinning the creation of Aboriginal art. In this culminating discussion I am particularly concerned to show that the idealistic narrative of Aboriginal art that sees art, and fine art in particular, as a forum for Aboriginal cultural resurgence struggles to accommodate the economic objectives that have driven the Aboriginal art movement's evolution.

A Historical Overview of Aboriginal Art

The following provides a brief historical account of the Aboriginal art movement, and is likely to only be of value to readers not familiar with Aboriginal art.[3] To understand the reasons for the eclecticism of the category of Aboriginal art, we need to both recall the precolonial foundations of Aboriginal expressive forms and consider how current forms of Aboriginal art have been shaped by the uneven history of colonialism in Australia. Prior to colonisation, a highly complex visual language, in conjunction with song, dance and performance, articulated totemic identities, ancestral histories, and the moral infrastructure of Indigenous society. These forms narrate the 'Dreaming', a temporally unbounded body of religious knowledge that explains the origin of all life, recognises the natural environment as embodying the essence of creation beings and defines people's obligations as custodians of the land.[4] Indigenous people had ties to strictly differentiated areas of land. While it has long been thought that there was a hunter-gatherer society, there is growing recognition of Indigenous agriculture and aquaculture, including the systematic and timely use of fire that ensured the regeneration of varied plant species and preserved open pastures for grazing (by kangaroos and other animals). Thus across Australia, Aboriginal groups kept animal and plant-based foods in abundance and defended against the unpredictability of rain (Pascoe 2014; Gammage 2012). There were hundreds of linguistically distinct nations, and the practicalities of survival within each distinct territory were founded in an inalienable familial, moral and legal order (Sutton 1988; Rose 1996).

The first British colonies were established in the south-east of the continent in the late eighteenth and early nineteenth centuries. Many Indigenous nations in these areas were partially or wholly destroyed by frontier warfare, disease and the depletion of food sources. Vast areas of the desert interior and the northern tropics remained relatively free of European incursion well into the twentieth century. Until the 1920s, Aboriginal people were subject to ad hoc policies of racial segregation or 'protection', which were in part underpinned by the belief that they would eventually die out. Between the 1930s and the early 1970s, assimilation policies instituted by governments throughout Australia led to the forced removal of entire communities from traditional lands to centralised reserves, missions and towns and the removal of Indigenous children from their families to be placed with white carers or in institutions. Aboriginal people became wards of state, subject to a web of intrusive and often punitive state and church control rationalised by the goal of eradicating Aboriginal cultural consciousness and practices and bringing Aboriginal people into the fold of white society (Stanner 1968; National Inquiry 1997; Haebich 2000).

From the first decades of colonisation, pastoralists, government officials, navy and army servicemen, naturalists, anthropologists, museum collectors and travellers acquired cultural objects from Indigenous people, often by trading them for tobacco and other goods. At the mission stations, Indigenous wards were often encouraged to produce artefacts, paintings on bark (unique to Arnhem Land), curios and small craft and textile items decorated with Indigenous motifs to be sold in the larger towns, usually to raise money for the settlements (Jones 1988; Moore 2006; Taçon and Davies 2004). These objects were widely circulated from the early years of the twentieth century, particularly in the interwar years.

The first Aboriginal artist to receive wide acclaim was Albert Namatjira, a Western Arrente man based in Hermannsberg in Central Australia. In 1936 Namatjira received a small amount of painting tuition from the visiting non-Indigenous watercolourist Rex Batterbee, and was encouraged to paint by Friedrich Albrecht, the pastor of the Lutheran Mission within which Namatjira had been born and raised. His watercolours of the region quickly gained attention and became extremely popular among the non-Indigenous public, partly due to the influx of domestic tourists visiting Alice Springs and the inland regions at this time (Haynes 1998). Many people were attracted to his singularity as an Aboriginal person participating in white society, and in the 1940s and 1950s he attained celebrity status as a kind of exotic icon of assimilation. The Australian art establishment was sceptical however: in general they regarded him as a skilled imitator of Western technique, and through the emerging lens of modernism he was seen to have forsaken his tribal artistic traditions for a naturalistic genre of painting that was becoming passé (Thomas 1992; Kleinert 1992). It was some years before his work was re-evaluated (Hardy et al. 1992; French 2002). Many of Namatjira's descendants and affiliates learnt from him and established what is now known as the Hermannsburg School, which has fostered both watercolour painting practices and a distinctive style of painted and figurative pottery. Beyond this he inspired generations of Aboriginal artists across the country and helped to generate the popular awareness that much of Aboriginal art expresses a deep connection with the land.

What is now known as the contemporary Aboriginal art movement began in 1971–72, when Papunya Tula Artists was incorporated as a nonprofit company by Aboriginal men in Papunya, a remote government settlement that had been established in 1959 to administer a number of Central Desert tribes. Several of these men had been producing carvings, artefacts and paintings in previous years and/or were affiliated with the Hermannsburg watercolour school. Geoffrey Bardon, an erudite, sympathetic and idealistic school art teacher, then helped to galvanise the Papunya painting movement in 1971–72.

Bardon encouraged the men to produce paintings of their Dreamings on small boards in a strictly symbolic and nonrepresentational style drawn in part from sacred ground and body paintings.

These events overlapped with the election of the progressive Labor government of Gough Whitlam and the introduction of the policy of Aboriginal self-determination, which was premised upon recognition of Indigenous cultural autonomy and agency. As will be explored in Part I, this policy entailed that Indigenous people in remote regions were encouraged to return to their traditional lands, a move made possible by welfare support. At the same time, the Aboriginal Arts Board (AAB) was formed within the Australia Council for the Arts. The board provided financial and logistical support to Papunya Tula Artists, and with the efforts of a few pioneering collectors, art centre coordinators and museum professionals, Papunya paintings eventually found a place in the contemporary Australian art world (Bardon 1999; Myers 2002; Johnson 2007; 2010). In the following decades, art production spread to other parts of the country and was taken up by women, and many more art centres and art collectives were established across the country. Distinctive practices and styles emerged in the Kimberley region of Western Australia, in Northern Queensland and the Torres Strait, and other areas (Lüthi and Lee 1993). The bark painting tradition, which had its origins in the decoration of the walls of bark shelters, rock art and body painting, flourished in Arnhem Land, and wood carving traditions from around the country were increasingly seen in sculptural terms (Taylor 1996a; Morphy 2008). During the 1970s and early 1980s, the Aboriginal Arts Board and a suite of government trading outlets facilitated the sale and exhibition of Aboriginal art works at outlets in major cities and underwrote the fledgling art centres (Peterson 1983; Altman et al. 1989). A young generation of artists who had grown up in or moved to the cities as young adults also began creating politically astute and formally diverse works, taking advantage of unprecedented opportunities to study art at colleges and universities, and in some cases forming collectives like the Boomalli Aboriginal Artists Co-operative in Sydney and the Campfire Group in Brisbane (Croft 1999; Eather 2005).

Indigenous artists take a variety of approaches to representing and interpreting Indigenous knowledge and ancestral traditions and to exploring those aspects of Australian history and politics that have shaped their experience and the experiences of their families and communities. As Indigenous curator Hetti Perkins writes: 'The possibilities of Aboriginal art practice are infinite and can have relevance and resonance outside their immediate cultural context while maintaining the integrity of speaking from within that context. We belong to this country; always have, always will' (1997, 19). These words are drawn from the catalogue of the *fluent* exhibition that represented Australia at the 1997 Venice Biennale, which included the work of the three Indigenous women artists: Yvonne Koomatrie, a weaver and member of the Ngarrindjeri people based in the Murray River region in South Australia; Judy Watson, a Waanyi woman and multi-disciplinary artist based in the city of Brisbane; and Emily Kame Kngwarreye, an Anmatyerr painter from the Utopia community in Central Australia.[5] Perkins's description points to the unity and diversity of contemporary Aboriginal art and how difficult it is to characterise its many strands – typified by these artists' practice – in a summative way. Thus Aboriginal art today encompasses paintings that are produced with both natural and synthetic mediums and supports. There are also locally specific art forms such as pearl shell and emu egg carvings, possum-skin cloaks, hollow log coffins, carved or woven spirit figures, shell necklaces, painted ceramics and various forms of fibre art. Printmaking and fabric design are widely practiced, as are installation, photography, video, animation and a range of other digital forms, and numerous artists have been commissioned to create temporary and permanent public art works. All of these approaches are brought into dialogue with the heterogeneous practices that comprise the field of global contemporary art.

In the last twenty years the number of art centres that facilitate art production in remote areas has fluctuated, however the most recent research documented 87 as operational in 2012 (Woodhead and Acker 2014). Almost all rely on government funding. Modelled to some degree on the Papunya Tula Artists cooperative they have evolved to be 'part business, part community centre, part creative studio' (Acker and Sullivan 2014, 168). As Jon Altman writes:

> [they are] invariably incorporated organisations that have artists as their members. The members elect management committees that form the governing body and this governing body employs staff. These are hybrid organisations, at once cultural and commercial, local and global, Aboriginal and non-Aboriginal – fundamentally inter-cultural and operating between thoroughly different locales. (2005a, 6; see also Wright 1999; ORIC 2012)

These management committees elect art centre coordinators, or art advisors, who in almost all cases are non-Indigenous. These coordinators are required to mediate between the markedly different domains of remote communities and the cosmopolitan art market. Many artists also sell directly to dealers, wholesalers and other intermediaries who either visit the artists, or are based in Alice Springs, the largest town in Central Australia, which has a large, transient Indigenous population (Acker et al. 2013).

The history of the Aboriginal art market and the emergence of the category of Aboriginal fine arts are the subject of later chapters; however, here I will highlight one further characteristic of the Aboriginal art world to conclude this brief history and set the stage for later discussions. Even though Aboriginal art is remarkably heterogeneous, 'remote' and 'urban' Aboriginal art are strongly differentiated, and it is usually very easy for art audiences to place an Aboriginal art work in either of these categories. Remote Aboriginal art tends to be understood as art that is produced in the Central and Western Deserts, the 'Top End' and Alice Springs. It is created by artists who do not have an art school education and who tend to draw on traditional knowledge, ceremonial designs and the teachings of elder artists to make work about their particular Dreamings and Country, though there is also a flourishing movement of figurative and new media works. Urban Aboriginal art refers to art produced by Aboriginal artists who reside in metropolitan centres and who, for the most part, have had a tertiary-level art education. The most successful of these are cosmopolitan in their outlook and traverse multiple idioms of contemporary art, and their work is often seen to be overtly political. The moniker *urban Aboriginal art* endures despite being heavily disputed. For example, artist Richard Bell argues that the work it names 'often speaks of contemporary injustices against our people' and that because of this, 'Liberation art is a far more accurate term that may also help to discourage the perpetual attempts to ghettoise us' (Croft 2007a, 59). As Bell implies here, the opposition of urban and remote reproduces essentialist ideas about Aboriginal culture and who 'has it' and who doesn't. In addition, the crude geographic distinction presumed by urban and remote bears little relation to the life-paths of many Aboriginal artists, not least because it excludes rural towns, where a large proportion of Aboriginal people live or have lived (Mundine 2009a; Gibson 2013).

Hope and Disenchantment

As I researched this book, I found that *hope* and *disenchantment* captured something of the contrasting moods I encountered again and again in Aboriginal art discourses. In 1987 Geoffrey Bardon, who had played a pivotal role in the establishment of the Aboriginal painting movement in the Central and Western Deserts, made the following statement at an exhibition opening in Melbourne:

> The painting movement articulated once more with immense brilliance the relationship of these [people] to their land. It gave them pride of self and let them once more become men and women speaking in their own right and their own traditions [...] I sense that 200 years of neglect and discrimination cannot be reversed within one generation or even two, yet the painting movement points for all of us toward a great resurgence of the human spirit in this country. (Quoted in Ryan 2004, 73)

This quotation expresses the sense of optimism and utopianism that can be found in many Aboriginal art discourses. As we will see throughout the book, Aboriginal art has anchored a range of aspirations, including the desire to rejuvenate an ancient culture, empower Aboriginal people in the face of injustice and racism and alleviate Aboriginal poverty. It has also been a source of hope for those who wish for a reformed, inclusive and less homogenous national culture that does not always favour Anglo-Saxon identities over the numerous other ethnicities that make up Australian society. And within the art world, Aboriginal art's unanticipated success has appeared to signal that the trenchant cultural prejudices of the Western fine arts system are weakening. However, counterposed to these there have been a range of pessimistic and dystopian perspectives. For example, the Aboriginal art movement has been characterised as the final frontier of colonial oppression due to the unbridled commodification of various images and motifs, and Aboriginal artists have been portrayed as enslaved to the market. It is also frequently suggested that Aboriginal art is popular largely because it allows non-Indigenous Australians to sustain a fantasy of postcolonial virtue. These countervailing perspectives reveal how the complexities inherent in Indigenous/non-Indigenous relations in the post-assimilation era, particularly around the figurations of Aboriginal victimhood and agency, suffuse the Aboriginal art arena.

The poles of hope and disenchantment also remind us that Aboriginal art has been configured as an ethical project for so many people (Indigenous and non-Indigenous) who have participated in the art's development. Throughout the book I maintain a preoccupation with ethical concerns, or matters of conscience, that have arisen in relation to Aboriginal art: efforts to facilitate meaningful cross-cultural dialogue, to redress historical wrongs and ameliorate suffering, to pursue justice and equality and so on. When these kinds of ethical concerns arise in the Aboriginal art arena, we are able to discern how affective forces have been consequential in Aboriginal art's story in both obvious and subtle ways. In particular, by tracing the imprint of altruistic and sympathetic sentiments, we can discern how Aboriginal art has been a vehicle by which non-Indigenous Australians have become invested in the problems that arise from the settler state condition.

The Romantic Artist and the Primitive

Some final remarks are needed to frame an art historical project of this kind. Much of my analysis in what follows takes place at a reflexive distance from some of the traditions of art history and criticism. It thus seems necessary to review the aesthetic values and the sensibilities associated with the idea of the artist that are presupposed by those traditions. I will focus here on the

interrelated figures of the Romantic artist and the primitive, which are reference points for several discussions in this book.

It is not always acknowledged that, notwithstanding postmodernism's decon-
struction of the humanistic faith that underpinned the Romantic movement,
our current understandings of the place of art in society and the subjectivity
of the artist retain many of the ideals of eighteenth- and nineteenth-century
Romanticism. As they faced the upheaval of the Industrial Revolution and
the associated decline of courtly and aristocratic patronage, artists, poets and
writers were compelled to participate in an impersonal marketplace as specialist producers. Their insecurity in these circumstances kindled a defensive
attitude: repelled by industrial capitalism, they sought to stand apart and insu-
late themselves from its effects. Many saw the artist as duty-bound to both
preserve aspects of humanity that were under threat and be champions of a
better world. The fulcrum of potential change was the imagination, 'the highest moral quality' (Calinescu 2006, 106). In the poet Percy Shelley's words, 'A
man, to be greatly good, must imagine intensely and comprehensively; he must
put himself in the place of another and of many others [...] The great instrument of moral good is the imagination' (1904, 34). At the same time, the liber-
tarian creeds of the French Revolution and its disruption of social, economic
and political institutions fomented a powerful drive not only to radicalise society but also to discover or create the self anew. All of these forces gave rise to
a highly idealised notion of the artist as a marginal and embattled member of
society endowed with heightened sensibility, imagination and insight (Hauser
1962 [1951]; Shiner 2001). In Raymond Williams' summation, Romanticism
characterised art as 'the embodiment [...] of certain human values, capacities, energies, which the development of society towards an industrial civilisation was felt to be threatening or even destroying' (1958, 36).

As Wolff writes, the Romantics' responses to industrialisation go some way
to explaining why we currently tend to see the artist as 'outside society, marginal, eccentric, and removed from the usual conditions of ordinary people
by virtue of the gift of artistic genius' (1981, 10, 26–27; see also Lunn 1982).
We have not relinquished the idea that it is the right and obligation of the
artist to create in absolute freedom in the service of, as William Wordsworth
declared, the 'embodied spirit of a people' (quoted in Williams 1958, 34).
These convictions accounted for the artists' contempt for the urbanised masses
and the bourgeoisie, and their hatred of the idea that they should accede to
any notion of the popular or seek to gratify an ignorant and capricious public
(Hauser 1962, 166).

So how does primitivism fit into this history? The Romantic artists drew inspiration from the writings of eighteenth-century scholars such as Giambattista
Vico, Jean-Jacques Rousseau and Johann Gottfried Herder, in which the

primitive subject was pictured as living freely within nature and as being most alive to their senses, emotions, imagination and attuned to the divine (Cocchiara 1981). These scholars refuted the interpretations of Enlightenment rationalist thinkers who had preceded them, who saw the customs and beliefs of 'primitive' and 'common' people as being pure superstition, irrelevant to history and anachronistic to progress. The Romantic scholars encouraged people to appreciate popular ancestral traditions as the repository of humanity's heritage and to admire the rustic and steadfast 'volk' of the peasant village as embodying the nationally distinctive roots of a universal human spirit. For their part, the Romantic artists shared the scholars' aversion to the Enlightenment concepts of reason, order and objective truth, feeling that they helped justify the utilitarian and economic rationalist processes of industrialisation. They too championed folkloric forms of culture over the formulaic yields of mass production (Williams 1958, 37–42; 1977, 14). They explored mysticism and mythology and formulated new understandings of the divine in the face of secularism that were often linked to an exalted sense of the natural world. Folklore poetry, tales and ballads that were either recovered from the past or documented from living traditions were gathered together, translated and published in several European countries. As Paul Jones writes, this material 'aided the formulation of a series of central critical tenets of Romanticism: the preference for "primitivist" or "exotic" artworks ('cultural primitivism'); the related hostility to the formal rules of neo-classicist composition and criticism ... [and] the celebration of spontaneous creativity' (2004, 32). Peasant societies were depicted as remnant examples of the 'organic community' of a utopian past; a domain of genuine fellowship and belonging within which art, music, storytelling and performance figured in the everyday (Leavis quoted in Jones 2004, 5).

Much has been written about primitivism as a paradigm premised on colonialism and Western practices of 'cultural and ideological appropriation' that affirm a self-serving logic of modern progress (Myers 2006, 268; Araeen 1987; Price 1989; Torgovnick 1990; Russell 2001). Less is written on the primitivist moorings of many of the affective and existential dimensions of the Western artistic project that most of us continue to cherish. Miller (1991) has argued that primitivism is a kind of ubiquitous modern ideology, suggesting that all art of the modern period can be characterised as 'a fragmented comment upon the nature of fragmentation' that never relinquishes the ideal of resolution (54). He remarks that 'Primitivism stands for that aspect of the Romantic movement which is based on the assumption that there exists a form of humanity which is integral, cohesive, and works as a totality' (54–55). As this book aims to illuminate the varied ethical problems that have arisen around Aboriginal art, and because much remote Aboriginal art is appreciated from a formalist, modernist vantage point, it seems essential to consider how and why people engage with Aboriginal art in relation to nostalgic and utopian currents of thought that contemplate the condition of modernity. At the risk of alienating some readers before this book has even begun, I am suggesting that we not forget that primitivism has been a vehicle for ethical and utopian thought as well as racist thought, and that it is approaching intellectual bad faith to ignore the threads of primitivist thought that comprise the heritage of current fine arts values out of a desire to disavow colonialism. As I will explain in the conclusion to this book, Aboriginal art has appealed to some audiences precisely because it resonates with compelling moral interrogations of capitalist modernity.

The Limitations of the Text

I wish to conclude with some important caveats. In seeking to offer a comprehensive and synthetic analysis of the Aboriginal art phenomenon and its place in Australian society, I have necessarily generalised across different domains of art creation that are in a state of flux. While I do my best to ensure that the examples I refer to are not isolated cases, local particularities have no doubt been overlooked. Further, given the rapidly changing dynamics of Aboriginal sociality and art practice, and the volatile history of the Aboriginal art market and funding arrangements, it is also possible that some changes have not been sufficiently accounted for.

While writing this book I was frequently asked whether I had visited remote community art centres and interviewed artists. When I began the project I recognised that to approach the subject in this way would pose insoluble ethical and practical problems for a book whose subject was the Aboriginal art movement in its entirety, and whose primary focus was the meaning that the movement had acquired within the Australian art world, and within Australian public culture in the post-assimilation era. Strange as it may seem, the decision not to visit communities and interview artists was one made out of respect for artists, given the history of white researchers who come and go, and the impossibility of doing justice to the social worlds to which the art is tied. My research draws on written sources that contain artists' discourses, as well as the writings of those who have worked within artists' domains, and I have learnt a great deal from the Indigenous artists, curators and academic colleagues whom I've worked with and in some cases interviewed over the years in association with other research projects. My 'fieldwork' was largely conducted in the arenas of the reception of Aboriginal art: exhibition openings and talks, public and private galleries and art auctions. I also interviewed a range of Aboriginal art collectors, art dealers, curators and auction house professionals in Australia, England, the Netherlands, France, Switzerland and Germany.

Although only a small number of these are quoted (anonymously) in this book, they all shaped my understanding immensely.

The question is: is this approach adequate for a book that aims to explore Aboriginal art as an *intercultural* phenomenon? Some might say no. However relations of interculturality in Australia take many forms, from the most immediate and mutually affecting to the very distant, momentary and selective (in the sense that the vast majority of non-indigenous Australians can choose whether or not to allow Indigenous issues to have any moral bearing on their lives) (Merlan 1998, 2013; Altman and Hinkson 2010). The accounts of Aboriginal art written by scholars like Fred Myers, Howard Morphy, Vivien Johnson, John Carty, Djon Mundine, Christine Nicholls, Françoise Dussart, Jennifer Biddle, Jon Altman, Luke Taylor and others are characteristically localist and arise from relationships of reciprocity, and they enlighten readers both to the ontological specificity of Aboriginal art practices and their responsiveness to non-Indigenous values, meanings and so on. This book pursues its questions largely in the latter sphere of interculturality, where Indigenous/non-Indigenous relations are heavily mediated by discursive and visual representations. In formulating my arguments I have relied upon the remarkable scholars, writers, art centre coordinators and professionals, Indigenous and non-Indigenous, who *have* made it possible for the rest of us to better understand Aboriginal art practices and who have ensured that Aboriginal artists who predominantly speak Indigenous languages or otherwise don't participate in the mainstream art arena have a voice within the domain of Australian art.

In sum, I hope that what has been gained by undertaking a 'meta' analysis and focusing on the field of reception compensates for what has been omitted and that this book can be read as complementing the many rich studies of particular strands of the Aboriginal art movement. I also hope that its weaknesses provide new departure points for Aboriginal art scholarship.

Part I

GOVERNANCE, NATIONHOOD AND CIVIL SOCIETY

In the post-assimilation era – dating roughly from the 1960s to the 2000s – the status of Indigenous Australians, and popular understandings of Indigenous identity and culture, underwent radical changes in Australian society.[1] As Attwood writes, at this time 'the problem of Australian national identity and Aboriginal rights became increasingly intertwined' (2005, 25). In this context Aboriginal art has been called on to broker two interconnected relationships: that which exists between Indigenous people and the state, and that which can be said to exist at a national level between Indigenous and non-Indigenous citizens. To put this another way, Aboriginal art has stood at the interface between the redemptive project of the settler state and the movements for rights and recognition that have been pursued by Indigenous people, both of which depend on the reflexive engagement of non-Indigenous civil society for their success. It is perhaps hazardous to take as a starting point three entities that are so internally fragmented and reciprocally entwined: the Indigenous community, the state and civil society. Nevertheless, we can only grasp the nuances of Aboriginal art's social meanings if we examine the rhetorical and symbolic communication that takes place between these three entities within the discourses and forms of visual culture that animate Australian public life.

It is important here to acknowledge the way the relationship between art and the state is shaped by settler state circumstances. Since World War II, arts and cultural policies in democratic societies have been underpinned by notions of civic virtue; that is, the conviction that through the subsidy of particular forms of culture, the best qualities of the human spirit and intellect are cultivated for the benefit of all. This means that such policies usually aim to foster artistic excellence, encourage culturally and socially diverse forms of self-expression, and stimulate pride in the heritage of the nation, locality or community. An additional priority is that disenfranchised members of society should be given the opportunity to participate in creative and fulfilling cultural experiences, in order to foster positive social relationships and an enhanced sense of self-worth (see Craik et al. 2000; Stevenson 2000). As scholars who have explored the cultural imaginaries of settler and postconflict societies have shown, in countries like South Africa, New Zealand and Australia these 'public good' aspirations are inflected with the particular problems that arise from historical injustice, ongoing inequality and ethnic difference (Thomas 1999; Marcus 2004; Coombs 2003; McCarthy 2007). With this in mind, in Part 1 I focus on cultural policies that have fuelled the production and circulation of Aboriginal art and made Aboriginal art an intensely symbolic form of visual culture.

Chapters 1 and 2 map the civic and political movements that have galvanised Aboriginal art's mobilisation by Aboriginal people, the state, and Australian civil society. They review how, from the 1980s in particular, the state's concern with overcoming Indigenous disadvantage and social exclusion was taken beyond matters of discrimination and equal opportunity and emerged as a responsibility of moral consequence for the nation as a whole. They also examine the powerful role played by art in advancing Aboriginal land rights, in consolidating Aboriginal collective identity, and in amplifying the objectives of urban Aboriginal activist movements.

Chapter 3 discusses the subsidisation of Aboriginal art production, particularly in remote communities. Here I am primarily interested in the fact that arts subsidies have since the 1970s been an avenue for addressing Aboriginal people's depressed economic status, and thereby created the conditions for Aboriginal art production to be configured as a form of work. Chapter 4 explores the way Aboriginal art has been pivotal to a sustained mobilisation of commemorative events, institutions, discourses and symbolically powerful forms of visual culture to address the tensions inherent to the settler state condition. Finally, Chapter 5 examines a range of exemplary discourses that arise at the nexus of state, civil society and Aboriginal personhood to delineate the particular way in which Aboriginal culture has been constituted in the post-assimilation era. Ultimately it suggests that Aboriginal art has become emblematic of Aboriginal culture as it is positively imagined in Australian public life.

Chapter 1

NEW INTERCULTURAL RELATIONSHIPS IN THE POST-ASSIMILATION ERA

The Aboriginal art phenomenon has been shaped by a range of cultural and Indigenous governance approaches that reflect the changing status of Aboriginal heritage, subjectivity and culture in Australian public life. In this chapter, I focus on the political events and legislative reforms that brought Aboriginal culture into being in Australian public life and came to anchor citizens' understandings of what it comprised. Fred Myers has aptly pointed out that Aboriginal fine art has been constituted by an intercultural process of 'culture making' through 'historically and institutionally specific mediations [...] of art, of Aboriginal administration, of governmentality' (2002, 351; see also Merlan 1998). In what follows I hope to shed light on the dialectic nature of this process. Not only has Aboriginal art acquired meaning and value as fine art through this process of culture making but it has also galvanized, through its circulation as a positive aesthetic signifier of Aboriginality, wider processes of culture making in the context of social and political negotiations of the settler state condition.

1.1 Cultural Trauma in Australian Public Culture

To begin, the history reviewed in this section can be appraised through the lens of cultural trauma, a concept theorised by cultural sociologists such as Jeffrey Alexander (2003) and Ron Eyerman (2004) to elucidate the lasting social ramifications of the Holocaust, the September 11 attacks and the history of slavery in the United States. The concept is usefully summarised by Alexander when he writes that 'it is by constructing cultural traumas that social groups, national societies, and sometimes even entire civilisations not only cognitively identify the existence and source of human suffering but "take on board" some significant responsibility in it' (2003, 85). The cultural dimension rests in the memorialising narratives and other representations that constitute this shared sense of victimisation in relation to a devastating event or process, representations that are created and disseminated within the arenas of the mass media, academia, policy, religion and the arts, for example. Together these mediations identify the victims, define the nature of the unjust act, present the victims' experiences in a way that corresponds to principles acceptable to the wider population and attribute responsibility for the past injustices to the state and particular social groups. Alexander suggests that eventually 'the heightened and powerfully affecting discourse of trauma disappears, [and] the "lessons" of the trauma become objectified' in a range of commemorative institutional, material and ritual forms (103).

The idea of cultural trauma is a useful one for comprehending the way Australia's history has been reconceptualised in the 40-year period that can be roughly traced from the 1967 Referendum to the 2008 National Apology to Australia's Indigenous peoples. During this time, a narrative of loss, suffering and injustice evolved that encompassed many kinds of Aboriginal victimisation dating back to the arrival of Captain Cook in 1770 and the First Fleet in 1788. This narrative melds several histories: experiences of frontier conflict; land dispossession; missionisation and institutionalisation; entrenched poverty and ill health; the fragmentation of families; violence and death in the criminal justice system; racism; loss of language and so on (Atkinson 2002; Haebich 2000; Johnston 1991a; Reynolds 1999; 'National Inquiry' 1997). Over the last several decades, all of these histories have been illuminated through a range of cultural representations and public dialogues.

One of the dictums of the final Declaration of Reconciliation is 'As we walk the journey of healing, one part of the nation apologises and expresses its sorrow and sincere regret for the injustices of the past, so the other part accepts the apologies and forgives' (quoted in Gordon 2001, 135). This statement is suggestive of the way these histories coalesce and foreground the Indigenous/non-Indigenous divide. However, it is important to point out that Australia's cultural trauma narrative has been very much entwined with a broader civic project of revisioning Australia as a culturally sophisticated and progressive nation (Merlan 1998). As will be elaborated later, this interrelatedness helped form the meanings that have accrued to Aboriginal art over the course of its emergence as a contemporary art movement. The following historical account lays the groundwork for this argument.

1.2   The End of Assimilation and the Rise of Aboriginal Culture

Since the mid-twentieth century, efforts to improve the relationship between Indigenous and non-Indigenous Australians and forge a respected place for

Indigenous Australians within the nation have taken many forms. In the 1920s and 1930s, the assimilation policy was viewed by many to be a progressive corrective to the formerly held belief that the Aboriginal population would simply die out; however, by the 1950s and 1960s, it was subject to greater scrutiny and criticism (Broome 2010). Assimilation was increasingly recognised to be founded on spurious racial classifications and fundamentally injurious to human dignity, a viewpoint inspired in large part by the international decolonisation movements and emerging human rights discourses of the post–World War II era. For example, as Jane Lyndon points out, the horrific photographic evidence of the cruelty of the Nazi regime that entered Australian newspapers in 1945 sensitised the public to race-based oppression and suffering (2012, particularly chapter 4). Indigenous activists and humanitarians were very effective in drawing analogies between the experience of the Jews and Aboriginal people's abject circumstances on missions, reserves and in police custody and helped to stimulate a reappraisal of Indigenous cultural, political and citizenship rights in Australia (Attwood 2005, 20–22; Sanders 2002). This shift in social attitudes drove the successful campaign for the 1967 Referendum, which led to the amendment of two sections of the constitution so that Aboriginal people would be counted in the census and Aboriginal affairs would become a federal (rather than state and territory) responsibility. When Gough Whitlam was elected as Labor prime minister in 1972, the policy of assimilation was explicitly terminated in favour of self-determination, and Indigenous affairs governance radically reconfigured through a variety of policy platforms.[1]

These changes took place against the background of Britain's decline as the foundation of Australian nationalism after World War II.[2] At the same time, the '50s, '60s and '70s witnessed the maturation of Australian anthropology, archaeology and prehistory as scholarly fields within universities and museums across the country. The Australian Institute of Aboriginal Studies (now the Australian Institute of Aboriginal and Torres Strait Islander Studies) was established as a statuory authority in 1964. These fields of research were a tributary to the Whitlam government's 'new nationalism' in the early 1970s and the associated ideal of building civic pride in the 'National Estate' (Curran 2004).[3] The activities of researchers in these disciplines and institutions helped to crystallise an image of the natural and cultural patrimony of the nation, and as a consequence, Aboriginal history, sites and art became interwoven with nationalistic impressions of the country that focused on its landscapes and ancient heritage.[4]

At the same time, the politics of contemporary Aboriginal identity – now interpreted through the lens of self-determination – altered the status of Aboriginal heritage from being a matter of historical and scientific inquiry to being meaningful in the cultural present. Alongside other Indigenous groups around the world, Indigenous Australians articulated a particular language of historicity to anchor their collective visions of resurgence in the political and cultural spheres (Clifford 2013, 23–35). They unraveled normative constructions of the nation's history that presumed the diminution of Aboriginal society and articulated alternative narratives of cultural transmission and survival within which the concept of heritage was central. Through these means, they were able to assert a collective right to inhabit the present on their own terms. As artist Julie Gough put it, Indigenous Australians have been 'regenerating the means to make our own future in our own country' (2006, 13; see also Ginsburg 1994). The growing body of evidence of the antiquity of Aboriginal occupation of the continent would become, and remains, a powerful signifier of Aboriginal rights (Ireland 2002; Russell 2001, 86–91).

The formation of the Aboriginal Arts Board in 1973 was a defining moment in the history of the Aboriginal art movement; however, the values enshrined within it were prefigured in the years immediately prior to Whitlam's election through the work of the Council for Aboriginal Affairs. This council had been established as an advisory body by the Holt Liberal Government following the success of the 1967 Referendum. The three men who were elected to the council were H. C. 'Nugget' Coombs (as chair), Bill Stanner and the diplomat and public servant Barrie Dexter. All three were progressives, informed about minority rights movements elsewhere and sympathetic to Aboriginal people's struggles for land rights and the retention of their culture. At that time, Coombs was the governor of the Commonwealth Bank (the highest economic post then). He was also the founding head of the Australia Council for the Arts when it was formed in 1968 and the chair of its Aboriginal Arts Committee, and in these roles (and within the council) he argued strongly for the protection of Aboriginal heritage and the support of Aboriginal art practices (Rowse 2000a). In his view, art was a keystone of contemporary Aboriginal culture because it could conserve and revive the interconnections between ceremony, sacred sites and land custodianship (Davis 2007, 282–85). Coombs was instrumental in the first official acknowledgement of an infringement of Aboriginal copyright in 1966, when he compensated and honoured the artist David Malangi after one of his bark painting designs was reproduced on the Australian one dollar note (Johnson 1996). He also helped to arrange an exhibition of bark paintings in Britain, which was curated by the newly formed Australian Institute of Aboriginal Studies as part of the 1965 Commonwealth Arts Festival (Rowse 2001). William Stanner, an esteemed anthropologist who was instrumental in the founding of the Institute and who had also served as a journalist and public servant, was a strident critic of assimilation. He gained a profile beyond academic circles through his influential 1968 *Boyer Lectures* 'After the Dreaming', in which he explained the reasons for Aboriginal disadvantage and refuted prevailing understandings of Aboriginal subjectivity that essentialised their powerlessness and anomie. He argued for the recognition of the distinctiveness of Aboriginal culture and appealed for a more honest and less self-serving account of Australian frontier history (Stanner 1968).[5] Stanner's writings continue to have currency, because they seem to presage the ethical consciousness of late twentieth century Australian society. Melinda Hinkson attributes the ongoing interest in his work to the fact that 'he provides us with a picture of Aboriginal social life that is unusually multifaceted, that documents and weighs up contradictory forces, while resisting the urge to generalize or reach some final point of judgement in accounting for that life' (2010a, 87; Stanner 2009).

Due to Holt's untimely death in 1967, the Council for Aboriginal Affairs was never made a statutory body as initially envisaged. The subsequent Gorton government was indifferent to Aboriginal rights, and the McMahon Liberal government that succeeded it marginalised the council, leaving it without a charter or formal set of responsibilities. However, Dexter, Stanner and Coombs still had access to Commonwealth funding, and they endured this hostile climate and formulated policies nevertheless. They travelled the country consulting with Indigenous groups and numerous government agencies at the state and federal level on Aboriginal health, housing, education, employment, the arts and other areas and advocated for Aboriginal land rights (Dexter 2008).[6]

As Tim Rowse (2000b) has pointed out, as the council assessed how Aboriginal affairs might be governed humanely and effectively, it became clear that two divergent senses of Aboriginal difference needed to be comprehended. On the one hand there was the undesirable difference associated with inequality and social exclusion, and on the other, the set of cultural differences that had endured since colonisation and were understood to form the basis of Aboriginal people's 'positive self-consciousness' (29). The latter was a striking departure from the assimilationist understanding of Aboriginal culture as anachronistic to contemporary Australian life and an impediment to Aboriginal people's integration into Australian society. As Rowse writes: 'Assimilation was a program of inclusion of indigenous Australians and it presumed and urged their ultimate sameness' (11, 17; see also Goot and Rowse 2007, ch. 1, Hollingsworth 2006). Up to this point, even progressive humanitarians had not usually looked beyond the objective of Aboriginal people achieving equal citizenship rights.

In the subsequent decade an extraordinary reversal of this view took place. From the sympathetic realisation that Aboriginal people were not submitting to the assimilation project arose the conviction that Aboriginal difference should be respected and that Aboriginal people's advancement depended on their ability to make choices based on a sense of pride in their identity. Aboriginal culture came to be embraced within official discourses as the basis for a right to self-determination and to one's traditional lands, and even as something that Australian society as a whole could enjoy and cherish. Further, it was seen to be the patrimony of any person 'of Aboriginal and Islander descent who identifies as an Aboriginal or Islander and is so accepted by the community with which he or she is associated',[7] entailing that there was no discrimination between so-called full or part Aboriginal people as before. Dexter, Coombs and Stanner, left with a remarkable degree of autonomy to follow their convictions as representatives of the Commonwealth government, ensured that an embryonic Aboriginal policy platform grounded in these ideas was laid out for the Whitlam government to consolidate when it was elected in 1972.

As Peter Sutton states, 'By the late 1970s, "culture" was central to the new verbal currency of Indigenous liberation politics' (2009, 63), and this unquestionably created the scaffolding for the Aboriginal art movement to attain the symbolic gravity it came to have in national public culture. In this respect it was of some consequence that Dexter, Coombs and Stanner were erudite men who admired Aboriginal cultural traditions. Given the tangibility of art for the positive configuration of culture that was now being disseminated, it is not surprising that art became a stage for Whitlam's self-determination policy. Five months into Whitlam's term, the Aboriginal Arts Board (AAB) was launched by the National Seminar on Aboriginal Arts in 1973, a week-long series of talks and discussions involving Indigenous and non-Indigenous Australians and overseas guests, accompanied by several exhibitions, performances and film screenings (Aboriginal Arts Board 1973). Whitlam opened the seminar, and his speech situated Aboriginal affairs at the centre of his government's agenda:

> [I]f there is one ambition we place above all others, if there is one achievement for which I hope we will be remembered, if there is one cause for which I hope future historians will salute us, it is this: that the government I lead removed a stain from our national honour and gave justice and equality to the Aboriginal people. (1973, 4)

Whitlam declared that Aboriginal people's difference, in terms of their cultural heritage and customs, would be respected and encouraged to flourish. His speech articulated the core principal of self-determination – Aboriginal people would be empowered 'to make their own decisions about their way of life within the Australian community' – and highlighted the board's exclusively Aboriginal membership and direct access to financial resources as testaments to this (4). The arts were essential to the exercise of self-determination, he argued, because they ensured the preservation and adaptation of cultural traditions and had the power to instil an emotional awareness of Aboriginal people's plight within non-Indigenous Australians. He also saw the arts as an avenue for the expression of protest by those Aboriginal people living in towns and cities who suffered from 'isolation, [...] prejudice, and a multitude of social and economic handicaps' (6).

In its early years (during which Coombs had a strong influence), the board largely focused on Aboriginal cultural survival and rejuvenation and Aboriginal people's rights to their heritage (Australia Council 1974; 1979; Myers 2002, 132–33; Berrell 2009). The restitution of what had been eroded by colonisation had far more weight than the concerns about professional artistic development that preoccupied the other boards of the Australia Council. The board's first chair was the artist Dick Roughsey from Mornington Island. Roughsey wrote that the board's ambitions were 'an expression of pride and confidence that stems from the fact that it will be decisions made by Aboriginal people that will ultimately determine the future of their art and culture, and its integration within the total spectrum of Australian art' (1976, 239). While initially this entailed a focus on the art produced in remote Australia, more eclectic art practices emerging in the cities and in other parts of the country gradually gained support. The board came to regard the variety of art forms as a reflection of the diverse experiences and aspirations that underpinned Indigenous identity in contemporary Australian society (Australia Council 1974, 41; Rowse 2000a, 516). Importantly, Robert (Bob) Edwards, who was the first (non-Indigenous) director of the AAB and shared Coombs's values, was instrumental in drawing connections between Aboriginal art and the maturing scholarly fields discussed earlier. He was able to do this due to his significant knowledge of Aboriginal rock art (an interest he pursued with the encouragement and guidance of the anthropologist Charles Mountford), anthropology and archaeology, as well as his museum management experience (Edwards 1979; Mulvaney et al. 2011; Johnson et al. 2011; Genocchio 2008, 76–80).

Thus the AAB typified the new Indigenous affairs paradigm. A vibrant political movement evolved alongside these developments, founded on a sense of shared oppression among Indigenous people nationwide and attracting many non-Indigenous supporters. Core issues that galvanised activism in the 1970s and 1980s were land rights, deaths in custody,[8] threats to sacred sites and the 1988 Bicentenary. As was presaged by the Council for Aboriginal Affairs, a shift 'from a racial to a cultural paradigm' for thinking about Aboriginal identity underpinned these movements (McLean 1998, 108). Aboriginality partly overcame the divisions associated with tribal affiliations and colonial racial classifications, and the emerging Aboriginal polity articulated a pan-Aboriginal concept of identity with which many Aboriginal people came to identify proudly. This solidarity arose from the increased mobility of and interaction between Indigenous people from different parts of the country (particularly in urban centres such as Sydney and Melbourne); the influence of North American civil rights and Black Power movements; the powerful unifying symbol of the Aboriginal Tent Embassy, which was established by Aboriginal activists on the lawns of Parliament House in 1972; and the design and widespread adoption of the Aboriginal flag. Lawyer Pat O'Shane captures the spirit of pan-Aboriginality when she writes:

> Aboriginal culture is what Aboriginal people today are, with all our collective experience. All of us carry our 40 000+ years of history within us. We lay on top of that our present experiences, and the outcomes are a mixture of pain, despair, bitterness, humour, optimism, resilience, anger, longing, a search for truth, a search for identity, a search for understanding. (Thompson 1990, n.p.)

The inclination to identify positively as Aboriginal and to proclaim one's membership of an Indigenous nation (e.g., Yorta Yorta, Wiradjuri, Warlpiri) or to use regional Aboriginal vernacular to identify oneself (as Koori, Murri, Nyoongar) served to subvert the homogenising discourse of the assimilation era that had made Aboriginal ancestry an object of shame. As Indigenous activist and scholar Mick Dodson writes, there was a need to deny the classifications employed by past governments, those 'ideological tools' that 'assist[ed] the state in applying its policies of control, domination and assimilation' (2003, 29).[9] As we will see, this is of great relevance to the urban Aboriginal art movement.

The imperative of cutting through the sense of shame associated with being Aboriginal underlines the role of racism in anchoring the sense of pan-Aboriginal identity described here. For much of the twentieth century, the State's ascription of undesirable difference to Aboriginal people ensured that habits of discriminating against and assuming superiority over Aboriginal people were highly normalised in non-Indigenous society. A range of forms of segregation and exclusion (in schools, bars, cinemas, public pools and so on) were part of the social fabric of Australian towns and cities and were upheld daily by white citizens (Gilbert 1977; Curthoys 2002). The advocacy for equality and self-determination and the rejection of racial discrimination in official policy in the 1960s and 1970s did not, of course, instigate a wholesale realignment of these habits and attitudes. What drove the activist movements of this period was the fact that many Aboriginal people's outlook on their opportunities, their successes and failures and the welfare of their families had been filtered through the formative experiences of contempt and discrimination, experiences that were part of simply going to school, visiting the shops, finding a job and so on (Grossman 2003; Cunneen 2001; Cowlishaw 2004).

Gradually sympathetic non-Indigenous Australians became accustomed to an idea of Aboriginality founded on the notion of a culturally distinct minority that had been dispossessed and had suffered at the hands of white society but had nevertheless survived the colonial project. This understanding of Aboriginal people's predicament was potently expressed in journalist John Pilger's landmark film *The Secret Country* (1985). As will be discussed later, the self-critical and remorseful tendencies of non-Indigenous members of civil society contributed to the formation of this identity. In other words, a morally culpable white society helped to construct a reciprocal Aboriginal society deserving of recognition, sympathy and generosity.

The solidarity that emerged between the Indigenous polity and non-Indigenous people who were sympathetic to their rights campaigns led to a very effective boycott of the Australian Bicentenary in 1988. Large numbers of Indigenous and non-Indigenous people participated in protests that signaled their refusal to celebrate the arrival of the First Fleet in 1788: they hailed 26 January as 'Invasion Day' and as a 'National Day of Mourning' and demanded national land rights and justice for black deaths in custody. The Bicentenary organisers were keenly aware of the moral paradox of the anniversary. They knew that – in Ghassan Hage's terms – 'a national memory or a non-contradictory plurality of memories of colonisation in Australia' was not possible (2003, 91). They were eager to demote conventional icons of Australian nationalism and treated national heritage, culture and identity as being characterized by diversity. In large part the events had a contemporary and futuristic rather than a historic focus and seemed to aspire to a celebration of celebrating itself (Sarah 1989; Cochrane and Goodman 1988). This approach reflected the pluralistic inflection of Australia's intellectual culture at the time and was intended to diffuse tensions around multiculturalism, republicanism, Aboriginal activism and other points of conflict. In addition, there was a strong emphasis on having the world's attention, something that distinguished the Australian Bicentenary greatly from the American Bicentenary staged in 1976 (Spillman 1994). Here the commemorations were seen to signify Australia's maturity as a nation-state within the international community, and various events, particularly those associated with the arts and sport, were treated as opportunities to display Australian culture and achievements on the world stage. This outward looking nationalism speaks to Australians' consciousness of their geographic and cultural marginality, a consciousness that has had considerable bearing on the reception of Aboriginal art in Australia and will be revisited in later chapters (Rowse 1985; Stevenson 2000). The Bicentenary was criticised for presenting an amorphous and corporatist image of Australian culture. As Healy writes, it 'placed unresolved questions around colonialism at the very centre of attempts to articulate the nation', leaving a kind of heritage vacuum in the nation's public culture (Healy 2001, 284; 2008; Carter 1994). This arguably inspired the nationalistic focus on Aboriginal culture that we find in the 1994 *Creative Nation* cultural policy and other cultural policy forums in subsequent decades, as will be discussed later.

Several significant juridical and legislative events pertaining to Indigenous issues came in the wake of the Bicentenary: the release of the *Deaths in Custody Report* (1991), the Mabo and Wik native title decisions (1992 and 1996),[10] the release of the *Report of the National Inquiry into the Separation of Aboriginal and Torres Strait Islander Children from their Families* (1997)[11] and the 10-year term of the Council for Aboriginal Reconciliation (CAR) (1991–2001). These events generated emotive public commentary and debate, amplified by partisan political conflict in which non-Indigenous Australian citizens were often confronted with highly compelling moral injunctions to recognise Indigenous people's experience of loss, trauma and injustice. In the case of native title, revelations about Aboriginal people's relationship to land were immensely effective in fostering public understanding of Aboriginal culture as vested in 'country'. However, concurrently Aboriginal land interests were being attacked by the pastoral and mining lobbies, which found platforms of support within the Liberal opposition party and some state governments. A fear campaign that misrepresented the threat native title posed to private land, public space and commercial interests would come to dominate the tenure of the Keating Labor government, a campaign that escalated following the Wik decision during the term of John Howard's Liberal government (Tickner 2001; Short 2008).

In the case of what became known as the Stolen Generations Inquiry, the publication of documentary sources and extensive oral testimony generated a great deal of sympathy and indignation among the Australian public. At the same time, the report's invocation of the concept of cultural genocide, and its use of the phrase 'Stolen Generations', were interpreted by the Howard government and some Australian citizens as being excessive and inflammatory (Manne 2001). The report's recommendation that the government issue a national public apology for past practices of the state was emphatically rejected by the federal government (even though apologies were eventually made by all state governments as well as many local governments, churches and community groups) (C. Dow 2008). The refusal to say 'sorry' came to dominate Indigenous politics and became symbolic, for those sympathetic to the cause, of the government's lack of commitment to the process of Reconciliation (Gunstone 2007; Goot and Rowse 2007, 137–39). Many decisions made by Howard and his ministers over the following years led to an irrevocable cleaving of the federal government from most of the Indigenous leaders, advocates and organisations with which previous governments had for the most part negotiated in a collaborative spirit. Most severe among them was the body of legislation rushed through Parliament in association with the so-called Emergency Intervention in 2007 to address the presence of child sexual abuse in remote Australia. The government discourse surrounding the Intervention had the effect of inculpating remote community life *per se* in the public imagination (and demonizing Aboriginal men), and many of the measures introduced were intended to weaken Indigenous personal and collective values vested in land and kinship in favour of neoliberal, individualist reforms (see essays in Altman and Hinkson 2007).

Finally, in conjunction with these events, Australia's history was being revised in both popular and academic historiography in light of contemporary notions of justice, equality and rights, the formerly neglected testimony of Aboriginal people, and a reassessment of Aboriginal resistance on the frontier. A prolonged and often acrimonious debate about frontier warfare, massacres, Aboriginal land dispossession and the effects of the assimilation policies on Indigenous families took place across academic, institutional and journalistic forums in the 1990s and 2000s. At the same time, Aboriginal history was proliferating in the public domain through oral histories, localised commemorations of place and heritage, biographical and autobiographical literature, theatre, film, TV, radio, exhibitions and other forms of public culture (see, for instance, Langford 1988; Australian Broadcasting Corporation 1996; Birch 2003).[12]

1.3 Paul Keating, Indigenised Settler Nationalism and Reconciliation

More than any prime minister before or after, Paul Keating, whose term as Labor prime minister overlapped with many of these events, embraced the prospect of catharsis and renewal within the national consciousness in relation to Indigenous affairs. His government established the Council for Aboriginal Reconciliation in 1992, under the Reconciliation Legislation that had been introduced the previous year by the Hawke Labor government. Under Keating's leadership, the acknowledgement of a shameful and repressed history became a civic duty on which the restoration of Aboriginal well-being depended. When Keating launched the UN International Year of the World's Indigenous People in 1992 with his 'Redfern Address', he declared that 'With some noble exceptions, we failed to make the most basic human response and enter into their hearts and minds. We failed to ask – how would I feel if this were done to me?' (2001 [1992]). In retrospect, the statement is emblematic of a significant adjustment that took place within Australian civil society at this time.[13] While some non-Indigenous citizens were antagonised by the Keating government's position on Indigenous issues and the very idea of a redemptive civic project, others were very receptive.[14] As Francesca Merlan writes of Keating's speech, 'such readiness to publicly acknowledge settler responsibility for shaping contemporary Indigenous conditions became an index of a conciliatory approach', and as a result, a range of protocols of acknowledgement were developed by government bodies, nongovernment organisations and corporations (2014, 301). Many people who identified with the spirit of Keating's statements sought some sort of rapprochement with Aboriginal people, whether on an interpersonal level or symbolically through cultural consumption, or by contributing to Aboriginal advancement through employment, mentoring, scholarships and other such initiatives (Gooder and Jacobs 2001; Moran 2002).

What is significant about Keating's leaderships is that sympathy for Aboriginal suffering and a preparedness to imagine things from an Aboriginal person's point of view moved from being the inclination of individuals and small social groups to being a normative civic discourse advocated by the *state*. This discourse sought to foster collective affective experience and engender a sense of moral responsibility on a grand scale and, in Anthony Moran's words, was constitutive of 'indigenising settler nationalism' (2002). In a passage that is highly evocative of Alexander's theorisation of cultural trauma, Moran offers the following explanation of this form of nationalism:

> It is characterised by an attitude of mourning and sorrow in relation to past and contemporary forms of oppression of the indigenous. It involves an honouring of, and a desire to make reparation to, the indigenous absent in earlier dominant forms of Australian settler nationalism [...] and views the actions of the settler nation in the past with a more critical eye. It adopts a position that calls upon the nation to reconstruct itself through a fuller recognition of the indigenous and their claims as a central component of national identity. (2002, 1014)

Complimentary to Moran's characterisation of this ethical stance are Emma Kowal's insights about white antiracists (2011; see also 2008). Drawing on her experience as both an employee and ethnographer in the Aboriginal health sector, Kowal adumbrates a particular kind of white subjectivity that has been shaped by the late twentieth-century political and cultural shifts in Indigenous affairs and aims to 'invert colonial power relations' in pursuit of a vision of postcolonial justice (316). People in this position self-ascribe a condition of white stigma, because they are painfully conscious of their privilege and see themselves as unavoidably implicated in the colonial processes that led to Aboriginal people's dispossession and poor well-being (317).

As will be illustrated later, the sentiments associated with the new civic discourse of recognition and atonement had an impact on cultural consumption, government programmes and forms of art industry subsidy and private sector decision making. The most important vehicle was the Council for Aboriginal Reconciliation, which placed some citizens in a position to employ the state's resources to appeal to the consciences and challenge the prejudices of other citizens. Alongside the many grass-roots Reconciliation collectives and initiatives, a range of projects targeted the media, local government, the school curriculum, the community sector and the private sector (Gunstone 2007; Short 2008). In general the Council's activities were predicated on the following interdependent objectives: bringing about more opportunities for Indigenous people to participate in mainstream society, changing the way Aboriginal people were treated by non-Indigenous Australians and changing popular representations of Aboriginality that shaped everyday attitudes about Aboriginal society and culture. Behind these objectives lay the ideals of finding paths to healing, developing a stronger sense of self-worth, forming mutually sympathetic relationships between formerly estranged people and constructing a new basis for a proud sense of nationhood.

The Reconciliation process ultimately generated a new way of thinking about the moral calibre of the settler state and the very idea of Aboriginality to which subsequent policies became accountable. It established a moral paradigm through which the various revelations about and revisions of Australian history, legal judgments and inquiries that have taken place since the 1970s have been refracted. To use Alexander's words, the events and public discourses explored previously generated 'a narrative about a horribly destructive social process, and a demand for emotional, institutional, and symbolic reparation and reconstitution' (2003, 93). These processes all contributed to the crystallisation of a new perspective on the place of Indigenous identity, culture and history within Australian society, one that arguably filled the vacuum that Healy (2001) identified as being left by the Bicentenary.[15] It is now time to situate Aboriginal art within this process of change.

Chapter 2

ABORIGINAL PEOPLE MOBILISING ABORIGINAL ART

There have been many cases in which Aboriginal people have used their art and material culture to pursue political agendas in the post-assimilation era. As we will see, Aboriginal art has played a powerful role in articulating Aboriginal land custodianship claims, in establishing a sense of Aboriginal collective identity or pan-Aboriginality and in defining the grievances and agendas that propelled urban Aboriginal activist movements. With respect to the triumvirate of relationships with which Part I is concerned (Indigenous people, the state and non-Indigenous citizens), the following will focus on the role of art in the Aboriginal community's efforts to communicate its demands to the state and non-Indigenous civil society.

2.1 Aboriginal Art Mobilised in Political and Legal Domains

On several occasions during the 1950s and 1960s when Aboriginal art was not yet securely ensconced within the Western category of art, the Yolngu of North East Arnhem Land mobilised their customary material culture (painted barks, sacred poles and sacred objects) to demonstrate to the Methodist missionaries who had jurisdiction over them the solidarity that existed between their clans, their sense of autonomy and the salience of their religion.[1] They installed these objects – objects in which clan identities, land custodianship and law were symbolically inscribed – near or within the missionaries' churches. In doing this, they were placing secret-sacred material in the public domain in an unprecedented way (Morphy 1983). During these and later years, they also presented paintings ceremonially to visiting representatives of the church, members of parliament, lawyers and police. In a much more famous example, the Yolngu of the settlement of Yirrkala presented a petition to the House of Representatives of the Federal Parliament in 1963 in response to the announcement that large tracts of their traditional country were to be excised for lease by the Nabalco Mining Company. Previously of no value to settler interests, the area had been found to be rich in bauxite. The petition, typed out in both a Yolngu language and English, was signed by clan leaders and affixed to a length of bark on which sacred clan designs painted in ochre created a border for the printed page. It stated the economic, social and sacred significance of the land on which their tribes had lived 'from time immemorial' and protested that the Yolngu had not been consulted over the planned excision and were fearful for their future (Attwood 2003, 227–30). As Faye Ginsburg and Fred Myers write, despite the fact that the Yolngu were unsuccessful in getting the government to change its policy:

> the bark petitions were a brilliant transformation of the longstanding cultural idiom of bark paintings into an emblematic form of cultural self-objectification as political performance […] [T]he intuitively valid claims of Yolngu people […] created greater sympathy throughout Australia for recognition of Indigenous rights to land, and created an Aboriginal culture and identity acceptable for national recognition: the 'traditionally oriented' Aboriginal with religious and spiritual links to the land – and far from white settlement. (2006, 100)

In other words, the petition gave credence to the idea of Aboriginal culture delineated by Dexter, Coombs and Stanner within the Council for Aboriginal Affairs. It also helped to galvanise many of the protest movements of the 1970s and 1980s and gave impetus to the process of developing land rights legislation for the Northern Territory.

The symbolic efficacy of the Bark Petition inspired members of the Northern and Central Land Councils to create the Barunga Statement, which they presented to Prime Minister Bob Hawke at the 1988 Barunga Sports and Culture Festival. The Barunga Statement also took the form of a collectively produced bark painting illustrating ancestral designs from several Northern Australian Aboriginal groups accompanied by a printed text. This text employed the language of Aboriginal sovereignty, self-determination and human rights and argued that a treaty needed to be negotiated (Barunga 2012). Hawke's acceptance of the statement marked the moment when he explicitly declared his support for a treaty, though this support was short lived. His last act as prime minister was to see the Barunga Statement hung in the Grand Hall of Parliament House.

In the 1990s Aboriginal art was again mobilised in a symbolic and performative way in the context of native title cases, in which claimants must prove the continuity of their traditional connections with the land. In 1997 Spinifex Art Projects was established to contribute to the documentation process required by the Spinifex people's Native Title claim over land in the Great Victorian Desert, Western Australia. Two large paintings that mapped the birthplaces of the male and female claimants provided evidence of their land custodianship. The claim was successful and these works were included in the preamble to the agreement, which was formalised in 2000. The Spinifex community honoured this resolution by bequeathing 10 major 'government paintings' to the state of Western Australia (Spinifex Arts Project 1999). Also in 1997, over fifty traditional owners of land in the Great Sandy Desert in Western Australia produced an enormous painting, the Ngurrara Canvas, for the purposes of presentation at the Native Title Tribunal. During the hearings claimants stood and sometimes danced and sang on their respective parts of the canvas to give evidence of ongoing connection to land through a translator. This native title claim was eventually successfully concluded in 2007 (Winter 2002, 66–68; National Museum of Australia 2012a).[2]

In reflecting on the gravity of these objects as political and legal instruments in intercultural settings, we need to remember that they were representative of a culture with no tradition of cartography or documentation commensurable with Western traditions, yet for whom law and lore have long been communicated through the poetic traditions of rock-wall, body and sand painting, carving, song and performance. This is why scholars like Jennifer Biddle (2012, 33) have argued for the recognition of these idioms as 'Aboriginal-specific forms of historiography and cultural memory', and Vivien Johnson has argued that we recognise Aboriginal paintings of the western desert as 'deeds of title' to land (2007, 40).

2.2 Aboriginal Art, Activism and Pan-Aboriginal Identity

[C]ontemporary Black artists confront the conscience of the global public with images of our modern reality [...] Too frequently, the subject speaks of pain. This is not, however, the artists' fascination with the morbid – it is the reality of Black modern life and visual representation of our recent history. The scenes are torn from the psyche of a people, and in their presentation the Black community can weep and begin the process of recovery. Our grief and pain **must be acknowledged**! [...] Our creative people [...] provide the vanguard of our relentless march towards justice, and depict for us the history of this march. (Bobbi [Roberta] Sykes 1984, n.p., original emphasis)

This passage, drawn from the catalogue introduction for the seminal exhibition *Koori Art '84*, is striking for its evocation of cultural trauma and its compelling illustration of the political importance of Aboriginal creative expression in urban settings. In cities like Brisbane, Sydney and Melbourne, Aboriginal art has been a critical site of Indigenous empowerment and identity formation. In these places a range of Indigenous, black or blak cultural forms flourished in the 1980s and early 1990s, including dance, music and theatre groups, artists' collectives, periodicals, conferences, exhibitions and radio and television productions.[3] Their swift emergence highlights the role the arts and media play in 'cultural revival, identity formation, and political assertion' (Ginsberg 1994, 374; Eyerman 2004; Hall 1990). As Gillian Cowlishaw (2004, 6) writes, Aboriginal people's sense of identity has been 'constructed under duress', and the urban Aboriginal art movement was essential to depicting Aboriginal people as strong, virtuous and as having legitimate grievances, generating a sense of solidarity and provoking empathetic reactions among the wider public.

Sykes' association of the expressive power of art with social justice exemplifies the attitude of many Indigenous practitioners at this time, and there was a strong historical and ideological relationship between these emergent art forms and the Aboriginal activist movements discussed earlier. As Hetti Perkins and non-Indigenous writer and curator Victoria Lynn write:

> It is the neo/post colonial context in which Aboriginal and Torres Strait Islander artists create their work that has led many artists to believe that (sic) are not artists only – they are cultural activists. This implies that making art is as much a political statement, if less overtly so, as the dramatic demonstrations and protest marches of recent times. (1993, x; see also Perkins and Fink 1997; Mundine 2006; Allas 2010)

Events such as the Bicentenary and the Royal Commission into Aboriginal Deaths in Custody stimulated a range of artistic responses, and there was also some crossover between art and activism in the production of posters and printed materials for various events. In a summation that is characteristic of many historical accounts of urban Aboriginal art, Indigenous curator and writer Margo Neale writes that the generation of artists who emerged in the 1980s in the south-eastern states 'were young, articulate and angry, fuelled by decades of dispossession and displacement' (2004, 487; see also 2000; Onus 1993; Croft 2007b). Warrior, battle and weaponry metaphors became a recurring feature in urban Aboriginal art discourses in a manner reminiscent of the artistic appropriation of the military term 'avant-garde' in association with nineteenth-century revolutionary politics. The pioneering Boomalli Aboriginal Artists Co-operative, established in 1987 by several Sydney-based artists (two of whom, Hetti Perkins and Brenda L. Croft, were daughters of prominent political campaigners for Aboriginal rights) draws its name from the Wiradjuri word 'to strike'. *Culture Warriors*, the name of the inaugural Indigenous Art Triennial exhibition at the National Gallery of Australia (Croft 2007a), and Tess Allas's (2010) discussion of 'history as a weapon' in the work of Fiona Foley provide further examples of such metaphors.

The activist spirit of the 1980s impacted on the Aboriginal Arts Board in interesting ways during the tenure of Gary Foley (director from 1983–86) and Chika Dixon (chair from 1982–86) (Rowse 2000a; Lambert 1984a; 1984b). Dixon and Foley had been prominent activists since the 1970s, participating in the (Aboriginal) Black Power movement, protests against the touring of the South African Springbok rugby team in 1971 and the establishment of the Aboriginal Tent Embassy on the lawns of Parliament House in 1972. They were also active in the Union movement and had been involved in pioneering Aboriginal controlled services relating to health, legal rights and employment. For Dixon and Foley, the AAB was another domain in which to assert Aboriginal rights to justice, equality and autonomy. Following the retirement of several members, an entirely new board was elected in 1983/1984, one that was more geographically representative. Several path breaking practitioners who asserted the cultural value of nonremote Aboriginal artistic practices were members in the 1980s, including Lin Onus, Bob Maza and Oodgeroo Noonuccal (Kath Walker).[4] The board began to place greater emphasis on consensual decision making, equity and representativeness in the distribution of grants. The salience of social democratic ideals was reflected in the fact that young people, women, the unemployed and prisoners were argued to have 'high priority when allocating funds' (Australia Council 1985b, 53). While the board remained committed to funding organisations, individual artists now also received a greater share of funding. Targets of this new focus were those artists practising in urban centres who were regarded as having been neglected in previous years. They received individual grants but were also beneficiaries of the board's support for key exhibitions such as *Koori Art '84* in Sydney and *Aratjara: Art of the First Australians*, a watershed international touring exhibition staged in 1993, which included artists from across Australia (Lüthi and Lee 1993, Mundine 2013).

Clearly then, the idea of pan-Aboriginality that was so crucial to the Aboriginal political movements discussed earlier was consequential for the Aboriginal art movement as well. As Ian McLean suggests, the concept permitted all forms of Aboriginal art to be treated as facets of a heterogeneous cultural arena with which white society was now engaged in 'dialogue' (1998, 108–9). A useful illustration of this change is the following statement from the non-Indigenous artist Tim Johnson in an essay in the 1986 *Sydney Biennale* catalogue:

From Alice Springs to Redfern, from the Warumpi Band to the distant ceremonies of surviving tribal groups, from murals that depict changing times to interwoven, inherited living mythology, Aboriginal art is undergoing a renaissance [...] Aboriginal artists have not abandoned responsibility for their world, their own country and their own lives. In other words, no matter what the settlers, missionaries, landowners, miners and industrialists have done, Aboriginal communities still retain their culture and the conviction that what happens to them is still within the realm of their own control. (1986, 64)

The iconic Aboriginal Memorial, an artwork created to mark the 1988 Bicentenary, is also illustrative of the cohesive influence pan-Aboriginal consciousness had on Aboriginal art. It comprises 200 traditional hollow-log coffins, brought together to create a cemetery of sorts, to honour all those Aboriginal people whose lives were lost over the 200 years of colonisation and dispossession. The coffins were created by 43 Ramingining artists and their arrangement is connotative of their clan estates. The memorial was conceptualised and orchestrated by Indigenous curator Djon Mundine, who was the Art Centre coordinator at Ramingining at the time. The work was partly inspired by the film *The Secret Country* in which John Pilger laments that, even though Australian servicemen who fought wars in foreign lands were honoured in Australia, there were no memorials to those Aboriginal people who had died trying to defend their homelands (Mundine 1988). The memorial was commissioned by the National Gallery of Australia, and its inclusion in the *Sydney Biennale* of 1988 was a defining moment in the high art world's acceptance of Aboriginal art (Mundine 2000; Smith 2001). It has remained on permanent display at the National Gallery ever since, while it also led to hollow-log coffins being created and sold as fine art objects (Morphy 2008, 200). The scope of the work's message and its collaborative nature means it is very much expressive of pan-Aboriginality, while also being a potent symbol of Aboriginal cultural trauma.

Yet pan-Aboriginality was always a fragile and contested thing, and both non-Indigenous and Indigenous Australians continue to draw strong distinctions between so-called urban and remote Aboriginal people based on their ideas about habits of life and skin colour. The deployment of images of Aboriginal poverty in remote areas to spur the conscience of non-Indigenous society has sometimes been damaging for the communities concerned, due to the shame associated with these depictions, revealing the unintended local repercussions of the strategies of broad social justice movements (Lyndon 2012, 203–7). And as identity politics sometimes produced essentialist visions of Aboriginality, the importance of defending an 'open and liberal Aboriginality' became clear to intellectuals such as Indigenous scholar Philip Morrissey, so as not to risk 'the reintroduction of authentic/inauthentic discourses' or the reification of political dispositions and cultural orientations (2003, 53). In Aboriginal art commentary specifically the relationship between urban and remote Aboriginality has been characterised by a mixture of affinity and discord.[5] As Ginsburg and Myers observed, the concept of Aboriginality that was embraced by Australian civil society in the 1970s was rooted in remote, traditional Aboriginal Australia and in a sense of incommensurate *difference*. It was not necessarily inclusive of people with lighter skin (with mixed ancestry), whose Aboriginal forebears had been dispossessed of their lands many generations ago, and who had suffered the most severe fragmentation of their families and communities.

Therefore the recognition that has accrued to remote Aboriginal culture in institutional contexts, public culture and in legislation such as the Land Rights Act (NT) has been regarded ambivalently by many Aboriginal people who know that they are outside, or on the periphery, of this domain of recognition.[6] Indeed, this exclusion can be regarded as another thread of cultural trauma for Aboriginal Australians who live outside remote Australia, particularly for those who have experienced racism throughout their lives. Artist Brownyn Bancroft has remarked on the sense of exclusion engendered by this partial recognition, writing that, '[f]or years we were punished for being black, now we're punished for not being black enough' (quoted in Perkins and Lynn 1993, x). Similarly, Bob Maza noted that 'we urban Aboriginals used to look on Aboriginal culture as being "over there" – just like we considered the white culture as being "over there" – and we were in a sort of no man's land' (Maza quoted in Thompson 1990, 161–62).

The artistic practice and advocacy of people like Bancroft, Maza and in recent years the artists Vernon Ah Kee and Gordon Hookey, give voice to a sense of Aboriginal identity that is relevant to the majority of Aboriginal people in Australia. This identity can be roughly (and cautiously) generalised as having a heritage in mission life, in urban 'fringe-dwelling' and in displacement and transience, while it has also arisen from circumstances of partial and sometimes successful integration into white society. In many cases it has been shaped by low levels of education, uneven employment and being part of an itinerant rural, urban and coastal labour force. This kind of Aboriginal identity is one forged through resilience in the face of racism and adversity. It is also vested in the retention of songs, stories, language and bush skills as well as the adaptation of distinctly Aboriginal social structures, norms and ideals to changing conditions. It is rooted in extended familial and communal ties that were relied on and reinforced by experiences of social exclusion and discrimination that ran across several generations (Gilbert 1977; Langton 1981; Ah Kee and Barkley 2009; Johnson et al. 2009/2010).

The urban Aboriginal arts movement was both a product of and helped to foment a new consciousness and sense of pride in these experiences, as the following artists' statements from Ricky Maynard and Brenda L. Croft attest:

We have seen the negative stereotyping of Aboriginal people either as passive fringe dwellers or the noble savage. I intend to redress this situation and show

> the strength, kinship and cultural pride within urban Black Australia from an Aboriginal perspective. (Maynard quoted in Queensland Art Gallery 1990, 57)

> I am fair, I am aware that I am not what people are looking for when they want something black, something real, something authentic, something truly Aboriginal, but I am here. (Croft 1998; see also Caruana and Isaacs 1990)

In both of these quotations we sense that art is imbued with an activist sense of purpose, such that the representation of one's identity and experience might have emancipatory potential for a collectivity, not just the individual. In recent years an equally powerful vision of urban Indigenous fortitude has been created by artist Richard Bell, who regularly performs an irreverent and satirical public persona to confront white society's prejudices and hypocrisies (Perkins 2007).

2.3   Urban Indigenous Aesthetic Public Spheres

Habermas's theorisation of the 'aesthetic public sphere' is a worthy reference point when thinking about the activities of these Indigenous artists and intellectuals. Habermas has argued that social arenas in which emerging aesthetic forms are shared and discussed have the potential to inaugurate broader spheres of dialogue in which people are collectively able to establish a critical stance on the exercise of state power (1974, 52). Habermas offers the example of the London coffee houses and salons which in the eighteenth century became settings where members of the newly formed bourgeoisie critically debated literature, art and culture (Jones 2007a, 76–78). In these contexts, the 'discussion of aesthetic matters provides the associative fora which are capable of turning their concerns to matters of state' (Jones 2007b, 120). We might characterise the committee of artists and activists on the AAB described earlier as a vital and consequential politicised aesthetic sphere or point to Indigenous art collectives and cooperatives such as Boomalli, the Campfire Group (Indigenous/non-Indigenous) and proppaNOW. As Andrea Fisher of proppaNOW has stated, that platform has been 'a way of empowering ourselves as people to understand [Australian history] and to think it through quite critically' (Campbell 2009, 83). We might also point to the long running *Awaye* program hosted by Indigenous producer and presenter Daniel Browning on ABC radio and publishing opportunities opened up by magazines such as *Art Monthly* and *Artlink* that have dedicated special issues to Aboriginal art and Aboriginal writers.

Beyond these examples of public spheres, in general urban Indigenous artists, curators, writers and professionals (and their non-Indigenous supporters) have treated the art arena as a surrogate state – a domain that can be radicalised and democratised and compelled to provide the Indigenous subject with the recognition that the actual state withholds. Here it is worth quoting Paine, who points out that 'much of Fourth world politics is about turning physical powerlessness into moral power'; finding symbolically powerful means of 'impugning the morality of the state' that engage the sentiments and imagination of the wider public (1985, 190–91; see also Garneau 2014, 320–22). By the force of their collective political will, their aesthetic innovations, humour and the weight of their social critique, these Indigenous actors have arguably exercised this moral power, persuading art institutions and their attendant professionals and audiences to create a space for their art and their message.[7] The following statement from artist Richard Bell may be interpreted in these terms: 'I came into art through politics [...] I discovered, as far as activism goes, there's no better forum than art' (Sorensen 2006, 8; see also Von Sturmer 2006). Bell's statement, recalling the activist and military vocabulary noted earlier, encourages us to recognise the performative properties of these artworks and discourses, as they depict and enunciate nonnormative truths as a form of strategic symbolic communication (Yúdice 2003; Alexander 2004). As Paine reminds us, entertainment and 'dramatic presentation' are 'the cutting edge of moral opposition' (1985, 191, 215). This is well illustrated by the phrase "always was, always will be" proclaimed in neon in the public artwork by Kamilaroi artist Reko Rennie that is depicted on the cover of this book. This artwork was installed in 2012 on a disused heritage building situated at Taylor Square, a busy intersection and pedestrian meeting place in the heart of Sydney. Its geometric forms are inspired by the traditional tree-markings of Rennie's ancestral country in Northwestern NSW and have an optically powerful presence that outrivals the signage and lighting that clutters its setting. An abbreviation of the time-honoured activist slogan 'Always was, always will be Aboriginal land', its repeated articulation in Aboriginal art contexts is a reminder that Aboriginal art must not become estranged from the project of Aboriginal cultural survival (Perkins and Thornton, 2010). The visibility of Rennie's work as a piece of public art commissioned by the City of Sydney council provides a good segue to the themes addressed in the following chapters.

Chapter 3

UNDERSTANDING ABORIGINAL ART SUBSIDY

In order to grasp the relationship between Aboriginal art and the state, it is necessary to approach the problem from two directions: to understand the principles that have informed the subsidy of Aboriginal art (to be discussed here) and to understand how Aboriginal art has been mobilised in symbolic ways in the sphere of cultural governance (to be discussed in the following chapter). One of the distinguishing characteristics of Aboriginal art subsidy is that it has in part been premised on the idea that a form of work is being undertaken and needs to be encouraged. My aim here is to show that Aboriginal art has been subject to much more complex governance agendas than other types of government funded art production, and further, to reveal how instrumentalist forces have shaped Aboriginal art practices, meanings, and the trajectory of the movement as a whole.

3.1 'Meaningful Work': Making Sense of Aboriginal Art Subsidy

> This is a good thing for these people. It is meaningful, culturally appropriate work in a place where there is none. They also like doing it. They paint Monday to Friday from 9am to 5pm. They don't paint weekends because the art centre staff need to rest, but if it weren't for us, they'd come and paint here every day of the week. (Gloria Morales, coordinator at Warlukurlangu Artists in Yuendumu, quoted in Genocchio 2008, 93)

In general, Aboriginal art's subsidy has been viewed by governments as a 'means to combine cultural maintenance with economic activity for both Indigenous and national benefit' (Altman et al. 2002, 2). Since the 1970s, the Aboriginal art industry has been subsidised by sources in state, territory and federal governments, including the Aboriginal Arts Board within the Australia Council, Aboriginal Affairs agencies, the Aboriginal and Torres Strait Islander Commission (ATSIC) (now defunct) and arts ministries within the cabinet. The industry was first formally subsidised by the federal government in 1970, when the Aboriginal Arts Advisory Committee was formed within the Australian Council for the Arts (which had been established two years prior).[1] The Committee's budget grew from \$60,000 in 1970 to \$500,000 in 1972 (Roughsey 1976, 236; Thompson 1972). In 1971, the Commonwealth also established Aboriginal Arts and Crafts Pty Ltd, to take responsibility for marketing Aboriginal art and wholesaling works obtained from remote communities to retailers or selling them in its own outlets in major cities (Peterson 1983).[2] In 1973, when the Whitlam Labor government presided over the ratification of the Australia Council for the Arts as a statutory body, the Aboriginal Arts Advisory Committee was formalised as the Aboriginal Arts Board. Significantly, it was the only one of the Council's seven boards to be dedicated to a particular social group rather than a category of the arts.

For close to ten years, the Aboriginal art sector relied wholly on the Aboriginal Arts Board for financial support (Altman et al. 1989, 21). In addition to paying the artists for the works they produced, the board provided funding for supplies, transportation and salaries for art advisors at the fledgling art centres and built a retail market for Aboriginal art through the city-based Government Company galleries. This market was slow to develop, however, and between 1973 and the early 1980s, the board took the radical but prescient step of staging exhibitions of Aboriginal art overseas (Berrell 2009). These exhibitions were often followed by donations of works to the hosting embassies and institutions, in an effort both to prevent the emerging market in Australia from being flooded and to stimulate market interest overseas.

As Altman et al. (1989, Chapters 8 and 9) document, during the 1980s, the Hawke Labor government made a commitment to achieving employment and income equity for Indigenous Australians, and the Aboriginal arts and crafts industry (often in association with the tourism sector) was treated as one of the few areas of real promise. At the time of the 1989 Review of the Aboriginal Arts and Crafts Industry, the Department of Education, Employment and Training was 'becoming the major agency providing industry support' (155). By the early 1990s the Aboriginal art sector had expanded significantly. The Government Company was recognised to be operating in competition with private galleries selling Aboriginal art and was closed. At the same time, the National Arts and Crafts Industry Support Strategy (NACISS) was established to fund the art centres, and rather than being administered by the Aboriginal Arts Board, it was made part of the economic strategy of ATSIC. This marked a significant shift in the rationale for subsidy. As Healy notes, it entailed that 'the sources of funds and the requirements for funding for art centres [shifted] from arts-based to predominantly economic criteria' (2005, 30). In subsequent years, the art centres were increasingly treated as enterprises competing in the marketplace, and many developed very sophisticated and successful marketing practices (Altman 2000b, 91–98; Wright 2000a; Acker et al. 2013).

The possibility that Aboriginal people's economic disadvantage might be ameliorated through the sale of their art – an intuitively uplifting prospect – has informed this policy trajectory at many levels, just as it has been a recurrent feature of celebratory accounts of Aboriginal art and underpinned utopian characterisations of it as an emancipatory movement (Altman 2005a; Fisher 2015). As Fred Myers writes of the early days of painting at Papunya, 'an important part of the administrative response to the continuing presence, poverty, and high mortality of Aborigines was to find them a place in the economy' (2002, 130). The ideals of self-determination gave credence to the hope that painting might constitute 'culturally meaningful work' (130). This is true of the Aboriginal art sector more broadly, and several art centres and collectives have their origins in government programs concerned with Aboriginal economic development and adult education, including the Utopia Women's Batik Project, which launched the career of Emily Kame Kngwarreye and other artists (Thompson 1972; Batty 2008; Bowdler 2009). While the framework of self-determination diminished, the objective Myers describes has remained part of Aboriginal art subsidy strategies ever since. Beyond the sphere of policy, the treatment of Aboriginal art production as a form of work, and the emphasis on Aboriginal art's value as an avenue for Aboriginal people to engage with the economy has been consensual terrain for governments, artists and Indigenous and non-Indigenous advocates and art professionals.[3]

The Aboriginal Arts Board has also regularly made the case that the arts are a means for Aboriginal people to overcome poverty and earn an income. As stated in one annual report: 'Members of the Board are aware of the demoralising effects on people who depend on hand-outs for their livelihood. The Board has therefore pursued a policy of encouraging Aboriginals to produce works in order to assure themselves of economic independence' (Australia Council 1977, 25; see also 1979; 1984). This was initiated at Papunya, where it became clear very early that cash flow to the artists was essential for the continuation of art production (Myers 2001, 182–83). In response, rather than following the conventional arts subsidy model of providing individual artists' grants, the board chose to commission and pay the artists for the paintings they produced. In relation to this idiosyncratic method, Robert (Bob) Edwards, the first director of the board, was known to say that Papunya 'was the most heavily subsidised art in the country!' (Kimber quoted in McCulloch 2001, 30,

32–33). In subsequent years, variations of the upfront payment method were adopted by many other art centres (Wright 1999, 313).

In the state of Western Australia, the incentive of immediate payment proved to have a similarly vitalising effect. In the early 1980s the Department of Native Welfare employed Mary Macha, a project officer who ran the Government Company gallery in the city of Perth, to visit Aboriginal communities in the Kimberley and desert regions of the state to see if cultural production could be a viable source of income for them. Macha was able to draw on government funds to pay people in the community of Balgo for artefacts and carvings that were then sold in the Perth gallery. In John Carty's view, Macha's introduction of a market model in Balgo was a vital catalyst of the Balgo painting movement:

> Painting was a way that Balgo people could assert, and enable, their own autonomy in exchange with kartiya [white people]. For the first time, the ultimate objectification of Aboriginal value – Country and the Tjukurrpa [Dreaming] – was able to be brought into exchange with the primary measure of kartiya value: money. (2011, 59)

As a representative of the Government Company, Macha became an influential broker of the work of other celebrated Aboriginal artists in the region, like Rover Thomas.

In the 1980s, as noted earlier, Aboriginal art sector funding was less focused on the cultural priorities that were so fundamental to the art centre model and oriented more to 'training and enterprise support to create full-time positions in the formal labour market' and fostering 'cottage industries manufacturing arts and crafts' (Altman et al. 1989, 156). This was true of the Department of Education, Employment and Training's funding allocation but also the Aboriginal Development Commission and other government agencies that directed funding to art centres under a range of training, employment and business development schemes, in some cases on the basis that they were Aboriginal enterprises that would eventually become commercially sustainable (114–22). The Aboriginal Development Commission also took over the running of the Government Company from the Aboriginal Arts Board in 1984. Meanwhile – as discussed previously with regards to the social justice agendas leadership of Chika Dixon and Gary Foley, within the board there was new attention to arts-related employment opportunities for Aboriginal people. The board's non-Indigenous staff were replaced by Indigenous staff, and organisations that were recipients of board grants were encouraged to do the same if they wanted to be credible candidates for funding (Rowse 2000a, 516; Australia Council 1986, 26).

The Community Development Employment Projects (CDEP), a kind of 'work for the dole' scheme established in 1977, has also contributed to the work-like quality of Aboriginal art production. In 2000, 10 of the 39 art centres surveyed by *The Art and Craft Centre Story*, a report commissioned by the peak art centre body Desart, were employing some or all of their artists as CDEP participants (Wright 2000b, 31). Similarly, in 2007 the Department of Employment and Workplace Relations reported that 'around 130 arts activities are currently undertaken by 95 CDEP organisations' (Senate Standing Committee on Environment, Communications, Information Technology and the Arts 2007, 64; see also Wright 2006; Altman 2006, 6). When plans to abolish the CDEP scheme were announced in 2007, the reliance of some quarters of the industry on it was made clear. Richard Birrinbirrin, chairperson of the Association of Northern, Kimberley & Arnhem Aboriginal Artists (ANKAAA), expressed the following concern:

> Nearly all of our art centre workers and artists rely on CDEP payments which have supported jobs in art centres for the past 20 years. Due to the years of underfunding of Indigenous education, many or [sic] our people are not (mainstream) job ready and some never will be. They do have meaningful work though; their job is the expression and teaching of our culture. They are artists. (Quoted in Kohen 2007, 1; see also Peatling and Gibson 2007; Owen 2007a)

In 2008, at a time when art centres were facing difficult market conditions due to the global financial crisis, CDEP underwent reforms designed to steer Aboriginal people toward 'real' jobs.[4] This saw many artists lose access to regular, small wages, but the creation of new jobs for Aboriginal arts workers through the Indigenous Employment Initiative (IEI), a strategy of the government's 'Closing the Gap' policy to address Aboriginal people's socioeconomic disadvantage. As a result, it is now sometimes the case that the greatest portion of government funding received by art centres is allocated to the salaries of Aboriginal arts workers (that is, those who contribute to the running of the art centre) (Woodhead and Acker 2014). As Altman has suggested, this has created a somewhat perverse situation: at a time when the Aboriginal art sector is very vulnerable, the moderate income CDEP used to provide to artists to support their practice has been supplanted by a subsidy strategy that seeks to 'cajole people into the mainstream labour market, even if no mainstream jobs exist' (2013, 19). Similarly, Woodhead and Acker stress that 'the purpose of Indigenous Employment Initiative funding is specifically not for art making', which means that 'many art centres are recalibrating their operations to become an employment service with art as an activity' (2014, 127). In other words, art centre subsidy has now become entangled with employment policy to the extent that a proxy of labour-force participation is prioritised over ensuring that the conditions are there for the continued creation of the kind of art that sustains the sector.

The emphasis on labour and income in Aboriginal art subsidy strategies has created a unique economy of art production in which pecuniary interest is treated as an understandable driver of artistic creation. Inherent to this method of governance is the awareness that, as Birrinbirrin suggested earlier, Aboriginal people in remote communities often lack the education and skills to enter the workforce, even where job opportunities do exist. Now that Aboriginal art and other practices such as dance, storytelling and performance are credited as being alternative realms of skill and knowledge, they have become an attractive target of policy. At the same time, as Carty demonstrates in the case of Balgo art, the convergence of painting, 'work' and discretionary money that was brought about by the art centre model was quite fluidly incorporated into the mixed economies and kin-based sharing practices that are characteristic of remote Aboriginal communities. As he writes, 'acrylic painting is most productively understood as an Aboriginal form of 'work' bound to local values and relational principles' (2011, 98).

Of course, when subsidy was first introduced, no one anticipated that Aboriginal art would attain the status of fine art. But given that it has, it is quite obvious that the uniquely calibrated arts economy discussed here subverts the fine arts ideals embodied in the figure of the Romantic artist as discussed in the introduction. It thus problematises Western conventions around art's value and integrity. As I will explore in greater detail later, the emphasis on economic outcomes, and on money as an incentive for art production, has turned out to be both a galvanising and destabilising force: essential to the flourishing of the Aboriginal art movement but equally something that has encouraged the production of a prodigious amount of work of varying quality.

3.2   The Ambiguity of Aboriginal Art Sector Policy

It is interesting to note that the amalgam of economic, cultural and social objectives that has underpinned the subsidy of Aboriginal art production at remote art centres was endorsed by both major parties during a period of highly adversarial politics in Indigenous affairs: when there was little consensus over the reasons and solutions for Indigenous disadvantage, over what is meant by Indigenous 'rights', and about the meanings and duties entailed by reconciliation. The following remarks by Liberal senator Richard Alston in 2003 are exemplary of the kinds of ministerial endorsements of the Aboriginal art industry that have been articulated across party lines: 'Given the employment, cultural, artistic and wealth-creating significance of the sector as well as its enormous potential to boost community self-esteem a whole-of-government approach is required' (Alston et al. 2003; see also Hill quoted in Milliken 2004, 24; Garrett 2010a; Office for the Arts 2011a). If, as Altman and Rowse note, policy disagreements have largely revolved around the core question of whether Indigenous policy should prioritise the facilitation of 'choice and self-determination' or 'equality of socioeconomic status', then it is clear that Aboriginal art is highly mutable with respect to these disputes and can be viewed as complementary to both priorities (2005, 159).[5]

The rapid growth of the Aboriginal art market in the 15 years prior to the global financial crisis ensured the continuation of subsidy, but points to further ambiguities. As has been often pointed out, the precise meaning of Aboriginal art's widely celebrated success is elusive (Myers 2001, 181–82; Healy 2005, 6). Is it a market success, an economic success, an 'artistic' success, or an 'Aboriginal' success? That this question cannot be easily answered is indicated by the fact that the motives for subsidy, particularly in the 2000s, have been shaped by impressions of both the success and fragility of the Aboriginal art industry. With regard to the former, governments have focused on the recognition Aboriginal art has received in fine arts circles and its success within the art market. This inspired, for example, the introduction of Resale Royalty legislation in 2010, which presumed that the strong resale market for Aboriginal art observed in the 1990s and 2000s would continue indefinitely. In addition, state and local governments across Australia have increasingly regarded Aboriginal arts-related initiatives to be good policy in the areas of Indigenous affairs, cultural planning and tourism. These initiatives show that governments have sought to mobilise the commercial success of Aboriginal art within their own jurisdictions and further, that they view such policies as a matter of equity and a means to fulfil their obligations to their Indigenous constituents.[6] Such initiatives reveal the way governments' cultural and commercial goals are tethered to the policy imperatives thrown up by identity politics (Yúdice 2003). As 'culture' becomes the 'foundation for claims to recognition and resources', the subvention of Indigenous art and the facilitation of public celebrations of Indigenous culture have provided the state with ways to enfranchise those citizens who assert their right to cultural citizenship outside the mainstream (56).

Counterposed to those strategies that have been premised on Aboriginal arts' success, there are many instances of ministers and bureaucrats being warned that if they pursue a particular policy line, or do not intervene in some way, Aboriginal art is in jeopardy. This was the case when plans to abolish CDEP were announced, when new restrictions were placed on art's inclusion in self-managed superannuation portfolios (subsidised through tax-breaks) and in arguments made *against* the proposed resale royalty scheme (because a tax would be likely to discourage buyers in the primary market).

Such warnings were also expressed in submissions to the 2007 Senate inquiry, which argued that the integrity of Aboriginal art could only be preserved if art centres received greatly increased support and the government cracked down on the unethical conduct of some dealers (discussed later) (Senate Standing Committee on Environment, Communications, Information Technology and the Arts 2007; Glenday 2010; Fulton and Morgan 2010). The ambiguity and contradictions underpinning these policy discourses and strategies attests to the unique burden Aboriginal art has carried in Australian public and political life, as I now move to explore in greater detail.

Chapter 4

THE STATE MOBILISING ABORIGINAL ART

4.1 The Acquisition, Endorsement and Appropriation of Aboriginal Art and the Growth of Aboriginal Public Culture

With this brief account of the subsidy strategies that have sustained the Aboriginal art movement in mind, we can now explore the other side of the coin: the heightened visibility of Aboriginal art in the context of state endorsed commemorative events, discourses and forms of public culture. Previously I drew attention to Chris Healy's proposition that the 1988 Bicentenary left a 'heritage vacuum' in Australian public culture. Healy makes the persuasive argument that this vacuum came to be filled by Aboriginal culture and that at the end of the twentieth century an 'intercultural zone' of 'Aboriginality and heritage' monopolised nationalistic forms of governance where civic culture was concerned (2001, 287). This is evinced by the flourishing of Aboriginal-produced and themed music, performance, festivals, film and literature in the 1990s and 2000s that had very little of the fringe quality that the Aboriginal arts had in the 1970s and 1980s, and in fact became a significant niche within the Australian Arts sector. This flourishing was undoubtedly connected to a growing public consciousness of Aboriginal cultural trauma, and with respect to arts subsidy, the state's need to publicly reconfigure the terms of Indigenous/non-Indigenous relations. An 'intercultural zone' was certainly envisaged in the landmark *Creative Nation* cultural policy launched in 1994, in which Aboriginal economic prosperity and well-being were married to the cultural enrichment of the Australian community and to national Reconciliation (DoCA 1994, 67, 75). This synthesis is pivotal to understanding the agendas that have driven the circulation of Aboriginal art (Craik 2007, 45; see also Langton and CAR 1994; Garrett 2010a).

The following discussion is concerned with the movement of Aboriginal art to the centre of Australian public life in the 1980s, 1990s and 2000s. It aims to show how Aboriginal art was facilitated, acquired, appropriated and endorsed by the state as a symbolic tool of transformation to instantiate a postcolonial catharsis and resolution that might be generative of a new kind of nationhood. As we will see, this involved 'complex networks and institutions of collaboration' that traverse the Indigenous/non-Indigenous divide (Myers 2005, 89). In a later chapter I will explore the forms of Aboriginal 'mass culture' that proliferated in commercial and corporate settings and that are of relevance to this nationalistic project; however, here I focus on those forms of Aboriginal culture that have a direct relationship with cultural governance.

It is worthwhile beginning with a fact that is often overlooked when the historical successes of the Aboriginal art market have been assessed; namely, that government agencies have been significant purchasers of Aboriginal art for several decades. For example, in the late 1980s public sector acquisitions provided respite in the then feeble commercial market for Aboriginal arts and crafts. As Myers writes, in 1986 the Government Company 'doubled the sales in just one year [...] mostly from sales to government offices such as the High Court of Australia, the Parliament House art collection and the government-owned Artbank (which rented out art to government offices)' (2002, 200–201).[1] Since that time, in addition to the national, state and regional galleries that have endeavoured to build representative Aboriginal art collections, government offices and agencies at the local, state and federal level (including overseas embassies) have purchased and commissioned many Aboriginal artworks, and most Australians are familiar with Aboriginal art works in these venues serving as backdrops for politicians and dignitaries facing the press. In addition, universities, the Aboriginal and Torres Strait Islander Commission, the Australian Institute of Aboriginal and Torres Strait Islander Studies, Land Councils and other Aboriginal organisations have all established large collections of Aboriginal art.[2] All of these agencies need to be recognised as comprising a public component of the private market in Aboriginal art.

Another setting in which government agencies gave sustenance to the Aboriginal art movement was the Australian Heritage Commission's *Art of Place* National Indigenous Heritage Art Award, which was first staged in 1994. With 1993 being the UN Year of Indigenous Peoples (marked by Keating's 'Redfern Address'), Commission staff were eager for Indigenous people to put forward nominations for the register of the National Estate. An art exhibition was conceived and curator Margo Neale recognised that the exhibition could be tailored to the commission's goals if the artists were encouraged to create works about places of heritage significance to them and elaborate on this significance as part of their submission (M. Neale, pers. comm.). Designed to affirm and raise awareness of the diverse ways Aboriginal people connected with their ancestral country, the awards were staged in an inclusive spirit and encouraged the participation of established, emerging and amateur Indigenous artists. They proved to be highly successful and were held at Parliament House in 1994, 1996, 1998 and 2000.

The *Art of Place* Awards are rarely mentioned in Aboriginal art histories because they are not seen to have been a staging post in Aboriginal art's journey to high art status. However, they supported the Aboriginal art movement at a time when its repertoire of styles and regions was expanding rapidly, and played an important part in the story I'm telling about the paradigms of cultural governance that helped to bring Aboriginal art into the public arena. The Australian Heritage Commission (established in 1975) was an initiative of the Whitlam Labor government, and its work around Indigenous heritage was continuous with the activities of the research community that was engaged with Aboriginal rock art, archaeology and anthropology in the 1960s and 1970s, as mentioned earlier. Among those who were instrumental in establishing the Awards were Sharon Sullivan (then director of the Australian Heritage Commission) and Betty Meehan (director of the Aboriginal and Torres Strait Islander Environment Section at the Commission between 1991–95), both of whom had long been involved in Indigenous archaeological and anthropological scholarship and heritage management.

What is significant about the *Art of Place* Awards (and touring exhibitions) is that they provided a government arena in which connections could be drawn between the gravity of Aboriginal land custodianship and nationalistic ideas about environmental and cultural heritage. They celebrated the nexus of land and art as a basis for Aboriginal pride and participation, and, if we have in mind the ambivalent cultural messages of the 1988 Bicentenary, we can see that they helped to present Aboriginal heritage as a new anchor of the distinctiveness and depth of the culture of the nation (Australian Heritage Commission 1998; 2000). Such is conveyed in Liberal Senator Robert Hill's 'Minister's message' in the 1998 catalogue:

> What the Australian Heritage Commission is doing through important initiatives like this Art Award and Exhibition is to bring to the public the notion that heritage includes a vast array of cultural and natural places that are dear to Australians and which we want to keep. And it's doing it through the vitality of the art of Australia's indigenous people. (1998, 3)

There have of course been many other Aboriginal art awards, and in the 2000s almost all state and territory governments established dedicated Indigenous arts strategies and/or regularly subsidised Indigenous art fairs, prizes and showcases. These events, as well as the opening of museum and gallery spaces dedicated to Aboriginal art and culture, exhibitions, and large corporate commissions, have been launched by government ministers, state premiers, and ambassadors and consulate representatives overseas. These are important, performative moments that instantiate the way Aboriginal art has mediated reciprocal agendas at the interface between the state, civil society and the Aboriginal community (Yúdice 2003, 31). For example, we saw that Prime Minister Gough Whitlam launched the National Seminar on Aboriginal Arts in 1973, and in 1985 Prime Minister Bob Hawke opened the exhibition *The Face of the Centre: Papunya Tula Paintings 1971–84* at the National Gallery of Victoria (Johnson 1997, 65). The Governor-General Bill Hayden (from 1988–1996), who was highly sympathetic to Indigenous people's campaigns for social justice, opened the *Great Australian Art* exhibition at the Art Gallery of South Australia in Adelaide in 1989. Hayden used his speech to acknowledge the 40,000-year history of the continent rather than the 200-year history being commemorated by the exhibition and remarked that 'I sometimes think that unless we obtain an understanding of the landscape and the truths as Aboriginal people know them we will always be aliens in Australia' (The Advertiser 1989, 3). When he retired in 1996, Hayden made a speech on Australia Day in which he declared:

> Aboriginal creativity has taken its place as a major influence in our national consciousness. We're receptive to what Aboriginal artists, dancers, writers and performers have to say. In a very real sense they are helping to reshape our own concept of self and of country – of the way we see and feel things as Australian – and as others see us. (quoted in Rothwell 1996)

Both statements treat Aboriginal culture, heritage and ecology as integral to a progressive formulation of Australian nationalism. They imply, as Lattas has argued, that 'a redemptive function is being assigned to Aborigines, with the process of knowing something about Aboriginal culture taking the form of a pilgrimage' (1997, 241). In a similar vein, Aboriginal Affairs minister Robert Tickner made the following statement at the launch of the first of three (created in 1994, 1995 and 2002) Qantas jets featuring Aboriginal designs, for which Qantas had commissioned the Aboriginal-owned Balarinji Design Studio: 'If we as a nation believe in the reconciliation process, if we believe in bringing greater understanding between Aboriginal and non-Aboriginal people, this [aircraft] must be seen as a flying beacon of hope in that process' (quoted in Black 2008, 340; Qantas 2012). All of these examples reveal the way state actors mobilised Aboriginal art, symbolically and rhetorically, to persuade the public of the authenticity of the idea of Reconciliation.[3] As such they are emblematic of Aboriginal art's instrumentalisation: while they harness Aboriginal art's rich aesthetic meanings to their cause, the aggregate effect of this appropriation has also been to furnish Aboriginal art with a set of quite specific connotations linked to this broad national project.

Within this narrative it is important to make note of the numerous Aboriginal art commissions scattered across Australia's public spaces. Among the most well-known is a mosaic designed by Michael Nelson Jagamara for the forecourt of the new Parliament House in the nation's capital, and Reconciliation Place in Canberra, which features works by several artists including Judy Watson and Thanakupi. Overseas, the Australian Indigenous Art Commission for the Musée du Quai Branly in Paris (composed of permanent installations of eight Indigenous artists' work within the architecture of the museum) was unveiled in 2006. It was funded by the French and Australian governments as well as some Australian private donors, with the Australia Council being a partner in the management of the project (Musée du Quai Branly et al. 2006; Clark et al. 2007). As I will explore in the following chapter in relation to Jagamara's mosaic, not all such public art commissions permit an easy synthesis of Aboriginal heritage and Australian nationhood. This seems most obviously the case with works like Reko Rennie's *Always was, always will be* in Taylor Square in Sydney, *Witnessing to Silence*, by Fiona Foley at the Brisbane Magistrate's Court, and *Yininmadyemi Thou Didst Let Fall* in Sydney's Hyde Park by Tony Albert (Allas 2008; Martin-Chew 2009; Kembrey 2015).

Small commissions have been no less significant in terms of their symbolic purpose and effect. Between 2007 and 2009, *The Storylines Project* researched approximately 600 biographies of Indigenous artists from the settled (nonremote) regions of Australia for publication on the Australian artists' biographies database Design and Art Australia Online (DAAO) (Johnson et al. 2009/2010). This research found that among many of those artists who had developed (usually modest) artistic careers in the 1990s and 2000s, small-scale commissions from government bodies, schools and businesses comprised a significant proportion of their paid practice. These commissions included organisation logos, graphic designs and decorative imagery for booklets and documents. They also included small public art projects such as murals and public sculpture to commemorate important individuals, local history and heritage and acknowledge Indigenous land custodianship.[4] All of these forms have contributed to the distribution of a recognisable Indigenous aesthetic in Australian public culture.

As the Musée du Quai Branly in Paris commissions exemplifies, the state's mobilisations of Aboriginal art have often had the dual function of locating Aboriginal culture in both Australian domestic and exported culture. During the 1980s and 1990s, Aboriginal tourism was established as a niche within Australian tourism policy, and strategies formulated by ATSIC and state and federal governments located Aboriginal art and culture within a cultural tourism paradigm. In subsequent years, Aboriginal art, performance and land custodianship became ubiquitous as visual representations of Australia in national as well as state tourism advertisements, particularly those promoting the Northern Territory (ATSIC 1995; Office of Northern Development 1993; Zeppel 1998; Hinkson 2004). The 2000 Olympic Games (the logo of which featured a boomerang) typified the relationship being established between tourism, Aboriginal culture and nationalism. Reconciliation was a vitally important theme in nationalistic discourses that circulated during the bidding process for the games and in anticipation of the event itself, and in many people's minds the games marked the apex of the Reconciliation movement (Elder et al. 2006; Hanna 1999). In 1997 the Sydney Olympic Arts Festival series, staged over four years, was launched with the *Festival of the Dreaming*, dedicated to Aboriginal Arts and culture and comprising a range of events and programs produced and performed by Indigenous people (Hanna 1999). Aboriginal culture retained a strong presence in the following festivals, and ultimately the opening and closing ceremonies were dominated by Aboriginal themes and performances. The Indigenous athlete Cathy Freeman became the icon of the games, both through her selection to light the cauldron-flame (with a boomerang-shaped torch), and as a result of her victory lap following her 400-metre sprint, in which she held both the Australian and the Aboriginal flags (Elder et al. 2006; Rowe and Stevenson 2006).

During the decade of Reconciliation a range of festivals, anniversaries and calendar events that celebrate aspects of Aboriginal culture through-out the year were initiated or consolidated.[5] It is now also commonplace for Aboriginal performance to be included in launches, media events and conferences.[6] These forms of Aboriginal public culture have been incorporated into town, city and regional cultural planning policies in which the commemora-tion of Aboriginal heritage, places of importance and the engagement of the Aboriginal community are invariably specified as objectives (see, e.g., Coffs Harbour City Council 2009; Dubbo City Council 2008–2012).[7] Like the *Art of Place* awards, these planning initiatives integrate the meanings Indigenous people attach to place within their definitions of Australian heritage. Since the 1980s, sacred sites across the country have been identified and protected, and Indigenous knowledge of flora and fauna, and the spiritual and social mean-ing of particular places have become part of the management and education programs associated with National Parks and State Forests. Indigenous place names have proliferated in the cartography of the country and Indigenous custodianship traditions are increasingly deployed within land management and conservation, most recently through the Indigenous Protected Areas and Working on Country programs (Langton and CAR 1994; Birch 2003; Merlan 2000; Altman and Kerins 2012).

In this account I've identified a range of Indigenous creative and expressive forms that, framed by cultural governance, heritage management and public commemoration, have become familiar features of public culture for many Australians. I don't propose that we see these forms as subsumed by the hegemony of the state. They function as regular reminders that Australia is an 'unfinished Western colonial project' and as spurs for intercultural dialogue, and they represent localised arenas for Indigenous agency (Hage 2003, 94). Nevertheless, these forms have proliferated in part due to their usefulness to the state's redemptive political project that has attempted to affirm Indigenous presences and stimulate new visions of nationhood, heritage and intercultural fellowship. Later chapters will examine how these morally inflected meanings influence the reception of Aboriginal fine art. We move now to an elaboration of the significance that ideas about Aboriginal culture acquired during this period, which will help us to understand the connotative capacities of Aboriginal art in this redemptive project.

Chapter 5

'ABORIGINAL CULTURE' AT THE NEXUS OF JUSTICE, RECOGNITION AND REDEMPTION

Government practices that are tasked with addressing cultural trauma must address the space where individual psychology imbricates with a socially constituted sense of collective victimisation (Alexander 2003, 100; Nagel 1994; Hall 1990). In order to foster a sense of healing and refreshed dignity among members of a formerly maligned social group, the state must not only address the victimised collective, but the wider society on whom that collective's sense of belonging and recognition depends. The Australian public servants who turned their energies to unravelling the ideology and policies of the assimilation era in the 1960s and early 1970s had to contend with precisely these problems, as did those people who became engaged in the Reconciliation movement. Having been essentially entombed in the public imagination, 'Aboriginality' had to be resurrected as a living thing, and the state's bestowal of recognition needed to be made manifest in the public domain. I have made the case that Aboriginal art and other cultural forms have been central to this process, and I wish here to extend this argument a little further and show that in many ways Aboriginal art became metonymic for 'Aboriginal culture' in this context.

5.1   Cultural Loss, Cultural Rights and Keeping Culture Strong

The events and discourses that have been traced thus far contributed to a post-assimilation constitution of Aboriginal culture at the nexus of justice, recognition and redemption. Aboriginal culture became a locus of meaning and intent in national discourse and public culture, due to the state's need for symbols of its bestowal of recognition, the consolidation of a pan-Aboriginal platform in advocacy discourses, and the fact that the growing but often anchorless goodwill of the non-Indigenous Australian public needed to find purchase in something tangible. Across these domains, public discourses on Aboriginal issues have consistently drawn a causative connection between evincing the worth of Aboriginal *culture* and evincing the worth of Aboriginal *personhood*.

Before we proceed to illustrations of this, we need to be honest about how difficult it is to pin down the meaning of such a ubiquitous referent as *Aboriginal culture*. As Raymond Williams wrote of the etymology and social history of the term *culture*, the various meanings that had assembled around it by the mid-twentieth century 'indicates a complex argument about the relations between general human development and a particular way of life, and between both and the works and practices of art and intelligence' (1988, 91). This complexity was intensified when the belief that *race* denotes essential, biological characteristics was debunked in the latter part of the twentieth century. This left a vacuum for the study of ethnicities and patterns of social differentiation; a vacuum which was filled in part by culture.

For anthropologist Gillian Cowlishaw, who has studied Australian race relations extensively (1999, 2004), the intellectual aversion to the idea of race (as if the very use of the term is racist) has created as many problems as it seeks to address. She reminds us that, while race is not a 'material fact', it exists nevertheless as 'a fact of the imagination, as are the identities, rivalries and hierarchies which surround it' (2004, 10). The fact that culture emerged as a favoured term in Australia (as elsewhere) to describe Aboriginal difference brought about a confusion of perceptions about Aboriginal identity and ways of being. It means that perceptions of Aboriginal people's difference are now often conflated with the West's exalted understanding of culture. In turn, as we know from the different ways remote and nonremote Aboriginal identity is configured, and as Elizabeth Povinelli's *The Cunning of Recognition* (2002) reveals with great acuity, this conflation has buttressed idealistic and conditional judgements about Aboriginality and Aboriginal tradition in national discourse that are very much at odds with Aboriginal ontology.

Lorraine Gibson (2013) reflects on the paradoxical effects of this convergence of ideas in her ethnography of art practices in the predominantly Aboriginal rural NSW town of Wilcannia, in which she probes the absurdity of the claim, made regularly by non-Indigenous citizens in the town, that the local Aboriginal people 'don't have any culture'. The toxicity of such statements is obvious, given that they are being made at a time of enhanced national recognition of Aboriginal society through Aboriginal art. They amount to 'a refusal of who Aboriginal people believe they are' (2013, 52). Such denials speak of local histories of agonistic coexistence while they also point to what has been left out of the visual and public culture idioms of national Reconciliation. Gibson asks, 'Since the majority of townspeople in Wilcannia are Aboriginal; where we might ask, if not in an Aboriginal community, is "real" Aboriginal culture thought to exist?' (2013, 36–41). Gibson was also made aware of the economy of cultural knowledge in Wilcannia: the way employment opportunities in heritage and land management, for example, drove the imperative of cultural retrieval. This meant that '[t]his thing called "culture" is actively being sought at the same time that it is actively asserted as present, real and alive' (57). Gibson's ethnography provides just one example of the way in which the concept of Aboriginal culture is negotiated interculturally – rebounding between local and national arenas of sociality and harnessed to perceptions about value and virtue. In Povinelli's terms, the paradox of Wilcannia Aboriginality lies in the 'difference between the traditions to which a cacophony of public voices pledge their allegiance and the indigenous people who are the alleged sociological referent of these traditions' (2002, 47, see also 48).

If we return to the arena of politics and social justice, it is clear that Aboriginal culture has been prominent in arguments advanced about the need to reverse the process of assimilation, to rehabilitate Aboriginal people's sense of self-worth and to correct the view that prevailed throughout much of Australia's history that Aboriginal people and their culture were inferior. This is illustrated in the rhetoric of prime ministers such as Whitlam and Keating, and the discourses surrounding Aboriginal Deaths in Custody, the Stolen Generations and Reconciliation. For instance, in the *Final Report of the Royal Commission into Aboriginal Deaths in Custody*, Commissioner Johnston writes that:

> [Aboriginal people] never voluntarily surrendered their culture and, indeed, fought tooth and nail to preserve it, throughout dispossession, protection, assimilation, [and] integration [...] They have the right to retain that culture, and that identity. Self-determination is both the expression and the guarantee of that right. (1991b, 1.7.21)

Similarly, in his Redfern address, Labor Prime Minister Paul Keating asked non-Indigenous Australians to recognise that '[w]e took the traditional lands and smashed the traditional way of life', and to 'imagine if ours was the oldest culture in the world and we were told that it was worthless'. He highlighted 'the demoralisation and desperation, the fractured identity' that had been revealed in the *Deaths in Custody* report, but suggested that:

> [w]e are beginning to more generally appreciate the depth and the diversity of Aboriginal and Torrest Strait Islander cultures. From their music and art and dance we are beginning to recognise how much richer our national life and identity will be for the participation of Aboriginals and Torres Strait Islanders. (2001[1992])

An important thread of the Stolen Generations Inquiry was that children who were removed had been deprived of 'community ties, culture and language' (National Inquiry 1997, 283, 296–314). As the report states:

One principal effect of the forcible removal policies was the destruction of cultural links. This was of course their declared aim. The children were to be *prevented from acquiring the habits and customs of the Aborigines* (South Australia's Protector of Aborigines in 1909); *the young people will merge into the present civilisation and become worthy citizens* (NSW Colonial Secretary in 1915). Culture, language, land and identity were to be stripped from the children in the hope that the traditional law and culture would die by losing their claim on them and sustenance of them. (202, original emphasis)

The inquiry found that this stripping away of culture was enforced not only by the children's separation from their families but by the punishment children experienced if they spoke or sang in their language. In general they were taught to be ashamed of their Aboriginality and to aspire to become white. This notion of cultural loss informed the argument put forward in the inquiry report that the policy amounted to 'genocide', because 'the predominant aim of Indigenous child removals was the absorption or assimilation of the children into the wider, non-Indigenous community so that their unique cultural values and ethnic identities would disappear, giving way to models of Western culture' (272–73; Curthoys and Docker 2001).

The grieving and sympathetic discourses that circulated in connection with the inquiry lamented the children's disconnection from their culture and the fact that they were left without a sense of identity. As one testimonial put it: 'Why was I made to suffer with no Aboriginality and no identity, no culture?' (National Inquiry 1997, 277). Such declarations of suffering attest to the importance of cultural loss in the Aboriginal cultural trauma narrative.

In official Reconciliation discourses, a recurrent claim has been that members of non-Indigenous society need to understand and respect Aboriginal culture as part of the 'distinctive character' of the nation if Reconciliation is to be achieved. The following statement found on the Reconciliation Australia website 'Share Our Pride' is exemplary:

It is important for all Australians to understand the essential features of Indigenous culture, including our special connection to the land and our commitment to family and community. So we can walk on this land together as friends and equals. So you can share our pride. Understanding and respecting our culture also gives you a better sense of the impact on our communities when life-sustaining structures are ignored or broken, as they have been and continue to be. (Bridge 2012; see also CAR 2000)

These discourses around cultural loss and respect for culture are often strongly inflected with the language of rights, including the concept of cultural rights. As we know, human rights became a powerful platform for advancing Aboriginal interests in Australia from the 1960s onwards and international law has been a fertile arena of progressive thought around Indigenous issues. ATSIC, the Council for Aboriginal Reconciliation, the Human Rights and Equal Opportunity Commission (now the Australian Human Rights Commission), political leaders like Gough Whitlam and Paul Keating and many other organisations and public figures have employed the language of human rights, the instruments of international law and the idea of a rights-cognisant international gaze to both criticise and justify state policy.[1] As stated by the Aboriginal Arts Board:

> The existence and operation of the Aboriginal Arts Board is based on the right of the indigenous people of Australia to determine the future of their own cultural heritage. The board's responsibility is to provide support to promote and develop activities which give expression to this basic right. (Australia Council 1979; see also 1982; 1985a)

Thus the concept of having a right to one's heritage and to enjoy one's culture, articulated by Commissioner Johnston earlier, has been formative of understandings of Aboriginal social justice, and human rights concepts have provided a vocabulary for both defining and advocating for the survival of Aboriginal culture in relation to past and present practices of the state.

The 'Share our Pride' quotation exemplifies the way Aboriginal culture is often depicted as being synonymous with healthy Aboriginal personhood. Across many discourses, Aboriginal culture is both portrayed as a resilient force that is indivisible from Aboriginal subjectivity, and a fragile thing on the brink of loss. It is also often nostalgically described as a domain free from the ravages of Western society (see for instance Reynolds 2006; Roberts 2011; Don't Forget Our Elders 2007). The concept of culture is also semantically powerful because it is the preferred term used by Aboriginal spokespeople from remote Australia (partly due to their having a limited English vocabulary) when they speak about their needs and their well-being. These ways of picturing Aboriginal culture are true of statements made in the art context, which is in fact one of the few domains in which remote Aboriginal peoples' voices are regularly heard by non-Indigenous Australians. Spokespeople for the Aboriginal Arts Board, ATSIC, art centres and Aboriginal artists themselves have consistently telescoped from taking about Aboriginal 'art' to Aboriginal 'culture'. In these discourses, the former is depicted as being embedded within the latter, such that, as the Australians Arts Board declared, 'the survival of skills in traditional art forms is […] vital to the survival of the social structure and beliefs' (Australia Council 1979, 2–3). The following statement from Yuendumu artist Valerie Napaljarri Martin is exemplary:

> The art means to carry on our stories, to know it belongs to my family and it belongs to my father and grandfather, so that everyone can know about us, so we can carry on, so our kids can carry on forever, even when we're gone. So non-Indigenous people can know about us in the future, how we fought to keep our culture strong for the sake of our children's future. (Quoted in Desart 2009)[2]

This description rings true in relation to Gibson's suggestion that 'art for culture's sake' is a far more felicitous notion than 'art for art's sake' among practitioners in Wilcannia, where art is 'a means to maintain, redefine, rediscover, remember, remake and teach culture' (2013, 202). The connection between art and culture is also drawn in the mottos of art centres (many of which are identified as 'art and culture' centres) and in exhibition discourses. Ananguku Arts, for instance, carries the motto: '*Arts kunpu, tjukurpa kunpu, munu waltja tjuta kunpu: Strong arts, strong culture, strong families*', and the motto of Tjala Arts is '*Nganampa Art. Nganana walytjangku. Business palyanu. Munula tjukurpa kanpu kanyini*' (Our Art. Our Business – keeps our culture strong). We might also recall that the first Indigenous Art Triennial Exhibition at the NGA was titled *Culture Warriors* and think of exhibition titles such as *Strong Women, Strong Painting, Strong Culture* (shown at the Casula Powerhouse Centre in Sydney in 2011).

The configurations of heritage discussed previously have of course also been integral to the constitution of Aboriginal culture at the nexus of justice, recognition and redemption. As Moran writes, the development of indigenised settler nationalism 'involved a discourse of sharing culture and heritage', which entailed that Aboriginal people's 'cultural heritage, their long and deep spiritual connection with Australian lands, given as a "gift" to the national community, would indigenise the Australian nation as a whole' (2002, 1030; Lattas 1997). Instances of this were surveyed previously, in relation to Whitlam's new nationalism, Bill Hayden's speeches, in the Reconciliation mantra that Aboriginal culture be seen as intrinsic to the distinctive character of the nation, and in nationalistic celebrations of Aboriginal culture being the oldest continuing culture on earth. This amalgam is often made explicit in funding announcements and media releases in which the allocation of monies to Indigenous art, culture and heritage projects is tied to the 'important position Indigenous history and expression occupies in Australia's cultural life' and the need for the nation to 'continue to protect, preserve and promote Indigenous arts, culture and heritage to help build a diverse and dynamic Australia' (Garrett 2010a; Australia Council 2014). Consequently, imperatives that may only be directly relevant to a small group of people, such as maintaining localised cultural practices, recording nearly extinct languages and songs, and documenting stories associated with particular areas of 'Country' have been facilitated by government grants and initiatives on the grounds that they are national imperatives. This is in part premised on a belief that the state might be able to halt the cultural destruction it has caused. It is also premised on the concern, one that has global resonances and is enshrined within institutions such as UNESCO, that a deficit is suffered by humanity as a whole should particular traditions and languages be lost to history.

In sum, the discourses cited here show us that Aboriginal culture has been constituted in the public imagination by a medley of hopes and moral arguments that are contingent on very particular political circumstances. Aboriginal culture has been characterised as a realm of plenitude and virtue made fragile by patently unjust acts. It is a fundamental human right, and the basis for a coherent Aboriginal identity and sense of collective self-worth. Its recuperation is a path to rehabilitating Aboriginal psychological well-being and settler society's atonement for the crimes of the past. It is rich and dynamic, deserves respect, and it is what most distinguishes Australian culture. It has remarkable antiquity and is a gem of the universal patrimony of humankind, the further erosion of which would be an indictment of Australian society.

As John Morton has argued, definitions of Aboriginal culture in Australian public life seem to always have moralistic intent and involve 'judgements of worth' (2006). We can attribute this tendency to the fact that being able to ascertain and celebrate the worth of Aboriginal culture has been pivotal to the state's and non-Indigenous civil society's negotiation of their obligations to Aboriginal people. This negotiation has tended to be oriented by the following types of oppositions: injustice and justice, oppression and empowerment, destruction and survival, loss and renewal, denial and recognition, shame and pride, despair and self-worth, trauma and remedy. As Peter Sutton has written with some disillusionment:

> A central focus of progressive politics and governmental thinking in Australian Indigenous affairs since the 1970s has been on recovery: recovery of lost political autonomy, lost property rights, lost regional integration, lost economic self-sufficiency, lost pride, lost languages, lost identities, lost sacred objects, lost human remains. Many have put their trust in the promise that 'culture' and its partial recovery will do more than restore dignity and the respect of others – it will work wonders more broadly by overcoming economic and social dysfunction. (2009, 65)

Within a narrative of cultural trauma that stretches back to the founding moment of colonisation, the state and hostile white society arguably stand accused with respect to all the former terms in the oppositions I have outlined and all of the losses in Sutton's list. Aboriginal culture, as a highly elastic and morally charged idea inflected with the West's elevated understanding of creative and intellectual pursuits, has been viewed as the vehicle for making amends and reversing the effects of unjust policies of the past.

5.2 Aboriginal Art as Metonymic for Aboriginal Culture

I make the suggestion that Aboriginal art has become to some degree metonymic for Aboriginal culture in Australian public culture because the art has been one of the most potent and amenable means of circulating positive images of Aboriginality in the public domain and symbolising the redemptive intentions of non-Indigenous civil society and the state. This can be illustrated on four fronts.

First, it is clear that positive conceptions of Aboriginal culture that were so essential to the task of drawing a line under the era of assimilation ultimately found the most traction in the domains of the arts and land custodianship. Both resonate with the predispositions of left-leaning civil society and further, the arts and ecology enable the complexity of the dreaming to be authenticated and the value of Aboriginal knowledge and skill to be honoured with the greatest cogency. In these domains, Aboriginal culture is recognised as an entity of sophistication and intelligence that can be compared to other great traditions around the world.[3] To focus on the arts specifically, it is unquestionably the case that the revered status of art within Western culture opened up a sphere of value with which Aboriginality could be affiliated by the state and by sympathetic non-Indigenous civil society. As James Clifford points out, 'one of the most effective current ways to give cross-cultural value (moral or commercial) to a cultural production is to treat it as art' (1991, 241; see also Amato 2006). On this point it is pertinent to recall that the polymath economist and bureaucrat H. C. 'Nugget' Coombs whose career traversed the Holt, McMahon and Whitlam governments was a persuasive advocate of both Indigenous interests and the arts and that both Gough Whitlam and Paul Keating were art lovers who made the arts *and* Indigenous affairs central and highly nationalistic platforms of their leadership. Therefore the treatment of the arts and Indigenous affairs as kindred concerns has a long history, and ideas around their virtue suffused the intellectual culture of those members of the community and government who were sympathetic to these leaders.[4]

One way in which this cross-cultural value has been asserted is through the characterisation of Aboriginal art as a conduit for respect and understanding between Indigenous and non-Indigenous people, an idea that has frequently been reiterated in journalistic, political and art world discourses. For example in 2006 the high-profile collector Colin Laverty remarked that '[s]o far, art has been the key way that Australia at large has come to understand and learn about and have respect for Aboriginal people' (Rothwell 2006a). Laverty's remarks recall the aspirations of progressive thinkers in the 1940s and 1950s, who, in their efforts to dispel racist beliefs about Aboriginal people's primitivity and assert the intellectual and emotional parity between 'them' and 'us', would point to Aboriginal art and material culture to substantiate their claims. This was true, for instance, of A. P. Elkin, who was head of Anthropology at the University of Sydney between 1933 and 1956 and instrumental in establishing the assimilation policy (and here we must bear in mind the relevance of humanitarian principles to assimilation when it was initially conceived). Formerly a cleric and teacher of theology, Elkin had observed the tragedy of frontier relations in the Kimberley and became a passionate advocate for Indigenous justice and equality (Wise 1996). In a foreword to Charles Barrett's and R. H. Croll's 1943 publication *Art of the Australian Aboriginal*, Elkin argued that

> the more the art of the aborigines is publicised, the more appreciative we will all be of that race whose country we have usurped, and whose culture is capable of enriching our own literature and art [...] [T]hey find pleasure, beauty, and meaning in the result of their artistic efforts. Such a people consists of men and women of like passions as ourselves. (1943)

Similarly, in his preface to the popular publication *Australian Aboriginal Decorative Art*, which introduced Aboriginal artefacts and motifs to a generation of Australian artists and designers and was produced by anthropologist and Australian Museum curator Frederick McCarthy, Elkin declared his hope that the publication would

> contribute materially to the appreciation of the Australian aborigines both as a people possessed of artistic powers, and as human personalities. Moreover, in so far as we let the aborigines – the civilised ones in particular – know our appreciation, we shall help them to get rid of that feeling of inferiority for which contact with us has been responsible. (McCarthy 1952, 10)

As Carolyn Lovitt (2000) has explained, Elkin's views (which were shared by McCarthy) are indicative of an earlier phase of ethical consciousness in Australia. They arose from a confluence of relatively new ideas: the modernist appreciation of the beauty of objects made by 'primitive' peoples; the progressive anthropology associated with Franz Boas that rejected evolutionism in favour of universalist and culturally relativist principles; and the shift from the protectionist policies of the past that assumed that Aboriginal culture was incompatible with white civilisation to policies of assimilation and integration. Similar views formed part of the rationale of Aboriginal art subsidy, with Machmud Mackay noting in his 1973 report on the government's Aboriginal art marketing and wholesaling agency (which I have referred to previously as the Government Company) that a primary objective of the Aboriginal art industry should be that it generate 'in the viewing and buying public an awareness and deep respect for Aboriginals, their skills, culture and way of life' (1973, 28; see also Thomas and Baily 1973).[5]

Second, Aboriginal art embodies both the historicity and contemporaneity of Aboriginal culture, the marriage of which has become vital to picturing Australian nationhood as youthful and progressive yet with ancient roots. It is not possible to imagine a reconstructed, virtuous Australia without evidence of Aboriginal cultural survival, and the vitality of Aboriginal art makes it a powerful emblem of this. This perspective is the inverse of the dying race nostalgia that prevailed in Australian literary and visual culture in the late nineteenth and early twentieth centuries. At the same time, Aboriginal art is viewed in terms of ancient national heritage, the survival of which is significant to the nation and to the world. Declarations that Aboriginal culture is many decades old and that Aboriginal art is the 'longest continuing art tradition in the world' recur in the discourses of Aboriginal arts advocates, activists, art and museum professionals, writers and politicians (as exemplified by Paul Keating above). For instance in 1983, the Aboriginal Affairs Minister in the Hawke Labor government, Clyde Holding, stated in parliament that 'at a time when our European forbears still lived in caves, art and dance, song and ceremony, language and religion, had become an integral [part] of this great ancient culture'. He argued that this culture could 'now enrich and enhance all our lives', and that contemporary Aboriginal art was 'undoubtedly the most distinctively Australian cultural item that is produced by modern Australians' (Commonwealth of Australia 1983, 3488).[6] In a more recent example, the Australia Council for the Art's strategic plan opens with: 'Our culture is unique. It is a culture that is deeply shaped by more than 70,000 years of continued, unbroken Indigenous storytelling' (Australia Council 2014).

Somewhat provocatively, Paul Carter has suggested that the idea of Aboriginal antiquity is appealing because it enables an elevation of 'our own knowledge and thus control', where 'our' refers to non-Indigenous citizens. As he points out, 'it is we Europeans who associate antiquity with "a rich cultural heritage". In discovering the Aboriginal past, we demonstrate our piety towards the household gods of our own history' (2010, xviii). It might further be argued that the rhetorical power of such claims is that they generate a sense of kinship with these antecedent generations of Aboriginal people by enfranchising them – as a humanist corrective to primitivist portrayals – as cultured: as having always possessed *our* creative and intellectual faculties. Furthermore, these evocations of cultural richness have been mobilised to legitimise Indigenous claims to justice and recognition. Therefore, in addition to being able to encapsulate a sense of historicity and contemporaneity in both Aboriginal and Australian culture, Aboriginal art provides a rare platform for Aboriginal advocates and non-Aboriginal representatives of the state to sing in tune.

Third, the subsidisation and endorsement of Aboriginal arts by the state, and the discourses that promote Aboriginal art exhibitions, art centres, festivals, performances and so on, very often appeal to the latter terms in the oppositions listed above such as empowerment, pride and self-worth. Janet Holmes à Court who, with her husband Robert Holmes à Court (now-deceased), was a path breaking collector and supporter of Aboriginal art, makes the following exemplary statement in an explanation of why she became involved with Aboriginal art:

> If the rest of the world could see and appreciate the work of our indigenous people, it would help them gain self-esteem, self-respect – if they realised that they were able to produce things that were regarded as on a world scale then that would help lift their self-esteem and maybe lift them out of the dreadful circumstances in which many of them find themselves. (Hoy 2011)[7]

This statement echoes the wedding of Aboriginal cultural rejuvenation and well-being that we encountered in the Reconciliation and Stolen Generations discourses and the way Aboriginal people portray Aboriginal culture. It is also evocative of the sympathy and remorse felt by non-Indigenous people – the affective investments that have in many cases triggered the desire to acquire Aboriginal art works. In these kinds of remarks we see the way Aboriginal art has been incorporated into the broader narrative with which we have been concerned, in which Aboriginal culture is located at the nexus of Aboriginal social justice and well-being, state accountability and remedial duty, and reconstructed Australian nationhood.

Fourth, Aboriginal art has had particular magnetism as a positive image of Aboriginality because there are many other representations in Australian public culture that cannot be part of affirmative engagements with Aboriginal identity (Povinelli 2002). Much is omitted from the state-endorsed representations of Aboriginal culture. For instance, claims to sovereignty and enduring land ownership are aspects of Aboriginality that contest the authority of the state and the legitimacy of settler society. Furthermore, there are Indigenous traditions that have endured since colonisation that remain inassimilable and in some cases repugnant within the framework of liberal democratic Australia. Among these we might include young women being promised as brides to older men, corporal punishment such as spearing, and forms of superstition and sorcery to which cases of intracommunal violence have been attributed. We might add to this delineation of problematic Aboriginality the degree of disadvantage present in remote Aboriginal Australia in which the level of trauma that is presented in press reports seems unimaginable from the point of view of urban middle-class life. One of the most fraught and contentious questions encountered in Indigenous affairs discourses is whether aspects of Aboriginal culture or certain Aboriginal values can be understood to contribute to this trauma.[8] There is no doubt that Aboriginal art, and the Aboriginal arts in general, provide a powerful counternarrative to the story of chronic poor well-being that informs how many non-Indigenous citizens perceive Aboriginal Australia, and which often has a dehumanizing effect (Altman and Hinkson, 2007). Thus not only is Aboriginal art salient to the redemptive project of Reconciliation but it also offers a reprieve from the seemingly intractable 'problems' in Indigenous Australia.

A further important point to be made here is that Aboriginal art signifies Aboriginality without having to represent particular Aboriginal people. As Jane Lyndon points out, the history of demeaning photographic representations of Aboriginal people that appeared in journalistic and scholarly literatures prior to the 1970s meant that 'Australian visual culture has been shaped by a distinctive and powerful convergence of anxieties about picturing Indigenous subjects' (2012, 23). As I will elaborate later, the abstract elements of Aboriginal art have made it particularly amenable to being transferred to variety of visual culture forms, and this has generated a distributed visual regime of Aboriginality in Australian public culture.

5.3   Conclusion to Part I

The preceding discussions have sought to reveal how Aboriginal art mediates the relationship between Indigenous people, Australian civil society and the state. This line of inquiry was necessarily situated within a broader exposition of the ways in which the complexities inherent to Indigenous/non-Indigenous relations find expression in public life through the lenses of cultural trauma, Reconciliation, heritage, nationalism, Indigenous rights, Indigenous disadvantage and so on. It also required an adumbration of the linkages between, on the one hand, the structural and economic factors that underlie policy initiatives, subvention and the partial nature of Indigenous Australians' citizenship, and on the other hand, the symbolic, metonymic and rhetorical manifestation of ideas that are collectively negotiated in public culture. While the former can be identified in the intersections between Indigenous affairs policies, arts and cultural policies and the Aboriginal art movement, the latter is often fluid and elusive, and the examples provided here will be complemented through later discussions in this book. What I hope to have shown is that Aboriginal art has been mobilised and to some extent instrumentalised within a variety of activist, governmental, intellectual and affective processes through which Aboriginal people, Australian civil society and the state have addressed the exigencies of the settler state condition.

Part II

CONTEMPORARY ABORIGINAL ART IN THE 1980S

Introduction

In 1983 the non-Indigenous Australian artist and critic Ian Burn published an article in *Art Network* titled 'The Australian National Gallery: Populism or a New Cultural Federalism?', in which he reviewed the opening exhibition at the Australian National Gallery, which had been launched the previous year. In it he lamented the intransigence of modernism-inspired curatorial decisions and Australian art's subordinate placement in relation to the international collection in the exhibition. He also made clear that he saw the program of thematising Australia's national identity and heritage that the 'custodians of our national taste' had undertaken at the gallery as being deeply problematised by Aboriginal political issues (1983, 40). Indeed, the article begins with a description of a major land rights protest that had taken place in Brisbane the week before the official opening. Burn also noted that the 'Australian Art' hang in the opening exhibition only displayed a few Aboriginal works, and only those that had served as source material for non-Indigenous Australian artists. Regarding the juxtaposition of a 1946 bark painting by East Arnhem Land artist Djawa with two Margaret Preston works, Burn asked, '[W]hat does it do for our understanding of Djawa's art or Aboriginal culture?' (41). He went on to argue that 'unless the incorporation of bark paintings into the white Australian collection can be accomplished to reveal as much about black traditions, it must inevitably carry echoes of the assimilation policy, now so thoroughly discredited' (41). Burn also found it troubling that the more substantial showing of Aboriginal art was to be found in the 'Australian Aboriginal, Oceanic, Black African, Asian and Pre-Columbian American' section, not least because it implied that Aboriginal art was not part of Australian art.

I begin with Burn's article because it can be read as a précis of the main themes to be explored in Part II. The 1980s was a threshold era in Australian art for several reasons. Not only were Australian artists attempting to reconfigure their relationship to the wider art world but, internationally, the transition from modernism toward the more globalist, relativist and highly diversified field of contemporary art was well underway. As Wolff writes, feminist and postcolonial critiques were 'expos[ing] the myth of objectivity in Western aesthetics and art history', and demonstrating 'the very clearly *extra*-aesthetic principles and practices at work in excluding the work of women, minority, and non-Western artists from the canon' (2008, 19; see also Lüthi 1993). The micropolitics behind these ideas manifest the diversification of social identities in the late twentieth century, while they were also responsive to the fracturing effects and possibilities for invention and reconstruction that came with global commodity capitalism, new technologies and accelerated global mobility (Jameson 1991, 319; see also Hall 1993; Hall and Du Gay 1996; McLean 2014). These forces, and the influx of postmodern ideas, had an invigorating effect on the Australian art arena in the 1970s and 1980s. An unprecedentedly large, mobile and ethnically mixed generation of Australian practitioners (artists, writers, curators) were eager to interrogate old paradigms and embrace new ones, and a new landscape of arts subsidy created unprecedented opportunities to do so.[1] For example, the New York experience of curators and critics Ian Burn, Terry Smith and Paul Taylor (all discussed in Part II) inspired fresh vantage points from which to assess Australian culture and ensured they had the cultural capital among their Australian peers for their ideas to find purchase. Australian practitioners were also highly sensitive to the equivocal negotiations of nationalism taking place in Australian public culture at this time in relation to both multiculturalism and Aboriginality. It was into this milieu that Aboriginal art emerged as a form of contemporary Australian art. As is well illustrated in Burn's critique, Aboriginal art became ensconced within the critical and exploratory movements of that era.[2]

The following discussion provides an analytical account of those movements that were responsive to, or mediated, the emergence of contemporary Aboriginal art. It is primarily informed by 1980s art journal and magazine articles, exhibition catalogues and other ephemera which are the archival trace of the vigorous culture of intellectual debate that existed at the time. As rich as this archive is, it is of course only a partial representation of that era, and it would now be fruitful to gather the recollections of that generation of Australian practitioners. The history that I have composed from this archive is one of an art world digesting the implications of Aboriginal rights campaigns, Aboriginal disadvantage, the Australian Bicentenary of 1988 and the other politicized social issues discussed in Part I, *in addition* to the challenge posed by the unique aesthetic and conceptual properties of Aboriginal art itself. Part II culminates in a consideration of two interrelated concerns that recur across the literature of the day: how to empower Indigenous artists and the Indigenous voice and how to dismantle Eurocentric, primitivist and exclusionary structures within the fine arts domain.

Chapter 6

THE EMERGENCE OF ABORIGINAL ART IN THE 1980S

In the 1980s the Australian arts sector was reaping the benefits of the 1970s policy initiatives of the Whitlam Labor government. Several state galleries had expanded their spaces and, as was flagged in Burn's article, the new Australian National Gallery was launched (by the Queen) in 1982 (its name was changed to National Gallery of Australia in 1992). Art auction house Sotheby's Australia was established in the same year. Corporate investment in art increased throughout the 1980s and there was a boom in the Australian art market (Van den Bosch 2005, 63–64; Huda 2008, 103–107). At the same time, a growing number of tertiary education institutions began offering art courses, which produced an exceptionally large generation of art school graduates. Art journals such as *Art Network* (established in 1979), *Artlink* (1981), *Art & Text* (1981), *Praxis M* (1983), *Art Monthly* (1987) and *On the Beach* (1983) were in most cases made possible by subsidies from the Australia Council for the Arts and/or institutional affiliations and provided new fora for critical reviews and debates regarding contemporary art in Australia and overseas. The first *Sydney Biennale* was staged at the Art Gallery of NSW in 1973, and the *Australian Perspecta* – a biennial showcase of contemporary Australian art – was initiated by the same institution in 1981. Each was a watershed in legitimising the work of the new countercultural generation of Australian artists. The *Sydney Biennale* was a particularly important initiative. Not only did it establish an exhibition program in which the work of Australian contemporary artists was regularly displayed alongside that of prominent overseas artists but it created the conditions for unprecedented exchange between Australian artists, curators and museum professionals and their counterparts overseas.

The artistic, curatorial and discursive practices of this era were adventurous and reflexive (Taylor 1984a; Waterlow 1986; Lumby 1995). Postmodern and poststructuralist concepts were brought into dialogue with – and in some cases mobilised to challenge – the subcultural movements that were ongoing from the 1960s and 1970s.[1] Pluralist theorisations of identity had wide appeal, as they provided platforms for self-expression for migrant Australians from beyond the Anglosphere, but they were also salient for those Australians who wanted to unyoke themselves from the bland and derivative paths they associated with their British heritage. Many artists embraced an anti-establishment (which usually entailed antimodernist), anti-elitist and anticommodity ethos. The flourishing of conceptual and 'post-object' art practices led to a great diversification of art forms, as well as noncommercial exhibition methods and settings for collegial exchange. While some practices became highly esoteric, others were engaged in social critique and pursued activist and collectivist forms of expression.

6.1   The Cultural Cringe and Provincialism

It is difficult to overstate the significance of these changes. In the preceding decades, much of Australian art history and criticism had upheld the idea that Australian cultural life was unassailably conditioned by the country's marginal, dependent and envious relationship to the metropolitan centres of Europe and North America. In the absence of an endogenous aesthetic tradition, Australian artists and writers seemed to have no alternative but to emulate overseas trends. This meant that their work was often judged in the light of largely inscrutable international standards. In 1950, the literary critic Arthur Phillips coined the phrase 'Cultural Cringe' in a brief essay to refer to this condition. He pointed out that such judgements led to the 'estrangement of the Australian intellectual' and robbed artists and writers of 'a sympathetically critical audience' (1980 [1958], 113–16). Ultimately he proposed that 'the Cringe is a worse enemy to our cultural development than our isolation' (117).

The theme of Australia's artistic dependence on overseas developments had also infused Bernard Smith's seminal and highly influential Australian art history texts *Australian Painting* (1971 [1962]) and *Place, Taste and Tradition* (1979 [1945]). In the 1960s and 1970s he and other critics employed the concept of provincialism to explore this predicament (see B. Smith 1971[1962], 333–34; T. Smith 1969). For instance, Burn theorized provincialism in relation to what he regarded as the cultural imperialist implications of the American avant-garde's pre-eminence (1991 [1973]). He argued that in order to overcome the deferential attitude that prevailed in provincial settings, an attitude that sustained and naturalized American art's prestige, it was necessary to appraise the local conditions of art practices and stop treating aesthetic concerns as universal and ideologically disinterested. The most well-known example of the critique of Australian provincialism is Terry Smith's 1974 article 'The Provincialism problem', which was published in the New York art journal *Artforum*. Here he remarks that in Australia:

> [many overseas styles] have had small to quite large bands of advocates who devote their artistic maturity to mastering, then elaborating aspects of the initiatives of those they have imitated. This process continues unabated today, like a succession of faithful echoes, always open to replenishment at the sound of a new call from the other side of the divide. (55)

Smith noted that critics as well as artists were implicated in this 'pattern of provincialist submission' (59). He acknowledged that Australian artists were appearing in overseas exhibitions and international art magazines and identified several currents of local innovation, and like Burn he argued that art making is 'a thoroughly context-dependent activity' for which there are 'no ideologically neutral cultural acts' (59). Nevertheless, the message of the essay was that provincialism was an intractable Australian condition: '*As the situation stands, the provincial artist cannot choose not to be provincial*' (57, original emphasis).

The themes of the Cultural Cringe and provincialism were frequently debated in the 1980s and were the subtext of many of the reflexive activities of the period. The question of whether or not Australian art had left these afflictions behind was of concern to many commentators. For instance a 1983 edition of the London-based art journal *Studio International* was themed 'Australian Art: Beyond the Cringe'. In his editor's introduction, Michael Spens enthused: '[I]t now seem[s] that heads are turned, and return travel passes sought, to Australia; the one-way route to the mother country has now been dramatically reversed, and the flow of cultural escapees, refugees and prospectors has become legendary'. Spens proposed that Australia's 'exile' status has given way to 'sanctuary', and that the country 'has developed of late a new and ebullient cultural confidence': 'The Cringe, then, is no more [...] The Cringe has gone' (1983, 6).[2] Many Australian artists who engaged with these discourses sought to determine whether it was desirable to forge a specifically Australian art, and to ask what it might consist of, an endeavour sometimes described as regionalism. In general, a distinguishing feature of this era in Australian art was a widely shared concern with devising a new individual and collective relationship to the international art world.

6.2 The Emergence of Contemporary Aboriginal Art

The circumstances and debates discussed so far are critical to our understanding why Aboriginal art was radically reappraised by Australian art institutions and cognoscenti in the 1980s.[3] In the 1970s, Aboriginal art from Arnhem Land and the Central and Western Deserts had been acquired by only a small number of private collectors and state galleries. It also remained relatively marginal within the Australian fine arts market, with Sydney's Hogarth Galleries (which established a dedicated Aboriginal art wing in 1976) and the Government Company galleries being among the only vendors (Peterson 1983). It was not until artists from Papunya and Arnhem Land were included in the 1979 and 1982 *Sydney Biennales* and the 1981 and 1983 *Australian Perspecta* exhibitions that Aboriginal art really entered the sphere of contemporary art. For instance, the 1979 *Biennale* included work by artists from Ramingining alongside prominent non-Indigenous Australian and European artists such as Bea Maddock, Imants Tillers, Joseph Bueys and Gerard Richter. And the 1981 *Perspecta* included the extraordinary piece *Warlugulong* (1976) by artists Clifford Possum Tjapaltjarri and Tim Leura Tjapaltjarri (at which time it was acquired by the Art Gallery of NSW). Among other things, we can see the inclusion of Aboriginal art in these exhibitions as being inspired by the heuristic and ethical tendencies of the conceptual art practices that were widely represented within them, and which inspired the efforts of pathbreaking curators like Nick Waterlow and Bernice Murphy (*Biennale of Sydney* 1979; Murphy 1981; 1983a; 1983b).

In 1980 both the Australian National Gallery and the Art Gallery of South Australia acquired paintings from Papunya, and the latter become the first gallery to include this work in a display of contemporary Australian art. In the following year, James Mollison, then director of the Australian National Gallery, declared that the Papunya artists had produced 'possibly the finest abstract art achievements to date in Australia' (quoted in Johnson 1990, 16). A dedicated collection program was initiated and by 1987 the gallery's holdings of Aboriginal art numbered 700 works (Ward 1987; Philp 2007). Other state galleries began to establish Aboriginal art departments, collections and curatorial roles and to stage substantial exhibitions of Aboriginal art from remote regions, while the *Perspecta* and *Sydney Biennale* exhibitions continued to feature Aboriginal art and performance from both remote and urban areas (Biennale of Sydney 1986; Nairne et al. 1987). As Vivien Johnson describes in relation to the 1986 Biennale (directed by Nick Waterlow):

> The Ramingining Performance Group danced a public mortuary rite in the sand before their own paintings on the gallery wall, confronting the audience's unspoken misgivings about the relationship between their artmaking and their ritual life by enacting their continuity in the most direct way. The collective strength of the exhibiting artists' presence asserted that in the right hands art could still be a form of cultural resistance, transforming the context in which it was displayed, rather than being transformed by it [...]. (1997, 66)

At the same time, the number of Aboriginal art showings in elite commercial galleries grew, as did noncommercial art spaces' forays into mixed showings of Aboriginal and non-Indigenous art (Tasmanian School of Art Gallery 1981; Johnson 1986a; Ewington 1986). The years 1987 to 1990 marked the period in which Australian art journals began including articles on Indigenous art to a significant degree, with several journals marking the shift by publishing special issues. Statistical research carried out by Ian McLean and Jon Stanton found that in the case of *Artlink*, articles with Indigenous and mixed Indigenous/non-Indigenous content accounted for 3 per cent of their issues between 1981 and 1987. In 1990 Indigenous content spiked at 50 per cent, and over the following decade around 18 per cent of articles had some Indigenous content (McLean 2009).

6.3   Artistic and Critical Approaches to Aboriginal Art

Clearly then, Aboriginal art's entry into the field of contemporary Australian Art was aided by the fact that non-Indigenous artists, art writers and intellectuals were reimagining Australian culture, identity and art traditions in the 1980s. Mediating this reimagining were a set of discussions that were oriented not only to the presence of Aboriginal art, but to the moral questions posed by contemporaneous Aboriginal rights campaigns and the growing public consciousness of the history of Aboriginal dispossession. I will begin by discussing the concepts of cultural convergence, rapprochement, cultural colonialism and ethnocide. While the first two had somewhat hopeful foundations in notions of dialogue and exchange, the last two were highly dystopian. All of them show us that formulating an ethical standpoint in relation to Aboriginal art and Aboriginality was a widely shared imperative in Australian art forums in the 1980s.

6.3.1   Cultural convergence and rapprochement

The concept of cultural convergence entered Australian art discourses as a result of *The Spectre of Truganini* Boyer Lecture series delivered by the aforementioned art historian Bernard Smith in 1980. These essays attest to the degree to which heroic narratives of the nation's history were being interrogated in academic and public discourse at this time.[4] Smith's analysis of the history of Indigenous/non-Indigenous relations and the aesthetic manifestations of this relationship was premised on the view that 'the country was acquired by the forcible dispossession of the Indigenous inhabitants of Australia from their ancestral lands, a process that might be more fittingly described as invasion and conquest' (1980, 8). By employing the vocabulary of dispossession, invasion and conquest, he was offering a controversial revision of prevailing historical discourses around settlement.

Smith was concerned with the 'psycho-cultural mechanisms' (16) of white Australia's efforts to forget these origins and argued that there was a 'close connection between culture, place and morality' (10). Consistent with his focus on place in his other writings, he suggested that a virtuous and authentic Australian culture was obtainable if the Australian people developed a cultural consciousness enlightened to the unique knowledge that emanated from 'this ancient land' (45). He hoped that a condition of cultural 'convergence'[5] might be catalysed by the non-Indigenous public's growing awareness of the many injustices Aboriginal people had experienced, a condition characterised by 'a relationship in which identities are maintained and even developed but relationships become more complex and fruitful, and beneficial to the Australian culture as a whole' (50).

Smith's lectures are redolent of the post-assimilation cultural adjustments explored earlier in this book and are an exemplary portrayal of the Aboriginal cultural trauma narrative. They are highly politicised meditations on the nation's conscience and present what were still relatively new conceptualisations of Australia's ancient cultural and national heritage. As with the Cultural Cringe and provincialism, the themes raised in *The Spectre of Truganini* were often echoed and debated in 1980s art critical literature, such that in 1988 *convergence* was described as a 'much overworked phrase' (Maughan et al. 1988, 25). For instance, non-Indigenous artist Imants Tillers refers to it in his well-known essay 'Locality Fails', which contains a critique of non-Indigenous art that, in his view, sought to appropriate the sheen of Aboriginality (as we will see later, Tillers was also appropriating from Aboriginal art, but he characterised it in different terms). He suggested that:

[Australian's resistance to forging] an authentic 'cultural convergence' can in part be explained by the deep guilt underlying Australian culture. For the history of white settlement in Australia in relation to the Aborigines is a story of homicide, rape, the forcible abduction of children from their parents and the methodical dispossession of the lands upon which their well-being, self-respect and survival have depended. 'Cultural convergence' is attractive as an *idea* because it offers a painless way to expiate our collective guilt of this history while simultaneously suggesting an easy solution to the more mundane but nevertheless pressing problem of finding a uniquely Australian content to our art in an international climate sympathetic to the notion of 'regional' art. The reality of 'cultural convergence' which necessitates that political and economic inequalities be rectified first is a less satisfying prospect. (1982, 53; see also Van den Bosch 1985; Adams 1987)

This passage provides an excellent example, like Burn's review, of the ways in which acknowledgements of Aboriginal cultural trauma were being brought into dialogue with considerations of what constituted Australian art in 1980s critical discourses.

A concept with which the idea of convergence was sometimes associated was rapprochement. For example, Bruce Adams writes of 'the European Australian's belated *rapprochement* with this continent' and states that '[t]he much vaunted appeal in Australian culture for a sense of place has adopted the notion of aboriginality (as quite distinct from Aboriginal culture) as a vehicle for a natural convergence of people and land' (1983, 31, original emphasis; see also 1987). Writing of the appropriation of Aboriginal art by non-Indigenous artists, Vivien Johnson noted that '[w]hite incursions onto the terrain of Aboriginal representations are now highly problematic. But they are equally imperative in order to contradict in practice the dismal doctrine that no *rapprochement* is possible' (1986b, 15, original emphasis; see also T. Johnson 1986; 1988). As will be elaborated below, the validity of non-Indigenous artists appropriating from Aboriginal art was the subject of serious debate at this time.

6.3.2 *'Killing me softly'*:[6] *cultural colonialism and ethnocide*

Another significant concept in 1980s critical discourses on Aboriginal themes was 'cultural colonialism'. In 1982 an article on Aboriginal art written by Canadian cultural critic and Inuit art expert Kenneth Coutts-Smith was published posthumously in *Art Network*. Coutts-Smith had visited Australia in the early 1980s in part to pursue theories about cultural colonialism that he had canvassed in an overseas journal in 1976 (Coutts-Smith 1991 [1976]). The spirit of his argument is captured in the following quotation: 'Cultural colonialism does not massacre and imprison and institutionalise a subservient people, but, more gently, it absorbs the values of a peripheral culture into the larger system of the dominant one' (Coutts-Smith 1982, 55). Although critics found flaws in his approach, Coutts-Smith's argument that colonisation operated in covert and insidious ways in the cultural realm was frequently echoed in other critical writings of the day.[7] Adrian Marrie, for instance, invoked the themes of cultural colonialism, assimilation, cultural genocide and the idea that Australia was 'not yet decolonised' in his critiques of the way Aboriginal art and cultural heritage were trapped within Western ethnocentric frameworks of expertise and institutional control rather than being under the control of Aboriginal people themselves (1985; 1987). Even when they are not explicitly cited, the concepts of 'cultural colonialism' and 'cultural imperialism' were implicit reference points for other critiques of the Aboriginal art world at the time. For example Kirby's essay 'Aboriginal Art and the New Patrons' (1982) analyses, in a Marxist vein, the sponsorship of a major Aboriginal art exhibition at the National Gallery of Victoria by American Express, and argues that Indigenous land rights movements and aspirations to maintain culture were enervated by such corporate opportunism (see also Megaw 1986, 52; Von Sturmer 1989).

An idea that was strongly affiliated with the concept of cultural colonialism was ethnocide. Ann-Marie Willis and Tony Fry wrote several articles published in the Australian journals *Artlink* and *Praxis M* and the overseas journals *Third Text* and *Art in America* (1988, 1989a; 1989b; 1989c), in which they employed this idea in their discussions of the commercialisation of Aboriginal art. These were written from an academic standpoint explicitly located outside the art world, notwithstanding their chosen sites for publication (see particularly 1989a, 5). They advance an extremely pessimistic polemic, arguing that the impact of commodification on Aboriginal culture was totalising in its degradation, and that colonial forces were simply tightening their grip through the various economic, cultural and social exchanges that were constitutive of Aboriginal art. They were incredulous of those who saw Aboriginal artists as being empowered in light of the racial inequalities that prevailed within the art world and in Australian society generally. They also suggested that a neocolonial form of primitivism was prevalent in the Aboriginal art world. In general their arguments were grounded in a critical Marxist perspective on capitalist relations and hegemony as well as ideas relating to ethnocentricism and Eurocentricism.

The reputation of these essays is particularly interesting. Their arguments were not endorsed at the time in the way that Coutts-Smith's were, and many took issue with their totalising cynicism and the fact that they effaced the agency of Aboriginal artists (this critique was articulated most elaborately in Roger Benjamin's riposte article in *Art in America*) (1990). In subsequent years however, these essays have been anthologized as typifying an uncompromising postcolonial critique of the Aboriginal art industry (see Butler 2004 [1996]; McLean 2011c; Araeen et al. 2002). The authors have recently written that they had intended to 'contest claims about [Aboriginal art] as a politically progressive activity – claims made loudly by non-Aboriginal voices' (Willis and Fry 2011, 286). They argue that '[g]iven the structurally subordinate position of Aboriginal people within Australian society, the question of the efficacy of a claimed cultural politics of Aboriginal art was (and still is, as far as we're concerned), the only ethically valid question to consider' (in McLean 2011c, 286). As I will discuss further later, these arguments signal that postcolonial critiques generated a highly problematic dichotomy for people who were sympathetic to Aboriginal artists and the cause of Aboriginal rights: Was the Aboriginal artist an agent of cultural survival and resistance, or a victim of commercial and cultural exploitation? There was a profound friction between people's optimism about the movement and their sensitivity to the insidious nature of postcolonial power and the inexorable proliferation of capitalist relations.

6.3.3 *Landscape and tribalism*

We move now to a discussion of other artistic and critical engagements with Aboriginal art and Aboriginal themes in the 1980s. Landscape had long been the dominant paradigm of Australian art, and many non-Indigenous artists and writers perceived the depth of the challenge that Aboriginal art posed to those traditions in conceptual, formal, affective and spiritual terms (Burn and Stephen 1986; 1992; Hoffie 1997). Non-Indigenous artists for whom land was a preoccupation were inspired by Aboriginal sacred sites, rock art sites and the role of narrative, song and performance in mapping and sustaining land custodianship. They were also responsive to Aboriginal ground (or sand) paintings, the topographical perspectives present in many paintings, the ceremonial context of traditional Aboriginal creativity and the use of natural materials such as bark and ochre.[8] Several painters engaged with the nature of the 'abstraction' in Aboriginal paintings, and drew on Aboriginal themes to imagine a deeper and more emotive connection with place. For those artists who were affiliated with the burgeoning schools of performance, installation, environmental and situation–based art, many features of Aboriginal art and ceremonial culture resonated with the ideals of authenticity and transience with which these schools were concerned, as well their disavowal of commodification. There was also a strain of artistic practice in which engagements with Aboriginal art were a facet of a broader exploration of non-Western culture and spirituality, tribalism, shamanism and the primordial (Adams 1983; Murphy 1981).[9]

6.3.4 *Appropriation*

Several non-Indigenous artists engaged with Aboriginal art through the medium of appropriation. For instance Charles Cooper was concerned with how the problematic coexistence of Aboriginal and settler society was manifest in the Aboriginal-themed imagery that circulated in Australian visual culture. He based a series of paintings on the photographs of rock art sites that were reproduced in popular books and stamps, particularly in association with the 1988 Bicentenary. These works juxtaposed the poetic communication methods in Aboriginal society with the territorial and uniformist symbology of settler society and highlighted the 'cultural annexation' of the former by the latter (Cooper 1987; Sisley 1988).

Other artists who practiced appropriation were Tim Johnson and Imants Tillers, both of whom were impressed by the layered, iconographic conceptualism of Papunya painting, and the way its optical features resonated with other forms of contemporary art. Interestingly, Johnson and Tillers were initially among those artists who turned away from painting, because they identified with conceptual art's repudiation of modernist aesthetics. However the complexity of the Aboriginal paintings they encountered was such that they were prompted to imagine how painting could be recast as a conceptual art practice.[10] Tim Johnson established an appropriative and collaborative practice in relation to Papunya painting, which arose from direct engagements with Papunya artists and was expressive of his concerns about Indigenous/settler relations and the political aspirations of Aboriginal people.[11] This practice was also expressive of his interest in spirituality, which has seen him appropriate from and collage a range of non-Western artistic traditions in his paintings (T. Johnson 1988; Lingard 1989a).

Imants Tillers began appropriating from Aboriginal art in 1982 and has continued to do so throughout his career. He has regularly made use of small canvas boards that allow him to deconstruct and reconfigure his variously sourced imagery (Tillers 1982; 1983; Hart 2006). In 1985 he produced a work titled *The Nine Shots* in which fragments of a well-known painting by Warlpiri Papunya artist Michael Nelson Jagamarra titled *Five Dreamings* from 1984 are interspersed with those of a figurative painting by German artist Georg Baselitz.[12] These two works (the latter bore the title *Possum Dreaming* at the time, and has also been entitled *Five Stories* in other contexts) were serendipitously illustrated on consecutive pages in the catalogue of the 1986 *Sydney Biennale* (due to the spelling of Jagamarra's name as Tjakamarra, thus following Tillers), even though in the exhibition itself Tillers was not in fact represented by *The Nine Shots* but rather by *Lost, Lost, Lost* (1985) (Biennale of Sydney 1986). Nevertheless, this juxtaposition in the catalogue was conspicuous and marked a particular moment in the intersection of Indigenous and non-Indigenous cultural expression in Australia (Johnson 1997; McLean 2010). Tillers was also commissioned to create work for the dome of the federation memorial in Centennial Park, Sydney, which was opened in 1988, and here again aspects of Jagamarra's work (his ground mosaic at the new Parliament House launched in 1988) were integrated into the commission (Baume 1988).

Tillers is one of Australia's most respected artists and his practice and commentary were central to wider negotiations of Aboriginal art as contemporary art, and to postprovincialist formulations of Australian art. His engagements with Aboriginal art have been explored in considerable depth by others (see, e.g., McLean 2010; Morphy 2006); nevertheless for my purposes it is worth remarking on the ambivalent motivation behind his appropriations. To some degree it seems that his appropriations were a transgressive impulse: he was keen to distance himself from the sentimentality of some of the conscience-driven engagements with Aboriginal art that were emerging at the time. However, this detached attitude is not so apparent in his refutation of the regionalist movement. In Tillers's aforementioned essay 'Locality Fails', published in *Art & Text* (1982), he extrapolates from a body of ideas associated with physicist John S. Bell regarding quantum mechanics. Tillers argues that artistic content is not wholly determined by the circumstances from which it emerges and that connections and causal relations can exist between events, ideas and expressive forms from disparate locations. In many ways this essay can be read as a critique of the views expounded by Ian Burn and Terry Smith in relation to provincialism. Tillers concludes his essay by remarking that '[l]uckily a world in which "locality fails" is far more interesting than the one in which we are limited to our immediate circumstances and which we are suffered upon to reflect in our art' (60).

Tillers's antipathy to regionalism had three dimensions. First, regionalism seemed to entail an acceptance of Australian art's peripheral relation to the centres of art in Europe and America. Second, it treated landscape as the most legitimate and meaningful form of nonderivative Australian art, which rendered this peripheral condition intractable. Bernard Smith had often affirmed the 'power of place' not only as inspiration for the most successful Australian art but also in cementing the Australianness of the many ethnic identities that formed Australian society. Tillers was the child of Latvian immigrants and was set on (and succeeded in) gaining entry to the international art world and was hostile to such a view. There was to be no fidelity to place for him: his aversion to the 'tyrannical' dominance of the landscape in the Australian artistic tradition was at the heart of his argument that 'locality fails' and his appropriative practice (Foss 1987, 132; see also Baume 1988; Nairne et al. 1987, 224–28). The third dimension brings us to Aboriginal art. According to regionalism's own principles, any overtly regionalist practice pursued by non-Indigenous artists was feeble in the face of the incontrovertible depth and sophistication of Aboriginal art. This had been suggested by Bernard Smith himself (1988 [1985], 301). Tillers was offended by the degree to which some practitioners seemed to be enthralled before this power. We sense this in his work *The Nine Shots* in which the circular icons of Michael Nelson Jagamarra's painting perforate the white male figure, an image which for Tillers evoked 'danger and dread' (Foss 1987, 136). At the same time, by reducing Papunya painting to mass-produced imagery that could be chopped up and manipulated, Tillers appeared to be seeking to diffuse the formidable authenticity of Aboriginal artists' cultural identifications with place.

6.3.5 *Postmodernism and conceptualism*

Postmodern and poststructuralist discourses were embraced by several non-Indigenous artists and critics in their negotiation of Aboriginal art and culture, Tillers among them. For example, the concepts of smooth space and rhizomes in Deleuze and Guattari's theory of nomadology were brought to bear on aspects of Aboriginal society and art and cross-cultural encounters (see for instance Muecke 1983; 1984; Tillers 1983). The ubiquity of semiotic theory in discourses on art and culture at this time meant that the language of signification was often employed in discussions of Aboriginal art, frequently in connection with non-Indigenous artists' appropriative practices (Foss 1987; McNeill 1987, 24–25; Murphy 1987).

The dissident anthropologist Eric Michaels offered the most sophisticated theorisations of Aboriginal art in relation to postmodernism. A recurring injunction in his writings is that, in view of their ability to transform ritual, transient and localised forms into commodities that are secular, permanent and portable, Aboriginal artists of the Western Desert should be recognised as innovative participants in the network of exchanges that was peculiar to the postmodern condition. He wanted people to see that, rather than occupying a discrete realm of exotic authenticity, Aboriginal works were produced within a 'dialogical space' and, furthermore, that Aboriginal painters and Aboriginal media producers had a unique facility for self-expression in a globalised world (2004 [1989], 220). In making these arguments, Michaels drew on Marshall McLuhan's ideas about the semblance between modes of information transfer in the 'electronic age' and tribal forms of communication. He also drew from Baudrillard's writings on art to critique the way notions of 'authenticity' and 'tradition' were being applied to Aboriginal art forms and to illuminate the nonindividualistic and anti-authorial methodologies of Warlpiri painting (with which his fieldwork at Yuendumu had made him very familiar) (Michaels 1994 [1988]).[13] In Michaels's view postmodern modes of critique that engaged on a conceptual level with Aboriginal artworks were essential to combat both the constraints of conventional anthropological expertise and the risk that Aboriginal art become 'fodder for Post-Modernism's consumerist appetite for the primitive' (2004 [1989], 220, 221).

Some non-Indigenous artists and writers who embraced postmodernist viewpoints enlisted the idea of Aboriginality as, in Tillers's words, 'a ubiquitous quality which is no longer the exclusive domain of "black" Aborigines' (1982, 51). On this point it is worth looking closely at the writings of Paul Taylor, an influential curator, writer and founding editor of the journal *Art & Text*, and a champion of Tillers's work.[14] Taylor had an irreverent and relativistic style of commentary that was explicitly poststructuralist. In his writings, he frequently depicted Australia as a site of simulacra and artifice, with a fragmented, multi-national citizenry and a forsaken interior. He also denounced 'social purpose' art and regionalism and rather endorsed art that played on the frivolous and the mass produced (Taylor 1982, 49; 1984a; 1984b [1981]; 1989).

In this vein Taylor saw Australian art as being uniquely placed to flourish under postmodern conditions. In 1983 he published an essay titled 'POPISM: the Art of White Aborigines',[15] which discussed the *POPISM* exhibition he had curated at the National Gallery of Victoria in 1982. The essay takes its name from a Tillers's work in the exhibition that was titled 'White Aborigines'.[16] Here Taylor suggests that '[a] search for a regional Australian culture, ulti-mately a worthless pastime, reveals a centrifugal impulse wherein our art, like the mythopoeic Dreamtime of the aborigines, is the flak of an explosion not of our detonation' (1983, 30). He praises, with specific reference to those art-ists who had embraced the medium of the camera, recent Australian art as 'an ab-original soulless, antipodal reflection' and asserts that POPISM, 'like the aboriginal nomads, can therefore find a metaphor for itself in its existence on the surface and edges of the existing landscape' (1983, 32). Taylor's rhetorical appropriation of Aboriginality thus buttresses his refutation of the qualities of authenticity and distinctiveness that had historically been coveted within Australian art. In Taylor's view, the absence of these qualities was a post-modern blessing. Though the concept of 'white Aborigines' was not favoured by many artists or critics,[17] the phrase was well aired at the time, and some authors echoed Taylor's views about the vacuity of Australian culture.[18]

In contrast to the irreverence of Tillers's and Taylor's writings, there were many more temperate conceptualist interpretations of Aboriginal art (Marcon 1986; McNeill 1987; Lingard 1989b). The curatorial writings of Bernice Murphy, for example, artfully communicate the purposefulness of the formal aspects of Aboriginal art works, explaining that they are precise and subtle renderings of social, mythological and geographical knowledge (see, for instance, Murphy 1981, 15; 1983b, 47). Nicholas Baume's article 'The Interpretation of Dreamings: The Australian Aboriginal Acrylic Movement' (1989) is a useful illustration of the way themes from conceptual art were brought into dialogue with Aboriginal art. Here Baume is critical of the ten-dency among some art writers to apply the frameworks of abstract expression-ism and minimalism to the desert painting movement. He questions the very idea that one can decode the meaning in Aboriginal paintings by examining their formal elements and discusses several points of correspondence between conceptual art and the work of Aboriginal artists. In reference to the primacy of *idea* over *object* in conceptual art, he points out that for Aboriginal artists, as is the case with conceptual artists, the idea on which a painting is based – from the artist's Dreaming – exists prior to and does not diminish after; it has been transposed into an art object. He notes that in their efforts to defy and transcend art history's fixation with the art object, conceptual artists seek just such an unfettered position. He writes that '[the] desire to look beyond the painted surface to its conceptual basis is gratified by Aboriginal art [...] It not only caters for the conceptualist taste, the social integration of its ideas makes the attempts of Conceptual art look amateur' (118, see also 116).

6.3.6 *Social justice*

As we have already seen in the writings of Ian Burn, Bernard Smith and Imants Tillers, Indigenous social justice issues impinged on many engagements with Aboriginal art at this time. For instance, when Vivien Johnson asks audiences to remember that they are part of 'the artistic dialogue of a subjugated people and their colonisers', the matter of justice is presented as being embedded in the intercultural exchange that is instigated by Aboriginal art (1986b, 14; see also 1987). Land rights movements, deaths in custody, the repatriation of Aboriginal human remains from museums, cultural property issues, the treaty campaign and the implications of the Bicentenary were often remarked on in non-Indigenous writers' commentary about Aboriginal art.[19] Many non-Indigenous artists and art professionals were sympathetic to Aboriginal political aspirations and participated in protests or advocated for Indigenous rights. For example, in 1981 and 1982 a group of Indigenous and non-Indigenous musicians and artists in Sydney formed the group Apmira in support of Aboriginal land rights. Apmira organised several concerts and art exhibitions to raise money for state land councils, and dozens of artists composed pieces and donated works to the cause (Register of Australian Archives and Manuscripts 2002). An exhibition of photographs of Aboriginal life and events during the decade 1972–82 taken by non-Indigenous photographer Wesley Stacey titled *After the Tent Embassy* was toured nationally in 1982 and 1983, accompanied by an essay by Indigenous scholar Marcia Langton. A promotional piece on the exhibition published in the journal *Art Network* states:

> The exhibition is a statement by us about our Aboriginality which since colonisation has been under threat. The photographic essay explains why we have a strong sense of identity, unity, and why we want real land rights. The statement is what every black person wants to say. (Australian Institute of Aboriginal Studies 1983, 30)

Stacey also assisted conservation and anti-logging movements, seeking to protect forests in the south-east of New South Wales that were of significance to Aboriginal communities (Stacey 1983, 152–54). The non-Indigenous artist

Peter Kennedy created videos, installations and painted banners that addressed Indigenous social justice issues as well as issues faced by other disadvantaged groups (Kennedy 1979; 1983).

6.4   The Overseas Reception of Aboriginal Art

Aboriginal art's enthusiastic reception overseas in the 1980s provoked interesting responses within Australian critical writings. Some people had concerns about the way Aboriginal art and culture were being interpreted in other countries, and the way non-Indigenous Australian art was positioned as subservient to Aboriginal art in overseas exhibitions as well as in local exhibitions that had an internationalist rationale. For instance, Imants Tillers wrote that at the 1979 *Sydney Biennale*, 'Australian artists were often dismayed by the interest in and knowledge of Aboriginal culture shown by visiting artists and critics and the almost aggressive indifference they displayed to the Australian urban environment and its culture' (1982, 54; see also Cameron 1988, 14; Baume 1989, 110). Artist Lyndal Jones made a similar point about an exhibition of Australian contemporary art (which included her own work) titled *Continuum* held in Tokyo in 1983. There was no Aboriginal art in this exhibition, nevertheless at the associated symposium Jones found that Aboriginal art and culture was the primary topic of interest for the audience, and perceived that it was widely assumed that non-Indigenous Australian artists *must* be influenced by Aboriginal art. For Jones the 'uninformed desire for an exotically decorative and pseudo-Aboriginal notion of "The Australian Art" by people of other cultures' was a serious matter. She goes on to remark that '[t]his simplistic homogenisation of the many cultures that make up Australia will continue to patronise, to marginalise, the art of Aborigines and white artists alike where such notions go unchallenged' (1983, 49).

The *D'un autre continent: l'Australie le rêve et le reel* exhibition (translated as *From another continent: Australia – the Dream and Reality/the Real*) provoked the greatest censure along these lines. This exhibition took place at the Musée d'Art Moderne de la Ville de Paris during the 1983 Autumn Festival in Paris, at which Australia was the theme country. It comprised works by dozens of Australia's most prominent contemporary non-Indigenous artists, as well as a ground painting created on site by 12 Warlpiri male artists (Phipps 1984). What is perhaps most interesting about the exhibition is that even though we see French poststructuralist thought being mobilised to assert the progressiveness of non-Indigenous Australian artistic and critical practices, French intellectuals engaged with Aboriginal art through a primitivist lens that was by this stage regarded as anachronistic in Australian intellectual circles.

The exhibition's literature reveals that postmodern discourses could be double-edged when brought to bear on non-Indigenous contemporary artists. Australian scholar Meaghan Morris provided a kind of critical portrait of Australia in her catalogue essay.[20] A motif of this essay, which echoes Paul Taylor's imagery discussed above, is that an explosion has taken place elsewhere, scattering cultural debris on the Australian continent from which such things as a national identity and aesthetic traditions are derived. Indeed her essay is titled 'Jetsam', and she writes that 'a compilation culture of borrowed fragments, stray reproductions, and alien(ated) memories is what we already have *to begin with*' (1983, 39, original emphasis). She suggests that our formative 'explosion' is in part 'a myth of origin for a culture created in the disintegration of the great European schemas that produced the idea of this country' (38). Morris pictured Australian culture as capricious and improvised: 'The strangeness, the absurdity of the Australian nation is that for most of its inhabitants it may exist only as a fictitious generalisation from the local environment – or as a mass-media experience' (37). Implicit in these characterisations is a contrasting vision of France as a country of antiquity and depth, the development of which has had considerable bearing on the evolution of Western culture. Instead of civil wars, revolutions and other catalytic incidents, Morris writes that 'the surface of Australian history is pitted with isolated revolts, stray riots, strikes, and fleeting acts of defiance'. In Australia, 'political militancy' has not corresponded to epic events, only 'the "movements" of minority and specific-interest group [sic]'. And, in the absence of iconic 'saviours' and 'liberators', Australia has only 'guerrillas' in the form of convicts and bush-rangers (38). In some ways, by presenting Australia as a quintessentially postmodern space and trivialising the '"movements" of minority and specific interest groups', Morris's essay presented another incarnation of the Cultural Cringe.[21]

French curator Suzanne Page's effusive introduction offered a lighter interpretation of Australia as a final frontier of adventure and romance in the European imagination, and as having a youthful and agile culture ready to assert 'its entirely original identity' (1983, 10). Page's text unfolds via several dichotomies, which build an exotic picture of Aboriginal society and landscapes. She speaks of the 'coexistence of an aboriginal civilisation over 40,000 years old and the shortest history in the world (less than 200 years)' and writes that the interior spaces that exist beyond the settled coastline offer 'the vertiginous prospect of an eternal commencement, a featureless immensity as far as Darwin'. Against the 'mass of contradictions' that constitute settler society, 'Aboriginal society, divided as it is into many tribes, stands with serene permanence and timeless transcendence' (10–11). She suggests that non-Indigenous Australian artists are fortunate to be isolated from Europe and to be part of a young and culturally mixed society. However such affirmations read somewhat as a foil for statements such as 'the necessarily ephemeral ground painting of the Aborigines, in clear and unshakable terms, bears witness to the timeless permanence of a solid religious tradition which finds its life and purpose in an unspoilt landscape' (13).

Other parts of the catalogue echo this deference to the Warlpiri participants. Warlpiri leader Maurice Jupurrula Luther contributed an essay as a representative of the Executive Council of the Aboriginal Cultural Foundation, an organisation that worked extensively with Pagé to establish the terms of the elders' involvement in the exhibition. Another (non-Indigenous) foundation member, Lance Bennett, provides in-depth descriptions of the sacred sites, creation ancestors and ceremonies that informed the ground paintings. Bennett's text has an ambiguous voice, with some passages articulating a first-person Warlpiri point of view and others reading as the insights of a close and knowledgeable affiliate. The catalogue also includes photographs taken by Axel Poignant (the only colour images in the catalogue) of Aboriginal ritual performance and a lengthy explanatory essay by anthropologist Nicholas Peterson. This content creates an impression of a self-confident society founded on disciplined adherence to antiquated values and religious beliefs. The following passages, in which Bennett refers to the ground painting the Warlpiri men created for the exhibition, exemplifies the sober tone of his text:

> We Warlpiri present you here in Paris not with a 'show-piece' [...] Instead, we present you with a glimpse of the way we venerate the sacred Heroes who have given us our identity, so that Europeans can have some understanding of what we are, and of how strongly we feel about being allowed to remain ourselves [...] We will **never** put this kind of painting on to canvas, or on to artboard, or on to any 'permanent' medium. The permanence of these designs is in our minds. We do not need museums or books to remind us of our traditions. (49, original italics)

Readers who took these texts at face value would not necessarily discern that such statements were being made in the face of immense upheaval in Warlpiri society as a result of contact with white society and that these elders and the Aboriginal Cultural Foundation were working extremely hard to maintain tribal traditions.[22] Without contextualisation, such texts could be read as evidence of a surviving, unpolluted realm of tribal culture.

This hermetic image of tribal life was enhanced by Klaus Rinke's essay, which is situated between these sections on the Aboriginal participants and the 'Plasticians' section dedicated to the non-Indigenous Australian artists in the catalogue. A French artist and professor at the Académie Nationale des

Beaux-Art, Rinke had participated in the 1979 *Sydney Biennale*. This essay narrates his two visits to the Australian bush in 1977 and 1979:

> [I became familiar with] the symboles [sic], the totems, the taboos, the world of men, the tasks of women, the clan, the tribes, the mystical instruments for sacred ceremonies in secret places [...] [O]ne who has had an insight into prehistory's creativity, cannot, from that instant, continue to create and still remain faithful to the art in which he believed before. (1983, 83)

A strong primitivist and psychoanalysis-inspired sensibility is expressed here, and in Rinke's use of the phrase 'pre-embryonic memories' to describe what he gleaned from his experiences with Aboriginal people in remote Australia (it is the title of the text).

A review of the catalogue as a whole leaves the impression that the contributions of the non-Indigenous Australian artists were of secondary importance to the honour of being shown 'how art and life can be integrated, [the] nostalgia of our modern age' by the Warlpiri ground painters (Pagé 1983, 13).[23] There was also the implication that Paris was going to be the venue for a mature rapprochement between Indigenous and non-Indigenous Australians. In Jill Montgomery's account of the responses of the French press, she writes that the official exhibition speeches and the lecture tour of the show often echoed the remarks made by Pagé that most of the non-Indigenous Australian artists 'will be meeting an Aboriginal tribe for the first time in Paris'; that the exhibition will display 'side by side two realities which are still foreign to each other' and that 'this is the first time a museum outside Australia presents this double participation' (1983, 9–10; see Pagé 1983, 11, 13).

Several non-Indigenous artists greatly resented the way they had been presented as the antithesis of both European and Aboriginal culture. Participating artists Richard Dunn, Juan Davila and Philip Brophy, all of whom were pursuing experimental and conceptualist art practices, voiced their disillusionment in a 1984 issue of *Art Network* (see also van den Bosch 1985). Dunn critiqued the exhibition's premise as it was captured in the title:

> White Australia was to be characterised as a dream; interlopers of other's imaginary space, colonisers of the Real place (the unFrench and the Aboriginal) *and* as purloiners of European Art. Forty thousand years of the Real in the form of the Warlpiri ground painting was to be set against the two hundred year dream: No contest! (1984, 52)

Dunn notes that the pluralist character of both Aboriginal and non-Indigenous society in Australia was effaced by this opposition and points to the aspirations of the Aboriginal Arts Board and other organisations as being far removed from the image of static tribal culture on show.

In an abrasive critique of the exhibition and discussion forums, Davila condemned the exhibition for including no works 'that convey the plight of Feminism, Art Workers, Alternative Spaces, Mural Movements, Gay Art, Migrant Culture, Urban Aborigines etc' (1984, 50). Objecting to the principle of 'eclecticism' that seemed to guide the treatment of the non-Indigenous Australian works, Davila argued that such an approach trifled with, and had the effect of 'cancelling out', the historically embedded, distinct identities that comprised Australia. He writes that '[t]he European public is drawn to the exotic and the novel and the Aboriginal presence fulfilled that role once again' (51). While Davila was irritated by the 'passivity' of the Aboriginal artists at the round table discussions (51), we can also sense that he wished for Aboriginal and other marginal identities in Australia to remain inscrutable to some degree.

Philip Brophy's similarly caustic response begins with the following sarcastic statement: 'In the domain of Arts and Culture, Australia is currently either embroiled, or calmly participating, in the intersection of Aboriginal and White Australian (otherwise known as "Not Aboriginal") art practices' (1984, 53). With regard to the Paris roundtable discussions (at which Claude Lévi-Strauss was among the participants), he remarked on the banality of listening to Warlpiri men explain in pragmatic terms how they adapted sacred ceremonies and ground paintings to public presentation, and 'French anthropologists (yawn) tell us about how Art functions differently in primitive tribal cultures from industrialised technological cultures' (53). Brophy's essay indicates that for him there was something highly contrived and undignified in the idea that a dialogue between black and white could take place in such a setting. Such a prospect was made meaningless by the 'schematic' frameworks through which it was arranged.

The *D'un autre continent* was a significant overseas exhibition of Australian artists that deserves a fuller retrospective investigation, one in which the context of the show's initiation and realisation is explored in depth and the recollections of artists and curators solicited. What the sources reviewed here illuminate are the interstices between divergent perspectives on Aboriginal art and Aboriginality, perspectives that were brought into unusually close contact at the *D'un autre continent* exhibition. They attest to the fact that, as will be explored below, the category of primitive art and the status of non-Western art in general were being critically and ethically renegotiated in the contemporary art world at this time.

6.5 Postcolonial Critique and Urban Aboriginal Voices

The *D'un autre continent* exhibition took place one year before the controversial *Primitivism in 20th Century Art: Affinity of the Tribal and the Modern* (1984) exhibition at the Museum of Modern Art (MoMA) in New York. The latter exhibition incited heated debate regarding the curators' rationale in juxtaposing artworks by revered Western modernists and non-Western cultural objects that had inspired them or with which they shared a formal or conceptual 'affinity'.[24] As McLean writes, critics argued that the exhibition 'reinforced rather than reevaluated the colonialist relationship between modernism and non-western art' (2011b, 334–35). These critical responses expedited a burgeoning movement of postcolonial critique in the fine arts world, of which Kenneth Coutts-Smith was an important forerunner. These transnational discourses, in conjunction with the arguments of urban Aboriginal artists and advocates, informed the way the components of progressive curatorship and commentary were being negotiated in Australia in the 1980s. For example, Bernice Murphy, who gave momentum to Aboriginal painting's incursion into the contemporary art sphere by including two works by Papunya artist Tim Leura Tjapaltjarri in the first *Australian Perspecta* (1981), attended the MoMA exhibition and reflected on its implications for curatorial practice concerned with Aboriginal art (1987). Willis and Fry drew on both Foster's and James Clifford's texts in their *Art as Ethnocide* article (1989a; see also Davila 2004 [1987]). These debates were also brought into dialogue with Aboriginal art in the British publication and TV series *State of the Art*. Its segment 'Identity, Culture and Power' used the 1986 *Sydney Biennale* to illustrate the mix of global identities that were present in the contemporary art field. In it, Tillers' appropriation of Michael Nelson Jagamarra's painting and the Ramingining performance from the *Biennale* exhibition were focal points for a review of art world debates surrounding issues of race, otherness and regionalism. In addition, the perspectives of people such as Thomas McEvilley, Paul Taylor, Gary Foley (Aboriginal activist, actor and then director of the Aboriginal Arts Board) and Imants Tillers are situated within discussions that traverse the MoMA exhibition, Edward Said's seminal postcolonial text *Orientalism* and Hal Foster's *Recodings* (Nairne et al. 1987).

The participation of Gary Foley in the *State of the Art* production is a measure of the degree to which urban Indigenous artists and advocates were finding forums for critique and political argument at this time (see also C. Dixon 1984; Onus 1988; Caruana and Isaacs 1990).[25] The following statement from Foley appears in the *State of the Art* text:

> I believe that any expression of Aboriginal art, be it traditional or contemporary, is an act of political defiance. So much time and effort, two hundred years of very concerted effort to destroy Aboriginality and Aboriginal culture, has gone into this country. The fact that Aboriginal culture does remain a living thing is in

itself an extraordinary political statement about their resilience, their adaptability and their tremendous willpower. (Quoted in Nairne et al. 1987, 216)

Foley's statement reminds us, as discussed previously, that the arts were an activist domain in which a pan-Aboriginal base of solidarity founded on concepts of agency and survival took shape in the 1980s. Other urban Indigenous practitioners (and sympathetic non-Indigenous commentators) commented on the struggle Aboriginal artists faced in getting art world exposure, and the ubiquity of racism in Australian society. Reflecting on the sense of shame he had experienced as a teenager coming to terms with his Aboriginal heritage, Gordon Bennett described his works as deconstructing the 'Eurocentric conditioning' that legitimized the racism that was the source of that shame, as 'a way to deconstruct the erroneous construction of my self' (Lingard 1989c, 39). Other artists spoke of their desire to wrest control of their cultural heritage and identity from European institutions and to escape the demeaning legacy of their photographic representation by Europeans in colonial and anthropological contexts.[26] They were also critical of the appropriative practices of non-Indigenous artists, designers and the tourist product industry (C. Dixon 1984; Tranby Aboriginal College 1984; Langton 1988). For instance Fiona Foley, one of the first Indigenous artists to attain a tertiary fine arts degree, stated in an interview that:

> At Sydney College [of the Arts] I didn't learn anything from them or any of the philosophies going around and didn't incorporate them in my work. They pushed – had respect for – Imants Tillers and Tim Johnson at that art school. They were for Post-Modernism [...] I was questioning that whenever I got the chance [...] Now Post-Modernists are stealing from other cultures. Those two artists are stealing from Aboriginal culture. They are held in high esteem by the art market and overseas. They sell their paintings for very high prices whereas the Aboriginal artists here in Sydney and throughout Australia find it hard to get recognition. (Quoted in Michaels 2004 [1989], 218)

Such claims made their mark as authentic local instances of concerns being raised in international theoretical debates about the objectification and subordination of the other within Western culture.

Non-Indigenous commentators had mixed responses to the deployment of post-colonial discourses and the emergence of urban Indigenous voices. John Von Sturmer questioned whether engaging in the 'politics of representation' was an effective means of changing the way Aboriginal people were perceived in the public realm. He proposed that a radical avoidance of othering relationships might lie in the occidental's 'willingness to be made over in relation to the group', to find means of 'immersion' and 'presence' rather than 'intervention' (1989, 127–28, 137). In her critique of an article written by Terry Smith, Bernice Murphy underlined the importance of diffusing Western epistemic authority and empowering the Indigenous voice, suggesting that it is 'not particularly helpful to Aboriginal culture, in a period when its internal dynamics of difference are being examined more comprehensively by Aboriginal people than at any time previously, for white interpreters (again) to rush in too quickly and ascribe roles of singular historical purpose for all to act out' (Murphy 1988, 2; see also 1987; T. Smith 1988). Burn and Stephen (1986) and Kleinert (1988a) raised similar concerns in their writings on Albert Namatjira's place in Australian art history, arguing that there needed to be a platform for Aboriginal perspectives that might rest on adaptation and cross-cultural exchange.

These writers were no doubt also conscious of the fact that essentialist and exotic interpretations of Aboriginality continued to circulate in Australian culture. Such interpretations were often characterised by idealisations of tribal spirituality and ecological harmony and in some cases advocated an Aboriginalised form of nationalism (Hamilton 1990; Lattas 1997; 2000 [1989]). For example, popular forms of primitivism were present in the appropriation of Aboriginal cosmology and mythology by New Age mystics and in Bruce Chatwin's bestselling book *The Songlines* (1988; Marcus 1997 [1988]; Michaels 2004 [1989]). Similarly, highly primitivist rhetoric appeared in the press in 1984 when the so-called last of the desert tribes (later known as the Pintupi Nine) came in to the remote outstation Kiwirrkurra in the Gibson Desert. Front page articles employed language such as 'Desert nomads come out of the stone age' and 'They arrived in the 20th century just a week ago' (Desert Nomads 1984; R. Dixon 1984; O'Neil 1984). We have also seen how salient primitivist ideas were to the *D'un autre continent* exhibition in Paris. Thus the target of postcolonial critique in relation to primitivism was still apparent in both popular culture and fine arts domains.

6.6   The Bicentenary

The 1988 Bicentenary provided a backdrop for many of the critical and aesthetic engagements reviewed above. Several exhibitions staged in that year cemented Aboriginal art's place within Australian contemporary art and addressed the theme of colonisation and the changing nature of Indigenous/non-Indigenous relations (Commonwealth Institute 1988; Sisley 1988). Artists' week at the 1988 Adelaide Festival had an Aboriginal focus, and the journals *Artlink* and *Agenda* dedicated issues to Aboriginal themes (Maughan et al. 1988; Langton 1988). The *Aboriginal Memorial*, shown as part of the 1988 *Sydney Biennale*, was widely embraced as an innovative and moving piece that captured people's ambivalent feelings about the Bicentenary celebrations. Its installation was in fact funded by the Australian National Gallery as part of an arrangement that has kept it on permanent display ever since and ensures that it will never be deaccessioned (Smith 2001, 646). *Biennale* curator Nick Waterlow felt it to be 'the single most important statement in this Biennale' and suggested that in the eyes of many artists 'the Aboriginal presence is the most civilising and creatively challenging element in our world' (1988, 12; see also Philp 2007).

As noted previously, Michael Nelson Jagamarra was commissioned in 1985 to create a large granite mosaic for the forecourt of the new Parliament House, which was opened in 1988. At the event of its opening (at which Nelson met the Queen of England), land rights protests were staged. Aboriginal activist, author and artist Kevin Gilbert, who coordinated the Treaty '88 activist campaign, was reported to have condemned the commission as being indicative of Aboriginal culture's cooption by the settler state. This act provoked a heated exchange of views between non-Indigenous writers Sylvia Kleinert and Vivien Johnson (Kleinert 1988b, 1988c; V. Johnson 1988). This dispute revolved around the question of Nelson's agency and the degree to which an individual artist's aspirations could or should be subsumed by the pan-Aboriginal cause or was nullified by the hegemony of the state. This exchange, and the event itself, highlighted the disjunctions between 'urban' and 'remote' Aboriginal people's perspectives and the tensions that arose from the fact that the remote (and black-skinned) Aboriginal person had been designated the authentic Aboriginal citizen to whom the state was prepared to bestow symbolic recognition.

6.7 Conclusion to Part II

In her book *Caging the Rainbow*, Francesca Merlan (1998) writes:

> Part of the process of coming of age in a former colony of settlement, but now a modernising nation, has been to conceptualise as a people those rendered marginal to the body politic through dispossession. The logic is one by which the Aboriginal, as a kind of political subject under construction (the searched-for 'self' of 'self- determination'), is produced and contested as a type of nationality, problematically related to the changing national subject itself. (153)

The writings discussed here reveal how disruptive Aboriginal aesthetics and the idea of the Aboriginal subject had suddenly become for Australian culture. As textual residues of a turbulent period in Australian art, they show us how artists and intellectuals were invested in the fraught process Merlan describes. As much as these individuals were responsive to the particularities of Australian and local histories, they were engaging with international trajectories of political change and critical thought arising from processes of decolonisation and globalisation that challenged the logic of European modernity. I wish here to offer a distillation of the key threads and tensions displayed in the 1980s literature.

First, Western and Central Desert acrylic painting posed a profound challenge to honoured Australian landscape traditions, while they also challenged conceptualist and postobject art practices. This work was grounded in ancient traditions, yet it was current: the artists were forging a new kind of painting largely independent of Western art practices. Furthermore, the inimitable depth of these artists' identification with their land was consistently being verified by the public discourses associated with land rights and treaty activism. Therefore, just as non-Indigenous artists were attempting to draw a line under the Australian provincialist past, there was a sense, typified in the responses to the *D'un autre continent* exhibition and the practice and writing of Imants Tillers, that they were to be derailed by a new kind of art that was novel, antique and uniquely Australian.[27] As critic Sasha Grishin wrote in 1989, 'The startling revelation [...] is that not only did white culture not move into an existing void, but that the artistic expression of black culture is richer than anything which has subsequently tried to replace it. If Australia has a great visual tradition, then it is black'. Thus Aboriginal art both inspired and problematised non-Indigenous Australian art practices at this time.

Second, Aboriginal social justice issues that were evolving in the public domain, and the links between Aboriginal art and land rights politics, loomed large for an art fraternity whose *raison d'être* was that art had 'political and social relevance' and offered fearless social critique (Baume 1989, 117). Moral concerns about Aboriginal political aspirations and the structural inequalities in Australian society were expressed in the writings of many Indigenous and non-Indigenous commentators, even though, as we have seen, there were a variety of viewpoints on the role Aboriginal art had to play with respect to these concerns.

Third, many non-Indigenous actors engaged with Indigenous social justice issues through the medium of emerging critical discourses on otherness, difference and postcolonialism. There was great sensitivity to the imperative of establishing an ethical means of engaging with minority cultures and facilitating the empowered expression of their difference. These actors were also keen to find ways of substantiating the burgeoning respect for and recognition of the Indigenous subject within Australian society. We have seen how these concerns crystallised around an ensemble of critical themes: cultural convergence, rapprochement, cultural colonialism and ethnocide.

Related to this was the program of diffusing white/Western/colonial power. Many non-Indigenous artists and audiences in Australia were responsive to Aboriginal art in a Romantic and sometimes primitivist vein: they envied Aboriginal people's deep attachments to place and the poetic means by which they communicated their lore and their spirituality. However, as the critical writings on the MoMA *Primitivism* exhibition and the *D'un autre continent* exhibition illustrate, cutting edge theoretical literatures were discrediting the sentiments of the disenchanted modern subject. Irrespective of whether these Romantic engagements were predicated on a sincere and pertinent critique of Western society, they were increasingly open to incriminating analysis as perpetuating a problematic modernist tradition and ignoring the flux of Aboriginal life and identity. Critics who echoed Coutts-Smith's approach theorised colonisation as being of the present and proposed that many individuals were, unwittingly or not, complicit with it. Notwithstanding the presence of some urban Indigenous voices (particularly later in the decade), and the fact that close relationships were being forged between Aboriginal artists in remote communities and a few non-Indigenous researchers and practitioners, most debates were conducted between non-Indigenous people exclusively and often articulated through the prism of theoretical discourses. In some of these writings we can perceive an urgent need to find an inviolable Aboriginal voice for which one might be a benevolent conduit and advocate. These desires were actualised in a range of ways: sometimes only rhetorically, sometimes in the realm of art making and curating, and sometimes in the use of one's professional position to create opportunities that were hitherto absent.

I wish to draw attention to the friction that arose between two prevailing tendencies, which points to a key dilemma with which this book is concerned. On the one hand there were recurring ethical injunctions to draw respectful and protective boundaries around the other: to affirm the other's incommensurability and stem the 'cannibalisation of Aboriginal culture' (V. Johnson 1989, 10; see also Sutton 1992b). On the other, we find the art realm being depicted as an autonomous space for uninhibited experimentation and inquiry, in which nothing should be off-limits. The iconoclastic styles of Paul Taylor and the more equivocal Imants Tillers can be read as a refusal to submit to the moral pressures I've just outlined. Appropriation was judged to be problematic by many commentators, particularly as the commercial exploitation of Aboriginal culture was a growing concern and thus artistic appropriation could be interpreted as another form of cultural theft (discussed in detail later; see also Cramer 1989). Nevertheless it was also recognised that such appropriative practices helped to break down the old institutional categorisations that were indicative of inequity and exclusion. The sieving of Aboriginal art through the arguments and anxieties that were attentive to

appropriation, and through concepts like 'white Aborigines' and 'rapprochement', and the associated theorisations of cross-cultural exchange, ensured
that conceptualist and interrogative art strategies were brought to bear on the
art. This, as McLean (2011a) makes clear, was undoubtedly progress in terms
of establishing Aboriginal art as contemporary art (see also Johnson 1989;
Michaels 2004 [1989]; Morphy 2006). Here we can perceive the tensions that
existed between different paradigms of advocacy, and the dilemma associated with exposing the myth of art's autonomy: it was necessary to employ
moral arguments to contest the exclusiveness of existing art values; that is, to
highlight the '*extra*-aesthetic principles and practices' that underpinned those
values (Wolff 2008, 19). Yet the overarching ambition was to consecrate new
art forms within that supposedly disinterested sphere. As Myers suggests, an
'underlying tension' in such projects is 'the necessary survival of the category
and institution of "art" for its own critiques' (1994, 27). We will have reason to
explore this dilemma further in Parts III and IV of this book.

The obvious interrelatedness of ethics and aesthetics in these discourses
encourages reflection on the poles of hope and disenchantment, which I argue
can assist us in understanding the tensions that have existed in the Aboriginal
art arena. Many of the debates discussed pivot on the distinction between
Aboriginal agency and victimhood, a distinction that goes to the heart of
the question of how non-Indigenous Australians might engage ethically with
Aboriginal art and Aboriginal people.[28] Key questions raised include: Did
existing interpretive frameworks elicit the artist's intentions satisfactorily, or
did they silence and/or distort those intentions? Was the art gallery a domain
of emancipation for Aboriginal art, or did its sanitised and individualising
spaces diffuse the challenging alterity of the art's makers? Did the art arena
enable cultural regeneration or was it yet another exploitative and corrupt-
ing force in Aboriginal communities? As we've seen, Aboriginal artists were
viewed as both victims and agents in the art arena, and there were reciprocal
arguments critiquing either position as naive, ethnocentric, racist, paternalis-
tic and so on.

The emergence of urban Indigenous voices inflected this distinction
between Aboriginal agency and victimhood with another set of problems.
Urban Indigenous artists and advocates placed issues of equality of participation and empowered professional involvement at the fulcrum of Aboriginal
art activities, particularly in association with the Aboriginal Arts Board. They
also encouraged an interrogation of white expertise *per se* (Onus 1989b; Sutton
1989). Furthermore, as concepts of Aboriginal identity came to be elasticised
in association with pan-Aboriginal discourses, some Aboriginal people felt victimised in settings that only validated remote Aboriginal art. This was illustrated in Kevin Gilbert's stance on Michael Nelson Jagamarra's mosaic, and

it is also expressed in Lin Onus's remarks about an Aboriginal art exhibition in which urban Aboriginal artists were not participants, titled *Renewing the Dreaming: New Directions in Contemporary Aboriginal Art*: 'The title of the show [...] speaks loudly and unequivocally to non-traditional and urban artists and says: "You are not Aboriginal your art is not real and does not belong here"' (1988, 29). These tensions between different formulations of urban and remote Aboriginal identity, political objectives and art will be pursued further in Part III.

Part III
NEGOTIATING DIFFERENCE

Introduction

Aboriginality (or Indigeneity) is a continually evolving identity that is shaped by both Aboriginal and non-Indigenous experience, knowledge and imagination. As Nagel writes, all ethnic identities arise from 'a dialectical process involving internal and external opinions and processes, as well as the individual's self-identification and outsiders' ethnic designations' (1994, 154; see also Hall 1990).[1] Aboriginal art is a category of art very much defined by the ethnic identity of its creators, and consequently it is drawn into the orbit of other forms of Aboriginal-focused culture and enmeshed in the dialectical process Nagel describes. Following Jules-Rosette who explored the trade of African tourist art, we might argue that Aboriginal art's circulation is modulated by the properties of 'cross-cultural interchange', which entails that '[t]he producers and consumers of [Aboriginal art] art live in quite different cultural worlds that achieve a rapprochement only through the immediacy of the artistic exchange' (1984, 8; see also Shiner 1994; Smith 2002, 149–52). This is most obviously the case when we are discussing Aboriginal art produced in remote Australia; however, something of this nature is also taking place in the case of urban Aboriginal artists who participate in the contemporary art milieu, because their Indigenous identity provides the framework for the interpretation of their art.[2]

We have already seen this dialectical process at work in the way Aboriginal art has been treated as a repository of cultural heritage, an anchor of collectivist consciousness, a means to engage in practices of cultural renewal and a political and legal instrument. It has also been a medium for ethical thought on the settler state condition among artists and intellectuals. And by being highly symbolic of Aboriginal identity within Australian visual culture it has been a focus of reflexive, sympathetic and remedial tendencies among non-Indigenous citizens, as well as nationalistic celebrations of inclusion and Reconciliation. Here I wish to expand on these discussions and explore how aspects of Aboriginal difference are negotiated in the realms of aesthetic taste, commerce, scholarship, curatorship and institutional practice.

Chapter 7

NEGOTIATING ABORIGINAL DIFFERENCE

7.1 Four Facets of Difference

Aboriginal difference is perceived and problematised in several ways in the art arena. First, Aboriginality exists as a site of disadvantage and injustice. This means that a range of parties advocate on its behalf on the basis of principles of equality and fairness, inclusion where there was once exclusion and respect where there was once stigma. As discussed earlier, Aboriginal art's subsidy and endorsement has been driven by the conviction that the restoration of Aboriginal culture is a matter of human rights and a means to alleviate disadvantage, and ethical concerns of this nature mediated many engagements between non-Indigenous practitioners and Aboriginal art in the 1980s. These issues are salient to the collecting practices of institutions, the opportunities available to Aboriginal artists and art professionals and the degree to which Aboriginal art gains acceptance in eminent contemporary art settings.

Second, Aboriginality is a site of exotic difference. Here we encounter all the ideas that underpin the objectification and commodification of otherness, which have revolved around notions of the premodern, the pre-industrial, the primitive, the tribal, the folkloric and so on. All of these currents of thought have been reference points for artistic and scholarly formulations of modernity (Enwezor 2003; Marcus and Myers, 1995; Clifford 1988). The sociologist Dean MacCannell offers some useful insights on this aspect of modernity in his seminal work *The Tourist* (1976), in which he argues that touristic experiences actualise the social differentiations that structure modern society. He argues that tourism produces a form of 'modern solidarity' (78) by packaging, in the service of the sightseer, aspects of nature, place, history and culture that signify what modernity is *not*. As he writes:

> The progress of modernity ('modernisation') depends on its very sense of insta-
> bility and inauthenticity. For moderns, reality and authenticity are thought to
> be elsewhere: in other historical periods and other cultures, in purer, simpler

lifestyles. In other words, the concern of moderns for 'naturalness', their nostalgia and their search for authenticity are not merely casual and somewhat decadent, though harmless, attachments to the souvenirs of destroyed cultures and dead epochs. They are also components of the conquering spirit of modernity – the grounds of its unifying consciousness. (3)

The pursuit of authenticity as a vehicle for self-discovery and enlightenment that MacCannell describes frequently involves 'cross-cultural interchange', while it also underlies Romantic and primitivist thought. Remote Aboriginal art and culture have a profound magnetism with respect to these tendencies and thus, as many scholars have pointed out, Romantic, primitivist and nostalgic ideas have dominated the landscape of reception of this art (Webb 2002; McLean 2002b; Lattas 2000). Conversely, as we saw in the previous chapter, Aboriginal art is a domain in which contemporary art practitioners, professionals and critics have sought to refute these othering tendencies and transcend the paradigm of primitivism that had formerly ghettoised non-Western art (Clifford 1988; Hiller 1991). Even when primitivism is not the target, the question of how to engage with difference without neutralising or appropriating it has been an abiding concern. For example, in his reflections on the illegitimacy of Eurocentric judgements of Emily Kame Kngwarreye's aesthetic achievements, Rex Butler suggests that it might be important that 'we think that this work is unspeakable within our discourse' (1997, 44). He proposes that the most ethical response may be to not seek to compensate for 'the failure of our critical language,' pointing out that immanent to that failure 'is the very experience of art itself, which is the contradiction, the antinomy, between the subjective and the objective, the singular and the universal, the formal and the social' (44; see also 2003 [1998]).

Third, the differences that exist *within* the Indigenous 'community' mean that, notwithstanding the efficacy of the idea of a pan-Aboriginal consciousness, it is always problematic to generalise about Indigenous identity and experience. Apart from the distinct Indigenous tribal groups, nations and regional groupings with which Indigenous Australians identify, Indigenous experience has been shaped by the uneven history of colonisation, pastoralisation and urbanisation across the continent; by differentiating policies of the state; and by the varying degree to which Indigenous people have partaken of the responsibilities and benefits of citizenship within a Western capitalist democracy. At the same time, across the domains of popular culture, news media, academic scholarship and remedial government policy discourses, dark-skinned Aboriginal people from remote areas are strongly distinguished from light-skinned Aboriginal people from rural and urban areas, and the latter are often excluded from the kinds of attention that validate Aboriginality as an identity (Anderson 2003; Lea 2005; Langton 1981; 2008b; Austin-Broos 2011). Consequently, a range of representations – sympathetic, voyeuristic or derogatory – of Aboriginality are active in the public domain as external and often conflicting determinants of this identity. And as Melinda Hinkson and Benjamin Smith point out, '[w]hether authentically traditional, politically resistant and autonomous, impoverished, drunk and demoralised, or aspirational, none of these representations recognises the fullness and complexity of Aboriginal people's ways of life, nor the possibility of articulating aspirations that reflect the contradictory experience of colonialism' (2005, 163). These representations influence the way audiences approach Aboriginal art and interpret its meanings, particularly because that 'fullness and complexity' is only perceived intersubjectively by a tiny proportion of non-Indigenous Australians. As we have seen, the impasses that arise from these circumstances emerge most clearly in relation to the tensions that underpin the opposition between urban and remote Aboriginal art (see Mundine 2009a; Iseger-Pilkington 2011).

As vexed as it might be, the differentiation of *urban* from *remote* tells us a great deal about how the political-geographic economy of Australia's colonisation process. European agricultural and urban development began in the south of the continent, and for a long time there was little economic or strategic incentive to bring about the social integration of Aboriginal people in the Northern and Central regions. This changed when the mineral wealth of those regions was targeted – for example, by the Nabalco Mining Company at Yirrkala in Arnhem Land – and as Rowse writes, this brought about 'a political contest between, on one side, government agencies allied with mining corporations and, on the other side, Aborigines, churches and others espousing, with much political success, a new global human right called "land rights"' (2014, 306; see also Langton 2013). The flourishing of Aboriginal art in these areas in the 1970s is thus linked in an important way to the timing of the state's and private industry's economic incursion into the north. As touched on in Rowse's remarks, it was at this time that international human rights concepts were becoming salient to domestic politics, and a progressive section of the Australian population were thus attuned to the moral conflict over land and resources taking place. Their responsiveness to Aboriginal people's disempowerment in these areas (with the Noonkanbah dispute in 1979–1980 in Western Australia being another early site of conflict over mining and Indigenous sacred sites) galvanised public awareness of Aboriginal culture and heritage. Those forms of Aboriginal art that are marked as 'remote', created within arid or tropical regions of the continent that would not yield to 'thoroughgoing productive domestication' as part of the national economy (Merlan 1998, 159), were thus able to flourish because 'the socio-economic assimilation' of

Aboriginal people that governments had aspired to in the southern areas and cities came to an end at this moment (Rowse 2014, 305). The assimilationist socioeconomic model was replaced in the 1970s with a different one: welfare, a model that gave credence to the burgeoning respect for Aboriginal cultural autonomy and enabled Aborigines to live – and make art – on their ancestral estates. The tertiary education that has underpinned the careers of some urban Aboriginal artists and to which those in remote areas have not had access is an analogous socioeconomic factor differentiating particular threads of Aboriginal art. Where mining is concerned, the political economy of Aboriginal art production remains complex. The previously mentioned scenario, in which mining threatened Aboriginal culture, has been somewhat inverted in recent years with mining companies such as Woodside Energy and BHP Billiton being significant funders of Aboriginal Art Centres and projects, due to land use and native title arrangements developed with traditional owners in resource-rich areas (Myers and Palmer 2015; Davis 2014; Cook 2013). We therefore can't ignore the different social and policy lineages, and their specific geography, that sit behind the paradigms of contemporary urban and remote Aboriginal art.

The degree to which urban and remote Aboriginal art are structurally differentiated in the Australian art arena can be illuminated in view of Bourdieu's model of the field of cultural production. Bourdieu's artistic field comprises a range of actors: artists, dealers, critics, curators, as well as institutions, styles, genres and movements, all of which compete for cultural legitimacy while simultaneously contributing to a field-wide consensus regarding what is legitimate (Bourdieu 1993, 30–36). Within the Aboriginal art field, urban and remote Aboriginal artists occupy paradoxical actor-positions, such that they have had markedly contrary experiences of marginality. On the one hand, urban Aboriginal artists, critics and advocates participate a great deal in competitive 'position-taking' within the field (Bourdieu 1993, 30), such that, as I proposed previously, it can be argued that they have established an urban Indigenous aesthetic public sphere in Habermasian terms.[1] However, because the field of Aboriginal art has been dominated by art from remote regions, measures of commercial success, exhibition activity, and institutional validation will identify most urban Aboriginal artists as marginal within the field. Remote Aboriginal artists, on the other hand, are very much at the periphery with respect to actor participation, even though their art has tended to find an audience and market more rapidly than the art produced by urban Aboriginal artists. We can attribute this to their inclination to remain in their communities, and to the fact that they do not have a sustained engagement with Western art or pay deference to (or create work in avant-gardist defiance of) a canon (Smith 2002, 148). Indeed, if we follow Bourdieu's reading of the way naïve French painter Le Douanier Rousseau was *constituted* by the artistic field in order for his paintings to be deemed art, a remote Aboriginal artist can be regarded as 'a "creator" who has to be "created" as a legitimate producer'; one whose art world trajectory depends to a large extent on how well he or she is 'produced' by 'impresario' figures – dealers, writers, and – in the case of Aboriginal art – Art Centre coordinators (Bourdieu 1993, 61, 275 [fn. 38], 177).

This differentiation between urban and remote Aboriginal art contributes to many of the tensions that surround the negotiation of Aboriginal difference in the Aboriginal art arena, because it means that a range of activities are problematised by identity politics. For instance, remote Aboriginal artists 'speak through' a range of non-Indigenous representatives. This generates a large body of non-Indigenous experts on Aboriginal art and Aboriginal identity that antagonise some urban Indigenous practitioners and professionals. It also means that the Aboriginal voice or cultural identity to whom non-Indigenous actors feel accountable can differ considerably depending on one's geographic location and one's affiliations within the field.

The problem of representing and advocating for the Aboriginal voice is highly pertinent to the fourth manifestation of difference with which I am concerned: the fact that many of the most knowledgeable people in the Aboriginal art arena (including the first people to promote the aesthetic merits of Aboriginal art) are associated with the traditions of Anthropology and Ethnography. Anthropologists cement art audiences' sense of Aboriginal difference in several conflicting ways. They are among the most strident advocates for the specificity of Aboriginal art and argue their case in ways that often affront traditional art discourses. Further, their research traditions invoke the histories and ideologies of colonialism and evolutionism, and their focus on remote communities has the effect of authenticating the Aboriginality of some Aboriginal people to the detriment of other Aboriginal people. These issues will be explored in detail later in Part III.

These four facets of difference cause the ethnicity of the Aboriginal artist to exist as a highly ambivalent component of the Aboriginal art object, a component that has both an attractive and repelling effect on audiences and consumers. We might understand this ambivalence from the point of view of Gell's suggestion that the power of artworks 'resides in the symbolic processes they provoke in the beholder', insofar as these symbolic processes involve rehearsing, testing and disrupting particular ideas about Aboriginality (1992, 48). For those involved in stewarding Aboriginal art within the contemporary art arena this poses a considerable challenge. As Indigenous curator Stephen Gilchrist observes, '[b]y focusing disproportionately on the racialised identity of Indigenous artists, the perceptual and cognitive engagement with their works is often completed far too quickly by the viewer' (2014, 57). And for others involved professionally with Aboriginal fine arts, asserting the value of the art object depends on managing the dissonances between Indigenous and non-Indigenous domains. This is captured in the following anecdote related to me by a Sydney fine art dealer regarding the reasons why their gallery began taking clients to remote communities to meet Aboriginal artists:

> *Dealer:* We developed the art touring education program because one of our really important clients came back from central Australia totally shattered and disillusioned about what he'd seen. On the cultural level, he went to the wrong place at the wrong time.
>
> *LF:* What do you mean by that?
>
> *Dealer:* He went to the wrong community at the wrong time. A lot of these communities *you do not go to*. They don't want you to go and you shouldn't go. You don't – just because Papunya Tula has an artist's association, I don't advise anyone to go to Papunya. It's a dangerous, unpleasant, unhappy, place.
>
> […]
>
> *Dealer:* You see everybody's left Papunya.[2] […] You know if you turn up at Papunya at the wrong time, you're possibly in danger! And you won't see any good art and all this kind of thing. So you can come back, and he did come back quite shattered, and that's when we realised that we in fact needed to go with our best clients to gently kind of dip them in or marinate them in the culture. And so it has to be about education and social conditions and stuff like that.
>
> *LF:* (asks whether artists are receptive to their visits)
>
> *Dealer:* [Yes, but with] some artists you won't. I mean we went to a community where they all just sat around on the floor and put their hands out, and we just said 'look' to the coordinator 'this is so dangerous and so damaging to them and to people's perceptions of what they do, you know, we don't want to meet people like this, we only want to meet people who want to meet us'. So yeah, there are other communities where people are a bit more geared to what we're trying to do and it was a much greater interaction. (pers. comm, June 2, 2008)

This exchange reveals the way Aboriginal art professionals face unique problems that arise from the fact that most remote Aboriginal artists do not directly participate in the art arena and, moreover, sometimes live in circumstances that their clients may find confronting. It reminds us that, as Cowlishaw states, 'most Australians are distant from radical difference, geographically, symbolically, and ideologically' (2004, 249). Thus, as mediators of 'cross-cultural interchange', the artists' advocates and representatives (art centre coordinators, anthropologists, government professionals, curators, commercial gallerists) are constantly required to improvise and compromise as they negotiate the discord between the artists' domain and the art domain.

7.2 The Cosmopolitan and the Tourist: Being an Outsider with Aboriginal Art

When Jules-Rosette writes that African tourist art provides 'a vicarious experience of the foreign and the exotic', she could just as well be describing the way many audiences engage with remote Aboriginal art (1984, 17). The taste for the exotic underpins a model of consumption that is inimical to contemporary fine arts sensibilities, and yet it is contemporary art audiences to whom those representing Aboriginal fine art (in institutional or art market settings) seek to appeal. This problem can be clarified by drawing an analogy between tourism and art consumption. As MacCannell points out, while it is an accepted feature of Western culture that we periodically escape from normal life and see the world, the tourist is also an object of ridicule. This is because we are disturbed by the tourist's apparent satisfaction with what we know to be contrived and recognise that we may be similarly deceived when we are in foreign places. The reflexive character of the modern search for meaning, whereby 'reality and authenticity are thought to be elsewhere', entails both a quest for the sincere and authentic, and the presentiment that some artifice will make a fool of us (1976, 3; see also Harkin 1995). As MacCannell suggests, 'touristic shame is [based] on a failure to see everything the way it "ought" to be seen' (1976, 9).

MacCannell's insights are arguably salient to many people's encounters with Aboriginal art. The fact that the art is produced for outsiders who are often compelled by a sense of curiosity about an exotic other makes many people suspicious that they may be a victim of the mystification that attends to those commodities that capitalise on the impression of authenticity (93). Just as tourists wish to 'see everything the way it "ought" to be seen', the ideal of contemporary art appreciation is competence with a particular aesthetic language, and membership of a collegiate of artists, art dealers, art professionals, collectors and connoisseurs. Contemporary Western art, and the apparatus of expertise that validates it, is produced for insiders: for peers and like minds who share, in Bourdieu's terms, a particular cultural competence. As he writes, 'the act of empathy [...] which is the art-lover's pleasure, presupposes an act of cognition, a decoding operation, which implies the implementation of a cognitive acquirement, a cultural code' (1984, 3, 86).

Aboriginal art generates a layered and uncomfortable apprehension of difference for many people, both with respect to the cultural difference inscribed in the art object that makes us feel like a foreigner as we try to comprehend it, and the sense that a commodified and perhaps contrived difference – a 'staged authenticity' to use MacCannell's phrase – underlies the object, one which invokes a kind of recipient or audience that we find distasteful and embarrassing. If we follow Gell's reasoning that art, as an index of social relations, 'can work by alienating the spectator as well as by producing identification' (1998, 31), we might argue that Aboriginal art can make one feel like a tourist in a domain in which we would like to think of ourselves as a cosmopolitan, a dupe and an outsider in a realm of intellectual and aesthetic pleasure in which we wish to feel 'at home'.

I will provide three examples of this insider/outsider dynamic. First, a Sydney art dealer once related to me a succinct riposte from one of Sydney's most prominent and longstanding contemporary art dealers to the question of why he did not represent Aboriginal artists: 'It's got nothing to do with me'. The comment conveys, very simply, an aversion to entering a realm in which he is an outsider (if all non-Indigenous people took this view, there would be no Aboriginal art market at all!). Second, when London-based artist and *The Times* arts commentator Grayson Perry reviewed the 2007 *Rarrk-London* exhibition of Maningrida works staged by the contemporary art dealer Josh Lilley, he asked why Indigenous artists should wish to be part of, and furthermore be allowed into, the contemporary art 'tribe'. He writes:

> The values of contemporary art are aesthetically and intellectually complex and have been refined through a long history of challenges and movements. Aboriginal art, whose value derives from a traditional folklore context, cannot just transfer that value into the more lucrative and far-reaching arena of contemporary art without having to work with and be judged by fine-art criteria. (2007)

By provocatively employing the trope of the tribe, Perry creates a potent image of insiders and outsiders and emphatically excludes Aboriginal art from a contemporary art context.[3]

Third, Georges Petitjean, the curator at the Aboriginal Art Museum in Utrecht, sought to take the institution in a new direction in 2008 soon after his tenure there began by exhibiting the work of Central Australian Aboriginal artists from the museum's collection – Kathleen Petyarre, Dorothy Napangardi, Lilly Kelly Napangardi and Jackie Giles – alongside that of renowned Belgian conceptual artist Marcel Broodthaers, in an exhibition titled *Nomads in Art*. He remarked to me during our interview that his intention was to attract audiences who may have regarded the gallery as having no connection to contemporary art. In other words, his curatorial strategy sought to circumvent the 'outsider' identity that the institution, by its very specificity, has transmitted to visitors (pers. comm. August 10, 2008; see also Petitjean 2008).

7.3 Authenticity and 'The Story'

As has been explored by many authors, authenticity plays a large part in shaping perspectives on cultural objects whose value inheres in their ethnic specificity, and Aboriginal art is no exception (Clifford 1988; Price 1989). In the mid-twentieth century, the archetypal Aborigine was an object of consumption in Australia because it accorded with essentialist constructs of desirable and enigmatic difference (Russel 2001; Franklin 2010). These constructs evoked many of the primitivist notions of authenticity with which we are now familiar; namely, that there exists a 'world of the unspoiled, pre-contact "natives" who live in another time than our own' (Shiner 1994, 229).

It is clear that the notion of authenticity has an ambivalent status in the Aboriginal art arena. The reasons for this return us to the insider/outsider dynamic discussed earlier and the tension between touristic and contemporary art modes of engagement with Aboriginal art. That is, while concepts of authenticity are sometimes a very important part of the explanation and brokerage of the art, in other contexts they are judged to impede the appreciation of the art, and to deter collectors. This can be illustrated by looking at the way 'the story' (the Dreaming narrative that is the reference point of most remote Aboriginal artworks) and, by extension, the spiritual content that denotes the alterity of the art feature in the brokerage of Aboriginal art. Following the lead of Geoffrey Bardon, it has been common practice for art centres to provide diagrammatic and/or narrative decodings of Aboriginal artworks to collectors (Bardon and Bardon 2004). As Myers writes, these decodings were initially ethnographic in intent, developed as a practice before Aboriginal art had caught the attention of the art world, while they also served the Indigenous artist's agenda of educating white audiences about the continued currency of the Dreaming and custodial relationships with the land (1994, 15).

'The story' is regarded by many to be an odious accompaniment to works of Aboriginal art. It signals that the work demands a different, and perhaps primitivist, framework of appreciation to Western art, and as Petitjean writes, the 'stress on the secret and sacred content in a painting often results in inaccurate and populist generalisations about Aboriginal culture, society, religious beliefs and art' (2000, 242). The provision of 'the story' may therefore indicate that the works are being made accessible to inerudite audiences, and that dealers are explicitly trading on the exotic, both of which are indicative of a touristic mode of engagement.

This was revealed to me in an interview I conducted with a particular Aboriginal art dealer. This dealer had had no art school training and had run a successful company in another industry before establishing his Aboriginal art business. Located in a high tourist traffic area, his outlet sells Aboriginal art, craft, and licensed product in-store and online. The following statement was preceded by the dealer describing how his interest in the art was partly inspired by visits to rock art sites around the world:

> [I realised Aboriginal art] was today's embodiment of what had been going on for many many millennia on rock walls. Just in a more modern format – modern media. And I started buying more. And looking at the people who I'm buying from and thinking: 'crikey, they're treating this as a whitefella's aesthetic. They've got no idea of the culture behind it [...] And, they don't know anything about the artist who's producing it [...] I felt that there was a better way to do it. Because you don't just sell the sausage, you sell the sizzle with the sausage'. (pers. comm. April 18, 2008)

These reflections convey the dealer's desire to make the art more accessible and interesting to audiences by focusing on the ancient heritage of Aboriginal art rather than the aesthetics, and throughout our interview he indicated that he thought the stories associated with particular paintings or particular artists were of great value to the brokerage process. A similar view is expressed in the following quotation from an art centre staff member in Wadeye regarding an exhibition staged in San Francisco in 1994:

> All the paintings we sold, we made sure the stories were there [...] I mean you look at some of the paintings and artistically they may or may not turn you on. But then when you hear the story you think, 'Oh, shit, that's really interesting,' and that's what sells the paintings as much as – as I say, the actual art work might not be terribly appealing, but when you hear the story, it's just so interesting. (Quoted in Belk and Groves 1999, 24)

These opinions can be contrasted to those of Beverly Knight, the owner of Alcaston Gallery in Melbourne, a long-established dealer in Aboriginal fine arts:

> Stories don't sell art, the aesthetics sell art. Where story is important is in the motivation and inspiration for the artist. People may have that deep cultural knowledge but their work is not selling. People who were collecting for that reason are no longer collecting, trust me, they're not. The contemporary collector is looking at the aesthetics. (Quoted in Finnane 2012)

In a similar vein, an esteemed dealer in Aboriginal fine arts made the following remarks to me regarding how his gallery first started showing Aboriginal art in the 1980s:

Dealer: We didn't show it to an Aboriginal audience, we showed it to a
contemporary audience because that's – I didn't *know* the Aboriginal
audience, I only knew the contemporary audience [...] I've never put wall
labels up next to paintings saying this is the such and such Dreaming. When
people ask me what galleries to go and see good Aboriginal art in, I send
them to the Art Gallery of NSW first, and then I say don't go to anything
that's got the words 'Aboriginal', 'Dreaming' or 'investment' in it.

LF: [...] [T]he wall text issue is such an interesting one when you're dealing
with cross-cultural art engagement, isn't it? Because, is something left out
then, in terms of what the artist might be wanting to communicate?

Dealer: People can find that out later. Emily Kngwarreye [would say] in her own
way 'this is my country, this is our *alhalkere*', and she'd touch that painting,
she'd sing a little song with that painting, which is you know, about her
country, and she believed that you should look at this painting [...] and you'll
understand. Now that's an artist who believes that they can put everything
they want into the painting. In the end, no matter what anyone says, if you've
got a painting that's hanging on the wall the only thing you've got to judge it
by is the painting. If the painting isn't any good, in that way that art is great
or not great ... no amount of blurb on the wall's going to improve it (pers.
comm. March 18, 2008).

A quotation from collector Colin Laverty provides another variation of this
way of seeing Aboriginal art. In an interview recorded on the occasion of
the publication of a monograph about the Laverty collection, *Beyond Sacred*,
Laverty says:

[W]e think it's a pity people can hardly look at Aboriginal paintings without first
saying 'what's the story?' And we would like people to look at them, as you look
at non-indigenous art and say 'this is a great painting' because, say, it has fantastic
visual impact, or it's beautifully painted, or it's beautifully colourful, or it's illustrative
of abstracted landscape mapping and that sort of thing. Rather than go straight to
wanting to know what the underlying story is. (Copeland and Laverty 2008)

All of these quotations reveal contestations over the way the *content* of Aboriginal
art – content that requires some explanation to be understood – is treated
within the art arena. Explaining this content in terms of sacred Country and
Dreaming stories may indeed open a door to greater understanding and appreciation and to a larger audience. However, two problematic consequences –
problematic from the point of view of some of the more elite dealers and
collectors – may follow from this. First, as I noted earlier, by evoking popular
stereotypes of the authentic and exotic Aborigine, a cohort of buyers that falls

outside the specialist sphere of contemporary fine arts appreciation is being engaged. This is conveyed for instance in the Sydney fine art dealer's grouping of the terms *Aboriginal, Dreaming* and *Investment*. Second, as is implied in Laverty's and the fine art dealers' remarks (and indeed in the title of Laverty's monograph), 'the story' may take primacy over form. Notwithstanding the short-lived conceptualist engagements with Aboriginal art of the 1980s, for these kinds of advocates it is the formal, usually abstract, beauty of Aboriginal work that underpins the art's value as contemporary fine art. Both fine art dealers quoted earlier in this chapter allude subtly to the acuity of their own connoisseurial judgement in this respect, in contrast to the Wadeye Art Centre staff member who is quite comfortable with the idea that 'the story' might be more appealing than the artwork itself. All of the individuals discussed earlier are concerned with making the art more appealing to clients. However, those engaged with fine Aboriginal art are speaking to erudite contemporary art audiences for whom aesthetics is a universal entry point: the cosmopolitans who are a world away from the touristic consumers to whom the dealer in the high tourist traffic area seeks to sell 'the sizzle with the sausage'.

Chapter 8

THE ART/ANTHROPOLOGY BINARY

'The story' is of great importance to another group of people who are professionally engaged in the Aboriginal art arena: anthropologists. Anthropologists are keen to convey the content of Aboriginal art to art audiences for quite different reasons than entrepreneurial dealers, yet these reasons have been just as aggravating for many people in the contemporary art arena.

As noted previously, art and anthropology (or ethnography) are often situated as being hostile to one another in Aboriginal art discourses. This binary is frequently presented in narrative form, such that Aboriginal art is understood to have journeyed from anthropology or ethnography to art. For example, in 1976, in a much cited *Art & Australia* essay titled 'Aboriginal Art as Art', Australian art historian and former NGA curator of Australian art, Daniel Thomas, wrote that 'Australian Aboriginal art became art, as far as the European-Australian art world was concerned, in the 1940s. Previously it had been anthropology' (1976, 281). Here Thomas alludes to the moment when modern Australian artists such as Margaret Preston began to promote and appropriate the formal properties of Aboriginal cultural objects, and the first art gallery exhibitions of Aboriginal art took place at locations such as the David Jones Art Gallery in Sydney (Edwards 2005; Thomas 1999, 121–24; Morphy 2001; Stephen 2006). Thomas goes on to write that:

> It was not until the 1950s, however, that the art museums of Australia began to form small collections of Aboriginal art, not in rivalry with the great collections that already existed in all the natural-history museums, but to give Aboriginal artists the dignity of an art-museum context, to make their large collections of Australian art more truly Australian and to give the art public, which might never visit a science museum, an opportunity to see work of great beauty. (281; see also 1988)

This view has been echoed many times in subsequent years, including by the current director of the National Gallery of Australia, Ron Radford, when he launched the gallery's dedicated wing for Indigenous art in 2010 (Hinkson

2010/2011; see also Neale 2014). For example curator Judith Ryan writes that '[t]he best Aboriginal works are no longer trapped in an ethnographic category but possess a unique aesthetic aura born of truth' (2006, 10, see also 2010). Similarly, art journalist Miriam Cosic states that the art dealer Gabrielle Pizzi 'was one of the first dealers to take Indigenous art out of the ethnographic ghetto and promote it as an intellectual and spiritual force in contemporary culture' (2004, 18). Another example can be found in journalist Nicolas Rothwell's review of John Mawurndjul's 2006 retrospective exhibition *Rarrk* at the Museum Tinguely in Basel, in which he commends the artist for moving away from figurative imagery that is appealing because it 'persuade[s] the viewer that it brings them near the heart of something sacred' (2006b, 12). For Rothwell, Mawurndjul's embrace of abstract designs whose spiritual derivation is unintelligible to Western audiences is a significant milestone for Aboriginal art:

> Mawurndjul and his fellow masters of North Australian Aboriginal art are thus staking a claim to be regarded as artists without adjectives, contemporary painters who just happen to be from a particular cultural background. This momentous decision on their part goes some way towards dethroning anthropology as the key litmus of indigenous art and may yet herald the beginning of a legitimate school of critical appreciation of Aboriginal painting. (12)

Here Rothwell suggests an intriguing chain of causality: only when the artists adjust their *practice* to a Western-contemporary idiom can anthropology be jettisoned and real art criticism become possible. It is also worth noting that individualism is posited as the condition of Mawurndjul's art's contemporaneity. In keeping with the Western convention of deifying great individual artists, such a view counterposes the anthropological focus on community to the iconic artist-as-pioneer.

Before we further explore the context and subtext of these examples, let us first be clear about what is meant by the terms *anthropology, ethnography* and *art* in these contexts. The first two terms typically allude to the evolutionist perspectives that once presented Aboriginal and other 'races' as primitive and provided the rationale for the display of tribal artefacts in natural history museums in the nineteenth and early to mid-twentieth centuries. In these institutional settings, the worth of cultural objects rested in their revelation of the practices of an historic or declining culture; it was this 'salvage' imperative that allowed early anthropologists to advocate for the significance of their field of study (Coombs 1991). The earlier examples also convey the understanding that the primary focus of an ethnographic or anthropological framework is the way cultural traditions are *encoded* in an object, which means that objects are presented as authentic exemplars of a community (rather than individual) practice – that is, that the artist has adhered closely to tradition (Mulvaney 1982/1983; Jones 1988). In contrast, the term *art* conveys the understanding that we have encountered 'a distinct realm of works or performances of elevated status' that are the creation of an inspired individual (Shiner 1994, 225). Accordingly, individual artworks can be celebrated for their artistic merit, irrespective of the conditions of their production or the identity of their makers. With warm acknowledgement of the contribution made by anthropologists to the Aboriginal art field, Bernice Murphy locates this approach institutionally in the following terms: 'Art museums favour a *non-determined encounter* with Indigenous art. They seek to present Indigenous cultural objects *as* human creativity manifested directly, and thereby to some extent cross-culturally – that is, as bearing signs of art *already articulate* and capable of engaging a broader audience' (2011, original italics).

Any inquiry into the history of Aboriginal art reveals that the art/anthropology binary, as invoked in the previous examples, is apposite in many respects. The first forms of Aboriginal cultural production that caught the attention of Europeans were indeed collected by anthropologists and ethnologists, presented in museums as historical artefacts and treated as verifying the influential evolutionist theories of the likes of James Frazer and Sigmund Freud.[1] It is also true that individuals like Gabrielle Pizzi broke ground in their efforts to gain recognition for Aboriginal art as contemporary art. As late as 1997, Pizzi was rejected in her bid to bring Aboriginal artworks to the Basel Contemporary Art Fair because, as Throsby relates, the 'selection committee felt that letting in recognisably indigenous works from Australia would open the floodgates to "primitive", "tribal" and "folk" art from all around the world' (1997, 32). This snub attests to the obstacles dealers faced in cultivating a market for Aboriginal art. Indeed, late twentieth century Aboriginal art from remote areas occupied an institutional no-man's land for a number of years. For example, in 1977 the Australian Trade Commissioner in New York rejected the Government Company's bid to introduce Arnhem Land artworks into the American market, because museum directors judged the works (because they had been produced for sale) to be inauthentic and unable to be assimilated by the primitive art market (Morphy 1994, 214–15). Papunya paintings faced the same impasse in Australia for a decade following the establishment of Papunya Tula in 1972. As Johnson writes:

> These paintings were seen, at best, as anthropological curios, at worst, as tourist kitsch. Over the same period, the museums (with some notable exceptions) also declined to collect them on the grounds that they were 'non-traditional' – that is, ethnographically speaking, 'unauthentic'. This judgment showed at least a finer

appreciation than that of the art 'experts' of the quality of innovation in these paintings. (1991, 19)

These exclusions are indicative of the way institutions negotiate the identities of the objects under their care and define the ambit of their patronage in contradistinction to other institutions (Karp and Lavine 1991). Authenticity is the key fault-line in this context around which perceptions about pre- and post-colonial activity, commercial/noncommercial production and the sincerity of artistic intent coalesce. Clearly, even though Arnhem Land bark paintings had a greater monopoly on authenticity in the 1970s and 1980s, both they and the Papunya paintings were judged to bear the stain of commercialism because they were *produced for money*. This meant they were not deemed suitable for museum collections, and nor could they be consecrated as art in the way "outsider art" forms such as primitive art and asylum art had been, because the value of these forms was premised on the belief that such art objects sprang from inner necessity, produced for unique psychological or cultural reasons (Bowler 1997, 28–29).

These cases point to the verity of the art/anthropology binary as it appears in the quotations earlier, however, this history does not exhaust the binary's meaning. In these and many other examples, the terms *anthropology* and *ethnography* appear as euphemisms for an unjust exclusion from the domain of art. The implication is that they name marginal, undignified, circumscriptive spaces; while art is depicted as an unequivocally progressive space. This treatment sometimes appears to be historically informed; sometimes it is ahistorical in nature, while in other contexts it clearly implicates contemporary affiliates of the discipline of anthropology.

As others have argued (see, e.g., Morphy [2001] and Myers [1994, 1998] whose insights have informed the following discussion), this understanding of anthropology and ethnography warrants interrogation on many fronts. We can first identify an obvious hypocrisy in the contemporary art field: most contemporary art is opaque without elucidating texts. As Myers points out, '[art] criticism has significant parallels with anthropology as an interpretive activity which has culture as its objects', and indeed critics such as Nicholas Baume – as we saw in Part II – have amply illuminated the parallels between Aboriginal art and conceptual art (1994, 11; Baume 1989). Similarly, Gell argues that there is 'no need to apologise' for the provision of ethnographic information to present the 'complex intentionalities' of non-Western cultural objects: '[S]ince Duchamp it has gone without saying that written notes and commentary in the form of interviews and suchlike are necessary for the comprehension of contemporary artworks' (2006 [1996], 229–30). Second, members of the art establishment were dismissive of Aboriginal art works that are now much admired and valued, right up to the 1980s (McLean 2011a). In contrast, many Australian anthropologists promoted Aboriginal art as art from the early years of the twentieth century, befriending and collaborating with non-Indigenous modernists to bring Aboriginal art to the attention of art audiences.[2] And third, since the 1980s, anthropologists such as Eric Michaels, Peter Sutton, Jennifer Biddle, Christine Nicholls, Fred Myers, Luke Taylor, Howard Morphy and Jon Altman have participated in the field of Aboriginal art as curators, artists' representatives, translators and as writers of catalogue essays, art criticism and art historical essays (see, e.g., Nicholls 2006; Altman 2005b; Morphy 2003; Biddle 2013). Indeed, artists in remote communities have often made it clear that they regard anthropologists to be trusted representatives who can and should convey the significance of their cultural traditions to art audiences (Anderson 1991; Sutton 1989; 1992b; Myers 2011). Further, it tends to be these same anthropologists who have assisted Aboriginal communities with land rights and native title claims in the judicial system. Given that anthropologists have been so consequential to Aboriginal art's emergence as fine art and continue to use their expertise to the benefit of Aboriginal artists and their communities, we must ask why the art/anthropology binary is invoked so often and an anti-anthropology stance adopted so readily? The answer lies in the amalgamation of several conflicts, which I will now explore.

8.1   The Disciplinary Relationship between Art and Anthropology

'Without its meaning an object, however well executed, is dead, absolutely and irrevocably dead'. (Berndt and Berndt 1950, 187)

One of the conflicts that orient the art/anthropology binary derives from a long surviving tension between formalist-aesthetic interpretations of cultural objects and interpretations that focus on the meaning and purpose of those objects. This tension is fundamental to the adversarial character of the disciplinary relationship between art history and anthropology (Marcus and Myers 1995; Morphy 2001). The examples of the art/anthropology binary discussed earlier are predicated on a set of qualitative oppositions between form and content/meaning, aesthetics and utility, autonomy and context, individual and community, that have been formative of Aboriginal art's path to recognition as a form of high art. As Losche suggests (1999), while the disciplines of art history and theory promote the idea of the autonomy of art, both in terms of the purpose of its production and the viewer's experience of its aesthetic qualities, the discipline of anthropology refutes the idea that any sphere of human life is discrete from others. Furthermore, as Morphy and Perkins write, a tension 'remains between the avant-garde view that art speaks for itself and is open to universalistic interpretation, and an anthropological perspective, which requires an indigenous interpretative context' (2006, 5). If given the task of adumbrating the subjectivity of the creator, an adherent of the former view might draw the following contrast: The artist is the master of his or her conceptual universe and is one with whom the art writer, curator and audience shares some experiential and intellectual fellowship. Meanwhile, the subject of the anthropologist's attention is the servant of social norms and supernatural forces – and the true significance of the object can't be known unless it is illuminated by the expert interlocutor. As Marcus and Myers point out, this opposition became entrenched due to a 'division of labour between the study of "primitive", small-scale societies and complex contemporary Western ones' that has been perpetuated over several decades now, due to the boundaries between the disciplines and institutions of museum and art gallery (1995, 8; see also Morphy 2001, 38).

An early Australian critique of the antagonistic relationship between art and anthropology can be found in the work of anthropologists Ronald Berndt and Catherine Berndt, who were passionate about the need to adopt a contextual and meaning-focused approach to Aboriginal art. In an illustrated article published in 1950 in the literary journal *Meanjin* they write that

> [In Arnhem land] we find a society which has been concerned vitally with its own particular canons of beauty, having a social structure elastic enough to permit of individual treatment and variations on traditional themes, and the energy to have developed through the ages its own "school of art". (Berndt and Berndt 1950, 183)

Such a statement seeks to persuade readers of the intrinsic value of Aboriginal art as a vital and sophisticated form of art. However, the Berndts refuted the prevailing modernist focus on form and argued that Aboriginal art should be recognised as 'the external expression of the "soul" of the people' and the 'living representative of [a group's] own social order' (183, 188). Berndt's emphatic declaration that without its meaning an object is "dead" (quoted earlier) suggests that both "relics of the past" museology and the decontextualising paradigm of formalist aesthetics enervate the Aboriginal art object.

We find similar arguments in the 1964 volume *Australian Aboriginal Art* (edited by Ronald Berndt), a publication that marked a profound shift in Aboriginal art's reception. The book documented the works (with 73 colour reproductions) that had comprised the landmark exhibition of the same name staged by curator and artist Tony Tuckson at the Art Gallery of NSW, which toured all the state galleries in Australia in 1960–61 (and was part of the inaugural Adelaide Arts Festival in 1960). Tuckson was the first curator to display Aboriginal works in a state gallery, a decision in part inspired by his own admiration for Aboriginal art as an abstract expressionist painter. Besides contributions from Tuckson and Berndt, the publication contained chapters by several anthropologists and ethnologists: A. P. Elkin, Frederick McCarthy, Charles Mountford and T. G. H. Strehlow.

Berndt's preface conveys his concern with the fact that Aboriginal art was being integrated into a Western–European art paradigm in such a way that the intentions of the artists were being jettisoned. He emphasised the complex 'utilitarian' nature of Aboriginal art, the importance of engaging with it on its own terms, and the need to understand that '[u]nless we know something about [the art's meaning], we cannot pretend to understand Aboriginal art' (1964, 7–10). Berndt also commented on the 'gross inadequacy' of the suggestion made by Herbert Read and others that Aboriginal art 'remains at a childish stage of development' and that it might therefore be instructive with respect to the origins of art in Palaeolithic Europe. As he writes, 'this is a mature, adult art, reflective of a people's social and cultural life, and of their underlying values and view of the world' (7).

The book concludes with a weighty but polite dispute between Tuckson and Berndt. Tuckson's essay 'Aboriginal Art and the Western World' is very much written in a modernist spirit. He refers to European modern aesthetic theories and artists and links modern artists' interest in primitive art with 'man's search for fundamental values'. As he writes: 'the artist is returning, as it were, to the genesis of art – its means and meaning' (1964, 61). He also argues that art audiences can draw on 'the same sense of intuition as the artist' and that 'it is possible for us to appreciate visual art without any knowledge of its particular meaning and original purpose' (63–64). Such comments speak to the Kantian notion of disinterested contemplation, and the idea that universals reside in the practice of formal decision making and judgement. Berndt's epilogue– riposte argues that Tuckson's approach is problematic because it meant 'evaluating and interpreting [Aboriginal art] in our own idiom, within the climate of our own aesthetic traditions' (71). In this exchange we find the essence of the art/anthropology binary.

It is noteworthy that views similar to Tuckson's were expressed in previous years by Margaret Preston, the most high profile modern Australian artist to embrace Aboriginal imagery. Preston published widely on the need to forge an authentic Australian modernism from local sources of inspiration, and she turned to Aboriginal art to devise its principles (Edwards 2005; Preston and Butel 2003; Moore 2006). In 1930 she wrote that students of Aboriginal art should not 'bother about the myths the carver may have tried to illustrate. Mythology and religious symbolism do not matter to the artist, only to the anthropologist' (1930). Art historian Deborah Edwards situates Preston's perspective within an 'Ethnography to Art' narrative in the following statement:

> [I]t was Preston's privileging of formal compositional qualities, of abstract Aboriginal artforms over the figurative, which was crucial in the recoding of Aboriginal art by white Australians. This diverged from what was seen (by subsequent abstractionists) to be a content-ridden ethnography. (2005, 97)[3]

Preston clearly typifies the kind of formalist treatment of Aboriginal art that antagonised Ronald Berndt, and correspondingly, it may be that Berndt's polemical arguments galvanised Tuckson, clearly another adherent of modernist formalism, to defend the autonomy of the Aboriginal art object in a universalist spirit. In art historian Terence Maloon's view:

> [Tuckson] laid the foundations of the earliest public collection of Aboriginal art to be acquired for aesthetic rather than for ethnographic reasons. In the role of Aboriginal art expert, he had to take an opposing position to the anthropologists who to put it crudely, generally argued for the radical dissimilarity of all things traditionally Aboriginal to all things traditionally European. In refutation of them, Tuckson asserted that Aboriginal artists make their paintings with pleasure, imagination and intuition ... Once we see Aboriginal works of art as *inspirited*, as Tuckson advocated we should, we recognise that they are the unique creations of particular individuals. (2000, n.p.)

The dispute of which the Berndts and Tuckson are representative has been echoed many times. On the one hand, the Berndts' concerns about the silencing effect of formalistic treatments of Aboriginal art have been reiterated by a range of other anthropologists (see, for instance, Sutton 1990, 178; Morphy 2001, 43). On the other hand, as we saw in the case of Beverly Knight, Nicholas Rothwell and the fine arts dealer discussed previously, many art writers, professionals and dealers have pointed to the superfluidity and exoticising effect of explanations of content and meaning.[4] Clearly then, despite the many curatorial and scholarly activities that traverse them, a rift remains between anthropology and art in the Aboriginal art arena. This rift has likely been perpetuated by adversarial personalities, polemical writings and the disciplinary 'division of labour' described by Marcus and Myers earlier, which means that the oppositions between form and content/ meaning, aesthetics and utility, autonomy and context and individual and community have become overblown, infused with defensive and protective tendencies and ultimately embedded within the respective disciplines and institutions.

8.2 Western Secularisation and the Differentiation of Primitive Art

Another conflict on which the art/anthropology binary is founded, and one that intersects with the hostile disciplinary relationship described earlier, has its origins in the way primitive art was negotiated by the Western art world in the context of modern secularisation. As I noted in the introduction, secularisation was one dimension of the social tumult that fuelled the Romantic movement in nineteenth-century Europe and reconfigured the status of art and the artist in society. With the ascendency of scientific over religious explanations of life in modern thought, faith found a new home in the artist's *raison d' être* and in the language of Kantian aesthetics. Indeed as Bennett points out, Kant endowed humanity with 'all of those qualities that the Christian tradition had attributed to God' (2013, 19). David Inglis offers a useful summation of this transformation:

> [I]n many ways 'Art' had come to function as a substitute for religion in a society that was becoming in certain ways ever more secular, for Art was seen to be almost 'holy' in nature and 'above' ordinary social considerations [...] [T]he artist replaced religious figures such as prophets as the figure whom one should venerate because of his privileged insights into 'spiritual' and extra-mundane matters. (2005, 17; see also Shiner 2001)

However, faith also found a home in the primitive. As Thomas points out, the celebration of 'esoteric ritual, mystical transgression and spirituality' was central to primitivist thinking (1995, 15). Among the reasons why primitive art remained categorically distinct from modern European art, despite the avant-garde's admiration for it, was the fact that primitive subjectivity and the primitive art object were seen to be steeped in religiosity. By being reduced to the dimensions of spiritual life that had been demystified by scientific and technological developments in the West, primitive objects became symbolic of peoples and practices left behind by modernity, and the focus of intrigue and desire for the disenchanted subject of the capitalist West (Araeen 1987 [1985]).

The following paradigmatic contrast emerged. On the one hand, the iconic Western artist was a unique reflexive agent with purely aesthetic or existential concerns, producing 'art for art's sake', a calling which was confirmed by the new austere yet palatial settings for the display of art (Duncan 1991). It is the peculiar hallmark of the Western art tradition to have sacralised itself as transcending other aspects of life in this manner, despite the evidence that all art is socially contingent and purposeful in some way (Gell 1992; 1998; Bourdieu 1993; Ingold 2013). On the other hand, the primitive artist was anonymous within the tribe, bound to tradition and law and enthralled to his or her Gods, producing cultural objects heavily inscribed with social and religious mores. As art critic Robert Hughes famously remarked in a review of an Aboriginal art exhibition in 1988: 'Tribal art is never free and does not want to be. The ancestors do not give one goanna spit for "creativity"' (1988, 80).

Therefore religiosity was cloven into two paradigms of faith, the one founded on ideas about transcendent aesthetics, the other founded on ideas about primitive spirituality. This cleaving entailed that primitive art was constituted in a negative and oppositional guise in relation to Western art, and to some extent this has underpinned the intransigent primacy of Western cultural forms in the contemporary art arena. This history provides us with another means of comprehending why the content of Aboriginal art, which very often has a spiritual derivation, is difficult to reconcile with the ostensibly secularist paradigms of fine art that currently prevail. As suggested earlier in relation to 'the story', for many participants in the contemporary art arena the foregrounding of sacred content feels anachronistic and harnesses Aboriginal art to the domain of exotic otherness and primitivism.

8.3 Anthropology, Colonialism and the Urban Aboriginal Art Movement

Another set of problems that has helped the art/anthropology binary endure derive from, as Coombs states, anthropology's 'tarnished reputation as a product and perpetrator of the colonial process' (1991, 187). Claude Lévi Strauss made the following evocative comment about the relationship between the field of anthropology and colonialism in 1966:

> Anthropology is not a dispassionate science [...] It is the outcome of a historical process which has made the larger part of mankind subservient to the other, and during which millions of human beings have had their resources plundered and their institutions and beliefs destroyed, whilst they themselves have been ruthlessly killed, thrown into bondage, and contaminated by diseases they were unable to resist. Anthropology is the daughter of this era of violence; its capacity to assess more objectively the facts pertaining to the human condition reflects, on the epistemological level, a state of affairs in which one part of mankind treated the other as an object. (1966, 126)

This distillation is highly pertinent to the history of Indigenous/non-Indigenous relations in Australia. The pioneering work of anthropologist Baldwin Spencer and ethnologist Frances Gillen, for example, was influential in scholarly circles precisely because the Aranda people with whom they conducted their research were seen to be such a rarity as a remnant primitive race (see footnote

1, ch. 8). The discourses, images and museum displays produced by anthropologists and affiliated scholars and institutions during the nineteenth and early twentieth centuries provide disturbing evidence of the way Indigenous people were treated by colonial power in Australia (Mulvaney 1982/1983; 1990; Russell 2001; I. Anderson, 2003; W. Anderson, 2002). Through their 'scientific' explanations for the peculiarity and inferiority of the 'race', these researchers helped to rationalise the policies to which Indigenous Australians were subjected. Furthermore, only certain types of Indigenous subjects and cultural objects have been considered worthy of anthropological attention. There was (and largely still is) a strong disciplinary bias toward communities that could be regarded as pure: untouched by Western modernity – a favouring that entailed a de-authentication of the Indigenous identity of Aboriginal people from the south-eastern rural and urban regions who had mixed ancestry and whose communities had suffered colonisation most intensively. For these reasons, Anthropology and Ethnography have long been treated with suspicion by many Indigenous people outside of remote Australia.[5]

Many of the Aboriginal artists, activists and critics associated with the urban Aboriginal movement are very mindful of this history, and their grievances have unquestionably contributed to the circulation of the art/anthropology binary. Indeed, the refutation of anthropological expertise about, and museological representations of, Aboriginal identity and culture has arguably been foundational to the formation of the urban Aboriginal artistic and intellectual consciousness as well as trends of postcolonial critique (see, for instance, Moreton-Robinson 2003). This is implied by Margo Neale in her discussion of the marginalisation of Aboriginal artists from south-eastern urban areas during the 1980s. She states that '[w]hile those from the south remained outside the ethnographic gaze, invisibility was assured' (2004, 489; see also 2000). The reference to the ethnographic gaze in this quotation, which is not uncommon in urban Aboriginal discourses, very much suggests a fixation with the pure, traditional Aboriginal subject.

We find other illustrations of this perspective in the context of *Aratjara*, a highly successful exhibition of urban and remote Aboriginal art that toured in Europe in 1993/1994. Gary Foley writes that '*Aratjara* was born when a Swiss artist called Bernhard Lüthi approached the AAB in 1984 and expressed the view that Australian Indigenous art should be exhibited in the modern art galleries of Europe rather than the ethnographic museums where at that time they languished' (Foley 2005, 186; see also Lüthi 1993). While it aimed to subvert the exclusionary tendencies of European art institutions, it was also a response to the landmark *Dreamings* exhibition staged at the Asia Society Gallery in New York in 1988. Curated by anthropologists based at the South Australian museum, the *Dreamings* exhibition and catalogue were criticised for focusing on 'classical' cultural traditions and excluding the work of urban Aboriginal artists.[6] As Djon Mundine recalls, the activist intent of Gary Foley and Chicka Dixon shaped the way *Aratjara* was conceived: 'their strategy was to push the concept of Aboriginal society as a sovereign people by shunning the bicentennial celebrations in Australian but taking ATSI [Aboriginal and Torres Strait Islander] art exhibitions overseas to speak directly to the world' (2013, 52). The subtitle of the exhibition was 'Art of the First Australians', and many of the catalogue essays bear the tone of political activism (Lüthi and Lee 1993). A diverse range of Indigenous artists, curators and writers participated in *Aratjara* and the exhibition was pivotal to legitimising the art practice of Aboriginal people from the South-East (Edmonds 2010). In the discourses that surrounded the exhibition we can discern the feeling that anthropologists perpetuate racist ideas about the other, ghettoise Aboriginal art from the fine arts world, and unjustly define the limits of so-called authentic Aboriginal identity and art.

Aboriginal artists continue to critique the ways in which ethnographic museology and anthropological scholarship have transmitted ideas about authentic Aboriginality to the public. Many have drawn on archival material from museum collections, or appropriated ethnographic modes of picturing the subject, in order to deconstruct the way Aboriginal identity has been imagined within settler and European society.[7] There is often a poignant duality to these works: they at once speak to the artist's sense of identification with the Indigenous people who were objectified and demeaned in these settings, while they also confront the fact that their own narratives of Aboriginal experience are elided by these representations of Aboriginality.[8] And this practice of cultural erasure of course lives on in non-Indigenous Australians' interrogation of the validity of urban Indigenous identity (Bennett 2011; Browning 2010).

Postcolonial critiques of anthropological discourses and institutional methods have found other forums in addition to these artistic practices. For instance Indigenous artist Richard Bell, in the well-known polemic that accompanied his 2003 work '*Scienta E metaphysica (Bell's Theorum), or Aboriginal Art it's a White Thing*', criticises the '"Ethnographic" approach to Aboriginal art' that he suggests associates it with spirituality and the 'Dreamtime'. He suggests that '[m]any Urban artists have rejected the ethno-classification of Aboriginal art to the extent that they don't participate in Aboriginal shows. They see themselves as **artists** – not as *Aboriginal* artists' (2002, 3, original emphasis; see also Mundine 2009a). Such positions imply that the Aboriginal identity that is evoked by Aboriginal art, attributed by many to a fetish for the 'ethnographic', invokes a hierarchy of legitimacy that subordinates artists from urban areas to such an extent that some would rather be located outside that paradigm altogether. This circumstance evinces the structure of the Aboriginal art field as discussed earlier, in which urban Aboriginal artists, writers and professionals feel oppressed by the ubiquity and authority of non-Indigenous experts on remote Aboriginal art. Bell also suggests that Aboriginal art from remote regions should be marketed by drawing on 'purely Western construct[s]' and argues that we should '[d]emand that it be seen for what it is – as being among the World's best examples of Abstract Expressionism. Ditch the pretense of spirituality that consigns the art to ethnography' (2002, 2; see also Isaacs 2002, 549–50). These comments echo the tendency we have seen illustrated throughout this chapter, to regard the prioritisation of form over content/meaning, and the eschewal of spiritual content, as being fundamental to a progressive approach to remote Aboriginal art.

The grievances discussed here exemplify the ways in which objectives relating to recognition, justice and redemption have underpinned Aboriginal art's mediation of the relationship between the Aboriginal polity, Australian civil society and the state. They form part of the critical discourses and practices of the urban Indigenous aesthetic public sphere and reveal how Aboriginal art has been mobilised to instantiate particular formulations of Indigeneity within settler society, and to provoke members of settler society to interrogate their assumptions about Indigenous identity. The art/anthropology binary can be treated as a rhetorical 'artefact' of these negotiations. Clearly, for urban Aboriginal practitioners as well as non-Indigenous writers and professionals, to reject Anthropology and embrace Art is to make a political statement of opposition to primitivism and racism.

8.4   Conclusion to Part III

It is worth concluding with some remarks on the ethical inflection of the mediation of Aboriginal difference discussed here, recalling that this chapter sought to differentiate between four facets of difference: Aboriginal disadvantage and injustice, exotic Otherness, the differences that exist within the Aboriginal community, and the dominance of anthropological expertise. Each of these confront us with the histories of colonisation and racism that are both particular to Australia and entangled with the global story of modern imperialism. They also evoke the politics of recognition and equality that have been central to the restorative intentions of the settler state and civil society and the postcolonial discourses and artistic practices of the 1980s. While there is now robust critical thought in the contemporary art sphere around colonised, subaltern, 'Southern' and otherwise marginalised identities, it is clear that the principles of transcendent aesthetics and artistic autonomy are, often problematically, equally robust and circumscribe the kinds of ethical actions and discourses that are possible. In Part IV we will see how these norms are manifested in the tensions that play out in the Aboriginal art market.

The insider/outsider dynamic that I initially outlined in relation to the cosmopolitan and the tourist is useful for thinking through the ethical problems that pertain to Aboriginal difference. This dynamic elicits themes of inclusion and exclusion, belonging and exile, the experience of being recognised and validated or being ignored or maligned. There is an emotive subtext to many of the disputes discussed earlier that resonates with these themes. For instance, it is clear that the popularity of remote Aboriginal art among non-Indigenous audiences and collectors, and the large, expert pool of non-Indigenous representatives of that art, makes some urban Aboriginal artists feel like outsiders in the Aboriginal art world. Poignant and often unspeakable issues around cultural loss are brought to the surface by this predicament. For an urban Aboriginal person, this circumstance suggests that one's identity is not being validated in the public domain and worse still, a privileged non-Indigenous person knows the components of Aboriginality better than oneself.[9]

There is also an emotive subtext to the insider/outsider dynamic for some non-Indigenous people engaged with Aboriginal art. In the antagonistic relationship between art and anthropology, we can discern a profound ethical dilemma between, on the one hand, having fidelity to the specificity of another's view of the world within the context of the dominant and dispossessing culture, and on the other hand seeking, in a humanist vein, to bring about some equality of treatment through a universalist lens that transcends the discriminatory paradigms of the past. By disavowing anthropological/ethnographic expertise and articulating formalist modes of engagement, many non-Indigenous art writers and professionals are resisting being characterised as *outsiders* in relation to Aboriginal art and are adhering to the latter pole in this ethical dilemma (Fisher 2012). It is undoubtedly distressing to be associated with any discourses or curatorial strategies which have been accused of giving succour to colonialist and racist paradigms of thought, and the discourses and practices of anthropology are perceived to have done this. This is despite anthropologists' close and sympathetic affiliation with remote Aboriginal artists and their commitment to conveying artists' intentions and aspirations to the non-Indigenous public. We could argue that these non-Indigenous writers and professionals are concerned with being *insiders* within the project of bestowing value on Aboriginal identity and culture, and they are able to do this by arguing for the existence of shared territory across cultures on the grounds of empathy and the universality of artistic virtuosity.

In sum, I see the art/anthropology binary as being a highly consequential discursive product of the Indigenous polity's struggles for recognition and empowerment. An anti-anthropology or ethnography stance signifies the resilience and legitimacy of an eclectic Indigenous identity that has withstood the colonial project and the discriminating authenticity fault-line that accompanied it within the cultural domain. It is clear that many non-Indigenous professionals feel morally culpable when faced with the grievances articulated within the urban Indigenous aesthetic public sphere.[10] In this context the binary has considerable rhetorical weight; or in Bourdieuan terms, it is mobilised as part of people's competitive position taking within an art 'field' that has been sensitised to postcolonial critique. The binary allows one to repudiate anthropology to indicate one's abhorrence of the forces of colonialism, which establishes a reactive dynamic whereby art, which is antagonistically related to anthropology for other reasons, becomes an unequivocally progressive space.

It may be that the policing effect of the art/anthropology binary is serving to *affirm* rather than subvert simplistic views about remote Aboriginal art. In a range of settings it appears that the desire to, in Langton's terms, 'deny the viewer any opportunity to apply old modernist and premodernist categories' (2003, 90) encourages superficial forms of engagement that elide the art's conceptually intricate and demanding content and preclude meaningful cross-cultural exchanges. Philip Jones has recently remarked on the superficial character of Aboriginal art discourses; noting their decontextualised presentation of the art and their evasion of its social and religious bearings (2011b, 22). He suggests that '[f]or many museum and gallery visitors, Aboriginal art remains an amorphous and generalised cultural and political expression. Without clear insights into the artist's world, Aboriginal art symbols seem to invite this function' (24). We seem to be facing a situation in which Aboriginal art must be denuded of many of its properties, even those that might be intrinsic to its meaning and its uniqueness, if it is to be enfranchised as contemporary art.

I do not wish to overstate this point however, given the complexity of the cross-cultural encounter taking place, and the relative infancy of this field of art research. As Bernice Murphy has recently pointed out, significant progress could be made simply by resourcing the translation process: 'It is time to commission proper translations from native-fluency thought … [and] to liberate the nuanced orality of Indigenous *speech*.' As she notes:

> [I]t is still received practice to render remotely located Indigenous artists' thought in Kriol – that is, in a reductive language, acquired in addition to sometimes three or four Indigenous languages spoken already, and therefore a language that cannot convey the richness of concept that is possible only in the layered reference of first-language speech, by which thought itself is fully encoded culturally (2011).

As Murphy suggests, John Mawurndjul is an exemplary case of an Indigenous artist whose biography and conceptual and formal investigations have been richly elucidated in print through the sustained engagement of Kunwinjku linguist Murray Garde and anthropologists Luke Taylor (e.g., 1996b, 2005) and Jon Altman (e.g., 2005b).

At the same time there have been several fresh inquiries that explore rather than evade Aboriginal art's complexities and that, to use Myers's words, 'imagine conditions of cultural heterogeneity, rather than those of consensus, as the common situation of cultural interpretation' (1994, 13). Henry F. Skerritt, for instance, bridges anthropological and aesthetic insights in his writings, noting of Aboriginal paintings that 'while their indexicality to the land is intrinsic to their meaning, the precise nature of this meaning is forged in the confluence of exchange, negotiation, and relation' (2014a, 14, see also 2014b; 2010). This view provides a welcome entry point for appreciating Aboriginal abstraction as an aesthetic that arises from turbulent cultural forces, whether they be intimate cross-cultural relationships, art market catalysts or the Dreaming itself as it is kindled by new conditions of Aboriginal being. On another front, the *Same But Different* exhibitions and fora have showcased new art practices emerging from art centres and organisations in the Central and Western Desert, including fibre arts, animation, digital comics, short films and festivals. The experimentation and collaboration driving the works showcased through *Same But Different* invites a comprehension of the art as 'social practice and cultural process', with conveners Jennifer Biddle and Lisa Stefanoff arguing that Indigenous aesthetics be defined by 'the complex ways in which both the past and the present are activated and enlivened' (2015, 101–2; see also Myers and Palmer 2015). Similarly, exhibitions such as *Roads Cross* (Radok 2012) and *The World Is Not a Foreign Land* (Spraque 2014) are among several astute curatorial projects that offer compelling vantage points from which to give considered attention to individual Aboriginal artists and contemplate the dialogical relationship between Indigenous and non-Indigenous art. These recent projects are suggestive of the kind of critical engagements that might now be possible in the breathing space left by the subsidence of the speculative Aboriginal art market, which is discussed in Part IV.

Part IV

ABORIGINAL ART, MONEY AND THE MARKET

Introduction

In 1996 the Campfire Group, a collective of Indigenous and non-Indigenous artists based in Brisbane, staged an interactive installation outside the Queensland Art Gallery during the Asia-Pacific Triennial. Titled *All Stock Must Go!*, the installation consisted of a cattle truck painted with Aboriginal designs and laden with items of Aboriginal art, cultural objects, kitsch and tourist souvenirs, all with price tags. It was staffed by members of the collective who, along with various signs around the truck, encouraging onlookers to 'buy buy buy'. All the objects were sold by the end of the Triennial (Neale 1996; 2014; Eather 2005). Margo Neale, a member of the group who was also a curator at the Queensland Art Gallery at the time, recalls its 'carnivalesque character' and liminal occupation of the gallery grounds: 'This theatre of cultural transaction not only parodied itself, the Aboriginal art industry and our place in the intersection between museums and art galleries, but also undermined and dismantled codes of entry by which Aboriginal artists gain acceptance into white power structures' (2014, 297).

All Stock Must Go! is a wonderful testament to the escalation of demand for Aboriginal art from the late 1980s onwards, a growth that really only abated following the global financial crisis in the late 2000s. During this time, the Aboriginal fine arts and crafts market expanded in association with the proliferation of Aboriginal art centres, several key Australian and international exhibitions, the acquisition policies of state galleries and the leadership of a few high profile collectors in Australia, Europe and America.[1] Sotheby's began to stage contemporary Aboriginal art auctions in the mid-1990s and dominated the secondary market for the next 15 years (these auctions reached their peak in 2007).[2] Interest in other forms of Aboriginal art, such as decorative and inexpensive paintings, souvenirs and licensed products, also increased during this period, and a mixed – and characterful – group of commercial operators took their place in the market in response to this demand.

My aim in Part IV is to analyse the way Aboriginal art has been com-modified in conjunction with the other trajectories of its emergence that I have explored so far. This entails doing more than examining the growth of the Aboriginal art market: we need to foreground money *per se* in this analy-sis, acknowledging that Aboriginal art is a kind of interface between social spheres characterised by great wealth disparity. Specifically, I aim to reveal how money has been configured in both the elite and commercial sectors of the Aboriginal art market, how it has been seen as both empowering and damaging for Aboriginal people in places like Alice Springs who have very few income streams, and how money and the desire for it sits in vexed rela-tion to fine arts ideals (Fisher 2015). By exploring these threads of Aboriginal art's relationship to money we can further illuminate the hopeful and disen-chanted faces of Aboriginal art.

The public's understanding of the cultural and aesthetic value of Aboriginal art has been mediated by both agonistic and celebratory discourses around money. As the demand for Aboriginal art of all kinds grew, the Aboriginal art market's 'success' became a source of intrigue in national public culture, and the market became highly speculative.[3] Indeed, it bears comparison to the 1980s New York art boom: in both cases the availability of money and people's eagerness to participate in a rising and sensationalised market fuelled the competition over artworks as much as (or more than) interest in the works themselves (Sullivan 1995). Commentators have often noted the scarcity of Aboriginal art criticism relative to the interest in the art, and this can in part be explained by the fact that market forces have disproportionately motivated people to become involved with it (Benjamin 2000; Acker 2008; Smee 2006). Arguably, the speculative nature of the market has had the effect of truncat-ing many of the meaning-making practices that contribute substantially to the value of a fine artist's oeuvre over time (and this is not unique to the Aboriginal art market). Meanwhile, there was an energetic discourse around investment and collectability, and interestingly art *market* discourses have provided a forum for the explanations of art works, styles, subject matter and artists' biographies. Sotheby's Aboriginal art auction catalogues, for example, have provided elabo-rate and highly illuminating explanations of artworks in the absence of more conventional art literatures (see also Newstead's AIAM100 2015).[4]

Due to the rapid expansion and volatility of the market, and as *All Stock Must Go!* implies, Aboriginal art acquired a public profile of being highly mercenary (Moore and Eccles 1999; Four Corners 1999; Dwyer 1999; Gennocchio 2008). As early as 1989, pioneer Aboriginal fine arts dealer Gabrielle Pizzi complained:

[There has been] an indiscriminate flooding of the market with work of alarmingly poor quality [...] The curatorial ineptitude and greed of some get-rich-quick dabblers in Aboriginal art is responsible for New York City currently being inundated with an avalanche of alarmingly banal and outrageously overpriced paintings. (Quoted in Ryan 2005, 507)

This mercenariness seemed to saturate all stages in the chain of value creation and extraction, from the artist to the auction house, implicating both Indigenous and non-Indigenous actors. Many artists became the object of competition among dealers, and their families came to reap the benefits of the cash they earned through painting. Some artists became accustomed to painting for several dealers at once, producing works of variable quality depending on the acumen and expectations of the agent they were negotiating with. Particularly in Alice Springs, paintings have been created and sold as part of a hand-to-mouth cash economy – as a source of disposable income for people who are otherwise heavily reliant on government welfare. In the case of one of the most loved Aboriginal artists, Emily Kame Kngwarreye, it is estimated that she produced between three thousand and four thousand works between 1988 (when she began painting) and her death in 1996, by which time she was represented by around seven agents (Cadzow 1995; Batty 2007). Kngwarreye's case typifies the oversupply of works of varying quality that has exasperated fine art dealers since the 1980s (Cadzow 1987; Kronenberg 1995; Mossenson in Hamlyn 2015). At the same time, by the 1990s art centres were no longer only suppliers to the primary market, but competing within it as businesses themselves. Some were very proactive in finding new markets across the spectrum from fine art to tourist art, making use of online platforms and facilitated visits from groups of 'art tourists' for example. Their own need for cash flow has meant that the imperative of making sales has at times taken precedence over fostering the practice of their artists (Healy 2005). Finally, the mercenary reputation of Aboriginal art was exacerbated in the late 1990s when a series of scandals over works that were attributed to and carried the signature of celebrated artists but were either partially or fully painted by family members, or forged by outsiders, was aired in the press, often as sensationalist front page exposés (see, e.g., McCulloch 1997a; 1997b; 1999).[5]

While these circumstances have ensured that the profitability of Aboriginal art has been viewed in negative terms by many people, it is also true to say that this profitability stimulated a range of altruistic responses. The sense of dynamism and hope that has surrounded the Aboriginal art movement and market, and the art's status as metonymic for Aboriginal culture, has made it the target of numerous charitable projects relating to Aboriginal well-being. Many people have been motivated to acquire Aboriginal art by the belief that some remedial effect will flow from their support. This is not only true of artworks but also inexpensive craft and other commodities adorned with licensed images of Aboriginal art that are sold within the fair-trade and third world goods market. Dozens of charity auctions of Aboriginal art have been staged to fund various programs and in addition, percentages of the profits raised from mainstream Aboriginal art auctions have been allocated to charitable projects.[6] For example the Gamarada Indigenous Scholarship Program, which was established by Shalom College at the University of NSW in Sydney in 2005, has seen the proceeds of Aboriginal art exhibitions and auctions (with works donated by artists and galleries) fund college residency scholarships for Aboriginal students undertaking medical degrees (Shalom College 2012). Between 1996 and 2010, World Vision Australia ran an Aboriginal art gallery in Sydney (Birrung Gallery) and other organisations such as the Aboriginal Benefits Foundation have seen Aboriginal art dealers and advocates mobilise their networks and resources to fund programs that seek to ameliorate Aboriginal disadvantage.

In addition, the introduction of Australia's resale royalty legislation (which applies to all artists) in 2010 was also clearly triggered by concerns about the discord between the growing value of Aboriginal artworks and the poor life circumstances of the artists themselves. Even though many art dealers and professionals disputed its efficacy, it was launched in the presence of a group of Aboriginal women artists in Alice Springs, an event at which Arts Minister Peter Garrett made specific mention of the anticipated benefits for Aboriginal artists (Martin 2004; S. Dow 2008; *Indigenous Law Bulletin* 2006; Garrett 2010b).

These altruistic and charitable initiatives remind us once again of the ethical concerns that have propelled the Aboriginal art movement. These ethical concerns have manifested in many other ways. The press coverage of the art boom frequently made a spectacle of the contrast between the poverty of remote communities, on the one hand, and, on the other, the glamour of the auction house, the wealth of collectors and the extraordinary prices achieved for paintings that had been sold cheaply decades earlier (see, e.g., Ceresa 1997; S. Dow 2008). This kind of coverage spoke to a widely shared sense of moral discomfort with the incongruity of Indigenous poverty and non-Indigenous wealth and the anxiety that Indigenous people were not necessarily benefiting from the escalating value of their work. However, ethical concerns extended further than this. Aboriginal people were increasingly viewed as victims of deliberate exploitation by non-Indigenous dealers, as victims of unequal power relationships and enslaved to painting.

These discourses about ethics that have circulated in connection with the Aboriginal art market are a core concern of this part of the book, and in the following I survey some examples, with a particular focus on the Senate Committee Inquiry into the Indigenous Visual Arts and Craft Sector, which reported in mid-2007. While I am interested in the troubling market behaviors to which these discourses refer, I see it as essential that these discourses also be recognised as being entangled with an array of problems associated with the challenge of making Aboriginal art 'fit' as fine art. I examine the rift that existed at this time between a small and elite collegiate of Aboriginal art dealers and associates and the entrepreneurial dealers who are generally the target of these discourses, highlighting the two groups' radically different approaches to selling art. This discussion, informed by sociological perspectives on fine arts principles, serves to show that the commercial models adopted by the entrepreneurial dealers are immensely damaging to the edifice of Aboriginal fine art. My objective here is neither to vilify or defend these dealers. Rather, I want to establish a somewhat detached vantage point from which to appraise the meaning of the normative discourses around ethics and consider how they were a mechanism for addressing a range of ambiguities and crises around Aboriginal art's value. I also consider the significance of the institution of the art centre in attesting to the cultural integrity of works of Aboriginal fine art and analyse the ways in which art world actors negotiate the cash imperative that is a powerful motivator for some artists.

Part IV also contains expositions of two other economic forces that destabilise Aboriginal fine arts. First, I provide a critical account of the evolution of Aboriginal mass culture: a sphere of popular commodities and varieties of visual culture in which we find images that reductively connote Aboriginality and impede the specialisation of works of Aboriginal fine art. Second, I offer some reflections on how Australia's adoption of the cultural industries model of cultural policy in the late 1980s and early 1990s impacted on the Aboriginal art phenomenon. The chapter concludes by discussing the specificity of art making practices in Aboriginal communities, taking into account the distinctiveness of Aboriginal artistic labour and Aboriginal people's treatment of their art as a means to earn money. The intention here is to show that the social and economic calibrations of Aboriginal art practice are at odds with the conventions to which those actors who chaperone Aboriginal artworks through the consecrative pathways of the fine arts world try to remain faithful. My hope is that by illuminating this discordant relation, and by showing that the discord cannot always be resolved, we can better understand the fragility of Aboriginal fine arts and further, the anxieties that inflect the discourses around ethics with which we began. In addition to being informed by a range of journalistic, scholarly and policy sources, the following arguments are informed by interviews with art dealers, collectors, auction house professionals and attendance at a range of auctions and events, for the most part in the years 2007 to 2010.

Chapter 9

ETHICS AND EXPLOITATION IN THE ABORIGINAL ART MARKET

In 2006 the government announced that a Senate Inquiry into the Indigenous Visual Arts and Crafts sector would take place to establish a better understanding of the sector's scope, the creative and market practices that took place within it, and ultimately to assess its sustainability and recommend strategies for its growth. The committee received hundreds of submissions, visited several art centres and art galleries and staged a series of hearings in different cities before reporting in mid-2007. The first paragraph of the report's introduction offers an exemplary articulation of the celebratory narrative of the Aboriginal art phenomenon:

> Australian Indigenous art is a story of the flowering of one of the world's greatest contemporary movements in art. It is a story of cultural reinvigoration and communication within, between and beyond Indigenous communities. It is a story of successful links being forged across areas of Indigenous policy and need, particularly between culture and health. And it is a story of economic growth and prosperity amidst poverty and economic disadvantage. (The Senate Standing Committee on Environment, Communications, Information Technology and the Arts 2007, 1)

While the Inquiry was tasked with addressing a range of matters, the issue of 'unscrupulous or unethical conduct' was of greatest interest to those engaged with the sector. The majority of those who made submissions and participated in the public hearings were representatives of fine arts dealerships, art centres and arts institutions.[1] Most of these advocated for the art centre system and condemned the conduct of a cluster of dealers, wholesalers, agents and intermediaries who were engaged with the production and sale of art outside this system. Put simply, the agendas and methods of the latter were presented as antithetical to the ethical conduct exemplified by the relationships between art centres and fine arts dealers.[2]

One of the triggers for the inquiry was Nicholas Rothwell's 2006 broadsheet feature article 'Scams in the Desert' in which he speaks of the 'rotten, morally decayed state of the indigenous art trade' (2006a). He declared that the art trade had 'become a gold-rush scene where money chases the dream of profit, where forgers, con men and thieves with plausible eyes greet you at the entrance of smart shopfronts, while Aboriginal artists sit cross-legged in back-yard sheds, daubing hack works for paltry sums' (22). He writes:

> [T]he problem, of course, is not just technical or legal, it is moral. The dark side of the desert painting trade is a national disgrace and it is also destroying the broader Aboriginal art industry, the one viable source of income and the one productive economic activity for Indigenous people across remote Australia [...] Art buyer, as you read this weekend paper, is your conscience clear? (22)

In a similar vein, Indigenous scholar Marcia Langton offered the following synopsis in a broadsheet op-ed piece: 'Indigenous art, the great economic lifeline for bush communities, is being undermined by its own success and parasites feeding off its lifeblood'. She asks: 'How many children have gone hungry – and become ill, terminally ill – in these exchanges while carpetbaggers pay off their mortgages, spruce up their equity portfolios, dine out with clients, buy a new BMW?' (2007). These are particularly polemical variations of a discourse about unscrupulous and exploitative dealing that circulated for many years prior to the inquiry.[3] Will Stubbs, art centre coordinator at Yirrkala (in Arnhem Land), provides an earlier example: '[A] customer who thinks that they are doing themselves a favour by bypassing [art centre] channels really deserves what they get [...] The product of other people's misery, as opposed to something that enhances their lives or the lives of the artists' (quoted in Coslovich 2003). More generally, in a manner somewhat similar to the reiteration of the art/anthropology binary, nonspecific claims about unethical and exploitative conduct, and the derogatory characterisation of 'carpetbagger' were reiterated frequently in journalistic contexts in the 1990s and 2000s.

It was in the atmosphere of these discourses that I undertook most of the research, and conducted many of the interviews, for this book. It was also the peak of the market: art dealers with whom I conducted interviews in the pre-GFC period of 2006–2007 described the situation as 'frenzied' and 'chaotic', 'an art market on steroids'. Some artworks were being sold at auction only a few years after they had appeared on the primary market, and some re-entered the auction market after relatively short intervals.[4] My notebooks are full of reflections on conversations I had with artworld insiders in which I tried to understand the relationships and exchanges that structured the market. I also spent many hours reviewing the submissions to the inquiry. I was struck by the severe moral differentiations made between different classes of commercial operators. As implied in Rothwell's article, a battle between good and evil – between virtuous and malevolent conduct – appeared to be taking place. These discourses also spoke very overtly to the broader politics of Indigenous/ non-Indigenous relations with respect to racism, injustice and disadvantage. Indeed, it was while deliberating on these sentiments, and reflecting on the impression that something special, miraculous even, was being ruined, that I fixed on the terms *hope* and *disenchantment* as a way of thematising the concerns that underpin the book as a whole.

The intensity of feeling that I observed at this time seemed to confirm, as I've noted previously, that the Aboriginal art movement has in many ways been viewed as a *social movement*, in Jon Altman's terms, as 'a cultural renaissance spearheaded by visual arts practice' (2005a, 4). The flourishing of art centres during the 1990s and 2000s had meant that hitherto unknown communities, fresh styles and exciting new artists were introduced to the public on a regular basis. The later phase of this era of successive revelations of 'new great art' was contiguous with a period in Australian public debate dominated by the contestation of Aboriginal native title by populist voices and commercial interests. As those sympathetic to Aboriginal rights observed the legislative weakening and extinguishment of Aboriginal native title under the Howard Liberal government, it was difficult not to see the Aboriginal art movement in political terms. The proliferation of nuanced and intensely subjective land images disproved the suggestions that Aboriginal people's connection to land had been severed and seemed to manifest the resilience of a marginalised people in defiance of the maleficence of a right-wing government and its supporters.

As the first paragraph of the Senate Inquiry illustrates so well, the optimism that has underpinned the vision of the Aboriginal art movement as a social movement is premised on the marriage of the idea that art has been a vehicle for the resurgence of an ancient culture, and that it has been an economic base for Aboriginal empowerment in contemporary Australia. We saw this articulated by the Aboriginal Arts Board and Gough Whitlam in the 1970s, and it has been reasserted many times since. As the quotations from Rothwell, Langton and Stubbs convey with great potency, the degrading image of Aboriginal artists immured in exploitative relationships, producing quick art for quick cash, vitiates the utopianism of this narrative.

The submissions to the inquiry tended to paint the following extremely disenchanting picture. Aboriginal artists are not getting a fair share of the income generated by their work. They are being compelled to leave their homelands and live in places like Alice Springs where they become prey to relatives who demand money from them while also being exposed to the deprivations, alcoholism and violence that is a daily reality for disenfranchised

Aboriginal people in such towns. Profiteering agents take advantage of their poor literacy and numeracy skills and exploit the power of the obligation they have to their kin by manipulating artists' relatives. Naive buyers are acquiring debased art in the belief that artists are benefiting from that sale and that the work is valuable.

These concerns were continuous with a range of other discussions of unethical conduct in the Aboriginal art market in the years leading up to the inquiry. For example, the concepts of 'authenticity' and 'provenance' had acquired a particular kind of efficacy in differentiating market players. In the case of the former, while a handful of people had been convicted for engaging in fraudulent art production and trading in fakes, there were many additional cases where the authenticity of particular works and the integrity of dealers were merely impugned in the public domain or conspiratorially within the social scene of the art world. The term *authenticity* is rhetorically consequential in these settings precisely because of its ambiguity: the implication is not necessarily that fraud is taking place, but merely that questions are being raised and that one is at risk of being conned (Newstead 2014, 304–5; Korman 2006; Borham 2006; McCulloch 2000; Money 2011).[5] The concept of 'provenance' has worked in a similar way, serving to erase thousands of Aboriginal artworks from the fine arts ledger. Good provenance flags an elite pedigree and standard of professionalism and is critical to art's resale value on the auction market and its future collectability by major art institutions (Caruana 2006). The high-end auction houses and state art institutions have very rarely consigned, exhibited or acquired work whose provenance is not traceable to an art centre – and they have been censured if they break this rule.[6]

In addition, several voluntary ethical codes were developed; though none achieved industry-wide support or reflect industry-wide consensus regarding what constitutes ethical conduct (Wilson 2011; Boland 2010; Indigenous Art Code 2012). The art centre advocacy organisations Desart and ANKAAA[7] also distributed extensive buyer awareness material on how to purchase Aboriginal art ethically, and the *Australian Art Collector* magazine has published Guides to Aboriginal Art Centres (2009; 2010). These guides were premised on the view that collectors needed to be informed about how to source their work ethically (and by corollary, source work that would have resale value in the future) so that a corrupt industry could be reformed. Finally, boycotting strategies were employed by some participants in the industry, most notably at the 2008 Telstra National Aboriginal and Torres Strait Islander Art Awards, the major annual prize for Aboriginal art. At this event, works by several finalists from six art centres were withdrawn as an act of protest against the fact that the Awards included works by artists who painted for John Iannou of

Agathon Galleries, a private dealer much maligned for having undermined the art centre system (Wilson and Perkin 2008).

All of these discourses and measures have arisen from benevolent concerns about artists being taken advantage of and were part of an effort to stem unscrupulous and nontransparent trading practices and to protect the institution of the art centre. But they reflect much else besides. As I argue later, the anger and anxiety that found expression through the inquiry involved a complex conflation of moral codes. In my view, these responses were as much about the despoliation of a fine arts movement through the widespread transgression of its core principles and standards as about people's concerns for the well-being of the artists.

9.1   The Bifurcation of the Aboriginal Art Market

As noted earlier, the Aboriginal art market came to be structured around a highly adversarial bifurcation between fine arts dealers, on the one hand, and what can be described as entrepreneurial dealers, on the other. To a great degree this split corresponds with what sociologist Olav Velthuis describes as the 'opposition between the sacred world of art and the profane world of commerce' (2005, 42). The opposition is particularly apposite for this discussion because it echoes the moral opposition enunciated by Rothwell and Langton earlier.

Sotheby's reputation as a (global) high-water market for integrity in the secondary market and its relationship with overseas collectors were essential in the consecration of Aboriginal fine arts in general (Huda 2008). By promoting the Papunya boards as the foundation stones of the contemporary Aboriginal art movement, Tim Klingender (who established the Aboriginal Art department at Sotheby's in 1996) gave credence to the 'fine' quality of more recent works emerging from art centres. Furthermore, Sotheby's brought historic bark paintings and artefacts into the ambit of 'contemporary art' sales. In the late 1990s and early 2000s, a collegial nexus developed between the Sotheby's-dominated auction market, the art centres, a small group of elite commercial dealers and art institutions. It is this collegiate that validated Aboriginal fine art and became the source of information and assurance for the educated collector. Importantly, they were a minority in a sector dominated by entrepreneurial dealers, wholesalers and commercial purveyors whose market has largely been tourists and occasional buyers.

Setting aside the explicit moral differentiation of these groups that I presented earlier, fine art dealers and entrepreneurial dealers can be very clearly differentiated in terms of the models of commerce they adopt. The former have for the most part been cultured elites based in cities who share a love of art. Such dealers collaborate with art centres in staging exhibitions and managing an artist's career; although in rare cases they have represented an independent Aboriginal artist who is not associated with an art centre. They are committed to upholding key fine arts conventions: First, they seek a long-term association with an artist and show only the best works in annual or biannual exhibitions. Second, they adopt the consignment model of artist representation, which entails that both the artist and art dealer take a percentage of the sale price for an art work, often at a 60/40 split. As fine arts dealer Christopher Hodges summarises, this means that 'every sale, every decision, is of mutual concern and benefit' (2007). Third, they dedicate themselves to cultivating artists' reputations and educating collectors with whom they have long-term relationships. Fourth, they are likely to accept that an artist might not sell well for the first few years, recognising that it takes time to introduce a new artist to collectors. Fifth, negotiations between all interested parties are ostensibly transparent and conducted according to strict professional standards. Collectively, these dealers in association with the art centres circulate 'well-provenanced' work.

The entrepreneurial dealers in the Aboriginal art market tend to take a competitive, opportunistic approach to the sale of Aboriginal art. In almost all cases they have had a professional background outside the arts or sell Aboriginal art as an adjunct to another business venture such as a caravan park, shop or taxi service. These vendors are usually located in Alice Springs and in tourist spots in major cities and typically cater to occasional buyers. They tend to treat the works they sell as revolving 'stock'. As one such dealer said to me: 'I try and make [my gallery] free and accessible to most people by having a range of product from, you know, five bucks up to a couple of hundred thousand. So there's something there for everyone' (pers. comm. April 18, 2008). The following (not unusual) newspaper advertisement has a similar message: 'ABORIGINAL ART SALE: hundreds of paintings, overflowing stockrooms & new works on the way! Take this opportunity to buy quality, authentic, contemporary aboriginal art at a seriously discounted price!' (Kate Owen Gallery 2010). While they may source work from art centres, entrepreneurial dealers generally do not have sustained relationships with them, and in some cases they may encourage an artist affiliated with an art centre to paint for them as well, or instead. There may not be thorough accounting, and transactions may be highly unconventional and nontransparent. For instance, artworks might be exchanged for a regular taxi service in Alice Springs, a secondhand car, weekly food drops or alcohol. In other circumstances an ongoing relationship of reciprocity between artist and vendor is negotiated, where an artist can 'drop in' or call to request cash, food or assistance anytime, and the vendor expects the artist to paint for them periodically.

9.2 Where Does the Value of Aboriginal Fine Art Reside?

The contrast between the two styles of commerce is obvious. To return to Velhuis's opposition of the sacred and the profane, we can see that the former's commercial model is veiled by, and contributes to the reproduction of, an explicitly noncommercial ethos founded in the disinterested 'love' of art. If we take a step back from the Aboriginal art arena for a moment, it is worth remembering that this ethos has its origins in the Kantian formulation of disinterested pleasure that emerged in association with the social, technological and economic transitions instigated by the Industrial Revolution. At this time, artistic creativity was increasingly differentiated from artisanal activity; untethered from the mundane and the functional and seen to be compelled by genius and inspiration. As Larry Shiner writes, the paradox in the concept of 'disinterestedness' is that the concept 'involved an intense "interest", in the sense of focused attention, but a complete absence of an interest, in the sense of a desire for possession or personal satisfaction, even of a moral or religious kind' (2001, 144). These are the foundations of the notion of aesthetic autonomy. It is because the art encounter is fundamentally disinterested that art can be a revelatory and ennobling experience that 'makes us aware of our freedom as moral agents' (147).

It is essential to understand how these ideas about the autonomy of the aesthetic modulate fine art's duplicitous relationship with money and agonistic relationship with the world of commerce. As technologies of mass production evolved in the West, cultural forms could be produced and disseminated in new ways and were directly responsive to the market's demand for entertainment. As Fredric Jameson notes, this led artists of the modern period 'to resist the commercial categories of the genres in an effort to distinguish themselves from commodity forms at the same time as they invent various mythic and ideological claims for some unique formal status which has no social recognition or acknowledgement' (2002, 159; see also Greenberg 1939). This is true of the Romantic poets and writers who, as I noted at the beginning of this book, insisted that an autonomous realm for art, insulated from the volatility of popular trends, commercial imperatives, and the ideological forces of the political realm, must be preserved in an industrial capitalist world.

Notwithstanding the many art movements and cultural leaders that have challenged the autonomy of art, and the iconoclastic, materialistic interventions within the art/money relationship exemplified by Andy Warhol and Damien Hirst, for instance, these ideas continue to govern the fine arts market (McQuilten and White 2012; Galenson 2007; Stallabrass 1999). In other words, the financial value of fine art continues to be gleaned from the aesthetic's negative and critical relation to money. And yet, as Bourdieu explores in his theorisations of distinction and the field of cultural production, the kind of distancing associated with the Kantian aesthetic disposition corresponds to, and is in fact dependent on, one's distance from economic need (1984; 1993). It is the very particular skill of the fine arts dealer to hold this contradiction in suspension: they must advocate for the art they represent in 'disinterested' terms, yet ensure, through discreet strategies and the reputation of their connoisseurship, that the art becomes desirable to those with wealth. This enabling wealth must be misrecognised because, as Daniel Miller remarks, the 'role of art as moral and critical commentary upon modern life [...] is threatened by the amoral and quantitative qualities of money' (1991, 52).

The degree to which the strategies of entrepreneurial dealers in the Aboriginal art market are 'profane' from the point of view of these fine art norms is well illustrated by the two overtly commercial statements earlier. Ensuring that there is 'something there for everyone' and offering 'contemporary Aboriginal art at a seriously discounted price' ruins the impression of exclusivity and connoisseurship that contemporary fine art dealers work so hard to cultivate and reduce art to a mundane commodity. Outside the Aboriginal art world, these two models of commerce rarely compete, because they serve different sets of clients and engage with different kinds of objects. The reason they are in competition here is because entrepreneurial dealers entered the Aboriginal art market in response to the increased demand for Aboriginal art. Some of them discerned that Aboriginal people's pursuit of income to serve their and their family's most basic, short-term needs and desires worked in their favour. These dealers also recognised that many of the artists with whom they worked were building respectable exhibition histories and had works in the collections of state institutions. This enabled them to sell works for high prices and point to the auction market to assure less informed buyers that the works had resale value.

Another obvious contravention of fine arts principles arises when Aboriginal artists have painting relationships with several outlets. In certain cases it has been possible to simultaneously source work by one artist from several outlets: an art centre, a wholesaler in Alice Springs, a prestigious art auction, an urban fine arts gallery, a tourist-oriented outlet and/or an online vendor.[8] From the point of view of fine art dealers, this transgresses the traditional artist/dealer relationship on many fronts and creates problems that rarely arise in the non-Indigenous art world, where a restriction on supply and consistency with respect to representation is critical.

The permeability of these two models of commerce has had chaotic repercussions.[9] This was poignantly conveyed to me in an interview with a fine arts dealer who at the time was extremely disillusioned and on the brink of ending his engagement with Aboriginal art. I will quote from him extensively because his observations demystify some of the strategies adopted by fine arts dealers. Having recognised the quality of a particular artist's work, this dealer proposed to the artist's art centre that he represent her works on consignment:

> My request [...] was that I would be the first person to actually group the works together, look at the substantial and most important works that she'd painted to date, and then place them in what I considered to be important collections and institutions. And that's exactly what I did [...] The first roll of paintings that I received from the community on consignment [...] went into the Yiribana collection at the Art Gallery of NSW. And several of those paintings also went into the Vroom collection in Amsterdam, and so on. But once the artist became noticed, and those images started to circulate through my advertising strategies [...] the demand for her work increased, and she moved from the community into Alice Springs with her husband, who chose to lead her into all of the other dealerships that exist in Alice Springs. So basically after investing all of that energy, I haven't received a painting for the last two years.

This dealer was immensely frustrated by the collapse in value entailed by the artist's decision to paint for other people. The following quotation illustrates the fine arts strategy of restricting supply and bringing only the highest quality art to the market:

> I've said [to Aboriginal artists] [...] *paint less, more money* [...] If an artist is capable of producing very fine work, then it shouldn't be over-produced. Ten paintings can hold the same value as a hundred paintings, by restricting the market for them. And so an artist doesn't have to be a slave to painting [...] [T]hat's the way I think it should function, but you just have artists running from caravan to caravan to backyard to backyard to painting shed to painting shed, from car yard to car yard just painting consistently, and never making any money!

This dealer also described the difficulties associated with taking work on consignment. He had frequently been accused of theft by members of the Aboriginal community because he did not buy paintings outright for cash but rather aimed to return 60 per cent to the artist once he had sold it for a high price: 'I've never spent a day in the community where I haven't been harassed, harangued and accused of robbery, accused of everything [...] [B]ut don't start me on the injustice of it all. I don't want to go there, I nearly had a nervous breakdown' (pers. comm., November 19, 2007).

This dealer's experience in many ways authenticates the perspective conveyed in the quotations from Rothwell, Langton and Stubbs and that found expression in other inquiry discourses. As discussed, those who embrace this perspective draw the following contrast.

While the fine art dealers support the art centre model which enables artists to stay close to country and family and produce high-quality works, the business-oriented dealers 'poach', or 'cherry pick' the most successful artists from the art centre and take them to demeaning locations and encourage them to produce works quickly with poor quality materials. These practices weaken the collectivist base of the art centre, where the income from well-established artists supports the practice of emerging artists who have not yet found a market and compel artists to cheapen their work and their reputation. And while the former have laboured to persuade collectors of the fine arts merit of Aboriginal art and ensure that an artist has a sustainable career, the latter are opportunistic and profit-driven, and have exploited the bullish auction market to trick naive buyers into believing that the substandard work they sell is valuable.

Before offering further analysis, I will share another illuminating anecdote about a very public encounter that involved a fine arts dealer and a highly esteemed elder artist from a remote community that she represented exclusively. The encounter took place at an airport after an Aboriginal art sector conference in central Australia. At the airport another dealer crossed paths with the artist, who was at that point in the company of the art centre coordinator from her community. This particular dealer had had no background in art but had been involved with Aboriginal communities throughout his life: both during his childhood in outback Australia and in his adult years when he had traded in a range of goods before entering the Aboriginal art market. He was a great admirer of the artist's work, and he went over to say hello to her. He was greeted warmly by the artist and asked the coordinator to take a photo of the two of them together. The photo was about to be taken when the fine arts dealer suddenly ran across the room, shouting, and prevented the photo from being taken. Also of note in the anecdote was the fact that while the artist and the fine arts dealer had been on the same flight, the former had travelled economy class while the latter had travelled business class.

At this time, the website of the second dealer featured numerous photographs of himself with Aboriginal artists and their families. While this was not uncommon, it is not something fine art dealers do: they judge the practice as serving to appeal to touristic consumers who seek a connection with the authentic, black-skinned Aborigine. The story conveys the importance, for the fine arts dealer, of controlling this artist's public image and preventing any link being drawn between her and someone who might be viewed as being associated with the entrepreneurial side of the Aboriginal art market.

9.3 Morality and Money in the Aboriginal Art Arena

I've sought to demonstrate that the opposition between the fine arts collegiate and the entrepreneurial dealers is almost always conflated with an opposition between ethical and unethical conduct, good and bad art, love of art and love of money, and strong Aboriginal culture and degraded Aboriginal culture. This conflation is so normalised in Aboriginal art scholarship, a great deal of which revolves around the work of artists associated with art centres, that to discuss the bifurcation of the market *without* making similar moral judgments feels counterintuitive. However, some counterintuitive thinking is precisely what we need to better understand the volatility of Aboriginal art's value and, by corollary, the precariousness of Aboriginal fine art. This is not the place to detail the many occurrences that implicate fine art dealers in unconscionable conduct, or to provide examples of entrepreneurial dealer relations that cut across the bifurcation outlined here. It is enough for us to note the remarks of art centre consultant Christine Godden in her submission to the inquiry:

> There are private dealers, commercial galleries and backyard production groups that operate with great respect and care for their Aboriginal artists. They pay fairly, support artists and their families with health and other issues, look after intellectual property issues, invest their artists' earnings, and manage their estates after they have passed away. It is important that such people are not tarred with the same brush as the very large number of unethical operators in the industry in Central Australia. (2006; see also Plunkett 2007)[10]

It is more instructive to ask the following question: is it possible for an artist and an entrepreneurial dealer to have a relationship that is humane and mutually beneficial but that configures the art object in a manner that offends fine arts principles and thereby restricts the object's potential to accrue value and find a home in a state institution? The answer is, of course, yes. This answer helps to reorient the lens through which we appraise the tensions at play in the Aboriginal art market. It allows us to recognise that individuals' appeals to ethics and claims about exploitation became a very potent tool in an arena made unstable by the conditions of an art boom, and by the distinctive social, economic and cultural environments in which Aboriginal art production takes place. One function of such claims is to exclude a large body of Aboriginal art works from the consecrative pathways associated with fine arts institutions, prizes and the high-end resale market. As a means of coping with the clash of commercial models discussed earlier, these claims have also been deployed as part of fine arts dealers' and representatives' attempts to maintain an exclusive association with artists, an association which allows them to better emulate the manner in which a non-Indigenous artist's career is managed.

Arguably, by dogmatically treating the pursuit of money as reprehensible, the unethical/ethical dichotomy has politicised what is a perfectly understandable condition: that Aboriginal artists should create paintings to make money. This paradox is highlighted by Adrian Newstead, an art dealer who has had a long history of engagement with Aboriginal fine arts, even though he has not always adhered to the principles and methods of the fine art market:

> [Fine arts dealers] may well have believed that Aboriginal artists should be professionally represented in the same manner as non-Aboriginal artists, but they failed to acknowledge that many independent artists had their minds on far more pragmatic and immediate concerns such as needing to hunt, go bush, or procure new tyres, petrol, food and other commodities. Many artists have received as much if not more money and practical assistance through these friendships [with entrepreneurial dealers] than they could ever expect from a city-based gallerist or an art centre catering to dozens, if not hundreds, of other individuals. (2014, 314)

By demonising the profit motive, in deference to fine arts principles, arguments about ethics have encountered a further problem: if the value of Aboriginal fine arts is vested in convictions about artists' cultural motivations, then Aboriginal artists can't be seen as agents in circumstances that undermine this image and thus devalue their art. In other words, it seems that the fine arts system can only accommodate Aboriginal artists' desire for money insofar as it is secondary to cultural preoccupations; that is, so long as money is the collateral of art making that is driven by an innate need to create.

The relationship between cultural values and the desire for money was explored provocatively in the 1999 ABC documentary *Art from the Heart?*, created by Richard Moore and Jeremy Eccles (note the question mark in the title). The film covered several of the issues around which the discourses about ethics have revolved: familial pressures to produce, the questionable provenance of many works and the fluid cash-based relationships artists have had with dealers in Alice Springs. Most controversially, it interrogated the supposition at the heart of the art centre rationale that Aboriginal art was made foremost for cultural reasons, and it presented scenes both within and outside art centre contexts in which artists indicated that they were motivated by the imperative of earning money. The film was heavily censured for its approach and was twice prevented from being screened. It was argued that it 'present[ed] negative stereotypes of Aboriginal people without context and without explanation' (Greene 1999, 2; see also Healy 1999; R. Moore, pers. comm 24 April 2014). The substance of the criticism and the filmmakers' defence is captured in the following comment from Jeremy Eccles:

> Although the white gatekeepers of the industry [...] have made careers and businesses out of the Indigenous arts industry, they are unhappy to witness scenes like the one at the start of *Art from the Heart?* – where a drunk Aboriginal man approached the film crew in Alice Springs with a painting for sale. Why didn't they like this scene? – Jacqueline Healy states, 'because it is demeaning to us all'. Healy's moral judgment begs the question of whether it was demeaning to the artist who was going about the business of survival in a scene repeated day in day out for tourists on Todd Mall. However unfortunate this may be – and in the context of other scenes we witnessed around Alice, this was mild, it is representative of a very real 'facet' of the market in Indigenous art. (Eccles 2000, 4–5)

I have often returned to *Art from the Heart?* and the backlash against it because it shows very clearly the way broader social tensions around Indigenous/non-Indigenous relations have been refracted through the Aboriginal art world. In particular, it seems to encapsulate some insoluble questions around Aboriginal victimhood and agency (*see* footnote 28, ch. 6). I admit that I remain ambivalent about the film. The irreverence of the film makers for the art centre model and the elite art world did elicit important truths about Aboriginal art practice – not least the artists' own ignorance of the way the art world operates and that there is a quotidian dimension to the making and sale of art for many Aboriginal artists that is sometimes elided in the celebratory narrative of the movement. And I'm troubled by the way the duplicitous economic logic of the fine arts world entraps Aboriginal artists in an absurd moral paradigm in which money is a completely understandable motive in some contexts but shameful in others. Yet, as Aboriginal people have so frequently been the victims of stereotyping and negative commentary in the media and public domain (the authenticity scandals of the 1990s are a case in point), I can see that there would have been every reason for those who opposed the film to fear another episode of sensationalism (see Hinkson 2010b). As they had a far more faceted knowledge of the artists concerned, they could see that the general public would be exposed to a very narrow representation of their lives. Those who opposed the film also knew that the sustainability of the Aboriginal art market depended on collectors' belief that the market has integrity, and thus something very tangible was at stake here.

Similar issues inform the following comment from Indigenous curator Hetti Perkins (speaking on behalf of several other Indigenous curators) at the 2007 Senate Inquiry:

> We take issue with those people that claim Aboriginal artists should be given free choice and that to do anything otherwise is racist and discriminatory. We feel that it is racist and discriminatory to presume that artists particularly in the more remote areas or the more disadvantaged areas are able to make free choices, given their circumstances. (DECITA 2007, 52)

Here Perkins speaks quite explicitly to the victim/agent question, pointing to poverty and unequal power relations to refute the argument that art centres are 'gatekeepers' that prevent artists from participating in the art economy as free agents. Her arguments stem from extensive knowledge of the exploitation of Indigenous artists and the artists' disempowered position more generally, as well as the understanding that art centres have created remarkable community benefits that cannot be replicated by a 'free agent' scenario. As Acker and Sullivan point out, art centres enfold 'cultural values *within* their business models,' and thus working 'with and for remote artists involves recognising and incorporating into art centres the values of culture, country, family and the interrelationships at the nucleus of remote life' (2014, 170). Further, as Wright et al. argue:

> [T]he two sides of the coin – the cultural and the commercial – are necessary to each other. The saleability of art centre product stems from the cultural conditions of its production, so the successful art centre supports those conditions of production to a commercial end. On the other hand, it is in the interests of the community and the artists that the art centre should be as successful as possible in commercial terms. (2000, 106)

And yet, for the reasons highlighted by Newstead earlier, artists clearly have reasons to participate in a cash economy in which their art may be valueless from a fine arts point of view, but valuable for them in the short term; they are deriving an income from the assets they have at their disposal. The point I am (cautiously) making here is that, from the vantage point of the Western artistic tradition, this agency is at odds with the virtue they are assumed to have as fine artists. This means that arguments about the exploitative practices of white dealers, while they undoubtedly speak to real cases of unethical dealing, also serve to externalise the moral offence to fine arts values being practiced by the artist themselves in these transactions.

These circumstances encourage us to recognise how vital art centres have become, not only for their role in enhancing community well-being and as

Indigenous 'agencies of collective choice' (Rowse 2002) but also in attesting to the disinterestedness of fine Aboriginal art forms. In Western fine arts contexts, there are many signs of disinterestedness with which we are familiar: the artists' preparedness to forsake the benefits of normal working life in order to devote themselves to their art, their nomination by society as the providers of clear-eyed commentary on social and political matters of the day, and their preoccupation with formal and conceptual problems intrinsic to art itself. The art centre acts as a surrogate for these signs and as a trustee of Aboriginal art's integrity in several ways. First, their not-for-profit status ensures that the affirmation and rejuvenation of culture is recognised as a priority of art production. Second, the organisation acts as a buffer between the world of commerce and the world of the remote Aboriginal artist. Third, fine Aboriginal art is thought to be created by an artist deeply in touch with *country*, either experientially (by living within or proximate to their custodial lands) or in their memory and imagination, and the remote art centre provides the best conditions for sustaining this connectedness. 'Country', by being a deeply emotive referent for Aboriginal artists that is now widely respected, thus inflects Aboriginal fine art with a unique and precarious cultural characteristic in the eyes of audiences and buyers. Fourth, by providing a space in which elder artists can mentor young artists, and in which coordinators can exert quality control measures and convey fine arts expectations to artists, an art school scenario is simulated to some extent. In trying to pin down the parameters of the art centre that make it so vital, I am reminded of Julian Stallabrass's insights regarding the Young British Artists in his critique *High Art Lite* (1999). These artists (Damien Hirst and Tracey Emin being among the most well known) have been so consistently irreverent of aesthetic values and normative ideas about quality that they are a particular target of the question: 'What makes it art?' Stallabrass's answer is direct and underwhelming: '[A]rt is something done by those who went to art school. The closed shop operates with remarkable effectiveness, and you will find very, very few artists endorsed by the gallery system, private or public, who have not been through an accredited course' (180). Given the idiosyncratic nature of Aboriginal art as a genre of contemporary fine art, and its susceptibility to that same question, it is clear that the art centre, configured as training institution, is critical.

In sum, art centres have existed as bulwarks against the irredeemable commercialisation of Aboriginal art and domains in which something akin to non-Indigenous fine arts practice is being fostered (Wright 2000a; 2000b; Healy 2002; Australian Art Collector 2009; 2010). In this sense, it is worth pointing out that they share some of the attributes of other more dominant institutions of liberal governance that validate practices of culture making and bestow virtue and value on the objects and artistic subjectivities that they steward (Bennett 2013; Duncan 1991). This helps to explain why, even when it is acknowledged that entrepreneurial dealing does not preclude conditions conducive to Indigenous agency, well-being and good art, the criticism of such dealing tends to focus on the fragility of art centres and their necessity to the movement as a whole (see, e.g., Lendon 2011).

Chapter 10

'ABORIGINAL MASS CULTURE' AND THE CULTURAL INDUSTRIES

I have thus far sought to show that while claims about unethical conduct have been responsive to concerns about Aboriginal artists' well-being, they have also arisen due to the interpenetration of very different models of commerce and manifest the problem of Aboriginal art's close relationship with money. In other words, the discourses around ethics have at least in part been symptomatic of the failure of the Aboriginal art movement to have been 'regularised' by the codes of the fine arts market (Shiner 2001). I wish here to widen the scope of this discussion and explore other economic factors that have destabilised the edifice of Aboriginal fine art. To this end I examine Australian cultural policy and visual culture, and some of the particularities of Aboriginal artistic work and the social worlds in which it takes place. My hope is that it will become clear that Aboriginal art is ensconced within commercial spheres and economic relationships (in addition to those already discussed) *in opposition to which* fine arts is typically defined.

10.1   A Critical History of 'Aboriginal Mass Culture' and Visual Culture

My efforts to develop a critical understanding of the tensions underlying the Aboriginal art market, and to better comprehend the status of those Aboriginal cultural forms that are embedded in the popular realm as opposed to, or in addition to, the fine arts realm, led me to formulate the concept 'Aboriginal mass culture' (Fisher 2014). Aboriginal mass culture can be summarised as an arena of cultural production that runs counter to, and poses ongoing problems for, the project of consecrating Aboriginal fine art. I see it as including those cultural forms that reproduce generic and stereotypical representations of Aboriginality and contain reductive and derivative variations of widely recognised Aboriginal art styles. These forms are immediately identifiable in the tourism souvenir market, but, as I will argue later, they have proliferated in a range of other contexts.

The concept of Aboriginal mass culture deliberately, and no doubt provocatively in the eyes of some readers, invokes the high/low culture dichotomy with its derogatory implications for the latter. I do not invoke this dichotomy uncritically: I am very mindful of the critiques of the hierarchical and ahistorical notions of high culture that have sustained the dichotomy (see, e.g., Clifford 1988; Shiner 2001; Wolff 2008). Indeed my aims are complementary to the project pursued in such critiques of demystifying the often opaque traditions of fine arts. My intention in formulating the concept is to delineate an arena of cultural production that operates as a countervailing force to the carefully constructed arena of Aboriginal fine art and, through doing this, help to establish a better understanding of the volatility of Aboriginal art's value.

I also believe we neglect a substantial dimension of Aboriginal art's cultural trace if we don't address the implications of the fact that Aboriginal art has been a visual cultural phenomenon as much as a fine arts phenomenon. As Lyndon has pointed out in reference to photography's relationship to Indigenous Australian rights movements, 'visual culture expresses shared meanings across professional and popular spheres' and shows us how particular ideas 'are widely circulated – or suppressed – at certain times' (2012, 25). While a classical art history approach singles out specific works for attention, the visual culture lens allows the researcher to recognise that 'low' and 'high' culture coexist within the visual sphere and to explore the ways 'visual meaning migrates from one form to another' (26). Here a kind of irreverent art history is needed, one guided by Gell's suggestion that cultural images and objects 'have indeed no essences, only an indefinite range of potentials' (2006, 234; 1998). Along similar lines Mitchell suggests that the forms of visual culture with which we are surrounded should be recognised as 'go-betweens in social interactions' and as both 'instrument and agency' (2002, 175). This entails apprehending the image 'as a tool for manipulation, on the one hand, and as an apparently autonomous source of its own purposes and meanings on the other' (175). These insights remind us that when we historicise the Aboriginal art movement, we need to take account of the prevalence of symbolic images of Aboriginality (both artistic and nonartistic) in Australian public culture that – as I've argued in earlier chapters – have ideological and affective weight. In building an understanding of the reception and interpretation of Aboriginal art, we need to consider how these images have been part of the visual milieu that has seen Aboriginal art consecrated as a fine arts movement. If we ignore the former we risk perpetuating a myopic kind of Aboriginal art history that does not sufficiently take account of the wider social significance of the movement.

The history of Aboriginal mass culture can be traced to the mid-twentieth century market for 'Aboriginalia', which included craft objects, carvings and artefacts made by Indigenous people living on missions and in settlements, Aboriginal-themed souvenirs, furnishings and graphic design made by Indigenous and non-Indigenous craftspeople in urban settings and symbolic renditions of Aboriginal people and culture that appeared in the context of tourism advertisements and major events such as the 1956 Melbourne Olympic Games (Moore 2006, Powerhouse Museum 2012a; 2012b; 2012c). As Thomas writes, the appropriation of Aboriginal themes and motifs by non-Indigenous artists and designers at this time was a form of 'settler primitivism' – a nativist inflection of the nationalism of the interwar period, when there was a strong desire to establish a firmer sense of Australia's independence from its colonial origins and find signifiers of Australia's uniqueness (1999, 12 see also Black 1964; Jones 1992a; Isaacs 1999; Franklin 2010).[1] The dissemination of the idea that the nation had ancient Indigenous heritage greatly enhanced the repertoire of material that could be designated authentically Australian. Indeed by the late 1980s, as McGrath (1991) and Marcus (1997) have argued, 'the Outback' and 'the Centre' had accrued immense symbolic and mythic potency in Australian culture, and the trend among non-Indigenous Australians of visiting Uluru and other remote destinations had acquired the qualities of a religious pilgrimage (see also Haynes 1998). These tendencies ensured that representations of Aboriginality became ubiquitous in visual and commodity culture in a range of settings.

The emergence of Aboriginal copyright in the 1960s and 1970s was a signal of the extent to which Aboriginal art was being appropriated for commercial purposes. Copying Aboriginal designs was first officially acknowledged to be an infringement of rights in 1966, when the artist David Malangi, from central Arnhem Land, was compensated by H. C. 'Nugget' Coombs when his artwork was reproduced on the one dollar note. In 1976 the Aboriginal Artists' Agency was established to protect Aboriginal copyright. Its founding was triggered by the discovery by Yolngu leader, artist and then chair of the Aboriginal Arts Board, Wandjuk Marika, of a tea towel and tablecloth decorated with paintings created by him and his father, Mawalan Marika (Marika 1976; Adams 1996). As we saw in Part II, in the 1980s the commercial and artistic appropriation of Aboriginal culture was censured by both urban Indigenous artists and critics and non-Indigenous supporters.[2]

As a consequence, the 1980s witnessed a gradual (but not complete) movement by non-Indigenous enterprises toward developing collaborative and licensing arrangements with Indigenous artists and enterprises.[3] At the same time, the global circulation of print reproductions of Aboriginal art works in books, calendars and other contexts provided rich material for further commercial appropriation. Several court cases relating to the infringement of Aboriginal artists' copyright took place during the 1980s and 1990s, with the most significant judgement being handed down in December 1994 (Johnson 1996).[4] In the 1990s the commercialisation and exploitation of Aboriginal culture became a concern across a range of industries, not only artistic and cultural (Wells 1996). A protracted government effort to find solutions to the problem of collectively owned Indigenous cultural patrimony led to the report *Our Culture: Our Future – Report on Australian Indigenous Intellectual and Cultural Property Rights* (Janke 1998; see also Altman et al. 1989; Altman and Taylor 1991).

By this time Aboriginality was increasingly central not only to the branding of inland Australia as a tourist destination but, as discussed previously, to Australia's exported self-image (Zeppel 1998; Craik 2001; Hinkson 2004). In response to the strictures on direct appropriation, a more oblique form of commercial appropriation evolved. During the 1980s and 1990s there was an escalation in the production of 'Aboriginal-look' designs (for clothing for instance) and 'pseudo Aboriginal art' (Johnson quoted in Maslen 1999, 104; Golvan 1992). These designs generally contained earthy colours or the colours of the Aboriginal flag (red, black and yellow), as well as cross-hatching derived from Arnhem Land bark painting traditions, the dots of Central and Western desert painting, boomerang shapes, 'x-ray' depictions of animals, and handprints (echoing those left in ochre on the walls of rock shelters). All of these elements connote Aboriginal art without being traceable to any particular work.

Interestingly, many of these signs of Aboriginality have been employed by Aboriginal artists and artisans who had no geographical or ancestral affiliation with the regions from which the signs originated.[5] This is particularly true of practitioners from the south-eastern states who have not attended university and had minimal training in art techniques. Thus stylised renditions of Aboriginal art styles like those listed earlier featured in the materials created for the pan-Aboriginal activist campaigns and in licensed imagery adorning objects created for the tourist market.[6] In addition, as noted earlier, the Bicentenary of 1988 and the decade of Reconciliation prompted local, state and federal government bodies across Australia to seek an Aboriginal aesthetic, which saw many Aboriginal artists and artisans being commissioned to create murals, logos, posters and banners for government agencies and corporations. The Aboriginal-owned Balarinji Design Studio, the company responsible for the globally familiar Qantas jets decorated with Aboriginal designs, has been at the forefront of this movement.[7]

Lin Onus (now deceased) and Richard Bell are significant urban Indigenous artists whose careers had their origins in the tourist market – in the former case in his father's company Aboriginal Enterprises in Melbourne (see footnote 4, chapter 2) (Allas 2008; Neale 2000). Onus once remarked on the irony of the fact that 'the area of the market that is widely perceived as the traditional enemy of fine art managed to keep the threads of a few ancient traditions intact' (1993, 290). An Indigenous artist's appropriation of another community's styles in the creation of commodities for the tourist market can be understood as an expedient adaptation to the tourist's desire for simple and contrived signs of Aboriginality but also, as Kleinert argues, 'as a form of cultural resistance, as a means of marking a space and claiming our attention in contested, cross-cultural settings' (2000, 28). Gibson (2013) similarly insists on an alternative reading of these kinds of Aboriginal art practices, noting that they have afforded a different kind of economic agency for Aboriginal people from the South-East and been part of processes of cultural consolidation and renewal at the subjective, familial and community level.

It is also important to note the role played by those models of art subsidy that have focused on Aboriginal labour-force participation in the proliferation of Aboriginal mass culture. In the 1990s, while in Central Australia, historian Philip Jones came across '[s]mall mass-produced terracotta lidded containers in the shape of sea shells and animals, embossed with motifs from Arnhem Land, [being] hand painted with acrylic dots by Central Australian women whose employment is subsidised under a Commonwealth scheme' (1992b, 142). Similarly, for a time Queensland Aboriginal Creations (one of the Government Company galleries located in the city of Brisbane), was employing Aboriginal people to paint replicas of bark paintings based on printed reproductions (Altman et al. 1989, 288). The creation of stereotypical and reductive Aboriginal art styles has also been facilitated through Aboriginal art courses in adult education and vocational training programs and in social work, prison and school contexts, simply because art is an obvious avenue for affirming positive conceptions of Aboriginal identity.

By the late 1980s a commercial realm of Aboriginal art and culture in which products were poorly differentiated in terms of authenticity, cultural integrity and quality was entrenched (Altman and Taylor 1991). In 1999 Vivien Johnson and her sociology students at Macquarie University compiled the 'House of Aboriginality' website and CD–ROM, which identified companies, products and websites that made unauthorised use of Aboriginal designs or reproduced Aboriginal cultural forms on mass produced commodities. Enough objects were found for a house to be 'entirely furnished with everyday items decorated with Aboriginal or "pseudo Aboriginal" designs', as a 'visual metaphor for the mass circulation of Aboriginal imagery in Australian popular culture' (Johnson 1999–2002; 1996). As Altman et al. (2002) document there is now an abundance of Aboriginal-themed commodities from which Aboriginal people derive economic return, including handmade and mass-produced items, clothing, cards, diaries and so on. At the same time, the growth of internet commerce, and the globalised nature of trade, means that it is possible for businesses to manufacture and sell goods that are marketed as authentic Aboriginal work but which have nothing to do with Aboriginal people (Gosford 2010).

What I hope this historical account makes clear is that Aboriginal mass culture encompasses an array of commodities and forms of visual culture, made by both Aboriginal and non-Aboriginal people, in which Aboriginality is symbolised in more or less stereotypical ways. The result of this proliferation has been the genericisation and duplication of particular formal components and motifs that are traceable to so-called traditional Aboriginal art practices, such as rock art, and seminal art objects that have been consecrated as fine art, such as Papunya 'dot' paintings. The circulation of these images in public culture poses an obvious challenge to the fine arts dealer seeking to assert the unique value of a particular artists' work. The examples I have provided have been connected to commercial as well as governmental objectives, and – as I will now argue, we can't account for the challenge Aboriginal visual culture poses to Aboriginal fine art if we don't engage substantively with the latter.

10.2 Aboriginal Art and Culture and the Cultural Industries

Australia's early implementation of the cultural industries model of cultural subsidy and governance is an underexamined factor in research on the Aboriginal art movement, even though it gave considerable momentum to the commodification of the varied forms of Aboriginal art discussed earlier. Understanding this policy shift also enables a clearer understanding of the mechanisms by which Aboriginal art has been instrumentalised to serve government agendas. Cultural industries policies began to be introduced within the United Kingdom, Australia and elsewhere in the late 1980s and early 1990s. For several decades prior to this, state support for the creative arts had largely embodied Keynesian welfare state philosophies and been justified according to the arts' cultural, heritage, national and 'public good' value (Throsby 2010, 64). The cultural industries model introduced economic measures of value into the policy agenda, and sometimes these measures came to prevail over these other, civic justifications. This change came about through an unlikely convergence of neoliberal principles of governance with a widespread cultural reassessment of the *a priori* value of the high arts. The latter was the fruit of the egalitarian and countercultural movements of the 1960s, '70s and '80s, which fostered an anti-elitist spirit and argued for the democratisation of arts funding. At the same time, the Marxist cultural critique of capitalist structures as being inherently disempowering was supplanted by the view (in part a consequence of the rise of Cultural Studies scholarship), that vital creative forms were in fact enabled by the competitive marketplace in the popular realm (Turner 2001). As David Hesmondhalgh remarks, there was growing recognition that 'most people's cultural tastes and practices were shaped by *commercial* forms of culture and by public service broadcasting' (2008, 555, original emphasis; see also 2002). Under the cultural industries umbrella, the arts came to be viewed by the state 'as part of a wider and more dynamic sphere of economic activity', able to cross-pollinate with other economic activities (Throsby 2010, 7). While art was still seen to be connected to civic ideals, it was no longer exempt from the need to measure up to economic arguments, nor was it treated as being more important than popular forms of culture.

As Jennifer Craik writes (2007), it was the Hawke Labor government that introduced economic rationalism into the sphere of Australian cultural policy. The government adopted an eclectic conception of culture that encompassed everyday activities, popular culture and sport, and showed some irreverence for the flagship arts companies and traditional notions of excellence in the arts. As Deborah Stevenson usefully summarises, the Hawke government was responsible for:

> the development of an industry approach to cultural policy whereby the language of subsidy came to be replaced by the language of economics with new emphasis being placed on 'demand' (i.e. consumption and audience development), rather than subsidising 'supply' (performance and creative development). In other words, it was during the Hawke years that the arts came to be regarded as an industry and not a part of the welfare state. (2000, 34; see also Gardiner-Garden 2009, 10–18)

The Keating Labor government's *Creative Nation* policy, launched in 1994, saw Australia lead the world in its programmatic embrace of the cultural industries model. The policy advocated the integration of 'cultural and economic life' and embodied Paul Keating's vision of a 'culture-led renaissance of the Australian economy' (DoCA 1994, 19; see also Craik et al. 2000, 190). It expounded a democratic view of culture that encompassed the traditional high arts and their institutions, commercial mass media, new communications, heritage and cultural tourism. A vibrant and diverse cultural sector, one that could serve both domestic and international cultural markets, might be able to withstand the 'assault from homogenised international mass culture' (DoCA 1994, 1). This imperative is conveyed in the following passage, which recalls the 'cultural cringe' history discussed in Part II:

> The revolution in information technology and the wave of global mass culture potentially threatens that which is distinctly our own. In doing so it threatens our

identity and the opportunities this and future generations will have for intellectual and artistic growth and self-expression. The measures we have taken in this cultural policy are substantially designed to meet this challenge, and ensure that what used to be called a cultural desert does not become a sea of globalised and homogenised mediocrity. (DoCA 1994, 6–7)

As much as it represented the changing face of Australian cultural policy, *Creative Nation* marked an important moment in the history of the state's endorsement of Aboriginal culture. Indeed, Aboriginal culture was treated as essential to the project of establishing a more inclusive and virtuous civic culture and a positive international image of Australianness:

As never before we now recognise the magnificent heritage of the oldest civilisation on earth – the civilisation of Aboriginal and Torres Strait Islander people. In literature, art, music, theatre and dance, the indigenous culture of Australia informs and enriches the contemporary one. The culture and identity of Aboriginal and Torres Strait Islander Australians has become an essential element of *Australian* identity, a vital expression of who we all are. (DoCA 1994, 6)

Aboriginal culture was presented as a rich asset around which could be built a lucrative sphere of consumer engagement – a platform both for Reconciliation and Aboriginal economic empowerment. The policy acknowledged that Aboriginal culture had been prey to market opportunism and argued that Aboriginal people would now be supported to re-appropriate their cultural resources for their own economic benefit. Aboriginal culture was also positioned as the flagship of the cultural tourism sector, which, as Craik points out, was argued to have 'the capacity to stimulate cultural production, annex tourism to diverse cultural industries, and promote the culture of the nation' (2001, 94).

This configuration of Aboriginal art and culture as a lynchpin of the Australian cultural economy had significant ramifications. The reliance of some kinds of Aboriginal art production on government subsidy has meant it has been susceptible to the ebb and flow of different policy ideologies. As I outlined previously, subsidy during the Whitlam era was linked to aspirations around Aboriginal cultural revival, and during the 1980s there was a greater emphasis on Aboriginal labour-force participation. The commencement of cultural industries policies in the 1990s similarly influenced the development of the Aboriginal art movement at a systemic level. As Hesmondhalgh notes, the cultural industries paradigm offered governments a way to categorise a range of social problems as manifestations of social and economic 'exclusion' that could be overcome by harnessing market forces (e.g., rather than by adopting welfarist measures) (2008, 556). In the Australian case, the cultural industries paradigm provided a rationale for amalgamating economic stimulus agendas with altruistic and nationalistic civic projects at a time when the Reconciliation era had focused considerable attention on Aboriginal socioeconomic disadvantage and on the injustices of the past. Many of the Aboriginal mass culture forms discussed earlier were facilitated and subsidised through policies developed under this umbrella, including those concerned with cultural tourism, cultural planning, cultural export and the 2000 Olympic Games.

In case such claims about the impact of the cultural industries model appear exaggerated and overly deterministic, it is worthwhile again mentioning a comparable but extremely different case of an art movement having been shaped by it: the Young British Artists. As Stallabrass argues persuasively, it is possible to identify numerous points of correspondence between the methods and styles of these artists and the enterprise model adopted by British art institutions in the 1990s, which, among other things, incorporated both business sponsorship and the sale of stylish merchandise. As he writes, 'The more exhibition-going has come to be seen as an extension of shopping activity, a leisure activity rather than an educational one, the more it can feature in lifestyle magazines' (1999, 173). The practice of the YBAs is 'highly suited to this new environment and makes the relation between art and commerce more visible, being a postmodern paradigm of such consumerism, especially in its unconcern with the activities of business' (173). Keeping in mind the importance of Aboriginal art to cultural tourism, the fact that the British government invested heavily in the export of British art to Europe and the wider world at this time (disproportionate to its support for the arts domestically), is also a salient point of comparison (188).

ATSIC's *Cultural Policy Framework* (1995) demonstrates the degree to which the cultural industries model typified by *Creative Nation* informed policy interventions that impacted on Aboriginal arts and culture. The *Framework* underlined the importance of advancing Aboriginal cultural development in the 'mainstream' to ensure maximum economic opportunity and control over the commercialisation of Aboriginal cultural forms and to help forge a respected place for Aboriginal culture within the Australian cultural landscape. In addition to the tourism and arts sectors, it saw this objective as being well served by the upcoming Olympic Games in 2000, the Centenary of Federation and the Year of Reconciliation. By means of a Value Production Chain Analysis, the *Framework* noted that the 'indigenous cultural industries' were hampered by being overly oriented toward the creative origins and production of culture, with little attention paid to 'circulation', 'delivery mechanisms' and 'audiences and reception' (12–13). This imbalance needed to be corrected, requiring a concerted focus on marketing strategies (17). In tension with this injunction were recurrent cautionary references to the importance of protecting cultural heritage, retaining cultural property, and preserving the integrity of Aboriginal culture.[8]

Ryan et al. have characterised the Aboriginal art market as an exemplary *creative industry* (a variation on the cultural industries model), in which 'the raw material of content creation is culture and knowledge, which is to say their everyday lives, beliefs and practices [...which] becomes a unique and distinctive intellectual property that finds its way into several markets' (Ryan et al. 2008, 285; see also 2005). Similar language can be found in a report prepared for the Economic Development Branch, Brisbane City Council, titled 'From Ceremony to CD-ROM: Indigenous Creative Industries in Brisbane' (Keane and Hartley 2001). Here it is argued that 'Indigenous culture functions as a "brand" among a range of creative products and experiences available to consumers' (9) and the authors remark on the 'social value-added effects' of Aboriginal culture in their discussion of the social benefits of economic development in this area (18).

The impact of the cultural industries model was felt in the late 1990s and 2000s when art centres who received funding through ATSIC's strategies were increasingly required to adopt business practices and competitive marketing strategies and meet high expectations with respect to annual turnover (Healy 2005; Altman 2005a). If we recall that discretion, differentiation and a restriction on supply are fundamental to the fine arts model of commerce, it must be noted that many art centres, in their pursuit of markets, have contributed to the abundance of work in circulation through these market strategies (Hamlyn 2015). Economic priorities were also foregrounded in the formation of the government-funded Cooperative Research Centre on Remote Economic Participation in 2010. In this model, 'Aboriginal and Torres Strait Islander Art Economies' is one of several enterprise development projects (CRC-REP 2012; Acker et al. 2013). All of these examples point to a particular way of conceptualising art that marks a considerable departure from the fine arts values we associate with the Romantic artist.

10.3   What Do 'Aboriginal Mass Culture' and the Cultural Industries Do to Aboriginal Fine Art?

My aim in surveying the phenomenon of Aboriginal mass culture and highlighting the influence of the cultural industries paradigm has been twofold. First, I wanted to substantiate one of the core arguments of this book: that Aboriginal art has been 'put to work' (in an economic as well as symbolic sense) at the nexus of the redemptive project of the settler state in the post-assimilation era, Indigenous movements for rights and recognition and civil society's reflexive engagement with both of these projects. Second, I wanted to show that the visual culture and structural-economic dimensions of this mediation have contributed greatly to the precariousness of Aboriginal fine art.

One way of drawing these threads together is to bring to mind the many cultural domains in which Aboriginal aesthetics are enfolded: Australian nationalism, tourism, heritage (environmental, cultural and ancient) and Reconciliation (among others). Each of these domains has unique but overlapping processes of meaning making and transmission in Australian society. The preceding discussion sought to clarify the way Aboriginal aesthetic forms have served to represent and amplify these meanings. As a consequence, the formal properties of Aboriginal art circulate beyond the remit of fine art in a manner that has few parallels in the mainstream contemporary art world. In Gell's terms, these properties have been acquiring the 'capacity to thematise and make cognitively salient' a range of cultural and social meanings in national culture (1998, 159). This phenomenon very much works against the efforts of fine arts dealers. The following comments made by a London fine arts dealer I interviewed, in which he refers to the excessive Australian spin of some Aboriginal art exhibitions he had seen in London, provides an illustration of this:

> You don't need to have those [gum] leaves burning in the corner, and the Australian commissioner and didgeridoo music, and – I'm not joking about these things, I've been to exhibitions in London with all three of those things happening [...] I mean that's just naff in my opinion, and unnecessary, and detracting from the beauty and the quality of the work. (pers. comm. July 9, 2008)

Because Aboriginal art is so frequently made to stand for the figure of Aboriginality, which is itself often constituted to enhance the image of Australianess, Aboriginal aesthetics are now linked in the popular imagination with a huge corpus of simplistic and exaggerated representations. Further, they have been incorporated into forms of visual culture that are propagandistic and often intended to trigger an affective response among non-Indigenous Australian citizens. If the value of fine art is predicated on our appreciation of it as unique, authentic and clearly differentiated from mass produced commodities – a special kind of object or experience that presupposes the specialisation of the community who admires it – we can see why Aboriginal *fine* art is enervated by these associations. As Russell Belk suggests, 'massification threatens us with anonymity in an impersonal marketplace' (2007, 738). What the London dealer's comments make starkly clear is that Aboriginal mass culture gives discerning audiences the impression that Aboriginal art is the province

of unsophisticated buyers and tourists, people without the 'cultural competence' that underlies the 'aesthetic disposition' (Bourdieu 1984, 4). Moreover,
by being tied to expectations around the settler state condition, it sometimes
seems to make a demand of its viewers in a dogmatic, sometimes fatiguing,
way.

10.4 Aboriginal Artistic Labour, the Economic Imperative and the Crisis of Aboriginal Art's Value

Now that we have widened the field of view to take in the broader social and
economic forces that impinge on the reception of Aboriginal fine art, let us
narrow it again and return to the conflation of moral values at play in the
Aboriginal art market. Anthropologists and sociologists of art have long been
concerned to show the cultural specificity and historically contingent nature
of Western aesthetic values. They remind us that while it is now the case that
these values repudiate, and are undermined by 'mercantile intent, commerce,
practicality, utility [...] both from the domain of the practical (artefact) and
from the domain of the commodity', this agonistic relation was not true of
the pre-eighteenth-century forebears of contemporary Western artists, nor is
it true of non-Western cultural traditions (Myers 2002, 294). It was only with
the differentiation of artist from artisan, art from craft, and the formulation of
the autonomy of the aesthetic that the value of art in the West came to reside
in a rarified domain that was understood to transcend the quotidian.

If we embrace these insights, we can shine a light on the circumscriptive
requirements made of Aboriginal art practice once it is institutionally enfranchised and commodified as fine art. For example, we might point to the prodigious output of the artists; that is, the problem of oversupply. In the discourses
around unethical conduct we find evocations of a degraded kind of artistic
labour generating copious low-quality works. The phrases *slave labour, production line* and *production chain* art are common, as we saw exemplified in the comments by the disillusioned art dealer earlier (Willis and Fry 1989b; Rothwell
2006a; Allam 2005; McDermott 2008). More than the problem of oversupply,
these phrases also signal the impression that another fine arts principle is being
breached: the expectation, to use Ryan's words, that there is an 'explicit separation and preservation of the creative phase of production from the reproductive phase' (1992, 41). However, the profusion of works and the repetitive
quality of some of them can of course not be seen exclusively in terms of
poverty, exploitation and external pressures to produce.

Many Aboriginal artists are not subjectively invested in the art object as
such, but in the ancestral knowledge on which the art object is a fleeting med-
itation. Nor do they necessarily subscribe to fine arts ideas around artistic

authenticity: as Michaels observed during his time with Warlpiri painters, 'Instead of an ideology of creative authority, there is an ideology of reproduction' (1994 [1988], 144). Similarly, Merlan writes that for many Aboriginal artists, 'great, even hieratic value is placed upon designs and images as manifesting a transcendent order to which people also belong, rather than upon the creativity of the maker' (2001, 212). This means that, as was well established following the authenticity 'scandals' of the 1990s, it is quite acceptable for the artist with cultural authority over particular designs to supervise the collective production of a work to which they will ultimately put their name (Nicholls 2002; Coleman 2001). It also means that recursive methods of painting have cultural potency: as with song, dance, ground painting and other Aboriginal cultural practices, it is a transient enactment of a fragment of a universe of knowledge held by the artist. This is illustrated in Biddle's discussion of the relationship between the painted canvas, skin and ancestral country in Central Australian women's painting:

> [I]f painting is to engender the efficacy of the Dreaming, it must reproduce marks as Ancestors themselves once did: as bodily imprints, as corporeal traces. Dreaming Ancestors made, marked, imprinted the country, the flora and fauna, the elements and the atmosphere, the weather and the people, and this is exactly what is repeated by women painters. (2006, 95)

Thus, rather than involving the debasement of iconic culture for pecuniary interest, the repetition of a design across many works can be interpreted as a continuum of cultural affirmation and revitalisation.

The issue of oversupply is interlinked, of course, with the relationship of Aboriginal artistic labour to money. As Altman pointed out in 1988, '[t]he commercialisation of art has played, and will continue to play, a significant role in its reproduction', and he further noted that 'innovative designs and art forms' can be triggered by market demand (1988, 48, 51; see also Morphy 2005). As I outlined earlier, and as many others scholars have explored in greater detail, Aboriginal people have been creating and trading objects of art and culture in order to earn cash and to meet the day-to-day needs of their families since the frontier days: on missions, reserves and pastoral stations; as fringe dwellers, itinerants and low-skilled workers; and in cooperatives and small businesses catering to the tourism industry and the Aboriginalia market (Mackay 1973; Berndt 1983; Moore 2006; Kleinert 2010). In the case of Albert Namatjira, for example, it was when he learned how much non-Indigenous artists Rex Battarbee and John Gardner were paid for their paintings of Aranda country that he proposed the radical idea that he could 'do the same' (Jones 1992c, 111). As Jones writes, 'In declaring that he could paint like Battarbee and Gardner, Namatjira was asserting his potential as an artist. More than this, he was making a bid for his own economic independence at a time when the Mission was gripped by poverty' (111).

Underpinning the economic imperative in much Aboriginal art production is the tribal social practice of 'demand sharing'. As Nicolas Peterson describes, demand sharing is a means of distributing food and other resources that is very much 'part of the habitus and of moral education in the management of interpersonal relations' in Indigenous communities across Australia (1993, 865; see also Altman 2011). Chrischona Schmidt (2011) has explored the way this social logic mediates Aboriginal art production in the community of Utopia, showing how it extends to artist-dealer relationships and serves as a foundation for reciprocity over a long period of time. 'Demand sharing' often means that artists' earnings are distributed rapidly within the community. In the case of Balgo Art Centre, Carty writes:

> The relatively constant flow of money into senior artists' accounts provides them with an equally persistent flow of demands, or expectations, and a consistent capacity to meet demands or obligations to extended family. Whilst these demands can become a source of frustration and familial conflict, the capacity to meet them is also a point of considerable esteem and cultural value [...] Beyond the fame of the art world to which they remain largely indifferent, Balgo artists create, through the work of art, a higher value through sharing money than money itself can ever hold for them. (2011, 96–97)

On this point, one dealer made the following remark in our discussion of a particular artist he new well whose work was much in demand in the fine arts market: 'Does _____ want to be an exclusive artist? Does she want to be a big name in the National Gallery of Australia? Or does she want to feed her family? I know the answer to that'. The observation is striking because it relativises the project of attaining high-art status for Aboriginal art to the more immediate and mundane needs to which this artist is responsive within her family and community, and which might, under different conditions, be more easily met. To use Myers' words, it reminds us that the 'hierarchy of values adhering to the objects' created by Aboriginal artists is always in flux due to the social and economic contingencies of Aboriginal art making (2005, 104).

The distinctive communal and cultural foundations of Aboriginal art practice brought into relief by the two examples of recursive painting and demand sharing remain largely irreconcilable with fine arts values. This fact has led Howard Morphy, in arguing for a more expansive, cross-cultural understanding of art, to suggests that 'in many ways the job of art history is to rescue art from its entanglement with the fine art category' (2008, 190).

If we look at the economic imperative specifically, the pecuniary nature of Aboriginal cultural production over the last century is largely effaced in the orthodox narrative of the contemporary Aboriginal art movement. This narrative usually sees the movement as being founded in Papunya in 1971 (with a retrospective acknowledgement of the bark painting tradition) and looks to the blossoming of art centres in the subsequent years. It depends heavily on the anointing power of the tragic-romantic figure of Geoffrey Bardon: the compassionate and aesthetically astute school teacher whose encouragement spurred an outpouring of cultural expression among the old men at Papunya who were otherwise largely treated with contempt by town administrators.[9] As Johnson (2010, 2015) and Healy (2008) have argued, this founding narrative neglects to acknowledge that the art practice of three of the most important figures at Papunya: Kaapa Mbitjana Tjampitjinpa, Clifford Possum Tjapaltjarri and Tim Leura Tjapaltjarri, preceded Bardon. These artists had links with the Hermannsburg watercolour school pioneered by Albert Namatjira, with Tjampitjinpa having taken up watercolours and started painting on board prior to Bardon's arrival, and the others having established reputations as skilled animal carvers (Johnson 2010). Indeed, Clifford Possum had been selling carvings for good money since the late 1950s, declining Albert Namatjira's offer to teach him how to paint because he was satisfied with his craft (Johnson 2003, 41–42). Other Papunya artists had produced boomerangs for trade and there was also a history of *churingas* (Aranda sacred objects for which Europeans developed an extraordinary acquisitive appetite) and other artefacts being produced and/or painted for sale in that region (Anderson and Dussart 1988, 97; Batty 2007; Jones 1995). Nevertheless, as the title of the landmark retrospective exhibition of Papunya painting *Papunya Tula: Genesis and Genius* (Perkins and Fink 2000) implies, the continuity between forms that are designated as being so-called low and high art is overlooked in favour of a founding moment of inspiration and innovation. This is not dissimilar to the disavowal of the souvenir and commercial art practices that are part of the pedigree of the urban Indigenous art movement (Neale 2000).

Beyond this, the treatment of mercenary interests as inherently 'profane' in the fine arts context is strikingly at odds with the fact that Aboriginal people have been actively encouraged to treat their art as a means to earn money. As we've seen, since the 1970s, the Aboriginal art movement has been championed precisely because it can empower people economically, and Aboriginal art production has repeatedly been construed as a form of work that yields income. If we look to the transactions that take place beyond the art centres, artists exercise their agency despite their disempowered position. Clifford Possum, for example, chose to paint for a range of dealers in Alice Springs, claiming the right 'to sell his work to whomever he wanted for whatever price he wanted to put on it' because he saw his art as '"my property, my private canvas"' (Johnson 2003, 167–68).

10.5   Conclusion to Part IV

In his book *The Invention of Art*, Larry Shiner asks, 'what if we wrote our history from a perspective more sympathetic to a system of art that tried to hold together imagination and skill, pleasure and use, freedom and service?' (2001, 9). Here, the latter terms distil those elements of art that are largely disavowed by Western fine arts values. In this appeal the distortions and omissions required to make Aboriginal art 'fit' as fine art become clear, and I am reminded of Terry Smith's point that Aboriginal artists 'originate their own structures of same and other, produce their own relations of distinction and difference, and then choose or not to act "in between" the cultures' (2002, 148). Adopting a reflexive position on the presuppositions of fine arts ideals enables us to perceive a recent history of Aboriginal art that both problematizes and complements extant histories of the movement and explains many of the tensions at play in the Aboriginal art arena. This history bears witness to the way members of the fine arts collegiate sought to affiliate Aboriginal art with the Kantian aesthetic tradition, within which ideas around autonomy and disinterestedness are axiomatic, but found themselves battling manifold economic and ideological phenomena that have anchored Aboriginal art to the realm of interest. Indeed, given how long Aboriginal people have been making money from their art, often simply to survive, we might say that the fine arts collegiate sought to *import* a highly specialised fine arts ethos into an arena of cultural production whose properties were antithetical to its value system. If we were to list the phenomena that have complicated this project, which pose a *systemic* challenge to fine arts, we would include the economic circumstances of Aboriginal people, which inspired a subsidy regime that treated art making as a form of work, and the fact that Aboriginal art practice is often interwoven with liquid economies that involve many dependent relatives. The list would also include the entrepreneurial dealers *and* the auction houses. The latter, while essential to the consecration of Aboriginal fine art, capitalised on the speculative character of the Aboriginal art market, ensuring that the public's appreciation of Aboriginal art's monetary worth prefigured or was contemporaneous with its appreciation of Aboriginal art's cultural and aesthetic value. We would then list the morally inflected economic, nationalistic and civil society projects of the post-assimilation era within which Aboriginal art has been immured and which the art has helped to amplify in Australian visual culture. And finally, we would point to the impact of the cultural industries model, which, in addition to other policy imperatives, has rationalised the commercialisation of Aboriginal art and culture as a means to address socioeconomic concerns and to recraft the national image.

Myers has frequently written about the competing 'regimes of value' that lay claim to Aboriginal art (2005; 2002), and similarly Morphy has pointed out that '[t]he success of Aboriginal art has depended on value creation processes that are both internal and external to Aboriginal society' (2006, 2; see also 2005). Along similar lines, my aim in this chapter has been to survey some of the communal, structural (cultural industries) and diffuse ('Aboriginal mass culture') forces that contribute to the density of Aboriginal art's meanings in Australian public culture, and impinge on the value and sustainability of Aboriginal fine arts. I initiated this discussion with a focus on the 2007 Inquiry because I wanted to show that the issues underlying the enmities and ethical disputes in the Aboriginal art market are not simply reducible to cases of exploitation and self-interested profiteering. To argue that Aboriginal artists are victims of the market as a means of accounting for their variable work and varied dealer relationships serves to mask the artists' own irreverence for fine arts principles. The apparent philistinism of some entrepreneurial dealers makes them the perfect foil in this argument. It seems essential to recognise that, whether or not they are poor, Aboriginal artists' priorities and expectations might never align with fine arts values. The autonomy of fine art is vested in a set of principles reproduced through the discourses of art history and criticism and the institutions of art schools and art museums. And while the fine arts system accommodates heterogeneous practices, certain institutional, discursive and commercial methods of consecrating art's value remain. Because many Aboriginal artists create their work outside of this system, they have no reason to share its prejudice against the idea that one might make art for the express purpose of making money, and that one might tailor one's practice to different trading opportunities that arise, and establish relationships with a wide variety of people to do so. Clearly, then, the discourses about ethics are partly symptomatic of the fact that Aboriginal art diverges so radically from other fine cultural forms that have an enduring pedigree, well-established traditions of professionalism and discretion, highly specified pathways to consecration and a high-culture-oriented audience. Acknowledging this can sharpen our understanding of the paradox that underpins the utopian vision of the Aboriginal art movement: that an Aboriginal art trade can benefit Aboriginal people economically and, at the same time, bring about a revitalisation of Aboriginal culture through the medium of fine art.

CONCLUSION

Three Ethical Projects Underpinning the Aboriginal Art Phenomenon

This book has its origins in a kind of crisis of interpretation that I experienced as a university student in the early 2000s, at which time my aesthetic sensibilities – which had drawn me to Aboriginal painting – were challenged by a new ethical sensibility that arose from my studies of various histories of colonisation and Indigenous social justice. I found myself looking at Aboriginal art in a compulsively reflexive way, trying to pick apart the foundations of my aesthetic judgments and asking what bearing the settler state context had on my interpretations. This book has been an attempt to come to terms with the fluidity of Aboriginal art's meanings, as it moves between the artists and their publics, between contemporary art spaces and the commercial sphere of touristic consumption, between local Indigenous domains and the noise of national visual culture. I am of course not alone in having been preoccupied with this problem, nor do I think my arguments necessarily chart new territory beyond the array of enlightening vantage points that other scholars of Aboriginal art have brought to bear on this problem. My priority has been to provide an empirical footing for understanding how the political relationship of Indigenous and non-Indigenous Australians underpins Aboriginal art's many valencies and to focus attention on the way fine arts has contended with the extra-aesthetic forces that make Aboriginal art such a unique entity.

In bringing this book to a close, I wish first to summarise the ethical problems that have been part of its analysis and which can be loosely divided into three categories. The first relates to the idea of redemptive nationhood. Not only has Aboriginal art been viewed as a platform for oppressed people to find a voice where they have otherwise been silenced, it has been viewed as something that can substantiate the worth of Aboriginal people in Australian society and stimulate sympathy for Aboriginal people's circumstances. We have seen these presumptions framed in nationalistic terms, such that the character of the nation and all of its citizenry can be ennobled through the redemptive process. This is conveyed by Aboriginal art collector Margaret Carnegie when she writes that '[w]e Australians need to arrive at a new vision of ourselves as neither settlers nor conquerors, but simply as Australians, since it is vital that we co-exist in harmony, justice and compassion with the earliest inhabitants of the continent, the Australian Aborigines' (1991, 5; see also other essays in the volume). These threads of goodwill, which have also been responsive to Aboriginal disadvantage, are very clearly identifiable in the charitable projects developed in response to the Aboriginal art market's success, as well as in the discourses around ethics. In more general terms, it can be argued that just as historical photographs of Aboriginal people were a vehicle for humanitarian and reformist ideas around Aboriginal rights (Lyndon 2012), Aboriginal art has been a vehicle for socialising late twentieth-century ideas around reconciliation and atonement.

The second category of ethical problems that has been explored is connected with the intellectual legacy of the decolonisation, civil rights and social justice movements of the twentieth century. These movements reverberated in the cultural spheres of Western democratic societies through the emergence of critical artistic practices that refigured the cultural status of Indigenous, minority and non-occidental communities. As we saw in Parts II and III in particular, Aboriginal art has been a medium for the negotiation of transnational postcolonial critique and for the assertion of Aboriginal people's rights, as founded in both their difference and their victimisation by a colonial power.

The third category of ethical problems is somewhat more difficult to summarise because it has had a kind of Janus-faced bearing on Aboriginal art. I will therefore elaborate on it in more detail. These problems arise around the figure of the disenchanted Western subject; that is, they relate to a reflexive movement in the West that is concerned with the destructive and inhuman aspects of industrial capitalist societies and that laments 'our' disconnection from nature, from a sense of community, from the sacred and indeed from culture itself. It is a movement that is both existential and poetic in nature. As I noted in the introduction, these ideas are to a certain extent present in contemporary fine arts ideals, while they are also linked to primivist thought and entangled with people's beliefs about Aboriginal people's ethnic specificity.

I will provide three examples of engagements with remote Aboriginal art in which the trace of Western disenchantment can be felt. First, in the following quotation, non-Indigenous Australian artist Fiona Hall draws a contrast between her own spatio-cultural location and that of artist Djambawa Marawili:

[I am located within a culture] in a continual state of flux, drifting without an anchor. It is an affluent place, foundering in the ocean of its superfluity. I have a sinking feeling. Djambawa's world is split in two. But it is not fractured. It is whole; everything in it is Yirritja or Dhuwa, which are the twin streams of the complex Yolngu clan and kinship system. They flow together through the land and coastal waters, through every person, every plant and creature, through Yolngu society and ancestry and sacred songs and ceremonies. Incredibly, Djambawa and I belong to the same nation. (2011, 6)

In the following passage, collector Ruth Hall describes her attraction to Aboriginal art that is 'produced within an Aboriginal communal ethos':

I am interested in how Aboriginal people work as a family, a community: the singing, the telling and retelling of stories, seeing works that are the sons and daughters of other stories, the now of the Dreamtime made present in the paintings. There's a continuity – nothing is lost in what is forever living, contemporary and eventful. Permeating all the images and stories, there is the land, timeless and evocative [...] What I respect and feel an affinity with is that their work reflects not only the traditions themselves but also the artists' efforts at maintaining those traditions [...] I believe that the Aboriginal people's sense of family, community, land and traditions allowed their skills to survive despite the last 200 years of white occupancy of this country. (Carnegie et al. 1991, 126–27)

A third example can be found in art critic Nicholas Baume's interpretation of Imants Tillers's commissioned work for the Federal Pavilion in Centennial Park (in Sydney), in which iconography drawn from Michael Nelson Jagamarra's work is part of the frieze decorating the interior of the Pavilion. He writes:

What the Federation Pavilion learns from Aboriginal culture is not the particular symbolic significance of its artistic expression, but man's need for a richly symbolic life. Mythology and symbolism are painfully absent from our lives, on all levels of culture. (1988, 83)

All three quotations depict a space of cohesion and continuity in which creative acts have meaning and purpose in daily life, and they all leave an after-image of the disenchanted Western subject. In these contexts, as Darren Jorgensen writes, Aboriginal art appears to instantiate a different social space of 'authentic relations [...] [which are] implicitly critiquing capitalism by pointing out that there is a viable alternative to it' (2008, 119).

Postcolonial critiques have encouraged us to view engagements with Aboriginal art that rest on disenchantment with the modern condition and a veneration of a halcyon Aboriginal culture as profoundly *unethical*: as primitivist, ahistorical and racist. And this is an apt assessment of many simplistic engagements. However, the philosophical and reflexive character of the earlier quotations shows that we should not allow the unethical dimensions of the project of the disenchanted Western subject to blind us to its ethical dimensions. Just as the Romantics looked to folk and medieval culture to distil those elements of art that might help them withstand the rationalising and dehumanising effects of industrialisation, so too do some audiences look to Aboriginal art to imagine more integrated ways of living, doing and making 'culture'; that is to understand how art might exist as 'a way of life' and be a basis for robust social bonds (Habermas 1996 [1981], 44; see also Symonds 1997; 2015, 178–81). In light of this, we might see Aboriginal art as a vehicle to protest two things: first, the erosive impact of capitalist systems on our creative and communal selves and on our relationship with the natural world, and second, the rarification of Western fine art: its elitism, its esoteric tendencies and its status as aloof from the day to day.

In drawing attention to the magnetism of certain kinds of Aboriginal art for this kind of idealism, I am not denying the truth or necessity of those critiques that denounce non-Indigenous Australians' romanticisation of remote Aboriginal art. The point is to recognise that Romantic engagements, on the one hand, and critiques of Romantic engagement, on the other, are discordant but coexisting currents of ethical thought that are responsive to different trajectories and scales of cultural change and thus need to be held in suspension. The gravity of the critique that urban Indigenous artists, writers and curators have directed toward non-Indigenous Australians, anthropology and the edifice of Aboriginal art as a whole, lies in its demand that they desist being 'enchanted' by remote Aboriginal culture and embrace the plurality of contemporary Aboriginal experience. It is a critique that registers the way 'Aboriginal art' is now a powerfully circumscriptive signifier of cultural identity in national culture. As Indigenous artist and curator Glenn Iseger-Pilkington asks, 'Is it possible for a curator or artist to escape the everstrengthening grip of ethnographic prescription, when it is this very prescription that the Indigenous visual arts sector relies upon to sell the Indigenous brand?' (2011, 36). Having moved far away from the pan-Aboriginal premise of the activist discourses of the 1980s, 'remote' and 'urban' Aboriginal art not only seem rigidly opposed but relativise each other: each appears to discredit the other way of being Aboriginal in Australia. This has been made explicit by some of the artists in the collective proppaNOW for whom, as Butler summarises 'the renaissance of Aboriginal art is part of the ongoing repression and exploitation of Aboriginal people and not any exception to it' (2010, n.p.). This configuration reveals a great deal about the way social meanings ramify in aesthetic spheres. The two idioms are connected with very different, locally contingent, Indigenous ontologies and values, as well as modernism's and postmodernism's respective negotiation of the non-Western other. At the same time, their differentiation bears the mark of the prejudicial constructions of Aboriginal personhood that prevail in the Australian cultural imaginary.

In many ways, it is by reflecting on this third category of ethical problems that we can hone our understanding of the most vexed ethical questions posed by Aboriginal art. Its Janus-faced insolubility attests to the 'intimate estrangements', to use Thomas's apt phrase, that arise from the moral paradox that sits at the heart of the settler state condition:

> [E]ven as new things become possible, old tensions find new expression. Sovereignty and dispossession, inclusion and exclusion, affirmation and denigration: the realities of cultural and political life in … settler societies are always somewhat in the muddy and uncertain no-man's-land between these contradictory conditions'. (1999, 279; see also Povinelli 2002, 46)

The rigid polarity of so-called urban and remote Aboriginal art idioms points to the fundamental contradictions inherent in the redemptive and inclusive nation making project with which this book has been concerned. And these contradictions are anchored to the following, simple truth: having decided to acknowledge the validity and value of Aboriginal culture in the post-assimilation era, non-Indigenous Australians then embraced those forms of Aboriginal culture in which the repercussions of the colonisation process were least evident. In Povinelli's terms, they have shown a desire to 'worship a traditional order stripped of every last trace of bad settlement history' (2002, 54). What the polemical voices in Aboriginal art are pointing to can be illuminated by recalling Indigenous scholar and activist Michael Mick Dodson's description of Aboriginal self-determination:

> It must include the right to inherit the collective identity of one's people, and to transform that identity creatively according to the self-defined aspirations of one's people and one's own generation. It must include the freedom to live outside the cage created by other people's images and projections'. (2003, 31)

Revisiting Hope and Disenchantment

In Thomas's insight we can recognise the dialectic nature of the ethical problems underlying the relationship between Indigenous and non-Indigenous culture and the place of Aboriginal art in that relationship. As Stuart Hall writes, cultural identities 'are subject to the continuous "play" of history, culture and power', and are 'constituted within, not outside, representation' (1990, 222–25). Thus certain forms of recognition – made manifest through practices of representation in public culture – have produced a sense of exclusion, but this experience has yielded new vocabularies for asserting difference and autonomy. Aboriginal art's entry into the high art arena and the fine arts market triggered a set of economic processes that brought chaos into that very value system. A dialectical approach underlies Chris Healy's revelations in *Forgetting Aborigines* (2008) about those Australian cultural forms which manifest divergent trajectories of remembering and forgetting the Aboriginal presence. And when Marcia Langton reminds us that '"Aboriginality" is primarily a textual or visual – and distant – experience for most Australians' and thus that 'the glut of Aboriginal images and metaphors' in recent years has 'amplified [the] paradox of our contiguity and our distance', we can also perceive dialectical thinking (2003, 91). Similarly, Ian McLean's *White Aborigines* sheds light on Australian artistic and intellectual cultures that have by turns sought to encompass and vitiate Aboriginality, a process that has been mediated by an ongoing discontent with Australia's antipodean condition. This is perhaps best illustrated in his analysis of Imants Tillers, in which he points out that the 'very lengths to which Tillers and other postmodernists went to dispel the myths of regional and Aboriginalist identities only showed the force of such myths in the contemporary arena' (1998, 119).

This book's attention to the hopeful and disenchanted faces of the Aboriginal art phenomenon hopefully also affirms the value of a dialectical approach. We have seen hope recur in discourses that celebrate Aboriginal art as a cultural renaissance and that view the art as a space of emancipation and empowerment, while disenchantment has resided in the critical tropes of ethnocide and cultural colonialism, in the allusions to sweatshops and slave labour, and in Richard Bell's assertion that Aboriginal art is 'a white thing'. When Sutton argues that Aboriginal art works have been 'made over into being "Australia's" in a keen collusion between artists, the market, scholars/ curators and the image machines of tourism and advertising', we have a sense not of a renaissance of Aboriginal culture, but of insidious processes of cultural subordination (1992b, 8). All of these variations indicate that Aboriginal art has been a locus for optimism, while also being the subject of narratives of disenchantment – of tragedy, exploitation, cynicism and futility.

This duality is of course symptomatic of the persistence of inequality in Australia. To engage in any depth with Aboriginal art is to comprehend the tragedy of dispossession and the subsequent phases of Aboriginal cultural trauma and to confront the level of disadvantage Aboriginal people currently experience. The high rates of suicide, early mortality, substance abuse and incarceration within Aboriginal communities testify to the suffering and sorrow that coexists with the vitality of the Aboriginal art phenomenon. This underpins the poignancy of the fact that some Aboriginal art centres have been conferred

Public Benevolent Institution status for tax purposes, which means that they are defined as 'a non-profit institution organised for the direct relief of poverty, sickness, suffering, misfortune, disability or helplessness' (ATO 2008). Indeed, as I suggested in Part I, the utopianism engendered by the Aboriginal art movement may be of such an intense nature precisely because of the distressing representations of Aboriginality that circulate in Australian public culture. The refrain that Aboriginal art has contributed and can continue to contribute to the economic empowerment of Aboriginal people in remote communities is challenged by the fact that the benefits of the Aboriginal art market 'have flowed back to artists, their families and communities unevenly and unpredictably' (Acker et al. 2013, 5) and broadly cannot be said to have reduced economic dependence on the state or alleviated the social ills just described. This gives rise to the deflating but obvious question: How could we expect an art movement to achieve such a radical transformation anyway?

I have made cautious use of the word *instrumentalise* throughout this book in pursuit of an understanding of the interrelatedness of ethics and aesthetics in the Aboriginal art arena, and to highlight the art's susceptibility to the appropriative nation building practices of the state. It might be useful to comprehend the hopeful and disenchanted faces of the Aboriginal art phenomenon as manifesting the mixed effects of the instrumentalisation of Aboriginal art. In other words, they reveal the charged meanings Aboriginal art has accrued as a consequence of its having been harnessed to a range of ideological and pragmatic projects across the domains of Indigenous activism, civil society and state governance. It is instructive to add the arena of fine arts to this list of domains even if this stretches the idea of 'instrumentalisation' a little too far, because Aboriginal art has also been harnessed to the project of dethroning the ethnocentric and imperialist architecture of the Western fine arts system (a project of which, it must be said, many Aboriginal artists remain ignorant).

In order to clarify the point I wish to make about the effects of this instrumentalisation, I refer the reader to the argument I made in Part I, in which I proposed that Aboriginal art has become metonymic for an affirmative figuration of Aboriginal culture in national public culture. This figuration was underpinned by an aspiration to achieve a confluence of strong Indigenous identity, revitalised culture, economic participation and a rich and inclusive sense of nationhood. Should these elements align, we would have a miraculous synthesis of the ideological, aesthetic and economic dimensions of the movements with which Aboriginal art has been affiliated. This synthesis has, however, not been achieved. Arguably, the stresses at play in the Aboriginal art arena are expressive of the limitations of these projects, and of the points where the avenues by which the logic and imperatives of each project clash. The tensions that I have described in relation to the art/anthropology binary, the relationship between urban and remote Aboriginal art and identity and the relationship between Aboriginal art and money are all exemplary in this regard.

Why Art Matters

I wish, finally, to break with what has been a relatively dispassionate style of analysis and offer some more personal reflections on the hope/disenchantment dialectic. Art – as an arena of social communication – remains one of the most important domains for giving expression to societies' utopian visions. Despite the transgressive and ironic idioms of contemporary art, much art practice is sustained by a collective sense of idealism about the pursuit of truth, the expression of human fellowship, and the belief that it offers respite from, and the strength to resist, the malevolent forces in society. The Aboriginal art movement has stimulated the altruism of non-Indigenous audiences, collectors, writers and art professionals at least in part because the idea that a profoundly marginalised minority has found a voice through art of remarkable beauty, originality and conceptual variety resonates very powerfully with these ideals. This book has interrogating the principles of fine arts for two key reasons. First, I believe it is important to 'make strange' the shared preoccupation that many who write about Aboriginal art have with ensuring that Aboriginal art attains the status of fine art. All intellectual writing and scholarly work is a project of persuasion in some way: an effort to introduce a new perspective or insight into an existing arena of understanding. However, to have been engaged in Aboriginal art research over the last 50 years is to have been involved in a very particular kind of project of persuasion, one grounded in ethical thought, because the creation of knowledge about Aboriginal art is an exercise in articulating the nature of Indigenous/non-Indigenous interrelatedness and resisting inequality. Thus, consistent with the broader aims of this book, I would argue that we need to acknowledge that writing on Aboriginal art, even when it is not activist or polemical in tone, has been an avenue for ethical action in the post-assimilation era. This writing should therefore be open to being studied as a cultural phenomenon along with all the other cultural phenomena we submit to analysis in order to formulate new understandings of Indigenous/non-Indigenous relations.

The second reason I have questioned the principles of fine art is that, while I do not dispute the virtuousness of the cause of attaining fine arts recognition for Aboriginal art, I do suggest that it has precluded certain lines of scholarly inquiry that might undermine the celebratory narrative of Aboriginal art. As was perhaps best demonstrated in my discussions of the art/anthropology binary and the discourses that have delineated the space of ethical art market conduct, some remarkable distortions and erasures have taken place in an effort to buttress Aboriginal art's status as contemporary fine art. These have taken place because the alterity of the artists' practice and social worlds is so inimical to many fine arts principles that it must be obfuscated or attributed to the artists' disempowered position. As David Hansen notes of some Australian museums, protocols of respect for contemporary Indigenous culture have curtailed certain kinds of truth telling about the colonial encounter (e.g., where social relations between Indigenous and non-Indigenous people contest overarching narratives of the latter's victimisation), and he warns against the subordination of historical inquiry to an 'abstract zone of retrospective judgement' (2010, 48). Along similar lines, I am cautiously proposing that deference to contemporary fine arts values may mean that some other, perhaps more enduring, ideals enshrined in fine arts – for instance the reverence for truth and the possibility of establishing dialogue between different theatres of experience – have been subverted.

In spite of having critiqued the way many fine arts values have been brought to bear in the Aboriginal art arena, I am by no means advocating that we dispense with them. I think we hold on to ideas about art's autonomy for very good reasons. The unethical conduct in the Aboriginal art marketplace has attracted considerable attention; however, equally concerning – though insufficiently acknowledged – are the systemic changes to cultural policy that have contributed to Aboriginal art's dispersed, genericised and symbolic presence in national culture. The forms of Aboriginal visual culture which became ubiquitous in Australian public culture in the late twentieth century attest to the need for continued interrogations of the cultural industries paradigm, and of government programs that seek to appropriate the vitality of artistic and cultural activity in order to, as Yúdice writes, 'solve problems that previously were the province of economics and politics' (2003, 25; Eyerman 2006; Hesmondhalgh 2002).

These critiques were of course prefigured by Horkheimer and Adorno's culture industry thesis as articulated in *The Dialectic of the Enlightenment* (2002 [1947]; see also Adorno 1991 [1938]; 1978 [1967]), in which they explore the way capitalism conditions objects and practices of culture to serve mercenary and administrative imperatives. They argue that, under these conditions, culture becomes a diversionary and incapacitating form of entertainment rather than something that encourages critical thought and imaginative engagement. They further suggest that the forces of mechanical reproduction that have allowed art and culture to be shared by a much larger community than was possible before have come to facilitate a repressive social order: mass oppression rather than mass emancipation. This is because the seductions of mass culture enervate our spontaneous and heuristic inclinations, ensuring that the 'autonomous' and 'authentic' works of art that resist the reifying 'principle of utility' and encapsulate the forces of truth and protest that are stifled in everyday life, have no power to compel us to change (Horkheimer and Adorno 2002 [1947], 128; Adorno 1978, 111). Adorno's potent summation of the problem in a 1936 letter to Walter Benjamin declared that high culture and popular culture comprise 'torn halves of an integral freedom, to which, however, they do not add up' (quoted in Paul Jones 2011, 49; see also Horkheimer and Adorno 2002 [1947], 127–28).

While Horkheimer and Adorno's thesis has been persuasively argued to be elitist and homogenising and to have less purchase in a digital age, it nevertheless provides a salutary departure point for bringing ethical questions to bear on the mingling of art, culture and commerce in contemporary life. It encourages us to think about what other meanings Aboriginal art might have had it not become ensconced in a new paradigm of culture that treated it as a resource to enhance commerce and serve economic agendas. The creative industries discourse – for instance, Ryan et al.'s argument that people's 'everyday lives, beliefs and practices' are the 'raw material for content creation' – constitute precisely the kind of rationalist synthesis of culture and enterprise that Horkheimer and Adorno feared would become the norm. The impact this synthesis has on Aboriginal art's meaning is addressed by Sutton, when he writes of the 'symbolic gulf' created by the 'projection of the local, intimate, and personally known onto the national and international stage' (1992b, 7). As he suggests, through this process the significance of Aboriginal cultural forms is 'directed away from their specificity' to serve the project of generating facile emblems of Aboriginality (7). Not only does this enervate these forms' aesthetic power and cause many art audiences to feel so jaded about Aboriginal art that they do not engage with it in any meaningful way, it has also, as I argued earlier, had considerable social consequences by circumscribing the properties of Aboriginal culture that are validated in national public culture.

There are some statements in ATSIC's 1995 *Cultural Policy Framework* to which I have returned many times while writing this book, because they seem to capture the pathos and perversity of Aboriginal art's predicament:

> It is unfortunate that we have had to allow the recognition of indigenous cultural forms and practices as valuable and saleable commodities – in Aboriginal art and cultural tourism – to be a key factor in their general recognition as integral and vital components in Australia's cultural resources. But nonetheless, since there is recognition at national and international levels, there is an agenda to be developed [...] A cohesive policy overview mechanism and structure for the production and marketing of indigenous cultural product is also imperative for

consolidating and increasing the *economic empowerment* and well-being of indigenous peoples. Of equal importance is the role of production, distribution, promotion and market development of this product plays [sic] in fostering an understanding by the broader Australian community of the unique nature of indigenous culture. (8, 17, original italics)

These declarations clearly articulate the rationales that have driven the dissemination of Aboriginal art within Australian public culture. They also present a poignant paradox: while they acknowledge the problems inherent in commodification, they are suffused with marketing vocabulary and articulate an overt 'means-and-ends' instrumentalism. There is something profoundly disillusioning about the way grave issues relating to survival, identity and recognition give way to cheery industriousness, as if good commercial strategy can ensure that everyone wins.

NOTES

Introduction

1 The Aboriginal and Torres Strait Islander Commission was established as a statutory body in 1989 to enable Aboriginal people to participate in the design and delivery of Indigenous affairs policy and programs. It was abolished by the Liberal government in 2005.

2 The phrases 'Aboriginal art', 'Indigenous art' and 'Indigenous Australian art' are now commonly used interchangeably in Australia, and in this book I do the same. I mean for all three phrases to refer to the art of Aboriginal and Torres Strait Islander peoples.

3 For more detailed surveys of Aboriginal art's history, see Morphy (1998), Caruana (2012) and Newstead (2014) and the anthologies of Kleinert and Neale (2000), Lüthi and Lee (1993) and McLean (2011).

4 'Dreaming' is the English word used to refer to this body of religious knowledge that is named in many different ways by Indigenous groups. The nature of Aboriginal people's relationship to their land is poignantly conveyed by Stanner:

> No English words are good enough to give a sense of the links between an aboriginal group and its homeland. Our word 'home', warm and suggestive though it be, does not match the aboriginal word that may mean 'camp', 'hearth', 'country', 'everlasting home', 'totem place', 'life source', 'spirit centre' and much else all in one [...] The aboriginal would speak of 'earth' and use the word in a richly symbolic way to mean his 'shoulder' or his 'side' [...] A different tradition leaves us tongueless and earless towards this other world of meaning and significance. (1968, 44)

5 *fluent* was curated by Hetti Perkins, Brenda L. Croft and Victoria Lynn.

Part I. Governance, Nationhood and Civil Society

1 I use the phrase 'post-assimilation era' to loosely frame the 40-year period covered by this book. Other researchers have referred to this period as the 'self-determination era', as this was the policy paradigm introduced by Whitlam to mark the end of the assimilation policy (see, e.g., Kowal 2008). However, while self-determination has been foundational to Indigenous social justice movements, it has always been contested in the sphere of Indigenous affairs governance, and it was significantly diluted as an idea during the term of the Howard Liberal government (1996–2007). The Rudd/Gillard Labor government (2007–2013) did not regenerate it as an ethos for Indigenous empowerment, focusing rather on socioeconomic disadvantage through its *Closing the Gap* policies.

1. New Intercultural Relationships in the Post-Assimilation Era

1 Legislative reforms included the establishment of the Department of Aboriginal Affairs as well as the National Aboriginal Consultative Committee, the latter of which enabled Aboriginal spokespeople to formally advise the Commonwealth. A royal commission into Aboriginal land rights was launched that culminated in land rights legislation in the Northern Territory in 1976. The Racial Discrimination Act was passed in 1975, giving legislative force to Australia's ratification of the International Convention on the Elimination of All Forms of Racial Discrimination. The government also supported the formation of incorporated Indigenous organisations and councils across the country – 'agencies of collective choice' – to manage the delivery of government services and resources to Indigenous people and address matters of concern to their communities (Rowse 2002, 1, 17). A related body of measures gave momentum to the 'homelands movement' that had begun in Arnhem Land in 1970, which saw Aboriginal people move away from missions, reserves, pastoral stations and townships to form outstations on their traditional clan estates (Coombs et al. 1982). Welfare payments and grants to establish basic infrastructure, housing and services on remote outstations encouraged this decentralisation. A consequence of these initiatives and the land rights legislation was the redistribution of Aboriginal people into tiny communities across northern and central Australia. While in 1982 these numbered around two hundred with a collective population of 6,000 people, by 2005 there were 1,200 remote outstations with a population approximating one hundred and twenty thousand to one hundred and fifty thousand (Coombs et al. 1982, 427; Altman 2005a, 1).

2 The war itself contributed to these changes, as Aboriginal servicemen received equal pay and experienced an unprecedented level of fellowship with non-Indigenous Australians.

3 In 1974 the Whitlam government ratified the Convention for the Protection of the World Cultural and Natural Heritage. In that year Australia's heritage was formally investigated by the government for the first time with the Inquiry into the National Estate, and in 1975 the Australian Heritage Commission was established.

4 Of relevance here is Myers's (2001) discussion of the Whitlamist 'professional managerial class', which he suggests leveraged the status of Aboriginal art in the 1970s and 1980s due to its desire to create an authentic national culture (see also Philp 2007, 61–62).

5 The *Boyer Lectures* have been hosted by the Australian Broadcasting Corporation (ABC) since 1959. They involve a prominent Australian presenting a series of radio lectures on political, social, cultural or scientific matters.

6 Coombs's commitment to Indigenous social justice goals was such that he chaired the Aboriginal Treaty Committee between 1979 and 1983.

7 This definition of Aboriginality, devised by the Council for Aboriginal Affairs and accepted by cabinet in 1968, remains in place (Dexter 2008, 79).

8 In 1987 the Royal Commission into Aboriginal Deaths in Custody was established to investigate the deaths of 99 Aboriginal people in prison or police custody. Its findings brought to public attention not only cases of brutality, negligence and racial discrimination where Aboriginal prisoners were concerned but also the tragic life paths of disenfranchised Aboriginal people that had led to their overrepresentation and high rates of suicide in custody.

9 Dodson also writes poignantly of the relational way in which Aboriginality has been configured: '[O]ur subjectivities, our aspirations, our ways of seeing and our languages

have largely been excluded' from the social imaginary of colonial culture; 'It is as if we have been ushered onto a stage to play in a drama where the parts have already been written' (2003, 38).

10 The substance of the Mabo decision, handed down by the High Court after a 10-year battle, was that Eddie Mabo's title to land on the island of Mer in the Torres Strait, which his ancestors had occupied for generations, had not been extinguished by colonisation and, furthermore, that the claim that Britain had justly appropriated the Australian landmass because it had been essentially unoccupied was a falsehood. In 1993 the government passed the Native Title Act, giving all Aboriginal groups the right to prove that their native title had endured on Crown land. In 1996, just prior to the election of John Howard's Liberal government, the High Court found that the Wik peoples retained native title to leasehold land (land in use by pastoralists or miners, leased from the government) on their clan estates in Cape York. Native title became an increasingly divisive issue in Australian politics, and in 1998 the government passed the Native Title Amendment Act, which diluted Aboriginal rights considerably in favour of contesting interests.

11 The Human Rights and Equal Opportunity Commission presented the *Bringing Them Home* report in 1997. The inquiry had found that between 1910 and 1970 most Aboriginal families had been affected by policies of child removal that had targeted Aboriginal children specifically with the objective of assimilating them into the white population. These children had become wards of state in children's homes, missions, or were fostered or adopted by white families. The report revealed the trauma caused not only by the fragmentation of families but also by displacement and the harsh living conditions and disciplinary regimes found in many of the institutions (National Inquiry 1997).

12 It is also worth noting the popular readership of Henry Reynolds's highly accessible histories of frontier conflict, dispossession and state control of Indigenous Australians, which were written in a very personal, conscience-heavy style, as conveyed in titles like *This Whispering in Our Hearts* and *Why Weren't We Told?* (Reynolds 1982; 1998; 1999).

13 In 2007 Keating's Redfern address was voted third in an ABC public poll of 'the most unforgettable speeches' in history, following Martin Luther King's 'I Have a Dream' and Jesus's Sermon on the Mount, which gives some indication of its significance to recent generations.

14 Indeed, all the phenomena described here were contested by contrary social and political groups. For example the the populist One Nation Party emerged, and there was a strong backlash against the Stolen Generations Inquiry and native title from the Liberal government and other commentators (Povinelli 2002). The 'History Wars' were waged in the press, through the revisionist history of Keith Windschuttle, and in response to the National Museum of Australia's presentation of Australian history (Mulgan 1998; Macintyre and Clark 2003; Marcus 2004). As Indigenous scholar Anderson writes of the climate created by these events, 'In a relatively short space of time, the cultural possibilities of new, more inclusive forms of nationalism seemed to dissipate' (2003, 20).

15 To some extent this shift was aligned with, and arguably assisted by, a concurrent project being pursued by the state and civil society: the project of assimilating multiculturalism into Australian nationalism. As Lattas writes, Aboriginal culture, heritage and 'otherness' provided the ground on which emergent ideals about social inclusiveness and the accommodation of difference were able to find purchase (1997). Similarly, Povinelli suggests that Australian indigeneity provided the nation with 'an experience of a time before the failures and compromises of national projects' (2002, 26).

2. Aboriginal People Mobilising Aboriginal Art

1 These events are better understood as taking place in the spirit of reciprocity and negotiation rather than resistance to oppression, because many missionaries were sympathetic to Yolngu interests and respectful of Yolngu culture, and the Yolngu in turn accepted elements of their Christian teachings.

2 See also the Saltwater Collection, a group of paintings produced by Yolngu artists to articulate their clan rights to waterways in Eastern Arnhem Land, which were created after a non-Indigenous fisherman left the severed head of a crocodile at a sacred site affiliated with Bäru, a crocodile ancestor being (Buku-Larrngay Mulka Centre and Drill Hall Gallery 1999). Some of these works were presented during the Blue Mud Bay Native Title Case, which was won by traditional owners following a High Court decision in 2008.

3 For examples in the realm of art specifically, see Johnson (1984); Caruana and Isaacs (1990); Williamson and Perkins (1994); Eather (2005); and Croft (2007b).

4 Bob Maza was an actor, playwright and prominent activist who became president of the Aborigines Advancement League in 1968 and participated in the Aboriginal Tent Embassy protests of 1972. Oodgeroo Noonuccal (Kath Walker) was a writer and poet. Her history of campaigning for Aboriginal rights dated from her membership of the Communist Party in the 1950s and her senior position in the Federal Council for the Advancement of Aboriginal and Torres Strait Islanders in the early 1960s. Lin Onus was a painter and sculptor. His advocacy of Indigenous aspirations echoed the ambitions of his father, Bill Onus, who had played a leading role in several Aboriginal political organisations in the 1950s and '60s and founded the Melbourne company Aboriginal Enterprises, both of which shaped Lin Onus's youth (see Thompson 1990 for relevant autobiographical essays; Attwood 2003, 315–18; Kleinert 2010; Neale 2000).

5 For useful examples of engagements with the tensions around the urban/remote distinction, see Caruana and Isaacs (1990); Onus (2003); Bell (2002); O'Riordan (2009); Browning (2010); and Jones (2010).

6 This ambivalence is reflected in the biographies and stylistic developments of several pioneering Aboriginal artists such as Lin Onus, Bob Maza, Trevor Nicholls and Fiona Foley, who learned from and were mentored by elder Aboriginal artists in remote communities as they developed distinctive styles and *raison d'êtres* for their work in their own locales (see Mundine 1990; Onus 1989a).

7 These points can't be made without acknowledging that Aboriginal artists and art professionals have experienced paternalism and suspicion regarding their conduct amongst non-Indigenous art professionals and have often argued that they remain marginalised with respect to dominant discourses (such as Anthropology) (see Katona 2007; Foley 2006; Mundine 2009a; 2009b). While disempowering, I would suggest that these experiences also reflect the efficacy of the Indigenous aesthetic public sphere.

3. Understanding Aboriginal Art Subsidy

1 This decision was in part inspired by a 1965 report on the country's tourism industry that recommended that the government provide infrastructure support for the development of an Aboriginal Arts and Crafts sector (Altman 2000a, 461).

2 This organisation was reinvented and renamed several times before its demise in 1991. To avoid confusion I will refer to it as the Government Company, as it was colloquially known in the 1980s.

3 See, for example, the 1989 *Review of the Aboriginal Arts and Crafts Industry* (Altman et al.
   1989) and the *Report of the Royal Commission into Aboriginal Deaths in Custody* (Johnston 1991a,
   34.4.15–21). See also ATSIC's *Cultural Policy Framework* (1995) and Colin Mercer's *Creative
   country: Review of the ATSIC arts and craft industry support strategy* (1997), both of which are
   indicative of the turn toward a cultural industries model of arts subsidy (discussed in
   Part 4). It has been reiterated in the *Closing the Gap* strategy – a framework for improving
   Indigenous people's lives across the areas of health, life expectancy, education, employment and living standards launched by the Australian Labor government in 2008 (Office
   for the Arts 2011a; 2011b).
4 This was, of course, the premise of CDEP when it was established.
5 Rowse has elaborated on this distinction in his examination of the way both policy and
   public discourse on matters of Indigenous disadvantage and social justice have oscillated
   between characterising Indigenous Australians as 'peoples' and 'populations' (2012).
6 These motives appear to have driven the establishment of art fairs and prizes in recent
   years, such as the Parliament of NSW Aboriginal Art Prize, the Victorian Indigenous
   Art Awards and the Cairns Indigenous Art Fair in Queensland. Other relevant initiatives include the Queensland Indigenous Arts Marketing and Export Agency, the NSW
   Aboriginal Arts and Cultural strategy and the Victorian 'Tribal Expressions: The
   Business of Art and Culture' series of showcases.

4. The State Mobilising Aboriginal Art

1 Myers suggests that '[t]he Government purchases were clearly inspired by a changing
   national construction that embraced Aboriginal culture as part of Australia, a construction that must have been supported, if not among the majority of Australians, then at
   least among those involved in politics and cultural production' (2001, 189).
2 See the National Museum of Australia's *Off the Walls: Art from Aboriginal and Torres Strait
   Islander Affairs Agencies 1967–2005* exhibition of some of the 2000 of these objects that
   became part of its collection in 2007 (National Museum of Australia 2011; see also
   Chubb and Sever 2009).
3 An interesting counterpoint to these examples was the selection of the NGA exhibition
   Culture Warriors, curated by Brenda L. Croft, to tour to Washington, DC as part of a cultural diplomacy initiative in 2009. The Australian Embassy staged the cultural showcase
   Australia Presents to establish stronger ties between the Rudd Labor Government and the
   newly elected Democratic administration led by America's first black president, Barack
   Obama. As McDonald (2014) explores in detail, the then Australian Ambassador to
   the United States Denis Richardson selected *Culture Warriors* precisely because it 'dealt
   openly with Australia's troubled history of race relations' (2014, 28, see also Fisher and
   McDonald 2016).
4 See, for instance, Lander (2008) on 'Badger' Bates and Fisher (2011) on Mark
   Blackman.
5 These include the Dreaming Festival, staged annually in Queensland since 2001;
   the Garma Festival, which has been staged in Arnhem Land annually since 1999;
   Reconciliation Week; Sorry Day/Journey of Healing Day; the Deadly Awards and the
   Message Sticks Indigenous Film Festival.
6 The Roadmap for Reconciliation, one of the final documents of Reconciliation, stipu-
   lated that 'All parliaments, governments and organisations observe protocols and negotiate with local Aboriginal and Torres Strait Islander elders or representative bodies to

include appropriate Indigenous ceremony into official events' (CAR 2000). There has since been a widespread adoption of 'welcome to country' policies by government as well as nongovernment organizations and corporations (Merlan 2014). This involves a representative of the local Aboriginal community being invited to make some kind of presentation (a song, a smoking ceremony, a speech) as a mark of respect and to ensure that attendees are aware of Indigenous people's continuing custodianship of that land.

7   Cultural planning and development policies began to be adopted by local governments across the country from the early 1990s. Consistent with the country's embrace of a cultural industries model of arts subsidy and governance (to be discussed in Part IV), these policies encouraged holistic strategies of integrating arts and cultural activities into policies addressing areas such as tourism, urban rejuvenation, heritage, regional economies, environment management, unemployment, health and social inclusion (Craik et al. 2000, 195; Stevenson 2000, 108–114).

5. 'Aboriginal Culture' at the Nexus of Justice, Recognition and Redemption

1   For instance, in his 1972 Election policy speech, Whitlam claimed that 'Australia's treatment of her aboriginal people will be the thing upon which the rest of the world will judge Australia and Australians – not just now, but in the greater perspective of history' and spoke of removing 'a stain from our national honour' with respect to Aboriginal rights and justice (Whitlam 1972; 1973; see also Curran 2004; Kirby 2010). Since the 1980s, Aboriginal people have been instrumental in the drafting and resolution of the Declaration on the Rights of Indigenous Peoples at the UN (Dodson and Pritchard 1998). For other relevant literature, see Dodson (1996), Behrendt (2003), Janke (1998), CAR (2000) and HREOC (2003).

2   For other examples from Aboriginal artists and leaders, see Jagamarra (2000), Roughsey (1976) and Yunupingu (1997).

3   This form of recognition can be traced to the popular 1954 UNESCO World Art Series publication *Australia: Aboriginal Paintings, Arnhem Land* (Read et al. 1954; see also Miller 2004). Peter Bellew, who headed the UNESCO Arts division at the time, was assisted in producing the book by the Australian UNESCO Committee for Visual Arts. This committee was chaired by anthropologist Charles Mountford and also included Hal Missingham – artist, photographer and then director of the Art Gallery of NSW, Desiderius Orban, Margaret Preston and Wallace Thornton, the last two of whom shared an avid interest in Aboriginal art. The book's introduction was written by the esteemed British art historian and critic Herbert Read and reflected his interest in the psychology of the 'primitive' and the belief that tribal art elicited primordial truths – both of which informed his writings on the aesthetic of the modern avant-garde (Read 1954; 1957).

4   See for instance Myers's discussion of the collector Margaret Carnegie, who responded to the encouragement of Bob Edwards to acquire Papunya works (2006).

5   For other examples, see the collector Gantner, quoted in Neales (2004, 20), and the comments of former Federal Indigenous Affairs minister, Clyde Holding, quoted in Cadzow (1987, 3).

6   For other examples, see Aboriginal Arts Board (1975), Miller (2004); Russell (2001, 87) and Ryan (2008).

7 For other examples, see Carnegie et al. (1991, 126); Australia Council (1982) and Office for the Arts (2011b).

8 These complexities were debated in scholarship and commentary following the Northern Territory National Emergency Response, or 'Intervention', in 2007. For discussions that reflect a spectrum of views, see Altman and Hinkson (2007, 2010), Langton (2008b), Sutton (2009), Price (2011), Toohey (2008), Austin-Broos (2011) and Lea (2012).

Part II. Contemporary Aboriginal Art in the 1980s

1 The Whitlam Labor government brought to fruition the fledgling arts initiatives of previous governments and injected substantial subsidies into the sector (Gardiner-Garden 2009). As Craik suggests, the establishment of the Australia Council for the Arts and the dramatically expanded arts budget entailed that it was now, finally, viable to develop an artistic career in Australia (2007, 12; Murphy 1983b).

2 Burn was at the forefront of these changes, having been affiliated with the famed collective Art & Language in London and New York in the late 1960s and early 1970s. Art & Language played a significant role in formulating the precepts of Conceptual art, as a practice of immanent critique of Art itself, and one that engaged directly with processes of social change and treated ideas and argumentation as new kinds of artistic form. Burn returned to Australia in 1977. Notably, he was also instrumental in triggering the Australian art world's positive reevaluation of Albert Namattjira's work (Burn and Stephen, 1986; 1992). My thanks to Vivien Johnson for alerting me to the fact that Burn's association with Art & Language meant his arguments about Aboriginal art had considerable weight in the Australian context.

6. The Emergence of Aboriginal Art in the 1980s

1 These ideas were also embraced within the emerging discipline of Australian cultural studies, the writings of which often overlapped with the themes addressed in art theory and drew heavily on French poststructuralist thought (see for instance Morris 1983; Muecke 1983; 1984).

2 For other writings that refer to the Cultural Cringe and provincialism, see Waterlow (1983), Murphy (1988), Smith (1988) and Van den Bosch (1985). See also the artist Imants Tillers's retrospective insight in Johnson (1997, 71), and Montgomery (2008) and Butler and Donaldson (2009) for more recent reflections.

3 See McLean (2011a) for an illuminating account of the transition outlined here.

4 Truganini was a Tasmanian Aboriginal woman who, following colonial efforts to rid the island of its Aboriginal population, was iconised as the 'last of her race' when she died in 1876. Her skeleton was on public display at the Tasmanian Museum between 1904 and 1947 and repatriated for cremation nearly one hundred years after her death. A large Aboriginal population has survived in Tasmania, but as they are of mixed heritage, they have had to fight for recognition in the face of the intrigue and nostalgia evoked by the idea of the 'last full-blood'. Though Smith affirms the myth that she was the last Tasmanian in his lectures, this view is no longer sustained (Ryan 2011 [1976]; Hansen 2010).

5 Smith attributes the term to the Australian poet Les Murray and elaborated on his theory in the essay 'On Cultural Convergence' (Smith 1980, 50; 1988).

6 This phrase appeared in critical writings on Indigenous art concerned with the theme of cultural colonialism (Murphy 1987; Marrie 1985; 1987) and was also the title of a book on the heritage of the Pitjantjatjarra people published in 1977: *Killing Me Softly: The Destruction of a Heritage.*

7 See McNahon and Mackinolty (1983), V. Johnson (1987; 1989) and Davila (2004 [1987]).

8 Ground paintings appeared in several exhibitions, such as at the 1981 *Festival of Sydney*, the 1982 *Sydney Biennale*, the 1988 *Dreamings* exhibition in New York and *Magicians de la terre* (Magicians of the Earth) in Paris in 1989.

9 See Maloon (1982), Adams (1983; 1987), Marcon and Jones (1987) and Murphy (1981) on the artists David Aspden, John Davis, David Jones, Bonita Ely, Marr Grounds and Ingo Kleinert. See Bromfield (1988) and Banchflower (1988) on the artist Brian Banchflower. See Carroll (1984) regarding the exhibition *The Centre*. See also Tillers's discussion of the European performance artists Marina Abramovic's and Ulay's pilgrimage to Aboriginal communities following their participation in the 1979 Sydney Biennale (1982). See Lattas's discussion of the German artist Nikolaus Lang's work of 1987–88 (1997 [1990], 235–36).

10 My thanks to Vivien Johnson for sharing her recollections on the relationship between Aboriginal painting and Australian conceptual art.

11 Tim Johnson and Vivien Johnson visited Papunya frequently in the 1970s and 1980s, where they befriended artists, collected works and assisted artists in getting exposure in the art world. They also curated important exhibitions such as *Koori Art '84* (together with a curatorium of local Indigenous artists) and *Two Worlds Collide: Cultural Convergence in Aboriginal and White Australian Art* (1985).

12 Tillers made a point of appropriating from reproductions, that is, from imagery that was already in circulation as part of mass-produced culture. At this time Michael Nelson Jagamarra's *Five Dreamings* was in high circulation within the art world as representative of the emerging Papunya movement (Tillers 1986; Foss 1987, 138; Johnson 1997, 61).

13 Indeed, in answer to the criticism of appropriators of Aboriginal art (discussed later), Michaels argued that Western Desert artists were equally appropriative in their mobilization of Western painting practices (2004 [1989]).

14 Paul Taylor worked as an art journalist in New York between 1984 and 1992. He wrote for a range of publications, frequently on Andy Warhol (he was the last critic to interview Warhol before he died) and post-pop art movements. Taylor died prematurely in Melbourne in 1992.

15 This essay was commissioned by *Flash Art* (Milan) and published in a 1983 edition of the magazine, as well as in the Australian journal *On the Beach* (1983) – a short-lived homage to French poststructuralist ideas.

16 Tillers had a solo exhibition in 1983 at Matt's Gallery in London with the same title, for which Paul Taylor wrote the catalogue essay (Hart 2006: fn. 26).

17 It is interesting to note that the term 'white aborigines' was also interpreted by some as a metaphor for the way artists were marginalized in Australian society (Lingard 1989a, 48; Annear, 1986).

18 See for instance Adams (1987), Tillers (1983), Phipps (1984), Davila (2004 [1987]) and Johnson (1987).

19 See for instance Craig (1984), Stephen (1984), V. Johnson (1988), Hoffie (1988) and Kleinert (1988a).

20 Morris's essay was also published in *On the Beach* (1984).

21 This is consistent with the fact that the relativist and apolitical tendencies of postmodern critique sometimes made a mockery of the social movements that had given rise to conceptual art in the 1970s. We see this with Paul Taylor's aversion to 'social purpose' art, as noted earlier.

22 For valuable insights into the Aboriginal Cultural Foundation's history, see Eccles and Spencer (2013).

23 Montgomery suggested that '[i]t is obvious that, without the aboriginal participation – the dance spectacle at the "Bouffes du Nord", the ground painting by the Warlpiri tribe at the Museum of Modern Art, the aboriginal video programme and the acrylic paintings at the Australian Embassy – the Australian contribution to the Paris Autumn Festival would have been almost a "non-event"' (1983, 3).

24 See particularly Araeen (1987), Clifford (1988), Foster (1985), McEvilley (1984) and Lüthi (1993).

25 In 1984 Djon Mundine was the first Indigenous person to be appointed to a curatorial post by a state art gallery – the Art Gallery of NSW, a further indication of this shift.

26 See Onus (1989b), Croft (2011 [1989]), Marrie (1987), Fourmile (1987; 1989) and Maughan et al. (1988).

27 McLean has shown that these challenges reverberated beyond the space of the national and has suggested that they in fact obliged the international art world to embrace a discourse of 'contemporary art' that 'escapes both the geographical and teleological limits of Western modernism' (2011b, 334).

28 There is a complex history of debate around the fluctuating figures of Aboriginal agent and Aboriginal victim that recur in Australia's visual culture and public discourse (see, e.g., Cowlishaw 2003; Sutton 2005; 2009; Bell and Nelson 1989; Moreton-Robinson 2003 [1999]; Pearson 2007; Langton 2008; Kowal 2011). We can perceive the dialectical quality of these fluctuations when Cowlishaw writes that 'as Australia's bloodstained, oppressive, and secreted past began to be revealed, assertive land rights activists were gradually replaced by injured and suffering Aboriginal people as the central motif in Indigenous politics' (2004, 52). Debates around Aboriginal victimhood and agency reveal the disjunctions between the way Aboriginal people see themselves on the one hand, and the representations of Aboriginal subjectivity that enter the public domain through national narratives of recognition, remedy and social justice on the other (Cowlishaw et al. 2006). Indeed many articulated positions on Indigenous empowerment are uninformed about local contingencies and are thus very blunt instruments. The public images of Aboriginality generated by these contending forces both reflect and are productive of the diverse psychological and social realities that are at play in markedly different theatres of Indigenous/non-Indigenous coexistence.

Part III. Negotiating Difference

1 Valuable discussions of the formation of Aboriginal identity can be found in Beckett (1988); Langton (1993); Dodson (2003), Marcus (2000) and Russell (2001).

2 However, as will be discussed later, several high-profile urban Indigenous artists have objected to this, including Brook Andrew, Richard Bell, Tracey Moffatt and Gordon Bennett. See Williamson and Moffatt (1992) and Riphagen (2008) for useful discussions of this issue.

7. Negotiating Aboriginal Difference

1 See for instance Martin-Chew (2011); Browning and Allas (2010) and *Blakatak* (2005).
2 Most of the artists associated with Papunya Tula Artists work at an art centre in the neighbouring communities Kintore and Kiwirrkura. However, at the time of this interview a new art centre, Papunya Tjupi, had just been established in the community.
3 Perry's approach has been critiqued by several writers (see Moore 2007; Owen 2007b).

8. The Art/Anthropology Binary

1 The work of anthropologist Baldwin Spencer and ethnologist Francis Gillen had a considerable impact on the development of a range of seminal human and social scientific literatures premised on evolutionist theories of human development, including the writings of Freud, Marx, Durkheim, Mauss, Engels and Frazer. This attention was due in large part to the wide circulation of *The Native Tribes of Central Australia*, an account of Aranda (also spelt Arrernte and Arunta) society in central Australia (Spencer and Gillen, 1899). Spencer and Gillen's sustained fieldwork meant that the book distinguished itself from the composite theories produced by so-called 'armchair' anthropologists and, along with future works by the pair, clarified the purpose and methods of the discipline of sociocultural anthropology (Kuklick 2006, 537–42). Their ability to gather information from Aranda people had a lot to do with Gillen's status as sub-protector of Aborigines (and thus distributor of rations). Aboriginal people were also friendly to Gillen as a result of his 1891 arrest (as Alice Springs special magistrate) of Constable Willshire, who had led many deadly 'dispersal' expeditions in the area during the 1880s (Jones 1995).

   As Stanner points out, the European scholars who drew from Spencer and Gillen's work 'fastened on the aborigines a reputation of extraordinary primitivity' (1968, 35–37; see also Miller 1994; 1995). For example, James Frazer's *The Golden Bough*, an influential global survey of mythology and belief systems, contains the following extraordinary image:

   > Here, then, in the secluded heart of the most secluded continent the scientific inquirer might reasonably expect to find the savage in his very lowest depths, to detect humanity in the chrysalis stage, to mark the first blind gropings of our race after freedom and light (2010 [1890], 799).

   Frazer was a close friend of Spencer's: he championed his work in Europe and was instrumental in bringing his writings to publication (Mulvaney and Calaby 1985). Similarly, Freud's *Totem and Taboo* (1985 [1913]), which draws on the writings of Frazer and Spencer and Gillen, proposes that to some degree prehistoric man remains 'our contemporary' in the persona of the 'savage' who offers 'a well-preserved picture of an early stage of our own development'. He identifies Aboriginal Australians as the appropriate starting point for the book's exegesis, because they were 'the most backward and miserable of savages' (53–54).
2 Anthropologists were extraordinarily proactive in bringing Aboriginal art to the attention of the public and showing it to be worthy of aesthetic engagement (McLean 2011a, 22–24; Smith 2006, 17–19; Philip Jones 1988; 2011a). Anthropologists like Charles Mountford, A. P. Elkin and Frederick McCarthy were instrumental in staging early exhibitions of Aboriginal art outside of museums, argued for Aboriginal art's quality as art in a range of forums and had close relationships with modern artists and intellectuals, including artists Margaret Preston and Frances Derham in Australia and

in Britain the painter James Cant and the influential art historian and critic Herbert Read. See McCarthy (1952), Smith (1961), Read (1957), Mountford (1950, 1954) and Cant (1950). A. P. Elkin also assisted the Czech artist, writer and amateur ethnographer Karel Kupka who visited Australia several times to collect Aboriginal art for European museums and conduct research for the seminal primitive art text *Dawn of Art* (Kupka 1965; Elkin 1949; McMillan 2005). Anthropologists Ronald Berndt and Catherine Berndt and Leonard Adam wrote about Aboriginal art in the literary journal *Meanjin* (Berndt and Berndt 1950; Berndt 1951; Adam 1950) and the avant-garde art journal *Angry Penguins* (Adam 1944).

3   The art critic Robert Hughes echoed Preston and Tuckson's emphasis on form in his 1960 review of Tuckson's show: 'The barks can certainly be enjoyed as design; I can think of no large exhibition at the Gallery in recent years, except the French and Italian shows, which presented so huge and varied a vocabulary of unsuspected forms as this one' (1960, 23). Artist and critic James Gleeson offered praise along similar lines (Tuckson 1964, 63).

4   See also Myers (1998) for an extended discussion of these issues with reference to the disagreements that surrounded the 1993 exhibition *La peinture des aborigènes d'Australie* at the Musée National des Arts d'Afrique et d'Océanie in Paris.

5   Through a relatively recent process of external and internal critique, the spirit of which is conveyed in Levi-Strauss's statement earlier, anthropology has been to some extent forgiven, in part because anthropologists align themselves with the powerless and advocate for the interests of the minority groups with which they work (Kulick 2006; Sutton 2005).

6   See Sutton (1990; 1992a); Maughan et al. (1988) and Myers (2002, 241–42).

7   This is true of the work of R E A, Fiona Foley, Brook Andrew, Danie Mellor, Yhonnie Scarce and Judy Watson.

8   Brenda L. Croft speaks to this fraught history when she states that '[p]hoto-media and moving image provide Indigenous artists with the agency to re-present our stories, or dreams, our desires, our (literal and metaphorical) reflections as we see fit, not as others see (or do not see) us' (2012, 40).

9   Indigenous scholar and writer Ian Anderson (2003) offers an enlightening reflexive account of the experience of juxtaposing his subjective sense of his Aboriginal identity with expert ethnographic writings on Aboriginality. See also the writings of Indigenous artist Gordon Bennett (1993; 2011).

10   See Smith (2006, particularly 13–14; Lowish 2005; Thomas 2011) for discussions that indicate that Australian art historical scholarship has become politicized by debates around the recognition of Indigenous people's art, identity and status.

Part IV. Aboriginal Art, Money and the Market

1   For valuable insights into the development of the Aboriginal art market, see Altman (2005a), Johnson (2010) and Myers (2002). See also Newstead (2014) for a rich historical and biographical account of the market from a dealer's perspective.

2   Sotheby's success can to a great degree be attributed to the extraordinary rise in value of Papunya boards that had been painted in the 1970s (Johnson 2010). Serendipity played its part here. In most cases the boards had not been valued or exhibited as fine art but had rather been 'unearthed', as Tim Klingender (who instigated Sotheby's sales of Aboriginal art under the banner of contemporary art) described, 'in people's caravans

and under their beds and in cupboards and in the houses of people who'd worked as missionaries or nurses or policemen or whatever [...]' (Byrne 2004, 38). This meant they surfaced in the secondary fine arts market as just-discovered masterpieces, sanctified by a prestigious auction house during a period of economic prosperity.

3 The Aboriginal art auction market had grown from a value of $666,000 in 1988 to $26,455,000 at its peak in 2007; however, 2007 was an anomalous year for both the Aboriginal and the wider Australian art market. The 2006 result of $16,540,000 is a truer reflection of the upward curve in Aboriginal art sales value over that period. The value of the Aboriginal art auction market in 2013 was $11,094,000, in 2014 it was $5,694,000, and in 2015 it was $12,795 (Australian Art Auction Sales, 2016).

4 A German collector of historic bark paintings was so admiring of this presentation that he told me in our interview that he wished Sotheby's would create a 'catalogue' of his collection exclusively, as if the sales catalogue was as reverential a format as an art monograph.

5 Such practices were not problematic from the perspective of Aboriginal law in the Western and Central Desert, so long as the contributions took place under the direction of the artist who had authority over the depicted Dreaming narrative (Johnson 2000; Nicholls 2002; Myers 2005). Moreover, collectivized production is the very means by which younger artists are mentored by senior painters in communities. Nevertheless, a legacy of these scandals has been the widespread suppression of these practices in Aboriginal art discourses and curatorship (though the emphasis placed on collaboration in recent exhibitions like *Martu* at Sydney's Museum of Contemporary Art may signal a change [Davis 2014; see in particular Carty and Taylor 2014]).

6 See, for instance, the funding of dialysis units in Kintore by Sotheby's auctions in 2000 and 2007 (Ahmed 2007). See also the 'Ochre – Supporting Indigenous Health through Art' auction 2008, which raised money for the Menzies School of Health in Melbourne (Mossgreen Auctions 2008).

9. Ethics and Exploitation in the Aboriginal Art Market

1 There was a notable absence of artists' voices in the submissions (though senators did visit some artists in remote areas and a handful of artists participated in the public hearings).

2 For literature that documents and debates these issues, see Petitjean (2000), Warakurna Artists (2006), Eccles (2005; 2006) and Lendon 2011 (including the correspondence that follows his essay).

3 Indeed they date back to the 1989 Review of the Aboriginal Arts and Crafts Industry (Altman et al. 1989; Schwartz 1989; Johnson 2003, 166–67).

4 In one controversial case an emerging 'star' artist, Irruntju painter Tommy Watson, painted work for a dealership that was then sold directly through an auction house, by-passing the primary market (Eccles 2005).

5 In response to the controversies over fakes, many business-oriented art dealers routinely document the production process with photos and video to authenticate the work produced. Fine arts dealers never do this because their integrity is unquestioned. The paradoxical effect has been that the existence of such documentation has come to signal unconscionable dealing rather than the absence of it.

6 The exceptions have been a few fine arts dealers [.of' stellar reputation who have represented an Aboriginal artist on an individual basis.

7 ANKAAA stands for the Association of Northern, Kimberley and Arnhem Aboriginal Artists.

8 Ben Korman's (2006) submission to the 2007 Senate Inquiry provides an illustration of this phenomenon, in which he mention two artists who fit this description: George Ward Tjungarrayi and Ronnie Tjamptajinpa. See also Hills (2006) and Finnane (2012).

9 The exhibition *The Real Gloria Petyarre: An Honest Survey*, staged in 2010 by Utopia Art Sydney, provides a useful example of a fine arts dealer attempting to manage the repercussions of this kind of disloyalty. Gloria Petyarre is one of the most widely known and traded Aboriginal artists with an easily recognisable, decorative aesthetic. While Utopia Art Sydney has represented Gloria Petyarre since the 1980s, her work is sold through dozens of other vendors. It is also the case that her particular style has been emulated by many other artists. The title of the show reveals an effort by art dealer Christopher Hodges to elevate a select few pieces above the mass of works associated with entrepreneurial dealers, which he casts as false (not 'honest') and irrelevant (not the 'real' Gloria) (Meachem 2010; see also Fisher 2014 for a more elaborate discussion of the distribution of Petyarre's works).

10 It is also widely known that there have been cases of significant malpractice in the art centre system (see for instance Wright 2011). It must further be noted that fine art dealers engaged opportunistically in the Aboriginal art boom, and relaxed the standards customarily adopted in the mainstream fine arts market. The recurrent appearance of works of Aboriginal fine art in Sotheby's auctions, when they had been sold only a few years prior on the primary market, attests to this. As Velthuis notes, fine art dealers usually have a keen eye for buyers who are motivated by a quest for profit (at least in the short term) and often refuse to sell to them. This is because in their company, 'the art work fails to get rid of its commodity character' (2005, 43–44). The erratic market careers of Aboriginal artists can be attributed to many factors, but it can certainly be attributed in part to the neglect of the principles of patience and discretion on which the accrual of fine arts value normally depends.

10. 'Aboriginal Mass Culture' and the Cultural Industries

1 See Thomas (1999), Black's (2008, 165–67) discussion of the role of Aboriginal themes and design in Qantas Airways' highly nationalistic branding and marketing projects of the 1950s and 1960s. See also Factor (2000) for a relevant discussion of 1950s Aboriginal-style commodities, and Maynard (1999) for a discussion of Aboriginal-inspired fashion in the 1970s that accorded with the Whitlam government's 'new nationalism'.

2 For instance non-Indigenous art writer Ann Stephen wrote:
   The Aboriginal movement in a series of symbolic acts […] ha[s] forced us to see the land not as our national heritage but as a series of frontiers and sites of invasion. However white Australian culture has sought to deflect and absorb the Black movement's radical critique mythologising 'Aboriginality' as some timeless essence. This latest form of colonisation is evident in forms of [sic] diverse as high art, rock clips, high fashion and tourism. (1984, 28)

3 The changing regard for appropriation at this time was illustrated by the abandonment of an Aboriginal-inspired swimwear line created by swimwear company Speedo for Australian competitors in the 1988 Olympic Games. Designer Gloria Smythe had based the designs on drawings she had produced in the 1940s when the curriculum at the art school she attended directed students to make designs based on Aboriginal objects on display at the Australian Museum (Powerhouse Museum 2010).

4 This case involved substantial 'cultural damages' being paid to the artists concerned and the recognition that a commercial design derived from a small part of an Aboriginal work was as serious an infringement as designs that were complete copies.

5 Queensland Aboriginal Creations in the city of Brisbane, one of the Government Company galleries, historically 'employed Aboriginal people to paint copies of bark paintings from various publications' (Altman et al. 1989, 288).

6 See, for instance, the 'we have survived' series of posters produced in 1988 (NMA 2012b).

7 See Debenham (1995) and Qantas (2012). Balarinji's other clients have included Bank of America, British Airways, Lendlease, Renault France, Coca Cola Atlanta and City of Sydney.

8 The project coordinator for the *Framework* was Colin Mercer, an academic and cultural policy planner and consultant affiliated with the cultural industries and creative industries turn in cultural policy in Australia and other countries. Mercer also conducted a review into ATSIC's Arts and Crafts Industry Support Strategy (which subsidised the art centres) in 1997, which articulated a similar set of concerns framed by a cultural industries approach (Mercer 1997).

9 Bardon, who trained at the National Art School in Sydney in the mid-1960s when abstraction was the dominant aesthetic, was also instrumental in installing abstract expressionism as the favoured idiom through which the paintings could be appreciated as both aesthetically strong *and* authentic (Smith 2006, 24). He was inspired by Herbert Read's concept of hapticity and made eloquent arguments about Papunya painting being an embodied and uniquely conceptual kind of painting that was not reducible to visual or pictorial decision making (Bardon 1999 [1991], 125–36; Johnson 2010, 116–17). He also directed the artists to remove 'whitefella' elements from their work when they had initially included realistic forms and figures (Bardon 2000; Michaels 1988, 152–53).

REFERENCES

Aboriginal Arts Board, ed. 1973. *National Seminar on Aboriginal Arts*. Canberra: Aboriginal Arts Board, Australian Council for the Arts.

Aboriginal Arts Board. 1975. *Aboriginal Art from Papunya, Central Australia*. Pamphlet. Aboriginal Arts and Crafts Australia Pty Ltd & Aboriginal Arts Board.

Australian Broadcasting Corporation. 1996. *Frontier: Stories from White Australia's Forgotten War*. Documentary series. Sydney: ABC TV documentaries.

Acker, Tim. 2008. 'Aboriginal Art: It's a Complicated Thing'. *Artlink* 28, no. 3: 64–68.

Acker, Tim, Lisa Stefanoff, and Alice Woodhead. 2013. 'Aboriginal and Torres Strait Islander Art Economies Project: Literature Review'. Working paper. Alice Springs: Ninti One Limited.

Acker, Tim and Gabrielle Sullivan, 2014. 'More than a place to paint: the complicated business of Art Centres' [Special issue: Red dirt research in remote Australia]. *Journal of Australian Indigenous Issues* 17, no. 4: 168–72.

Adam, Leonhard. 1944. 'Has Australian Aboriginal Art a Future?' *Angry Penguins*, no. 6: 42–50.

———. 1950. Review of *Art in Arnhem Land*. *Meanjin* 9, no. 3: 231–34.

Adams, Bruce. 1983. 'Presence and Absence: The Gallery as Other Place'. *Art & Text*, no. 10: 26–33.

———. 1987. 'Traversing the Difficult Territory of Aboriginal Art'. *The Sydney Morning Herald*, 16 January.

Adams, Philip. 1996. 'Shame of the White Man'. In *Copyrites: Aboriginal Art in the Age of Reproductive Technologies*, by Vivien Johnson, 12. Sydney: National Indigenous Arts Advocacy Association & Macquarie University.

Adorno, Theodor W. 1978 [1967]. 'Cultural Criticism and Society'. In *Culture and Mass Culture*, edited by Peter Davidson, Rolf Meyersohn, and Edward Shils, 105–22. Cambridge: Chadwyck-Healey Ltd.

———. 1991 [1938]. 'On the Fetish Character in Music and the Regression of Listening'. In *Adorno: The Culture Industry*, edited by J. M. Bernstein, 29–60. London: Routledge.

Ah Kee, Vernon, and Glenn Barkley. 2009. 'Interview'. In *Born in This Skin*, 19–23. Brisbane: Institute of Modern Art.

Ahmed, Nabila. 2007. 'Sotheby's Makes Sure Aboriginal Artists are not Deserted'. *The Age*, 2 February. Online: http://www.theage.com.au/articles/2007/02/01/116991947215 6.html (accessed 3 May 2008).

AIAM100 (Australian Indigenous Art Market top 100). 2015. Website. Online: http:// aiam100.com/index.php (accessed 25 November 2014).

Alexander, Jeffrey C. 2003. *The Meanings of Social Life: A Cultural Sociology*. New York: Oxford University Press.

————. 2004. 'Cultural Pragmatics: Social Performance Between Ritual and Strategy'. *Sociological Theory* 22, no. 4: 527–573.

Allam, Lorena. 2005. 'Black Art Gold Rush'. *ABC Background Briefing*, 25 September. Online: http://www.abc.net.au/radionational/programs/backgroundbriefing/black-art-gold-rush/3354282 (accessed 4 November 2011).

Allas, Tess. 2008. 'Richard Bell'. *Design and Art of Australia Online*. Online: http://www.daao.org.au/bio/richard-bell/#artist_biography (accessed 25 January 2010).

————. 2010. 'History is a Weapon: Fiona Foley History Teacher'. *Artlink – Special Indigenous Issue Blak on Blak* 30, no. 1: 56–61.

Alston, Richard, Gary Hardgrave and Tony Abbott. 2003. 'Building a Stronger Indigenous Art Industry'. Government media release. Online: http://www.dbcde.gov.au/Article/0,,0_4–2_4008–4_116986,00.html (accessed 25 January 2009).

Altman, Jon. 1988. 'The Economic Basis for Cultural Reproduction'. In *The Inspired Dread: Life as Art in Aboriginal Australia*, edited by Margie West, 48–55. Brisbane: Queensland Art Gallery.

————. 2000a. 'Marketing Aboriginal Art'. In *The Oxford Companion to Aboriginal Art and Culture*, edited by Margo Neale and Sylvia Kleinert, 461–66. Melbourne: Oxford University Press.

————. 2000b. 'Aboriginal Art Centres and NACISS: An Appraisal of Performance Based on Financial Statements'. In *The Art and Craft Centre Story: Volume II, Summary and Recommendations*, edited by Felicity Wright and Frances Morphy, 74–103. Canberra: ATSIC.

————. 2005a. 'Brokering Aboriginal Art: A Critical Perspective on Marketing, Institutions and the State'. In *Kenneth Myer Lecture in Arts and Entertainment Management*, edited by Ruth Rentschler, 1–24. Geelong, VIC: Centre for Leisure Management Research, Bowater School of Management and Marketing, Deakin University.

————. 2005b. 'From Mumeka to Basel: John Mawurndjul's Artistic Odyssey'. In *Rarrk John Mawurndjul: Journey Through Time in Northern Australia*, edited by Christian Kaufmann, and Museum Tinguely, 30–39. Belair, South Australia: Crawford House Publishing.

————. 2006. *Submission to Senate Committee Inquiry into Australia's Indigenous Visual Arts and Craft Sector*. Canberra: Parliament of Australia. Online: http://caepr.anu.edu.au/system/files/Publications/topical/Altman_Arts.pdf (accessed 29 November 2013).

————. 2011. 'A Genealogy of "Demand Sharing": From Pure Anthropology to Public Policy. In *Ethnography and the Production of Anthropological Knowledge: Essays in Honour of Nicolas Peterson*, edited by Yasmine Musharbash and Marcus Barber, 209–22. Canberra: ANU E Press.

————. 2013. 'The Escalating Challenges of Doing Indigenous Arts Business in Remote Australia in the 21st Century'. Paper presented at Remote Indigenous Enterprises in Arts and Tourism: Research Exchange, Canberra, 31 October–1 November.

Altman, Jon, Boyd Hunter, Sally Ward, and Felicity Wright. 2002. 'Some Competition and Consumer Issues in the Indigenous Visual Arts Industry'. Discussion Paper no. 235. Canberra: Centre for Aboriginal Economic Policy Research, The Australian National University. Online: http://caepr.anu.edu.au/sites/default/files/Altman/Chapters/2002_CompetitionAndConsumer.pdf (accessed 6 June 2009).

Altman, Jon, Chris McGuigan, and Peter Yu. 1989. *The Aboriginal Arts and Crafts Industry: Report of the Review Committee, Department of Aboriginal Affairs*. Canberra: Australian Government Publishing Service.

Altman, Jon, and Melinda Hinkson, eds. 2007. *Coercive Reconciliation*. North Carlton: Arena Publications Association.

Altman, Jon, and Melinda Hinkson. 2010. 'Very Risky Business: The Quest to Normalise Remote-living Aboriginal people'. In *Risk, Welfare and Work*, edited by Greg Marston, Jeremy Moss and John Quiggin, 186–211. Carlton, VIC: Melbourne University Press.

Altman, Jon, and Seán Kerins, eds. 2012. *People on Country: Vital Landscapes, Indigenous Futures*. Sydney: The Federation Press.

Altman, Jon, and Taylor, Luke, eds. 1991. *Marketing Aboriginal Art in the 1990s*. Canberra: Aboriginal Studies Press.

Altman, Jon, and Tim Rowse. 2005. 'Indigenous Affairs'. In *Ideas and Influence: Social Science and Public Policy in Australia*, edited by Peter Saunders, and James Walter, 159–77. Sydney: University of New South Wales Press. Amato, Sarah. 2006. 'Quai Branly Museum: Representing France After Empire'. *Race & Class* 47, no. 4: 46–65.

Anderson, W. 2002. *The Cultivation of Whiteness*. Carlton: Melbourne University Press.

Anderson, Christopher. 1991. 'Of Myth and Symbol, the Art in the Everyday'. In *Aboriginal Art and Spirituality*, edited by Rosemary Crumlin and Anthony Knight, 113–17. North Blackburn, VIC: Dove.

Anderson, Christopher, and Francoise Dussart. 1988. 'Dreamings in Acrylic: Western Desert Art'. In *Dreamings: The Art of Aboriginal Australia*, edited by Peter Sutton, 89–142. Ringwood, VIC: Viking (in association with Asia Society Galleries, New York).

Anderson, Ian. 2003. 'Black Bit, White Bit'. In *Blacklines*, edited by Michelle Grossman, 43–51. Carlton: University of Melbourne Press.

Annear, Judy. 1986. 'Dust of Dreams in Biennale of Sydney'. In *Origins Originality + Beyond – The Sixth Biennale of Sydney*, edited by Biennale of Sydney, 66. Sydney: The Biennale of Sydney Limited.

Araeen, Rasheed. 1987 [1985]. 'From Primitivism to Ethnic Arts'. *Third Text* 1, no. 1: 6–25.

Araeen, Rasheed, Sean Cubitt, and Ziauddin Sardar. 2002. *The Third Text Reader on Art, Culture and Theory*. London: Continuum.

Atkinson, Judy. 2002. *Trauma Trails, Recreating Song Lines: The Transgenerational Effects of Trauma in Indigenous Communities*. North Melbourne: Spinifex Press.

ATO (Australian Tax Office). 2008. *Is Your Organisation a Public Benevolent Institution?* Online: http://www.ato.gov.au/nonprofit/content.aspx?doc=/content/26553.htm&page=2 (accessed 12 April 2009).

ATSIC (Aboriginal and Torres Strait Islander Commission). 1995. *Cultural Policy Framework*. Canberra: ATSIC.

Attwood, Bain. 2003. *Rights for Aborigines*. Crows Nest, Sydney: Allen & Unwin.

———. 2005. *Telling the Truth about Aboriginal History*. Sydney: Allen & Unwin.

Austin-Broos, Diane J. 2011. *A Different Inequality: The Politics of Debate about Remote Aboriginal Australia*. Crows Nest, NSW: Allen & Unwin.

Australian Art Auction Sales by Artist Source. 2016. *Australian Art Sales Digest*. Online: http://www.aasd.com.au/index.cfm/artist-nationality-totals/ (accessed 3 February 2016).

Australian Art Collector. 2009. *Guide to Aboriginal Art Centres*. Ultimo, NSW: Gadfly Media.

———. 2010. *Guide to Indigenous Art Centres and How to Ethically Collect Indigenous Art*. Ultimo, NSW: Gadfly Media.

Australia Council. 1974. *Australia Council for the Arts Second Annual Report*. North Sydney: Australia Council.

———. 1977. *Australia Council for the Arts Annual Report 1976/1977*. North Sydney: Australia Council.

————. 1979. *Aboriginal Arts Board Program Booklet*. North Sydney: Arts Information Program of the Australia Council.

————. 1982. *Aboriginal Arts Board Program Booklet*. North Sydney: Australia Council.

————. 1984. *Australia Council Annual Report 1983/1984*. North Sydney: Australia Council, Commonwealth of Australia.

————. 1985a. *Aboriginal Arts Board Programs of Assistance*. North Sydney: Australia Council.

————. 1985b. *Australia Council Annual Report 1984/1985*. North Sydney: Australia Council, Commonwealth of Australia.

————. 1986. *Aboriginal Arts Board Programs of Assistance*. North Sydney: Aboriginal Arts Board of the Australia Council.

————. 2014. *A culturally ambitious nation. Strategic Plan 2014–2019*. Online: http://www.australiacouncil.gov.au/workspace/uploads/strategic-plan.pdf (accessed 11 February 2015).

Australian Heritage Commission. 1998. *The Fourth National Indigenous Heritage Art Award*. Canberra: Australian Heritage Commission.

————. 2000. *The Art of Place: The Fifth Indigenous Heritage Art Award*. Canberra: Australian Heritage Commission.

Australian Institute of Aboriginal Studies. 1983. 'After the Tent Embassy: Aboriginal History since 1972 in Black and White Photographs'. *Art Network*, no. 9: 30–31.

Banchflower, Brian. 1988. 'Letter to Editor'. *Praxis M*, no. 20: 58.

Bardon, Geoffrey. 1999 [1991]. *Papunya Tula: Art of the Western Desert*. Marlston, S. A.: J. B. Books.

————. 2000. 'The Papunya Tula Movement'. In *The Oxford Companion to Aboriginal Art and Culture*, edited by Margo Neale and Sylvia Kleinert, 208–210. Melbourne: Oxford University Press.

Bardon, Geoffrey, and James Bardon. 2004. *Papunya: A Place Made after the Story: The Beginnings of the Western Desert Painting Movement*. Carlton, VIC: Melbourne University Press.

Barunga. 2012. 'Barunga statement'. *Barunga Sports and Culture Festival Website*. Online: http://www.barungafestival.com.au/statement.html (accessed 4 February 2014).

Batty, Phillip. 2007. 'Selling Emily: Confessions of a White Advisor'. *Artlink* 27, no. 2: 68–71.

————. 2008. 'The Gooch Effect: Rodney Gooch and the Art of the Art Advisor'. In *Gooch's Utopia: Collected Works from the Central Desert*, edited by Fiona Salmon, 26–31. Adelaide: Flinders University Art Museum.

Baume, Nicholas. 1988. 'Learning from the Dreamtime'. *Art & Australia* 26, no. 1: 77–83.

————. 1989. 'The Interpretation of Dreamings: The Australian Aboriginal Acrylic Movement'. *Art & Text*, no. 33: 110–20.

Beckett, Jeremy. 1988. 'The Past in the Present; the Present in the Past: Constructing a National Aboriginality'. In *Past and Present: The Construction of Aboriginality*, edited by Jeremy Beckett, 191–212. Canberra: Aboriginal Studies Press.

Behrendt, Larissa. 2003. *Achieving Social Justice*. Annandale, NSW: Federation Press.

Belk, Russell W. 2007. 'Consumption, Mass Consumption, and Consumer Culture'. In *Blackwell Encyclopedia of Sociology*, edited by George Ritzer, 737–45. Malden, MA: Blackwell.

Belk, Russell W., and Groves, Ronald. 1999. 'Marketing and the Multiple Meanings of Australian Aboriginal Art'. *Journal of Macromarketing* 19, no. 1: 20–33.

Bell, Diane, and Topsy Naparrula Nelson. 1989. 'Speaking about Rape Is Everyone's Business.' *Women's Studies International Forum* 12 (4): 403–416.

Bell, Richard. 2002. 'Bell's Theorem of Aboriginal Art: It's a White Thing'. *The Koori History Website*. Online: http://www.kooriweb.org/foley/great/art/bell.html (accessed 3 April 2012).

Benjamin, Roger. 1990. 'Aboriginal Art: Exploitation or Empowerment?'. *Art in America* 78, no. 7: 73–81.

———. 2000. 'The Brush with Words: Criticism and Aboriginal Art'. In *The Oxford Companion to Aboriginal Art and Culture*, edited by Margo Neale and Sylvia Kleinert, 446–70. Melbourne: Oxford University Press.

Bennett, Gordon. 1993. 'Aesthetics and Iconography: An Artist's Approach'. In *Aratjara: Art of the First Australians: Traditional and Contemporary Works by Aboriginal and Torres Strait Islander Artists*, edited by Bernhard Lüthi, and Gary Lee, 85–91. Dusseldorf and Cologne: Kunstsammlung Nordrhein-Westfalen & DuMont Buchverlag.

———. 2011. 'The Manifest Toe'. In *How Aborigines Invented the Idea of Contemporary Art*, edited by Ian McLean, 155–57. Brisbane & Sydney: Institute of Modern Art & Power Publications.

Bennett, Tony. 2013. *Making Culture, Changing Society*. Abingdon, Oxon: Routledge.

Berndt, Ronald. 1951. 'Aboriginal Ochre-Moulded Heads from Western Arnhem Land'. *Meanjin* 10, no. 4: 350–53.

Berndt, Ronald, ed. 1964. *Australian Aboriginal Art*. Sydney: Ure Smith.

———. 1983. 'A Living Aboriginal Art: The Changing Inside and Outside Contexts'. In *Aboriginal Arts and Crafts and the Market*, edited by Peter Loveday and Peter Cooke, 29–36. Darwin: The Australian National University North Australia Research Unit.

Berndt, Ronald, and Catherine Berndt. 1950. 'Aboriginal Art in Central-Western Northern Territory'. *Meanjin* 9, no. 3: 183–88.

Berrell, Nina. 2009. 'Inroads Offshore: The International Exhibition Program of the Aboriginal Arts Board, 1973–1980'. *reCollections 4*, no. 1: 13–30.

Biddle, Jennifer. 2006. *Breasts, Bodies, Canvas*. Sydney: University of New South Wales Press.

———. 2012, 'Making (not taking) history: Yiwarra Kuju The Canning Stock Route'. *Art Monthly Australia*, August, no. 8: 32 – 36.

———. 2013. 'Provocations from the Margins: The Production and Curation of the Warburton Arts Project'. In *Tu Di Shen Ti: Our Land Our Body*, pp. 16–31. Phoenix Science Press Ltd and Waburton Arts Project. Online: http://www.warburtonarts.com/english/essays.html?ex=2&es=4 (accessed 27 June 2014).

Biddle, Jennifer, and Lisa Stefanoff. 2015. 'What Is Same but Different and Why Does It Matter?' *Cultural Studies Review* 21 (1): 97–120.

Biennale of Sydney. 1979. *European Dialogue: The Third Biennale of Sydney at the Art Gallery of New South Wales, the Australian Centre for Photography and Other Venues*. Sydney: Biennale of Sydney.

———. 1986. *Origins Originality + Beyond: 16 May – 6 July 1986, Art Gallery of New South Wales, Art Gallery Road, Sydney, PIER 2/3 Walsh Bay, Sydney*. Sydney: Sixth Biennale of Sydney, 1986.

Birch, Tony. 2003. 'Nothing Has Changed: The Making and Unmaking of Koori Culture'. In *Blacklines: Contemporary Critical Writings by Indigenous Australians*, edited by Michele Grossman, 145–58. Carlton, VIC: Melbourne University Press.

Black, Prudence S. 2008. 'Lines of Flight: The Design History of Qantas Flight Attendants' Uniforms'. PhD diss., University of Sydney.

Black, Roman. 1964. *Old and New Australian Aboriginal Art*. Sydney: Angus & Robertson.

Boland, Michaela. 2010. 'Aboriginal Art Code Hits Snag'. *The Australian*, 29 November. Online: http://www.theaustralian.com.au/news/nation/aboriginal-art-code-hits-snag/story-e6frg6nf-1225962382741 (accessed 12 June 2012).

Borham, Susan. 2006. *Submission to Senate Committee Inquiry into Australia's Indigenous Visual Arts and Craft Sector*. Canberra: Parliament of Australia. Online: http://www.aph. gov.au/Parliamentary_Business/Committees/Senate_Committees?url=ecita_ ctte/completed_inquiries/2004–07/indigenous_arts/submissions/ AustralianArtCollectorresponse.pdf (accessed 24 June 2012).

Bourdieu, Pierre. 1984. *Distinction: A Social Critique of the Judgement of Taste*. Cambridge, MA: Harvard University Press.

———. 1993. *The Field of Cultural Production: Essays on Art and Literature*. Cambridge, UK: Polity Press.

Bowdler, Cath, ed. 2009. *Colour Country: Art from Roper River*. Wagga Wagga: Wagga Wagga Art Gallery.

Bowler, Anne E. 1997. 'Asylum Art: The Social Construction of an Aesthetic Category'. In *Outsider Art: Contesting Boundaries in Contemporary Culture*, edited by Vera L. Zolberg and Joni M. Cherbo, 11–36. Cambridge: Cambridge University Press.

Bridge, Kim. 2012. 'Understanding "Culture"'. *Share Our Pride, Reconciliation Australia*. Online: http://www.shareourpride.org.au/topics/culture/understanding-culture (accessed 15 November 2013).

Bromfield, David. 1988. 'Landscape into Art: Australia 1950–1986'. *Praxis M*, no. 19: 10–16.

Brophy, Philip. 1984. 'Not the Black and White Artist Show'. *Art Network*, no. 13: 53.

Browning, Daniel. 2010. 'The Politics of Skin: Not Black Enough'. *Artlink – Special Indigenous Issue Blak on Blak* 30, no. 1: 22–27.

Browning, Daniel, and Tess Allas, eds. 2010. 'Blak on Blak'. Special issue. *Artlink* 30, no. 1.

Buku-Larrngay Mulka Centre, and Drill Hall Gallery. 1999. *Saltwater: Yirrkala Bark Paintings of Sea Country: Recognising Indigenous Sea Rights*. Neutral Bay, NSW: Buku-Larrngay Mulka Centre in association with Jennifer Isaacs Publishing.

Burn, Ian. 1983. 'The Australian National Gallery: Populism or a New Cultural Federalism?' *Art Network*, no. 8: 39–43.

———. 1991 [1973]. 'Art is What We Do, Culture Is What We Do to Other Artists'. In *Dialogue: Writings in Art History*, edited by Ian Burn, 131–39. Sydney: Allen & Unwin.

Burn, Ian, and Ann Stephen. 1986. 'Traditional Painter: The Transfiguration of Albert Namatjira'. *Age Monthly Review* 6, no. 7: 10–13.

Burn, Ian, and Ann Stephen. 1992. 'Namatjira's White Mask: A Partial Interpretation'. In *The Heritage of Namatjira*, edited by Jane Hardy, John V. S. Megaw and M. Ruth Megaw, 250–82. Port Melbourne, VIC: William Heinemann.

Burn, Ian, Nigel Lendon, Charles Merewether and Ann Stephen. 1988. *The Necessity of Australian Art: An Essay about Interpretation*. Sydney: Power Publications.

Butler, Rex. 1997. 'The impossible painter'. *Australian Art Collector* (2):42–45.

———. 2003 [1998]. 'Emily Kame Kngwarreye and the Undeconstructible Space of Justice'. In *Art of the Twentieth Century: A Reader*, edited by Jason Gaiger and Paul Wood, 304–318. New Haven & London: Yale University Press.

———. 2010. 'Where to Put Aboriginal Art'. Catalogue Essay for 'Jus' Drawn' exhibition, Linden Centre for Contemporary Art. Online: http://espace.library.uq.edu.au/view/ UQ:215535/proppanow.pdf (accessed 16 October 2014).

———, ed. 2004 [1996]. *What Is Appropriation? An Anthology of Writings on Australian Art in the 1980s and 1990s* (2nd ed.). Brisbane: IMA Publishing.

Butler, Rex, and Andrew . D. S. Donaldson. 2009. 'Outside in: Against a History of Reception'. *Art & Australia* 46, no. 3: 432–37.

Byrne, Jennifer. 2004. 'Tim Klingender'. *The Bulletin* 122, no. 6435: 36–38.

Cadzow, Jane. 1987. 'The Art Boom of Dreamtime'. *The Weekend Australian Magazine,* 14–15 March.

———. 1995. 'The Emily Industry'. *The Sydney Morning Herald, Good Weekend Magazine,* 5 August.

Calinescu, Matei. 2006. *Five Faces of Modernity: Modernism, Avant–Garde, Decadence, Kitsch, Postmodernism.* Durham: Duke University Press.

Campbell, Steven, ed. 2009. *Conversations, Insights and Anecdotes: Proceedings of the Inaugural Cairns Indigenous Art Fair Symposium Centre of Contemporary Arts, Cairns, Queensland, 21 August 2009.* Brisbane: Arts Queensland, Department of the Premier and Cabinet.

Cameron, Dan. 1988. 'Showdown at the Southern Cross'. *Artlink* 8, no. 3: 10–14.

CAR (Council for Aboriginal Reconciliation). 2000. *Roadmap for Reconciliation.* Online: http://www.austlii.edu.au/au/orgs/car/roadmap/ (accessed 5 July 2009).

Carnegie, Margaret. 1991. Foreword to *Aboriginal Art and Spirituality,* edited by Rosemary Crumlin and Anthony Knight, 5. North Blackburn, VIC: Dove.

Carnegie, Margaret, Janet Holmes à Court and Ruth Hall. 1991. 'Collectors and Enthusiasts'. In *Aboriginal Art and Spirituality.* Rosemary Crumlin, and Anthony Knight, 124–27. North Blackburn, VIC: Dove.

Cant, James. 1950. *Australian Aboriginal Art: Paintings by James Cant.* London: Berkeley Galleries.

Carroll, Alison. 1984. *The Centre, Works on Paper by Contemporary Australian Artists.* Adelaide: Board of the Art Gallery of South Australia.

Carter, David. 1994. 'Future Pasts'. In *The Abundant Culture: Meaning and Significance in Everyday Life,* edited by David J. Headon, Joy W. Hooton and Donald Horne, 3–15. St Leonards, Sydney: Allen & Unwin.

Carter, Paul. 2010 [1987]. *The Road to Botany Bay: An Exploration of Landscape and History.* Minneapolis: University of Minnesota Press.

Carty, John. 2011. 'Creating Country: Abstraction, Economics and the Social Life of Style in Balgo Art'. PhD diss., The Australian National University.

Carty, John, and Ngalangka Nola Taylor. 2014. 'You Don't Go out in Country by Yourself.' In *Martu,* edited by Anna Davis, 30–37. Sydney: Museum of Contemporary Art.

Caruana, Wally. 2006. *Caruana Fine Art: Submission to Senate Committee Inquiry into Australia's Indigenous Visual Arts and Craft Sector.* Canberra: Parliament of Australia. Online: http://www.aph.gov.au/Parliamentary_Business/Committees/Senate_ Committees?url=ecita_ctte/completed_inquiries/2004–07/indigenous_arts/ submissions/sub31.pdf (accessed 24 June 2012).

———. 2012. *Aboriginal Art.* 3rd ed. London: Thames & Hudson.

Caruana, Wally, and Jennifer Isaacs, eds. 1990. *Art Monthly Australia Supplement: The Land, the City – the Emergence of Urban Aboriginal Art.* Canberra, A.C.T: Art Monthly Australia Pty. Ltd.

Ceresa, Marica. 1997. 'Master Painter Will Settle for a Toyota'. *The Weekend Australian,* 5–6 July.

Chatwin, Bruce. 1988. *The Songlines.* London: Picador.

Chubb, Claudette, and Nancy Sever, eds. 2009. *Indigenous Art at the Australian National University.* South Yarra, VIC: Macmillan.

Clark, John, Peter McCallum and Ian Maxwell, eds. 2007. *Australian Arts: Where the Bloody Hell Are You?: Australian Arts in an International Context.* Sydney: Sydney University Press & Research Institute for Humanities and Social Sciences.

Clifford, James. 1988. *The Predicament of Culture: Twentieth-Century Ethnography, Literature, and Art*. London: Harvard University Press.

———. 1991. 'Four Northwest Coast Museums: Travel Reflections'. In *Exhibiting Cultures: The Poetics and Politics of Museum Display*, edited by Ivan Karp and Steven D. Lavine, 212–54. Washington: Smithsonian Institute Press.

———. 2013. *Returns: Becoming Indigenous in the Twenty-First Century*. Cambridge, MA, London: Harvard University Press.

Cocchiara, Guiseppe. 1981 [1952]. *The History of Folklore in Europe*. Philadelphia: Institute for the Study of Human Issues.

Cochrane, Peter, and David Goodman. 1988. 'The Great Australian Journey: Cultural Logic and Nationalism in the Postmodern Era'. *Australian Historical Studies* 23, no. 91: 21–44.

Coleman, Elisabeth Burnes. 2001. 'Aboriginal Painting: Identity and Authenticity'. *The Journal of Aesthetics and Art Criticism* 59, no. 4: 385–402.

Commonwealth of Australia. 1983. Parliamentary Debates. House of Representatives. No. 134, Thursday 8 December.

Cook, Sam. 2013. 'Dancing the triple bottom line'. *Artlink* 33, no. 4: 38–41.

Coombs, Annie. E. 1991. 'Ethnography and the Formation of National and Cultural Identities'. In *The Myth of Primitivism: Perspectives on Art*, edited by Susan Hiller, 190–213. London and New York: Routledge.

———. 2003. *History after Apartheid*. Durham, NC: Duke University Press.

Coombs, Herbert C., Barrie G. Dexter and Lester R. Hiatt. 1982. 'The Outstations Movement in Aboriginal Australia'. In *Politics and History in Band Societies*, edited by Eleanor Leacock and Richard Lee, 427–39. Cambridge: Cambridge University Press.

Cooper, Charles. 1987. 'Metaphysical Graffiti'. Masters diss., City Art Institute.

Copeland, Julie, and Colin Laverty. 2008. 'Beyond Sacred'. Radio interview with Colin Laverty. *Artworks*, 16 November. ABC Radio National. Online: http://www.abc.net. au/radionational/programs/artworks/beyond-sacred/3172420 (accessed 14 January 2009).

Cosic, Miriam. 2004. 'Pizzi's World View'. *The Weekend Australian*, 15–16 May.

Coslovich, Gabriella. 2003. 'Aboriginal Works and Artful Dodgers'. *The Age*, 20 September. Online: http://www.theage.com.au/articles/2003/09/19/1063625217241.html (accessed 24 June 2010).

Coffs Harbour City Council. 2009. *Arts and Cultural Development Plan 2006–2009*. Online: http://www.coffsharbour.nsw.gov.au/our-community/Documents/Arts_Cultural_ Development_Plan_2006–12.pdf (accessed 12 October 2013).

Commonwealth Institute. 1988. *Stories of Australian Art*. London: The Institute.

Coutts-Smith, Kenneth. 1982. 'Australian Aboriginal Art'. *Art Network*, no. 7: 52–55.

———. 1991 [1976]. 'Some General Observations on the Problem of Cultural Colonialism'. In *The Myth of Primitivism: Perspectives on Art*, edited by Susan Hiller, 5–18. London: Routledge.

Cowlishaw, Gillian. 1999. *Rednecks, Eggheads and Blackfellas*. Ann Arbour: The University of Michigan Press.

———. 2003. 'Euphemism, Banality, Propaganda: Anthropology, Public Debate and Indigenous Communities.' *Australian Aboriginal Studies* no. 1: 2–18.

———. 2004. *Blackfellas, Whitefellas, and the Hidden Injuries of Race*. Malden, MA: Blackwell.

Cowlishaw, Gillian, Emma Kowal and Tess Lea. 2006. 'Introduction: Double Binds'. In *Moving Anthropology: Critical Indigenous Studies*, edited by Gillian Cowlishaw, Emma Kowal and Tess Lea. Darwin: Charles Darwin University Press.

Craig, B. 1984. 'Non-Violent Land Rights Claims from the Centre' *Artlink* 4, nos. 2 and 3: 19–20.

Craik, Jennifer. 2001. 'Tourism, Culture and National Identity'. In *Culture in Australia: Policies, Publics and Programs*, edited by Tony Bennett and David Carter, 89–113. Cambridge: Cambridge University Press.

———. 2007. *Re-Visioning Arts and Cultural Policy*. Canberra: ANU E Press.

Craik, Jennifer, Glyn Davis and Naomi Sunderland. 2000. 'Cultural Policy and National Identity'. In *The Future of Governance: Policy Choices*, edited by Glyn Davis and Michael Keating, 177–202. St Leonards, Sydney: Allen & Unwin.

Cramer, Sue, ed. 1989. *Postmodernism: A Consideration of the Appropriation of Aboriginal Imagery*. Brisbane: Institute of Modern Art.

CRC-REP (Cooperative Research Centre for Remote Economic Participation). 2012. *Enterprise Development*. Online: http://crc-rep.com/research/enterprise-development (accessed 23 October 2012).

Croft, Brenda L. 1998 [1993]. 'Artist Statement – Brenda L. Croft'. In *Retake: Contemporary Aboriginal and Torres Strait Islander Photography*. National Gallery of Australia. Online: http://nga.gov.au/Retake/artists/00000002.htm (accessed 14 September 2013).

———. 1999. 'Boomalli: from little things big things grow.' In *Painting the land story*, edited by Luke Taylor, 95–118. Canberra: National Museum of Australia.

———, ed. 2007a. *Culture Warriors: National Indigenous Art Triennial*. Canberra: National Gallery of Australia.

———. 2007b. 'To Be Young (At Heart), Gifted and Blak: The Cultural and Political Renaissance in Indigenous Art in Australia'. In *One Sun One Moon: Aboriginal Arts in Australia*, edited by Hetti Perkins and Margie West, 285–92. Sydney: Art Gallery of New South Wales.

———. 2011 [1989]. 'Controlling Our Own Images'. In *How Aborigines Invented the Idea of Contemporary Art*, edited by Ian McLean, 294–95. Brisbane & Sydney: Institute of Modern Art & Power Publications.

———. 2012. 'Changing times, timing changes'. In *Making Change*, edited by Michael Fitzgerald, 29–44. Paddington, NSW: Australian Centre for Photography. Cunneen, Chris. 2001. *Conflict, Politics and Crime: Aboriginal Communities and the Police*. Sydney: Allen & Unwin.

Curran, James. 2004. *The Power of Speech: Australian Prime Ministers Defining the National Image*. Carlton, VIC: Melbourne University Press.

Curthoys, Ann. 2002. *Freedom Ride: A Freedom Rider Remembers*. Sydney: Allen & Unwin.

Curthoys, Ann, and John Docker, eds. 2001. '"Genocide"?: Australian Aboriginal History in International Perspective'. Special issue. *Aboriginal History* 25: 1–172.

Davila, Juan. 1984. 'On Eclecticism'. *Art Network*, no. 13: 50–55.

———. 2004 [1987]. 'Aboriginality: A Lugubrious Game?'. In *What Is Appropriation? An Anthology of Writings on Australian Art in the 1980s and 1990s* (2nd ed.), edited by Rex Butler, 193–95. Brisbane: IMA Publishing.

Davis, Anna. 2014. *Martu*. Sydney: Museum of Contemporary Art.

Davis, Michael. 2007. *Writing Heritage: The Depiction of Indigenous Heritage in European-Australian Writings*. Kew, VIC: Australian Scholarly Publishing.

Debenham, I. 1995. 'Aircraft Model Decorated by Balarinji Studio, 1993–1994'. Powerhouse Museum. Online: http://from.ph/142106 (accessed 4 May 2011).

DECITA Department of Environment, Informational, Technology and the Arts, Senate Standing Committee. 2007. *Official Committee Hansard – Australia's Indigenous Visual Arts and Craft Sector, 9 February 2007, Canberra*. Canberra: Commonwealth of Australia.

Online: http://www.aph.gov.au/hansard/senate/commttee/S9975.pdf (accessed 29 June 2012).

Desart. 2009. Advertisement. In *Australian Art Collector Guide to Aboriginal Art Centres*. Sydney: Gadfly Media.

'Desert Nomads Come out of the Stone Age'. 1984. *Daily Mirror*, 24 October.

Dexter, Barrie. 2008. 'Stanner: Reluctant bureaucrat.' In *Appreciation of Difference: WEH Stanner and Aboriginal Australia*, edited by Melinda Hinkson and Jeremy Beckett, 76–86. Canberra, ACT: Aboriginal Studies press.

Dixon, Charles (Chika). 1984. 'Letter to the Editor: Fashion: The Last Frontier'. *Art Network*, no. 13: 6.

Dixon, Robyn. 1984. 'We Find the Lost Tribe'. *The Herald*, 24 October.

DoCA (Department of Communications and the Arts). 1994. *Creative Nation: Commonwealth Cultural Policy*. Canberra: Department of Communications and the Arts.

Dodson, Mick. 1996. *Assimilation Versus Self-Determination: No Contest*. H.C. (Nugget) Coombs Northern Australia Inaugural Lecture. Online: http://www.hreoc.gov.au/about/media/speeches/social_justice/assimilation_vs_selfdetermination.html (accessed 22 October 2011).

———. 2003. 'The End in the Beginning: Re(de)finding Aboriginality.' In *Blacklines: Contemporary Critical Writings by Indigenous Australians*, edited by Michele Grossman, 25–42. Melbourne, VIC: Melbourne University Press.

Dodson, Mick, and Sarah Pritchard. 1998. 'Recent Developments in Indigenous Policy: The Abandonment of Self-Determination'. *Indigenous Law Bulletin* 4, no. 15: 4–6.

Don't Forget Our Elders. 2007. *The Australian*, 8 October.

Dow, Coral. 2008. *'Sorry': The Unfinished Business of the Bringing Them Home Report*. Australian Parliamentary Library. Online: http://www.aph.gov.au/About_Parliament/Parliamentary_Departments/Parliamentary_Library/pubs/BN/0708/BringingThemHomeReport (accessed 4 February 2014).

Dow, Steve. 2008. 'Stolen Hopes, Broken Dreams'. *The Sun-Herald*, 27 July.

Dubbo City Council. 2008–2012. *Dubbo City Council Cultural Plan*. Online: http://www.dubbo.nsw.gov.au/_literature_32504/Dubbo_City_Council_Cultural_Plan (accessed 12 October 2013).

Duncan, Carol. 1991. 'Art Museums and the Ritual of Citizenship'. In *Exhibiting Cultures: The Poetics and Politics of Museum Display*, edited by Ivan Karp and Steven D. Lavine, 88–103. Washington: Smithsonian Institute Press.

Dunn, Richard. 1984. 'Other than What'. *Art Network*, no. 13: 51–53.

Dwyer, Carmel. 1999. 'Hammer and Stipple'. *The Bulletin* 117, no. 6177: 106–108.

Eather, Michael, ed. 2005. *Shoosh! The History of the Campfire Group*. Brisbane: Institute of Modern Art & Campfire Group.

Eccles, Jeremy. 2000. 'Art from the Heart? – A Rejoinder'. *Art Monthly Australia*, no. 127: 4–5.

———. 2005. 'Bagging Out'. *Submission to Senate Committee Inquiry into Australia's Indigenous Visual Arts and Craft Sector*. Canberra: Parliament of Australia. Online: http://www.aph.gov.au/Parliamentary_Business/Committees/Senate_Committees?url=ecita_ctte/completed_inquiries/2004–07/indigenous_arts/submissions/sub43.pdf (accessed 25 August 2009).

———. 2006. 'Now Who's Bagging Out Whom?' *Submission to Senate Committee Inquiry into Australia's Indigenous Visual Arts and Craft Sector*. Canberra: Parliament of Australia. Online: http://www.aph.gov.au/Parliamentary_Business/Committees/Senate_Committees?url=ecita_ctte/completed_inquiries/2004–07/indigenous_arts/submissions/sub43.pdf

Eccles, Jeremy with Barbara Spencer. 2013. 'Took Indigenous Culture to World (Lance Bennett, 1938–2013)'. *The Sydney Morning Herald*. March 2. http://www.smh.com.au/comment/obituaries/took-indigenous-culture-to-world-20130301–2fbn1.html (accessed 11 October 2014).

Edmonds, Fran. 2010. '"We Have Survived" – South-East Australian Aboriginal Art Exhibitions since 1988. *reCollections* 5, no. 1. Online: http://recollections.nma.gov.au/issues/vol_5_no_1/papers/we_have_survived (accessed 5 May 2011).

Edwards, Deborah. 2005. *Margaret Preston*. Sydney: Art Gallery of New South Wales.

Edwards, Robert. 1979. *Australian Aboriginal Art: The Art of the Alligator Rivers Region, Northern Territory*. Canberra: Australian Institute of Aboriginal Studies.

Elder, Catriona, Angela Pratt and Cath Ellis. 2006. 'Running Race: Reconciliation, Nationalism and the Sydney 2000 Olympic Games'. *International Review for the Sociology of Sport* 41, no. 2: 181–200.

Elkin, Adolphus P. 1943. 'Foreword.' In *Art of the Australian Aboriginal*, edited by Charles Barrett and Robert Henderson Croll, ix–xii. Melbourne: Bread and Cheese Club.

———. 1949. 'Art in Arnhem Land – A Notice'. *Oceania* 20, no. 1: 80–82.

Enwezor, Okwui. 2003. 'The Black Box'. In *Art of the Twentieth Century: A Reader*, edited by Jason Gaiger, and Paul Wood, 319–26. New Haven & London: Yale University Press, in association with The Open University.

Ewington, Julie. 1986. 'Two Worlds Collide: Cultural Convergences in Aboriginal and White Australian Art'. *Art Network*, nos. 19/20: 77–78.

Eyerman, Ron. 2004. 'Cultural Trauma: Slavery and the Formation of African American Identity. In *Cultural Trauma and Collective Identity*, edited by Jeffrey Alexander, Ronald Eyerman, Bernard Giesen, Neil J. Smelser and Piotr Sztompka, 60–111. Berkeley: University of California Press.

———. 2006. 'Toward a Meaningful Sociology of the Arts'. In *Myth, Meaning and Performance*, edited by Ron Eyerman and Lisa McCormick, 13–34. Boulder: Paradigm Publishers.

Factor, Brenda. 2000. 'Marketing an Australian Identity'. In *Picturing the 'Primitif': Images of Race in Daily Life*, edited by Julie Marcus, 177–94. Canada Bay, Sydney: LhR Press.

Finnane, Kieran. 2012. 'What Future for the Aboriginal Art Economy?'. *Alice Springs News Online*, 10 May. Online: http://www.alicespringsnews.com.au/2012/05/10/what-future-for-the-aboriginal-art-economy/ (accessed 13 September).

Fisher, Laura. 2011. Mark Blackman (biography). *Design and Art of Australia Online*. Online: http://www.daao.org.au/bio/mark-blackman/#artist_biography

———. 2012. 'The Art/Ethnography Binary: Post-Colonial Tensions within the Field of Australian Aboriginal Art'. *Cultural Sociology* 6, no. 2: 251–70. doi:10.1177/1749975512440224

———. 2014. '"Aboriginal Mass Culture": A Critical History'. *Visual Studies* 29, no. 3: 232–48.

———. 2015. 'Some Reflections on Aboriginal Art's Relationship with Money'. In *Art and Money*, edited by Peter Stupples, 35–57. Newcastle upon Tyne: Cambridge Scholars Publishing.

Fisher, Laura and Gay McDonald. 2016. 'From *fluent* to *Culture Warriors*: curatorial trajectories for Indigenous Australian art overseas'. *Media International Australia* 158, no. 1, pp. 67–79. doi: 10.1177/1329878X15622080

Foley, Fiona, ed. 2006. *The Art of Politics the Politics of Art: The Place of Indigenous Contemporary Art*. Southport, QLD: Keeaira Press.

Foley, Gary. 2005. 'The Inevitable Collision Between Politics and Indigenous Art'. In *rarrk John Mawurndjul: Journey Through Time in Northern Australia*, edited by Christian Kaufmann and Museum Tinguely, 185–88. Belair, South Australia: Crawford House Publishing.

Foss, Paul. 1987. 'Mammon or Millennial Eden?: Interview with Imants Tillers'. *Art & Text* 23, no. 4: 124–39.

Foster, Hal. 1985. *Recodings*. Seattle: Bay Press.

Four Corners. 1999. 'Dot for Dollar'. *Australian Broadcasting Corporation*, 31 May. Online: http://www.abc.net.au/4corners/stories/s27931.htm (accessed 28 June 2006).

Fourmile, Henrietta. 1987. 'Museums and Aborigines: A Case Study in Contemporary Scientific Colonialism'. *Praxis M*, no. 17: 7–11.

———. 1989. 'Some Background Issues Concerning the Appropriation of Aboriginal Imagery'. In *Postmodernism: A Consideration of the Appropriation of Aboriginal Imagery*, edited by Sue Cramer, 6–10. Brisbane: Institute of Modern Art.

Franklin, Adrian. 2010. 'Aboriginalia: Souvenir Wares and the "Aboriginalisation" of Australian Identity'. *Tourist Studies* 10, no. 3: 195–208.

Frazer, James. 2010 [1890]. *The Golden Bough*. Edinburgh: Canongate Books.

French, Alison. 2002. *Seeing the Centre: The Art of Albert Namatjira 1902–1959*. Canberra: National Gallery of Australia.

Freud, Sigmund. 1985 [1913]. 'Totem and taboo'. In *The Origins of Religion*. Middlesex, England: Penguin Books.

Fulton, Adam, and Clare Morgan. 2010. 'Not So Super: Investment Proposals Leave Art Market Reeling'. *Sydney Morning Herald*, 7 July. Online: http://www.smh.com.au/ entertainment/art-and-design/not-so-super-investment-proposals-leave-art-market-reeling-20100706-zyzf.html (accessed 4 February 2014).

Galenson, David. 2007. 'Artists and the Market: From Leonardo and Titian to Andy Warhol and Damien Hirst'. Working paper. The National Bureau of Economic Research. Online: http://www.nber.org/papers/w13377 (accessed 2 September 2014).

Gammage, Bill. 2011. *The Biggest Estate on Earth*. Sydney: Allen & Unwin.

Gardiner-Garden, John. 2009. *Commonwealth Arts Policy and Administration*. Canberra: Parliamentary Library. Online: http://www.aph.gov.au/binaries/library/pubs/ bn/2008–09/artspolicy.pdf (accessed 12 December 2011).

Garneau, David. 2014. 'Indigenous art: from appreciation to art criticism' in *Double Desire: Transculturation and Indigenous Contemporary Art*, edited by Ian McLean, 311–26. Newcastle upon Tyne: Cambridge Scholars Publishing.

Garrett, Peter. 2010a. '$42 Million Supports Australia's Indigenous Arts, Culture and Heritage'. Government media release. Online: http://www.environment.gov.au/ minister/archive/env/2010/mr20100609c.html (accessed 4 August 2013).

———. 2010b. 'Artists to Benefit under Resale Royalty Scheme Starting Tomorrow'. Media release. Online: http://www.environment.gov.au/minister/archive/env/2010/ pubs/mr20100608b.pdf. (accessed 15 June 2011).

Gell, Alfred. 1992. 'The Technology of Enchantment and the Enchantment of Technology'. In *Anthropology, Art and Aesthetics*, edited by Jeremy Coote and Anthony Shelton, 40–66. Oxford: Clarendon Press.

———. 1998. *Art and Agency: An Anthropological Theory*. Oxford: Clarendon Press.

———. 2006 [1996]. 'Vogel's Net: Traps as Artworks and Artworks as Traps.' In *The Anthropology of Art: A Reader*, edited by Howard Morphy and Morgan Perkins, 219–235. Oxford: Blackwell Publishing.

Genocchio, Ben. 2008. *Dollar Dreaming: Inside the Aboriginal Art World*. Prahran, VIC: Hardie Grant.

Gibson, Lorraine. 2013. *We Don't Do Dots: Aboriginal Art and Culture in Wilcannia, New South Wales*. Sean Kingston Publishing: Canyon Pyon.

Gilbert, Kevin. 1977. *Living Black*. Ringwood, VIC: Penguin Book.

Gilchrist, Stephen. 2014. 'Indigenising Curatorial Practice.' In *The World Is not a Foreign Land*, edited by Quentin Spraque, 55–59. Melbourne, VIC: Ian Potter Museum of Art.

Ginsburg, Faye. 1994. 'Embedded Aesthetics: Creating a Discursive Space for Indigenous Media'. *Cultural Anthropology* 9, no. 3: 365–82.

Ginsburg, Faye, and Fred Myers. 2006. 'A History of Indigenous Futures: Accounting for Indigenous Art and Media'. *Aboriginal History* 30: 95–110.

Glenday, James. 2010. 'Planned Super Changes Affecting Aboriginal Art'. *ABC News Online*, 27 July. Online: http://www.abc.net.au/news/stories/2010/07/27/2965624. htm?section=justin (accessed 21 February 2014).

Godden, Christine. 2006. *Submission to Senate Committee Inquiry into Australia's Indigenous Visual Arts and Craft Sector*. Canberra: Parliament of Australia. Online: http://www.aph. gov.au/Parliamentary_Business/Committees/Senate_Committees?url=ecita_ctte/ completed_inquiries/2004–07/indigenous_arts/submissions/sub41.pdf (accessed 25 June 2012).

Golvan, Colin. 1992. 'Aboriginal Art and the Protection of Indigenous Cultural Rights'. *Aboriginal Law Bulletin* 2, no. 56: 5–8.

Gooder, Haydie, and Jane M. Jacobs. 2001. 'On the Border of the Unsayable: The Apology in Postcolonising Australia'. *Interventions* 2, no. 2: 229–47.

Goot, Murray, and Tim Rowse. 2007. *Divided Nation? Indigenous Affairs and the Imagined Public*. Carlton, VIC: Melbourne University Press.

Gordon, Michael. 2001. *Reconciliation: a Journey*. Sydney: University of New South Wales Press.

Gosford, B. 2010. '"Fake', 'Genuine' and 'Authentic Aboriginal Art' All Have Their Day out in Court'. *The Northern Myth*. Online: http://blogs.crikey.com.au/northern/2010/01/12/ fake-genuine-and-%E2%80%9Cauthentic-aboriginal-art%E2%80%9D-all-have-their-day-out-in-court/ (accessed 13 August 2012).

Greenberg, Clement. 1939. 'Avant-Garde and Kitsch'. *Partisan Review* 6, no. 5: 1–13. Online: http://blog.lib.umn.edu/mulli105/1601fall10/Greenberg-AvGd%26Ktch. pdf (accessed 3 May 2012).

Greene, G. 1999. 'ABC in Storm over Art Film'. *The Age*, 21 April.

Grishin, Sasha. 1989. 'Complex Works of Excellence' *The Canberra Times*, June 7, p. 31.

Grossman, Michele, ed. 2003. *Blacklines: Contemporary Critical Writings by Indigenous Australians*. Carlton, VIC: Melbourne University Press.

Gough, Julie. 2006. 'Being collected and keeping it real'. In *Keeping Culture: Aboriginal Tasmania*, edited by Amanda Jane Reynolds, 9–18. Canberra: National Museum of Australia Press.

Gunstone, Andrew. 2007. *Unfinished Business*. Melbourne: Australian Scholarly Publishing.

Habermas, Jürgen. 1974 [1964]. 'The Public Sphere: An Encyclopedia Article'. *New German Critique*, no. 3: 49–55.

———. 1996 [1981]. 'Modernity: An Unfinished Project'. In *Habermas and the Unfinished Project of Modernity*, edited by Maurizio Passerin d'Entrève, and Seyla Benhabib, 38–55. Cambridge: Polity Press.

Haebich, Anna. 2000. *Broken Circles: Fragmenting Indigenous Families 1800–2000*. Fremantle, WA: Fremantle Arts Centre Press.

Hage, Ghassan. 2003. *Against Paranoid Nationalism*. Sydney: Pluto Press.

Hall, Fiona. 2011. 'Fiona Hall'. In *Djambawa Marawili, Liyawaday Wirrpanda, Nawarapu Wunungmurra*, edited by Australian Galleries, 6. Sydney: Annandale Galleries.

Hall, Stuart. 1990. 'Cultural Identity and Diaspora'. In *Identity*, edited by Jonathan Rutherford, 222–37. London: Lawrence and Wishart.

———. 1993. 'Culture, community, nation'. *Cultural Studies* 7 (3): 349–63. doi: 10.1080/09502389300490251.

Hall, Stuart, and Paul Du Gay, eds. 1996. *Questions of Cultural Identity*. London: Sage.

Hamilton, Annette. 1990. 'Fear and Desire: Aborigines, Asians and the National Imaginary'. *Australian Cultural History*, no. 9: 14–35.

Hamlyn, Charlotte. 2015. 'Indigenous art sector wrestles with downturn: 'Perfect storm' blamed for waning market'. ABC News, 11 October. Online: http://www.abc.net. au/news/2015–10–11/indigenous-art-sector-grapples-with-oversupply/6842926 (accessed 9 February 2016).

Hanna, Michelle. 1999. *Reconciliation and Olympism*. Petersham, Sydney: Walla Walla Press in conjunction with the Aboriginal Research and Resource Centre and the Centre for Olympic Studies, the University of New South Wales.

Hansen, David. 2010. 'Seeing Truganini – Calibre Prize Essay'. *Australian Book Review*, no. 321: 45–53.

Hardy, Jane, John V. S. Megaw and M. Ruth Megaw, eds. 1992. *The Heritage of Namatjira*. Port Melbourne, VIC: William Heinemann Australia.

Harkin, Michael. 1995. 'Modernist Anthropology and Tourism of the Authentic'. *Annals of Tourism Research* 22, no. 3: 650–70. doi: 10.1016/0160–7383(95)00008-T

Hart, Deborah. ed. 2006. *Imants Tillers: One World Many Visions*. National Gallery of Australia: Canberra.

Hauser, Arnold. 1962 [1951]. *The Social History of Art, Volume 3: Rococo, Classicism and Romanticism*. London and Henley: Routledge & Kegan Paul.

Haynes, Roslynn D. 1998. *Seeking the Centre*. Cambridge: Cambridge University Press.

Healy, Chris. 2001. 'Race Portraits and Vernacular Possibilities: Heritage and Culture'. In *Culture in Australia: Policies, Publics and Programs*, edited by Tony Bennett and David Carter, 278–98. Cambridge: Cambridge University Press.

———. 2008. *Forgetting Aborigines*. Sydney: University of New South Wales Press.

Healy, Jacqueline. 1999. 'Art from the Heart?'. *Art Monthly Australia*, no. 122: 13–15.

———. 2005. 'A Fragile Thing: Marketing Remote Area Aboriginal Art'. PhD diss., University of Melbourne.

Hesmondhalgh, David. 2002. *The Cultural Industries*. London: Sage Publications.

———. 2008. 'Cultural and Creative Industries'. In *The SAGE Handbook of Cultural Analysis*, edited by Tony Bennett and John Frow, 553–69. London: SAGE Publications Ltd.

Hill, Robert. 1998. 'Minister's Message'. In *The Fourth National Indigenous Heritage Art Award*, edited by Australian Heritage Commission, 3. Canberra: Australian Heritage Commission.

Hiller, Susan, ed. 1991. *The Myth of Primitivism: Perspectives on Art*. London and New York: Routledge.

Hills, Euan. 2006. *Art Mob – Submission to Senate Committee Inquiry into Australia's Indigenous Visual Arts and Craft Sector*. Canberra: Parliament of Australia. Online: http://www.aph. gov.au/Parliamentary_Business/Committees/Senate_Committees?url=ecita_ctte/

completed_inquiries/2004–07/indigenous_arts/submissions/sub65.pdf (accessed 23 June 2012).

Hinkson, Melinda. 2004. 'Rebranding Australia – In a Different Light?' *Arena Journal*, no. 22: 37–43.

———. 2010a. 'Thinking with Stanner in the Present'. *Humanities Research* 16, no. 2: 75–111.

———. 2010b. 'Media Images and the Politics of Hope'. In *Culture Crisis: Anthropology and Politics in Aboriginal Australia* edited by Jon Altman and Melinda Hinkson, 229–47.

———. 2010/2011. 'For Love and Money'. *Arena Magazine,* no. 109: 17–21.

Hinkson, Melinda and Benjamin Smith. 2005. 'Introduction: Conceptual Moves towards an Intercultural Analysis'. *Oceania*. 75, no. 3: 157–166.

Hodges, Christopher. 2007. *Submission to Senate Committee Inquiry into Australia's Indigenous Visual Arts and Craft Sector*. Canberra: Parliament of Australia. Online: http://www.aph. gov.au/Parliamentary_Business/Committees/Senate_Committees?url=ecita_ctte/ completed_inquiries/2004–07/indigenous_arts/submissions/sub85.pdf (accessed 29 April 2012).

Hoffie, Pat. 1988. 'Considering the Politics of Questioning: A Brief Summary of Artists' Week'. *Artlink* 8, no. 2: 21–23.

———. 1997. 'Landscape and Identity in the 1980s'. In *Lying about the Landscape*, edited by Geoff Levitus, 68–81. Sydney: Craftsman House.

Hollingsworth, David. 2006. *Race and Racism in Australia*. South Melbourne: Thomson/ Social Sciences Press.

Horkheimer, Max, and Theodor Adorno. 2002 [1947]. *Dialectic of Enlightenment*. Stanford, CA: Stanford University Press.

Hoy, Greg. 2011. 'One of Australia's Richest Women's Interest in Aboriginal Art'. Television broadcast. *7.30 Report*, 19 August. Australian Broadcasting Corporation. Online: http:// www.abc.net.au/7.30/content/2011/s3317958.htm (accessed 25 August 2011).

HREOC (Human Rights and Equal Opportunity Commission). 2003. 'Social Justice and Human Rights for Aboriginal and Torres Strait Islander Peoples'. Information sheet. Online: http://www.hreoc.gov.au/social_justice/infosheet/infosheet_sj.pdf (accessed 28 November 2012).

Huda, Shireen. 2008. *Pedigree and Panache: A History of the Art Auction in Australia*. Canberra: ANU E Press.

Hughes, Robert. 1960. 'Iron and Bark'. *Nation*, 10 September.

———. 1988. 'Evoking the Spirit Ancestors: The Ancient, Mythic World of the Aborigines Comes Alive.' *Time* 132 (18): 79–80.

Indigenous Art Code. 2012. Online: http://www.indigenousartcode.org/ (accessed 1 July 2013).

Indigenous Law Bulletin Special Focus Edition: Indigenous Artists. 2006. *Indigenous Law Bulletin* 6, no. 18.

Ingold, Tim. 2013. *Making*. London & New York: Routledge.

Inglis, David. 2005. 'Thinking "Art" Sociologically'. In *The Sociology of Art: Ways of Seeing*, edited by David Inglis, and John Hughson, 11–29. Hampshire: Palgrave Macmillan.

Ireland, Tracy. 2002. 'Giving Value to the Australian Historic Past: Historical Archaeology, Heritage and Nationalism'. *Australasian Historical Archaeology* 20: 15–5.

Isaacs, Jennifer. 1999. 'Indigenous Designs on Australia'. *Art and Australia* 37, no. 1: 66–74.

———. 2002. 'International Exposure of Aboriginal Art 1970–2001'. *Art & Australia* 39, no. 4: 548–57.

Iseger-Pilkington, Glenn. 2011. 'Branded: The Indigenous Aesthetic'. *Artlink* 31, no. 2: 36–39.

Jagamarra Nelson, Michael. 2000. 'I Am an Artist Not a Politician'. In *The Oxford Companion to Aboriginal Art and Culture*, edited by Margo Neale and Sylvia Kleinert, 482–83. Melbourne: Oxford University Press.

Jameson, Fredric. 1991. *Postmodernism, or, the Cultural Logic of Late Capitalism*. London: Verso.

———. 2002. *A Singular Modernity*. London: Verso.

Janke, Terri. 1998. *Our Culture: Our Future – Report on Australian Indigenous Intellectual and Cultural Property Rights*. Surry Hills, NSW: Prepared for Australian Institute of Aboriginal and Torres Strait Islander Studies and the Aboriginal and Torres Strait Islander Commission.

Johnson, Carole, John Moriarty, Chris Fondum and Jenny Isaacs. 2011. 'Foundation of the Aboriginal Arts Board'. Panel discussion at A Tribute to Bob Edwards, National Museum of Australia, Canberra, 22 March. Online: http://www.nma.gov.au/audio/detail/foundation-of-the-aboriginal-arts-board (accessed 23 September 2012).

Johnson, Tim. 1986. 'Theoretical Force (State of the Art) in the Sacred Land'. In *Origins, Originality + Beyond – The Sixth Biennale of Sydney*, 64–66. Sydney: The Biennale of Sydney Limited.

———. 1988. 'Paying the Rent'. In *Stories of Australian Art: Commonwealth Institute, London, 31 March-29 May 1988, the Usher Art Gallery, Lincoln, 25 June-31 July 1988*, edited by Commonwealth Institute (Great Britain), and Usher Art Gallery, 57–65). London: The Institute.

Johnson, Vivien, ed. 1984. *Koori Art '84*. Surry Hills, NSW: Artspace.

Johnson, Vivien. 1986a. 'A Contemporary Survey of Aboriginal Art'. *Art Network*, nos. 19/20: 54–55.

———. 1986b. 'The Art of Decolonisation'. In *Imants Tillers, Venice Biennale 1986 Australia*, edited by Kerry Crowley, 14–15. Sydney, Adelaide: Visual Arts Board of the Australia Council; Art Gallery Board of South Australia.

———. 1987. 'Our Appropriation Is Your Dispossession'. *Praxis M*, no. 17: 4–6.

———. 1988. 'Among Others: Reply to "Black Canberra"'. *Art & Text*, no. 30: 98–99.

———. 1989. 'A Whiter Shade of Palaeolithic: Aboriginal Art and Appropriation'. *Praxis M*, no. 22: 9–11.

———. 1990. 'The Origins and Development of Western Desert Art'. In *The Painted Dream: Contemporary Aboriginal Paintings*, edited by Tim Johnson, Vivien Johnson and Auckland City Art Gallery, 9–17. Auckland: Auckland City Art Gallery.

———. 1991. 'Mona Lisa and the Highway Blues: Aboriginal Art in the Museum Context'. *Eyeline*, no. 14: 19–21.

———. 1996. *Copyrites: Aboriginal Art in the Age of Reproductive Technologies*. Sydney: National Indigenous Arts Advocacy Association & Macquarie University.

———. 1997. *Michael Jagamara Nelson*. Sydney: Craftsman House.

———. 1999–2002. *The House of Aboriginality*. Online: http://pandora.nla.gov.au/pan/10459/20030312-0000/www.mq.edu.au/hoa/index.htm (accessed 4 July 2011).

———. 2000. 'The "Aboriginal Art scandals" scandal. *Artlink* 20, no. 1: 32–35.

———.2003. *Clifford Possum Tjapaltjarri*. Adelaide: Art Gallery of South Australia.

———. 2007. "When Papunya Paintings Became Art." In *Papunya Painting: Out of the Desert Catalogue*, edited by Vivien Johnson. Canberra: National Museum of Australia Press.

———. 2010. *Once Upon a Time in Papunya*. Sydney: University of New South Wales Press.

———. 2015. *Streets of Papunya*. Sydney: University of New South Wales Press.

Johnson, Vivien, Tess Allas and Laura Fisher. 2009/2010. *This Side of the Frontier: Storylines Full Report.* Sydney: College of Fine Arts. Online: http://www.storylines.org.au/wp-content/uploads/2009/12/STORYLINESFINAL.pdf (accessed 11 September 2013).

Johnston, Elliott. 1991a. *Final Report of the Royal Commission into Aboriginal Deaths in Custody* 4. Canberra: Australian Government Publishing.

————. 1991b. *Final Report of the Royal Commission into Aboriginal Deaths in Custody* 1. Canberra: Australian Government Publishing Services.

Jones, Garry. 2010. 'Vernon Ah Kee: Sovereign Warrior'. *Artlink – Special Indigenous Issue Blak on Blak* 30, no. 1: 44–51.

Jones, Lyndal. 1983. 'The Continuum Symposium on Australian Art'. *Art Network*, no. 13, 49.

Jones, Paul. 2004. *Raymond Williams's Sociology of Culture: A Critical Reconstruction.* Hampshire and New York: Palgrave Macmillan.

————. 2007a. 'Beyond the Semantic "Big Bang": Cultural Sociology and an Aesthetic Public Sphere'. *Cultural Sociology* 1, no. 1: 73–95.

————. 2007b. 'Antipodean Public Spherists'. *Southern Review* 39, no. 3, 111–28.

————. 2011. 'Culture industry'. In, *Key Concepts in Media and Communications*, edited by P. Jones and D. Holmes, 47–53. London: Sage.

Jones, Phillip. 1988. 'Perceptions of Aboriginal Art: A History'. In *Dreamings: The Art of Aboriginal Australia*, edited by Peter Sutton, 143–79. Ringwood, VIC: Viking in association with the Asia Society Galleries, New York.

————. 1992a. 'The Boomerang's Erratic Flight: The Mutability of Ethnographic Objects'. In *Power, Knowledge and Aborigines*, edited by Bain Attwood and John Arnold, 59–71. Bundoora: La Trobe University Press.

————. 1992b. 'Arts and Manufactures: Inventing Aboriginal Craft'. In *Craft in Society: An Anthology of Perspectives*, edited by Noris Ioannou, 131–152. South Fremantle: Fremantle Arts Centre Press.

————. 1992c. 'Namatjira: Traveller Between Two Worlds'. In *The Heritage of Namatjira*, edited by Jane Hardy, John V. S. Megaw and Ruth Megaw, 97–136. Port Melbourne: William Heinnemann Australia.

————. 1995. '"Objects of Mystery and Concealment": A History of *Tjurunga* Collecting'. In *Politics of the Secret*, edited by Christopher Anderson, 67–96. Oceania Monograph 45. University of Sydney, Australia.

————. 2011a. 'Inside Mountford's Tent: Paint, Politics and Paperwork'. In *Exploring the Legacy of the 1948 Arnhem Land Expedition*, edited by Martin Thomas and Margo Neale, 33–54. Canberra: ANU E Press.

————. 2011b. 'The Art of Contact: Encountering an Aboriginal Aesthetic from the Eighteenth to the Twentieth Centuries'. In *The Cambridge Companion to Australian Art*, edited by Jaynie Anderson, 22–37. Cambridge: Cambridge University Press.

Jorgensen, Darren. 2008. 'On the Utopianism of Painting from Remote Communities'. *Journal of Australian Studies* 32, no. 2: 197–205.

Jules-Rosette, Bennetta. 1984. *The Messages of Tourist Art: An African Semiotic System in Comparative Perspective.* New York: Plenum Press.

Karp, Ivan, and Steven D. Lavine, eds. 1991. *Exhibiting Cultures: The Poetics and Politics of Museum Display.* Washington DC: Smithsonian Institute Press.

Kate Owen Gallery. 2010. 'Aboriginal Art Sale'. Advertisement. *Sydney Morning Herald, Spectrum*, 13–14 November.

Katona, Jacqui. 2007. 'Activism in Aboriginal Art'. *Machine* 2, no. 4: 3–5.

Keane, Michael, and John Hartley. 2001. *From Ceremony to CD-Rom: Indigenous Creative Industries in Brisbane*. Brisbane: Brisbane City Council. Online: http://eprints.qut.edu.au/4759/1/4759.pdf (accessed 18 May 2010).

Kembrey, Melanie. 2015. 'Tony Albert's 'Confronting' Tribute to Indigenous Diggers Unveiled in Sydney's Hyde Park' *Sydney Morning Herald*, 31 March 2015. Online: http://www.smh.com.au/entertainment/art-and-design/tony-alberts-confronting-tribute-to-indigenous-diggers-unveiled-in-sydneys-hyde-park-20150331-1mbuzo.html (accessed 4 April 2015).

Keating, Paul. 2001 [1992]. 'Redfern Park Speech 10 December 1992'. *Indigenous Law Bulletin* 5, no. 11. Online: from http://www.austlii.edu.au/au/journals/ILB/2001/57.html (accessed 4 June 2008).

Kennedy, Peter. 1979. 'Peter Kennedy'. In *European Dialogue: The Third Biennale of Sydney at the Art Gallery of New South Wales, the Australian Centre for Photography and Other Venues*, edited by Biennale of Sydney, n.p. Sydney: Biennale of Sydney.

———. 1983. 'Peter Kennedy'. In *D'un Autre Continent: l'Australie la Rêve et le Réel*, 119–22. Paris: Association Francaise d'Action Artistique & Ministère des Relations Extérieures.

Kirby, Michael. 2010. *Whitlam as Internationalist*. University of Western Sydney Whitlam lecture. Online: http://www.michaelkirby.com.au/images/stories/speeches/2000s/2010_Speeches/2432.Speech-WhitlamLecture-25February2010.pdf (accessed 21 March 2011).

Kirby, Sandy. 1982. 'Aboriginal Art and the New Patrons'. *Arena*, no. 60: 28–35.

Kleinert, Sylvia. 1988a. 'Albert Namatjira: A Paradigm for the Present'. *Agenda* 1, no. 2: 27–29.

———. 1988b. 'Black Canberra'. *Art & Text*, no. 29: 92–95.

———. 1988c. 'Sylvia Kleinert Responds'. *Art & Text*, no. 30: 99–100.

———. 1992. 'The Critical Reaction to the Hermannsberg School'. In *The Heritage of Namatjira*, edited by Jane Hardy, John V. S. Megaw and M. Ruth Megaw, 217–247. Port Melbourne, VIC: William Heinemann Australia.

———. 2000. 'Rear-Vision Mirror'. In *Urban Dingo*, edited by Margo Neale, 25–31. Brisbane: Craftsman House in Association with the Queensland Art Gallery.

———. 2010. 'Aboriginal Enterprises: Negotiating an Urban Aboriginality'. *Aboriginal History* 34: 171–196.

Kleinert, Sylvia, and Margo Neale eds. 2000. *The Oxford Companion to Aboriginal Art and Culture*. Melbourne: Oxford University Press.

Kohen, Apolline. 2007. *The Abolition of CDEP & Indigenous Artists: A Working Paper to Outline the Threats Posed & the Responses of Artists and Art Centres*. Online: www.whatsworking.com.au/WomenforWik/pdfs/CDEP_Issues_Paper.pdf (accessed 11 March 2012).

Korman, Ben. 2006. *Submission to Senate Committee Inquiry into Australia's Indigenous Visual Arts and Craft Sector*. Canberra: Parliament of Australia. Online: http://www.aph.gov.au/SEnate/committee/ecita_ctte/completed_inquiries/2004–07/indigenous_arts/submissions/sub64.pdf. (accessed 25 June 2012).

Kowal, Emma. 2008. 'The Politics of the Gap: Indigenous Australians, Liberal Multiculturalism, and the End of the Self-Determination Era.' *American Anthropologist* 110 (3): 338–48.

———. 2011. 'The Stigma of White Privilege: Australian Anti-racists and Indigenous Improvement'. *Cultural Studies*, no. 25: 313–33.

Kronenberg, Simeon. 1995. 'Why Gabrielle Pizzi Has Changed Her Mind about Aboriginal Art'. *Art Monthly Australia*, 85: 7–9.

Kuklick, Henrika. 2006. '"Humanity in the Chrysalis Stage": Indigenous Australians in the Anthropological Imagination'. *British Journal of the History of Science* 39, no. 4: 535–68.

Kulick, Don. 2006. 'Theory in Furs: Masochist Anthropology'. *Cultural Anthropology* 47, no. 6: 933–52.

Kupka, Karel. 1965. *Dawn of Art: Painting and Sculpture of Australian Aborigines.* Sydney: Angus & Robertson.

Lambert, Anthony. 1984a. 'How Gary Foley Is Giving Aboriginal Artists More Control of What Happens to Their Art'. *Australian Artist* 1, no. 2: 34–35.

———. 1984b. 'Shattering the Myth that Aboriginal Art Exists Only in Traditional Forms'. *Australian Artist* 1, no. 4: 24–25.

Lander, Janis. 2008. 'William Brian Badger Bates'. *Design and Art of Australia Online.* Online: http://www.daao.org.au/bio/william-brian-badger-bates/#artist_biography (accessed 3 June 2009).

Langford, Ruby. 1988. *Don't Take Your Love to Town.* Ringwood, VIC: Penguin.

Langton, Marcia. 1981. 'Urbanising Aborigines: The Social Scientists' Great Deception'. *Social Alternatives* 2, no. 2: 16–22.

———. 1988. 'Aboriginal Art in 1988: A Complex Reality'. *Artlink* 8, no. 2: 30–32.

———. 1993. *'Well I heard it on the radio and I saw it on the television…': An Essay for the Australian Film Commission on the Politics and Aesthetics of Filmmaking by and about Aboriginal People and Things.* Sydney: Australian Film Commission.

———. 2003. 'Culture Wars'. In *Blacklines: Contemporary Critical Writings by Indigenous Australians*, edited by Michele Grossman, 81–91. Carlton, VIC: Melbourne University Press.

———. 2007. 'Dodgy Dreaming as Parasites Run Free. *The Australian*, 25 May.

———. 2008. 'Trapped in the Aboriginal Reality Show'. *Griffith Review*, no. 19: 145–62.

———. 2013. *The Quiet Revolution: Indigenous People and the Resources Boom*, Boyer Lecture series. Sydney: HarperCollins Publishers Australia.

Langton, Marcia and CAR (Council for Aboriginal Reconciliation). 1994. *Valuing Cultures: Recognising Indigenous Cultures as a Valued Part of Australian Heritage.* Canberra: Australian Government Publishing Service.

Lattas, Andrew. 1997 [1990]. 'Aborigines and Contemporary Australian Nationalism: Primordiality and the Cultural Politics of Otherness'. In *Race Matters*, edited by Gillian Cowlishaw and Barry Morris, 223–55. Canberra: Aboriginal Studies Press.

———. 2000 [1989]. 'Colonising the Other: Dreaming, Aboriginal Painting and the White Man's Search for His Soul'. In *Picturing the 'Primitif': Images of Race in Daily Life*, edited by Julie Marcus, 240–65. Canada Bay: LhR Press.

Lea, Tess. 2005. 'The Work of Forgetting: Germs, Aborigines and Postcolonial Expertise in the Northern Territory of Australia'. *Social Science & Medicine* 61, no. 6: 1310–19.

———. 2012. 'When Looking for Anarchy, Look to the State: Fantasies of Regulation in Forcing Disorder within the Australian Indigenous estate'. *Critique of Anthropology* 32, no. 2:109–124. doi: 10.1177/0308275x12438251.

Lendon, Nigel. 2011. 'Aboriginal Art Centres on Nicolas Rothwell's Frontier'. *Iconophelia.* Online: http://www.iconophilia.net/aboriginal-art-centres-on-nicolas-rothwells-frontier/ (accessed 12 April 2012).

Levi-Strauss, Claude. 1966. "Anthropology: Its Achievements and Future." *Current Anthropology* 7, no. 2:124–27. doi: 10.2307/2740022.

Lingard, Bob. 1989a. 'Appropriation of Aboriginal Art: The Case of Tim Johnson'. *Tension*, no. 17: 48–50.

———. 1989b. 'Appropriation of Aboriginal Imagery: Tim Johnson and Imants Tillers'. In *Postmodernism: A Consideration of the Appropriation of Aboriginal Imagery*, edited by Sue Cramer, 19–25. Brisbane: Institute of Modern Art.

———. 1989c. 'A Kind of History Painting: Gordon Bennett' *Tension*, no. 17, 39–42.

Losche, Diane. 1999. 'The Importance of Birds: Or the Relationship between Art and Anthropology'. In *Double Vision: Art Histories and Colonial Histories in the Pacific*, edited by Nicholas Thomas and Diane Losche, 210–38. Cambridge: Cambridge University Press.

Lovitt, Carolyn. 2000. 'Aboriginal Art as Decor: The Politics of Assimilation in White Australian Homes 1930–1970'. Masters dissertation, University of Melbourne.

Lowish, Susan. 2005. 'European Vision and Aboriginal Art: Blindness and Insight in the Work of Bernard Smith'. *Thesis Eleven* 82, no. 1: 62–72.

Lumby, Catherine. 1995. 'The Art of Flux: An Australian Perspective'. In *Antipodean Currents: Ten Contemporary Artists from Australia*, edited by Julia Robinson, 16–25. New York: Guggenheim Museum Publications.

Lunn, Eugene. 1982. *Marxism and Modernism*. Berkeley: University of California Press.

Lüthi, Bernhard. 1993. 'The Marginalisation of (Contemporary) Non-European/Non-American Art (as Reflected in the Way We View It)'. In *Aratjara: Art of the First Australians: Traditional and Contemporary Works by Aboriginal and Torres Strait Islander Artists*, edited by Bernhard Lüthi and Gary Lee, 15–31. Dusseldorf and Cologne: Kunstsammlung Nordrhein-Westfalen & DuMont Buchverlag.

Lüthi, Bernhard, and Gary Lee, eds. 1993. *Aratjara: Art of the First Australians: Traditional and Contemporary Works by Aboriginal and Torres Strait Islander Artists*. Dusseldorf and Cologne: Kunstsammlung Nordrhein-Westfalen & DuMont Buchverlag.

Lyndon, Jane. 2012. *The Flash of Recognition: Photography and the Emergence of Indigenous Rights*. Sydney: New South.

MacCannell, Dean. 1976. *The Tourist: A New Theory of the Leisure Class*. London and Basingstoke: Macmillan Press.

Macintyre, Stuart, and Anna Clark. 2003. *The History Wars*. Carlton, VIC: Melbourne University Press.

Mackay, Machmud. 1973. 'Marketing and Aboriginal Arts and Crafts: A Preliminary Report on the Production, Distribution and Marketing of Aboriginal Arts and Crafts in Australia'. Paper presented at the National Seminar on Aboriginal Arts in Australia, Canberra, ACT, 21–25 May.

Maloon, Terence. 1982. 'Aboriginal Paintings: Strong and Beautiful Abstracts Survive the Cultural Dislocation'. *The Sydney Morning Herald*, 9 January.

———. 2000. "Tuckson and Tradition." In *Painting forever: Tony Tuckson*, edited by National Gallery of Australia. Canberra ACT: National Gallery of Australia. Online: http://nga.gov.au/Tuckson/tradition.cfm (Accessed 12 March 2014).

Manne, Robert. 2001. 'In Denial: The Stolen Generations and the Right'. *Quarterly Essay*, no. 1.

Marcon, Marco. 1986. 'Papunya Tula Paintings: Gallerie Dusseldorf'. *Praxis M*, no. 12: 38–39.

Marcon, Marco, and David Jones. 1987. 'Territories of Experience: An Interview with David Jones'. *Praxis M*, no. 17: 26–29.

Marcus, George E., and Fred R. Myers. 1995. 'The Traffic in Art and Culture: An Introduction'. In *The Traffic in Culture: Refiguring Art and Anthropology*, edited by George E. Marcus and Fred R. Myers, 1–51. Berkeley: University of California Press.

Marcus, Julie. 1997 [1988]. 'The Journey out to the Centre: The Cultural Appropriation of Ayers Rock. In *Race Matters: Indigenous Australians and 'Our' Society*, edited by Gillian Cowlishaw, and Barry Morris, 29–51. Canberra: Aboriginal Studies Press.

———. 2004. 'What's at Stake?: History Wars, the NMA and Good Government'. *Cultural Studies Review* 10, no. 1: 134–48.

Marcus, Julie, ed. 2000. *Picturing the 'Primitif': Images of Race in Daily Life*. Canada Bay, Sydney: LhR Press.

Marika, Wandjuk. 1976. 'Aboriginal Copyright'. *Art & Australia* 13, no. 3: 242–43.

Marrie, Adrian. 1985. 'Killing Me Softly: Aboriginal Art and Western Critics'. *Art Network* 14:17–21.

———. 1987. 'The Politics of Aboriginal Heritage'. *Praxis M*, no. 17: 17–20.

Martin, Lauren. 2004. 'Sold on the Dream of a Better Deal'. *The Sydney Morning Herald*, 20 August.

Martin-Chew, Louise. 2009. 'The Guerrilla Operative in Fiona Foley's Public Art' in *Fiona Foley: Forbidden,* Sydney: Museum of Contemporary Art & University of Queensland Art Museum. Online: http://louisemartinchew.com/wp-content/uploads/2012/07/The-Guerrilla-Operative.pdf (accessed 12 September 2014).

———. 2011. 'GoMA Draws Fire From Critics'. *The Australian*, 16 December. Online: http://www.theaustralian.com.au/news/arts/goma-draws-fire-from-critics/story-e6frg8n6–1226223416988 (accessed 4 January 2012).

Maslen, Geoff. 1999. 'Dots and Robbers'. *The Bulletin*, 27 July.

Maughan, Janet, Vincent Megaw, Ruth Megaw and Polly Sumner. 1988. 'Landscape with Figures…? The 1988 Adelaide Festival and Aboriginal Art'. *Artlink* 8, no. 2: 24–29.

Maynard, Margaret. 1999. 'The Red Centre: The Quest for "Authenticity" in Australian Dress'. *Fashion Theory* 3, no. 2: 175–96.

McCarthy, Frederick D. 1952. *Australian Aboriginal Decorative Art*. Sydney: Trustees of the Australian Museum.

McCarthy, Conal. 2007. *Exhibiting Maori: A History of Colonial Cultures of Display*. Oxford: Berg.

McCulloch, Susan. 1997a. 'Revealed: Black Art Scandal'. *The Weekend Australian*, 15–16.

———. 1997b. 'Artistic License or Fraud?'. *The Australian*, 15 March.

———. 1999. 'The Hand that Signed the Paper'. *The Weekend Australian Review*, 24–25 April.

———. 2000. 'When Is a Fake not a Fake?' *The Australian*, 15 January.

———. 2001 [1999]. *Contemporary Aboriginal Art: A Guide to the Rebirth of an Ancient Culture*. Crows Nest, Sydney: Allen & Unwin.

McDermott, Q. 2008. 'Art for Art's Sake'. *ABC Four Corners*, 28 July. Online: http://www.abc.net.au/4corners/stories/2008/07/28/2314182.htm (accessed 23 September 2011).

McDonald, Gay. 2014. 'Aboriginal Art and Cultural Diplomacy: Australia, the United States, and the *Culture Warriors* Exhibition'. *Journal of Australian Studies* 38, no. 1: 18–31.

McEvilley, Thomas. 1984. 'Doctor, Lawyer, Indian Chief: Primitivism in 20th Century Art at the Museum of Modern Art'. *Artforum* 23, no. 3: 54–61.

McGrath, A. 1991. 'Travels to a Distant Past: The Mythology of the Outback'. *Australian Cultural History*, no. 10: 113–24.

McLean, Ian. 1998. *White Aborigines: Identity Politics in Australian Art*. Cambridge: Cambridge University Press.

———. 2002a. 'Global Indigeneity and Australian Desert Painting: Eric Michaels, Marshall McLuhan, Paul Ricoeur and the End of Incommensurability'. *Australian and New Zealand Journal of Art* 3, no. 2: 33–53.

————. 2002b. 'The Modernity of Tradition: Interpreting Acrylic Desert Paintings'. Paper presented at the Art Association of Australia and New Zealand Art Association Conference, Art Gallery of NSW, Sydney. Online: http://archive.artgallery.nsw.gov.au/aaanz_2002/__data/page/2340/ian_mclean.pdf (accessed 24 October 2011).

————. 2009. 'Cargo cult: the Art world craze for Aboriginal art'. In *Conversations, Insights and Anecdotes: Proceedings of the Inaugural Cairns Indigenous Art Fair Symposium Centre of Contemporary Arts, Cairns, Queensland, 21 August 2009*, edited by Steven Campbell, 47–55. Brisbane: Arts Queensland, Department of the Premier and Cabinet.

————. 2010. '9 Shots 5 Stories: Imants Tillers and Indigenous Difference'. *Art Monthly*, no. 228: 13–16.

————. 2011a. 'Aboriginal Art and the Artworld'. In *How Aborigines Invented the Idea of Contemporary Art*, edited by Ian McLean, 17–75. Sydney: Institute of Modern Art & Power Publications.

————. 2011b. 'How Aborigines Invented the Idea of Contemporary Art'. In *How Aborigines Invented the Idea of Contemporary Art*, edited by Ian McLean, 333–42. Sydney: Institute of Modern Art & Power Publications.

————, ed. (2011c). *How Aborigines Invented the Idea of Contemporary Art*. Sydney: Institute of Modern Art & Power Publications.

————. 2014. 'Theories.' In *Double Desire: Transculturation and Indigenous Contemporary Art*, edited by Ian McLean, 31–42. Newcastle upon Tyne: Cambridge Scholars Publishing.

McMillan, Richard. 2005. 'Karel Kupka in Australia: Artist, Collector, Writer, Anthropologist'. In *rarrk John Mawurndjul: Journey Through Time in Northern Australia*, edited by Christian Kaufmann, and Museum Tinguely, 193–97. Belair, South Australia: Crawford House Publishing.

McNahon, Marie, and Chips Mackinolty. 1983. 'Letters: Avoiding Traps'. *Art Network*, no. 8: 47.

McNeill, David. 1987. 'Tillers of the Soil'. *Praxis M*, no. 18: 19–25.

McQuilten, Grace, and Anthony White. 2012. *Art, Money and Society: Private Funding, Public Benefit and Creative Enterprise*. University of Melbourne.

Meachem, Steve. 2010. 'The Real Gloria Petyarre – An Honest Survey'. *Sydney Morning Herald*, 20 July.

Megaw, John V. S. 1986. 'Contemporary Aboriginal Art – Dreamtime Discipline or Alien Adulteration?'. In *Dot & Circle: A Retrospective Survey of the Aboriginal Acrylic Paintings of Central Australia*, edited by Janet Maughan, and Jenny Zimmer, 51–54. Melbourne: Communication Services Unit, Royal Melbourne Institute of Technology.

Mercer, Colin. 1997. *Creative Country: Review of the ATSIC Arts and Craft Industry Support Strategy*. Canberra: Aboriginal and Torres Strait Islander Commission.

Merlan, Francesca. 1998. *Caging the Rainbow*. Vol. Honolulu, Hawai'i: University of Hawai'i Press.

————. 2000. 'Representing the Rainbow: Aboriginal Culture in an Interconnected World'. *Australian Aboriginal Studies*, no. 1 and 2: 20–26.

————. 2001. 'Aboriginal Cultural Production into Art: The Complexity of Redress.' In *Beyond Aesthetics: Art and the Technologies of Enchantment*, edited by Christopher Pinney and Nicholas Thomas, 201–34. Oxford: Berg.

————.2013. 'Theorizing Relationality: A Response to the Morphys.' *American Anthropologist* 115, no. 4: 637–38.

————. 2014. 'Recent Rituals of Indigenous Recognition in Australia: Welcome to Country.' *American Anthropologist* 8, no. 2: 296–309.

Michaels, Eric. 1988. 'Para-Ethnography'. *Art & Text*, no. 30: 42–51.

———. 1994 [1988]. 'Bad Aboriginal Art'. In *Bad Aboriginal Art: Tradition, Media, and Technological Horizons*, edited by Eric Michaels, 143–62. Minneapolis: University of Minnesota Press.

———. 2004 [1989]. 'Post-Modernism, Appropriation and Western Desert Acrylics'. In *What Is Appropriation? An Anthology of Writings on Australian Art in the 1980s and 1990s* (2nd ed.), edited by Rex Butler, 217–24. Brisbane: IMA Publishing.

Miller, Daniel. 1991. 'Primitive Art and the Necessity of Primitivism to Art'. In *The Myth of Primitivism: Perspectives on Art*, edited by Susan Hiller, 50–71. London & New York: Routledge.

Miller, Steve, ed. 2004. *Our Place: Indigenous Australia now: Australia's Contribution to the Cultural Olympiad of the Athens 2004 Olympic Games*. Haymarket, NSW: Powerhouse Publishing.

Miller, Toby. 1994. 'When Australia Became Modern'. *Continuum* 8, no. 2: 206–214.

———. 1995. 'Exporting Truth from Aboriginal Australia'. *Media Information Australia*, no. 76: 7–17.

Milliken, Robert. 2004. 'Reconciled to Success: The Golden Age of Aboriginal Art'. *The Weekend Australian Financial Review*, 23–28 December.

Mitchell, W. J. T. 2002. 'Showing Seeing: A Critique of Visual Culture'. *Journal of Visual Culture* 1, no. 2: 165–81.

Money, Lawrence. 2011. 'Disputed Aboriginal Painting to be Auctioned'. *The Age*, 19 November. Online: http://www.theage.com.au/entertainment/art-and-design/disputed-aboriginal-painting-to-be-auctioned-20111118–1nnbg.html (accessed 23 June 2012).

Montgomery, Jill. 1983. 'Australia – the French Discovery of 1983'. *Art & Text*, nos. 12/13: 3–15.

———. 2008. 'The Strange Tale of the Lucky Country, the Cultural Cringe and the Flight of the Tall Poppies'. *Art Monthly*, no. 215: 32–35.

Moore, Catriona. 2006. 'Craftwork: Margaret Preston, Emily Carr and the Welfare Frontier'. *Australian Cultural History* 25: 57–81.

———. 2007. 'Grayson Perry on Aboriginal Art: Worthy but Uninspiring'. *Moore and Moore Art*. Online: http://www.mooreandmooreart.co.uk/articles/news.asp?news_id=964 (accessed 23 January 2008).

Moore, Richard, and Jeremy Eccles. 1999. *Art from the Heart?* Canberra: Ronin Films.

Moran, Anthony. 2002. 'As Australia Decolonizes: Indigenising Settler Nationalism and the Challenges of Settler/Indigenous Relations'. *Ethnic and Racial Studies* 25, no. 6: 1013–42.

Moreton-Robinson, Aileen. 2003 [1999]. 'Tidda's Talkin' up to White Women: When Huggins et al. Took on Bell'. In *Blacklines: Contemporary Critical Writings by Indigenous Australians*, edited by Michele Grossman, 66–77. Carlton, VIC: Melbourne University Press.

Morphy, Howard. 1983. '"Now You Understand": An Analysis of the Way Yolngu Have Used Sacred Knowledge to Retain their Autonomy'. In *Aborigines, Land and Land Rights*, edited by Noel Peterson, and Marcia Langton, 110–33. Canberra: Australian Institute of Aboriginal Studies.

———. 1994. 'Aboriginal Art in a Global Context'. In *Worlds Apart: Modernity Through the Prism of the Local*, edited by Daniel Miller, 211–39. London: Routledge.

———. 1998. *Aboriginal Art*. London, Phaidon Press.

———. 2001. 'Seeing Aboriginal Art in the Gallery'. *Humanities Research* 8, no. 1: 37–50.

————. 2003. 'Buwayak: Surface and Inner Form'. In *Buwayak = Invisibility*, 16–17. Sydney: Annandale Galleries.

————. 2005. 'Indigenous Art as Economy'. In *Culture, Economy and Governance in Aboriginal Australia*, edited by Diane Austin-Broos and Gaynor Macdonald, 19–28. Sydney: University of Sydney Press.

————. 2006. 'Impossible to Ignore: Imants Tillers' Response to Aboriginal Art'. In *Imants Tillers: One World Many Visions Exhibition Catalogue*, edited by Deborah Hart, 85–94. Canberra: National Gallery of Australia.

————. 2008. *Becoming Art: Exploring Cross-Cultural Categories*. Sydney: University of New South Wales Press.

Morphy, Howard, and Morgan Perkins. 2006. 'The Anthropology of Art: A Reflection on Its History and Contemporary Practice'. In *The Anthropology of Art: A Reader*, edited by Howard Morphy and Morgan Perkins, 1–32. Oxford: Blackwell Publishing.

Morris, Meaghan. 1983. 'Jetsam'. In *D'un Autre Continent: l'Australie la Rève et le Réel*, 33–40. Paris: Association Francaise d'Action Artistique & Ministère des Relations Extérieures.

Morrissey, Philip. 2003. 'Aboriginality and Corporatism'. In *Blacklines: Contemporary Critical Writings by Indigenous Australians*, edited by Michele Grossman, 53–59. Carlton, VIC: Melbourne University Press.

Morton, John. 2006. 'Aboriginal Culture: Who Wants It, Who Needs It?'. *Online Opinion*. Online: http://www.onlineopinion.com.au/view.asp?article=4508 (accessed 12 November 2012).

Mossgreen Auctions. 2008. *Ochre: Supporting Indigenous Health through Art*. Casuarina, N.T., South Yarra, VIC: Menzies School of Health Research & Mossgreen Auctions.

Mountford, Charles P. 1950. 'Introduction'. In *Australian Aboriginal Art: Paintings by James Cant*, edited by James Cant, n.p. London: Berkeley Galleries.

Mountford, Charles P. 1954. 'Preface'. In *Australia: Aboriginal Paintings, Arnhem Land*, edited by Herbert Read, UNESCO, & New York Graphic Society. New York: New York Graphic Society by arrangement with UNESCO.

Muecke, Stephen. 1983. 'The Good Oil Company and the Bad Oil Company'. *Art & Text*, no. 9: 3–13.

————. 1984. 'The Discourse of Nomadology: Phylums in Flux'. *Art & Text*, no. 14: 24–40.

Mulgan, Richard. 1998. 'Citizenship and Legitimacy in Post-Colonial Australia'. In *Citizenship and Indigenous Australians*, edited by Nicolas Peterson and Will Sanders, 179–95. Cambridge: Cambridge University Press.

Mulvaney, D. John. 1982/1983. 'Museums'. *Australian Cultural History*, no. 2: 38–45.

————. 1990. "The Australian Aborigines 1606–1929: Opinion and Fieldwork." In *Through White Eyes*, edited by Susan Janson and Stuart Macintyre, 1–44. Sydney: Allen & Unwin.

Mulvaney, D. John, and John H. Calaby. 1985. *So Much that is New: Baldwin Spencer, 1860–1929, a Biography*. Carlton, VIC: Melbourne University Press.

Mulvaney, D. John, Mike Smith, Dick Kimber, Nic Peterson, Robin Hirst and Philip Jones. 2011. 'Bob Edwards: Museums and Archaeology'. Transcript of panel discussion. *A Tribute to Bob Edwards*. Canberra: National Museum of Australia. Online: http://www.nma.gov.au/audio/detail/bob-edwards-museums-and-archaeology/ (accessed 2 February 2014).

Mundine, Djon. 1988. 'Aboriginal Memorial'. In *1988 Australian Biennale: From the Southern Cross: A View of World Art c. 1940–88* edited by Biennale of Sydney, 230–33. Sydney: The Biennale of Sydney and the Australian Broadcasting Corporation.

————.1990. 'Black on Black'. In *Art Monthly Australia – Supplement 'The Land, the City – the Emergence of Urban Aboriginal Art'*, edited by Wally Caruana and Jennifer Isaacs, 7–9. ACT: Art Monthly Australia Pty. Ltd.

————. 2000. 'The Aboriginal Memorial: We Have Survived'. In *World of Dreamings*. National Gallery of Australia. Online: http://nga.gov.au/Dreaming/Index.cfm?Refrnc=Ch2aCroft (accessed 25 January 2012).

————. 2006. 'Aboriginal Art – It's a White Thing'. In *The Art of Politics the Politics of Art: The Place of Indigenous Contemporary Art*, edited by Fiona Foley, 57–64. Southport, QLD: Keeaira Press.

————. 2009a. 'White Face/Blak Mask (Apologies to Franz Fanon)'. *Artlink* 25, no. 3: 17–22.

————. 2009b. 'One Writers' Week'. *Art Monthly*, no. 222: 7.

————. 2013. " Ich Bin Ein Aratjara: 20 years later." *Artlink* 33, no. 2: 52–55.

Murphy, Bernice. 1981. *Australian Perspecta*. Sydney: Art Gallery of New South Wales.

————. 1983a. *Australian Perspecta 1983*. Sydney: Art Gallery of New South Wales.

————. 1983b. 'The Whitlam Years'. *Studio International* 196, no. 1002.

————. 1987. 'Curating Contemporary Aboriginal Art'. *Praxis M*, no. 17: 21–24.

————. 1988. 'Provincialism "Refigured" or Culture Disfigured?' *Art Monthly*, no. 15: 1–3.

————. 2011. 'Transforming Culture: Indigenous art and Australian art museums' in *Understanding Museums: Australian Museums and Museology*, edited by Des Griffin and Leon Paroissien. National Museum of Australia. Online: nma.gov.au/research/understanding-museums/BMurphy_2011.html (accessed 12 October 2013).

Musée du Quai Branly, Brenda Croft, Harold Mitchell Foundation, and Australia Council. 2006. *Australian Indigenous Art Commission = Commande Publique d'art Aborigene: Musée du Quai Branly*. Paddington, NSW: Art & Australia.

Myers, Debra, and Dave Palmer. 2015. 'What the World Needs Now Is Love, Sweet Love (punks).' *Cultural Studies Review* 21 (1): 249–61.

Myers, Fred. 1994. 'Beyond the Intentional Fallacy: Art Criticism and the Ethnography of Aboriginal Acrylic Painting'. *Visual Anthropology Review* 10, no. 1: 10–43.

————. 1998. 'Uncertain regard'. *Ethnos* 63, no. 1: 7–47.

————. 2001. 'The Wizards of Oz: Nation, State and the Production of Aboriginal Fine Art'. In *The Empire of Things: Regimes of Value and Material Culture*, edited by Fred R. Myers, 165–204. Santa Fe, NM: School of American Research Press.

————. 2002. *Painting Culture: The Making of an Aboriginal High Art*. London: Duke University Press.

————. 2005. 'Some Properties of Art and Culture: Ontologies of the Image and Economies of Exchange'. In *Materiality*, edited by Daniel Miller, 88–117. London: Duke University Press.

————. 2006. 'Collecting Aboriginal Art in the Australian Nation: Two Case Studies'. *Visual Anthropology Review* 21, nos. 1 & 2: 116–37.

————. 2011. 'Disturbances in the Field: Exhibiting Aboriginal Art in the US'. Paper presented at the Antipodean Fields conference, University of Western Sydney.

Nagel, Joane. 1994. 'Constructing Ethnicity: Creating and Recreating Ethnic Identity and Culture'. *Social Problems* 41, no. 1: 152–76.

Nairne, Sandy, Geoff Dunlop and John Wyver. 1987. *State of the Art: Ideas and Images in the 1980s*. London: Chatto & Windus, in collaboration with Channel Four Television Company Limited.

'National Inquiry into the Separation of Aboriginal and Torres Strait Islander Children from Their Families'. 1997. *Bringing Them Home: Report of the National Inquiry into the*

Separation of Aboriginal and Torres Strait Islander Children from their Families. Sydney: Human Rights and Equal Opportunity Commission.

National Museum of Australia. 2011. Off the Walls: Art from Aboriginal and Torres Strait Islander Affairs Agencies 1965–2005. Online: http://www.nma.gov.au/exhibitions/ off_the_walls/collection_background (accessed 27 October 2012).

———. 2012a. *Ngurrara: The Great Sandy Desert Canvas*. Online: http://www.nma.gov.au/ exhibitions/ngurrara_the_great_sandy_desert_canvas_/home (accessed 11 February 2014).

———. 2012b. *Aboriginal and Torres Strait Islander Art Collection*. Online: http://www.nma.gov. au/collections-search/atsiaa/results.php?search=adv&type=Posters (accessed 6 July 2013).

Neale, Margo. 1996. 'Campfire Group: All Stock Must Go!' In *The Second Asia-Pacific Triennial of Contemporary Art, Brisbane Australia 1996*, edited by Q. A. Gallery, 110. Brisbane: Queensland Art Gallery.

———. 2000. 'United in the Struggle: Indigenous Art From Urban Areas'. In *The Oxford Companion to Aboriginal Art and Culture*, edited by Margo Neale and Sylvia Kleinert, 267–78. Melbourne: Oxford University Press.

———. 2004. 'The Politics of Visibility: How Indigenous Australian Art Found Its Ways into Art Galleries'. In *Art and Social Change: Contemporary Art in Asia and the Pacific*, edited by Caroline Turner, 483–97. Canberra: Pandanus Books.

———. 2014. 'Whose Identity Crisis? Between the Ethnographic and the Art Museum.' In *Double Desire: Transculturation and Indigenous Contemporary Art*, edited by Ian McLean, 287–309. Newcastle upon Tyne: Cambridge Scholars Publishing.

Neales, S. 2004. 'Art Direction'. *The Australian Financial Review Magazine*, July.

Newstead, Adrian. 2014. *The Dealer in the Devil: An Insider's History of the Aboriginal Art Trade*. Blackheath, NSW: Brandl and Schlesinger.

Nicholls, Christine. 2002. 'Indigenous Australian Art: The Case for Law Reform'. *Feminist Studies* 28, no. 1: 212–15.

Nicholls, Christine. 2006. *Yilpinji: Love Art and Ceremony*. Victoria: Craftsman House.

Office for the Arts. 2011a. *Indigenous Visual Arts Industry Support (IVAIS) Fact Sheet*. Online: http://www.arts.gov.au/sites/default/files/indigenous/ivais/ivais-factsheet.pdf

———. 2011b. *Culture and Closing the Gap Fact Sheet*. Online: http://www.arts.gov.au/sites/ default/files/indigenous/closing-the-gap/ccg-factsheet.pdf (accessed 2 February 2014).

Office of Northern Development, ed. 1993. *Indigenous Australians and Tourism: A Focus on Northern Australia*. Darwin: ATSIC, the Northern Territory Tourist Commission and the Office of Northern Development.

O'Neil, M. 1984. 'The Great Sandy Desert's Ancient People Step Cautiously Towards Today'. *The Age*, 24 October.

Onus, Lin. 1988. 'On the Location of Aboriginal Art, its Promotion and Reception: Some Current Issues'. *Agenda* 1, no. 2: 29–30.

———. 1989a. 'Copyright and Issues of Appropriation'. *Artlink* 10, nos. 1 & 2: 38–39.

———. 1989b. 'A Clockwise Stroll through Australia'. *Tension*, no. 17: 38.

———. 1993. 'Southwest, Southeast Australia and Tasmania'. In *Aratjara: Art of the First Australians: Traditional and Contemporary Works by Aboriginal and Torres Strait Islander Artists*, edited by Bernhard Lüthi and Gary Lee, 289–96. Dusseldorf and Cologne: Kunstsammlung Nordrhein-Westfalen & DuMont Buchverlag.

———. 2003 [1990]. 'Language and Lasers'. In *Blacklines: Contemporary Critical Writings by Indigenous Australians*, edited by Michele Grossman, 92–96. Carlton, VIC: Melbourne University Press.

O'Riordan, Maurice. 2009. 'Telstra Blues'. *Art Monthly*, no. 224: 30–32.

ORIC. 2012. At the Heart of Art, edited by Office of the Registrar of Indigenous Corporations. Canberra: ORIC. Online: http://www.oric.gov.au/sites/default/files/documents/06_2013/11_0327_Corp_Visual_Arts_Sector_v3–3.pdf (accessed January 19 2015).

Owen, Will. 2007a. '"It's not Really Your Art Centre": Life Today in Ltyentye Apurte.' *Aboriginal Art & Culture: An American Eye*, 9 September. Online: http://aboriginalartandculture.wordpress.com/2007/09/09/its-not-really-your-art-centre-life-today-in-ltyentye-apurte/ (accessed 4 May 2008).

———. 2007b. 'Bad Aboriginal Art Criticism'. *Aboriginal Art & Culture: An American Eye*. Online: http://aboriginalartandculture.wordpress.com/2007/09/29/bad-aboriginal-art-criticism/ (accessed 28 January).

Pagé, Susan. 1983. 'Introduction'. In *D'un Autre Continent: l'Australie la Rêve et le Réel*, 10–15. Paris: Association Francaise d'Action Artistique & Ministère des Relations Extérieures.

Pascoe, Bruce. 2014. *Dark Emu*. Broome, Western Australia Magabala Books.

Paine, Robert. 1985. 'Ethnodrama and the 'Fourth World': The Saami Action Group in Norway, 1979–1981.' In *Indigenous Peoples and the Nation-State: 'Fourth World' Politics in Canada, Australia and Norway*, edited by Noel Dyck, 190–235. Newfoundland, Canada: Institute of Social and Economic Research, Memorial University of Newfoundland.

Pearson, Noel. 2007. 'White Guilt, Victimhood and the Quest for a Radical Centre' *Griffith Review* no. 16, Winter: 11–58.

Peatling, Stephanie, and Joel Gibson. 2007. 'Aboriginal Art Under Threat'. *Sydney Morning Herald*, September 17. Online: http://www.smh.com.au/news/national/aboriginal-art-under-threat/2007/09/16/1189881342944.html (accessed 25 September 2008).

———. 1997. 'Fluent'. In *Fluent: Emily Kame Kngwarreye, Yvonne Koolmatrie, Judy Watson: XLVII esposizione internazionale d'arte La Biennale di Venezia 1997*. 11–20. Sydney: Art Gallery of New South Wales.

———. 2007. 'Richard Bell.' In *Culture Warriors: National Indigenous Art Triennial*, 60. Canberra, ACT.: National Gallery of Australia. Perkins, Hetti, and Hannah Fink. 1997. 'Editorial'. *Art & Australia* 35, no. 1: 60–63.

Perkins, Hetti, and Hannah Fink, eds. 2000. *Papunya Tula: Genesis and Genius*. Sydney: Art Gallery of New South Wales in association with Papunya Tula artists.

Perkins, Hetti, and Victoria Lynn. 1993. 'Blak Artists, Cultural Activists'. In *Australian Perspecta 1993*, edited by Victoria Lynn, x–xii. Sydney: Art Gallery of NSW.

Perkins, Hetti, and Warwick Thornton. 2010. *Art + Soul* Collingwood, VIC: Madman Entertainment.

Perry, Grayson. 2007. 'Aboriginal Art: Worthy but Uninspiring'. *The Times*, 19 September. Online: http://entertainment.timesonline.co.uk/tol/arts_and_entertainment/visual_arts/article2482234.ece (accessed 15 January 2008).

Peterson, Nicolas. 1983. 'Aboriginal Arts and Crafts Pty Ltd: A Brief History'. In *Aboriginal Arts and Crafts and the Market*, edited by Peter Loveday and Peter Cooke, 60–65. Darwin: The Australian National University North Australia Research Unit.

———. 1993. 'Demand Sharing: Reciprocity and the Pressure for Generosity among Foragers'. *American Anthropologist* 95, no. 4: 860–74.

Petitjean, Georges. 2000. '"Where is the Story?": Paradoxes in Western Desert Art'. PhD diss., La Trobe University.

———. 2008. 'The AAMU in Utrecht'. *Museum Aktuell* no. 294: 13–15.

Phillips, A. A. 1980 [1958]. *The Australian Tradition*. Melbourne: Longman Cheshire.

Philp, Angela. 2007. 'Life and Art? Relocating Aboriginal Art and Culture in the Museum'. *reCollections: Journal of the National Museum of Australia* 2, no. 1: 48–70.

Phipps, Jennifer. 1984. 'Entre Deux Mondes'. *The Age Monthly Review* 3, no. 9: 11–13.

Pilger, John. 1985. *The Secret Country.* Video recording. Great Britain: Central Independent Television (production company).

Plunkett, Ian. 2007. *Submission to Senate Committee Inquiry into Australia's Indigenous Visual Arts and Craft Sector.* Canberra: Parliament of Australia. Online: http://www.aph. gov.au/Parliamentary_Business/Committees/Senate_Committees?url=ecita_ctte/ completed_inquiries/2004–07/indigenous_arts/submissions/sub21.pdf. (accessed 25 June 2012).

Povinelli, Elizabeth A. 2002. *The Cunning of Recognition: Indigenous Alterities and the Making of Australian Multiculturalism.* Durham & London: Duke University Press.

Powerhouse Museum. 2010. 'Swimwear Designed and Made by Speedo, 1988'. Online: http://from.ph/371869 (accessed 5 July 2012).

———. 2012a. 'Discover … Australia', poster by Eileen Mayo. Online: http://from. ph/102595 (accessed 12 June 2012).

———. 2012b. 'Corroboree Australia', poster by Gert Sellheim. Online: http://from. ph/161490 (accessed 12 June 2012).

———. 2012c. 'Australia', poster by Gert Sellheim. Online: http://from.ph/8683 (accessed 12 June 2012).

Preston, Margaret. 1930. 'Away with Poker-worked Kookaburras and Gum Leaves.' *Sunday Pictorial.* 6 April.

Preston, Margaret, and Elizabeth Butel. 2003. *Art and Australia: Selected Writings 1920–1950/ Margaret Preston.* North Sydney: Richmond Ventures.

Price, Bess. 2011. 'Bess Price: Welcome to My World' ABC Radio National *Background Briefing* (transcript), 1 May 2011. Online: http://www.abc.net.au/radionational/ programs/backgroundbriefing/bess-price-welcome-to-my-world/2949706#transcript (accessed 3 August 2013).

Price, Sally. 1989. *Primitive Art in Civilised Places.* Chicago: University of Chicago Press.

Qantas 2012. *Flying Art.* Online: http://www.qantas.com.au/travel/airlines/aircraft- designs/global/en (accessed 5 July 2012).

Queensland Art Gallery. 1990. *Balance: Views, Visions, Influences.* South Brisbane, Qld: Queensland Art Gallery.

Radok, Stephanie (ed). 2012. *Roads Cross: Contemporary Directions in Australian Art.* Adelaide: South Australia Flinders University Art Museum.

Read, Herbert. 1954. 'Introduction'. In *Australia: Aboriginal Paintings, Arnhem Land,* edited by Herbert Read, UNESCO, & New York Graphic Society. New York: New York Graphic Society by arrangement with UNESCO.

———. 1957. Review of *Records of the American-Australian Scientific Expedition to Arnhem Land: Art Myth and Symbolism,* by Charles P. Mountford. *The Burlington Magazine* 99, no. 655: 351.

Read, Herbert, UNESCO and the New York Graphic Society (eds). 1954 *Australia: Aboriginal Paintings, Arnhem Land* New York: New York Graphic Society by arrangement with UNESCO.

Register of Australian Archives and Manuscripts). 2002. 'Summary: Records of Apmira: Artists for Aboriginal Land Rights'. Online: http://trove.nla.gov.au/work/32065177 (accessed 14 March 2014).

Reynolds, Amanda, ed. 2006. *Keeping Culture: Aboriginal Tasmania.* Canberra: National Museum of Australia Press.

Reynolds, Henry. 1982. *The Other Side of the Frontier: Aboriginal Resistance to the European Invasion of Australia*. Ringwood, VIC: Penguin.

———. 1998. *This Whispering in Our Hearts*. St. Leonards, NSW: Allen & Unwin.

———. 1999. *Why Weren't We Told?: A Personal Search for the Truth About our History*. Ringwood, VIC: Viking.

Rinke, Klaus. 1983. 'Pre-Embryonic Memories'. In *D'un Autre Continent: L'Australie la Rêve et le Réel*, 81–83. Paris: Association Francaise d'Action Artistique & Ministère des Relations Extérieures.

Riphagen, Marianne. 2008. 'Black on White: or Varying Shades of Grey? Indigenous Australian Photomedia Artists and the "Making of" Aboriginality'. *Australian Aboriginal Studies*, no. 1: 78–89.

Roberts, Rhoda. 2011. *Perspectives with Rhoda Roberts*. Online: http://artsnorthernrivers.com.au/pages/news-features?page=3 (accessed 25 November 2012).

Rose, Deborah B. 1996. *Nourishing Terrains: Aboriginal Views of Landscape and Wilderness*. Canberra: Australian Heritage Commission.

Rothwell, Nicolas. 1996. 'Whose Culture Is It Anyway?' *The Weekend Australian [Weekend Review]*, 30–31 March.

2006a. 'Scams in the Desert'. *The Weekend Australian*, 4–5 March.

———. 2006b. 'How the West Was Won Over'. *The Australian*, 19 January.

Roughsey, Dick. 1976. 'The Aboriginal Arts Board'. *Art and Australia* 13, no. 3: 235–39.

Rowe, David and Deborah Stevenson. 2006. 'Sydney 2000: Sociality and Spatiality in Global Mega Events.' In *National Identity and Global Sporting Events: Culture, Politics, and Spectacle in the Olympics and the Football World Cup*, edited by Alan Tomlinson and Christopher Young. Albany: State University of New York Press.

Rowse, Tim. 1985. *Arguing the Arts*. Ringwood, VIC: Penguin Books.

———. 2000a. 'Aboriginal and Torres Strait Islander Arts Board'. In *The Oxford Companion to Aboriginal Art and Culture*, edited by Sylvia Kleinert and Margo Neal, 516–17. Melbourne: Oxford University Press.

———. 2000b. *Obliged to be Difficult – Nugget Coombs' Legacy in Indigenous Affairs*. Cambridge: Cambridge University Press.

———. 2001. 'The Arts Advocacy of H. C. Coombs'. In *Culture in Australia: Policies, Publics and Programs*, edited by Tony Bennett and David J. Carter, 114–34. Cambridge: Cambridge University Press.

———. 2002. *Indigenous Futures: Choice and Development for Aboriginal and Islander Australia*. Sydney: UNSW Press.

———. 2012. *Rethinking Social Justice: From 'Peoples' to 'Populations'*. Canberra: Aboriginal Studies Press.

———. 2014. 'Indigenous Heterogeneity'. *Australian Historical Studies* 45, no. 3: 297–310.

Russell, Lynette. 2001. *Savage Imaginings*. Melbourne: Australian Scholarly Publishing Pty Ltd.

Ryan, Bill. 1992. *Making Capital from Culture: The Corporate Form of Capitalist Cultural Production*. Berlin, New York: Walter de Gruyter.

Ryan, Judith. 2004. 'The Quick and the Dead: Purchasing Indigenous Art 1988–1990'. *Art Bulletin Victoria*, no. 44: 71–81.

———. 2005. 'Gabrielle Pizzi'. *Art & Australia* 42, no. 4: 507.

———. 2006. 'Of Paint and Possession'. *The Australian*, 7 February.

———. 2008. 'Shock of the Ancient Made New'. In *Beyond Sacred: Recent Paintings from Australia's Remote Aboriginal Communities*, edited by Colin Laverty and Elizabeth Laverty, Prahran, VIC: Hardie Grant Books.

————. 2010. '"The Raw and the Cooked": What Makes Aboriginal Art so "Deadly"' in *Remembering Forward*, edited by Kasper König, Emily Joyce Evans and Falk Wolf, 126–135. London: Paul Holberton Publishing; Cologne: Museum Ludwig.

Ryan, Lyndall. 2011 [1976]. 'Trugernanner (Truganini) (1812–1876)'. *Australian Dictionary of Biography*. National Centre of Biography, Australian National University. Online: http://adb.anu.edu.au/biography/trugernanner-truganini-4752/text7895 (accessed 2 June 2011).

Ryan, Mark D., Michael Keane and Stuart D. Cunningham. 2005. 'From Remote "outback" Beginnings to Cultural Export Phenomenon: A Case Study of Finance and the Internationalisation of Indigenous Australian Visual Art'. In *Information Society or Knowledge Societies? UNESCO in the Smart State*, edited by Rhonda Briet and Jan Servaes, 93–110. Penang, Malaysia: Southbound.

Ryan, Mark D., Michael Keane and Stuart D. Cunningham. 2008. 'Australian Indigenous Art: Local Dreamings, Global Consumption'. In *Cultures and Globalisation: The Cultural Economy*, edited by Helmut Anheier and Yudhishthir Raj Isar, 284–91. Los Angeles and London: Sage Publications.

Sanders, William. 2002. 'Towards an Indigenous Order of Australian Government: Rethinking Self-Determination as Indigenous Affairs Policy'. Discussion Paper no. 230. Centre for Aboriginal Economic Policy Research, The Australian National University. Online: http://caepr.anu.edu.au/sites/default/files/Publications/DP/2002_DP230.pdf (accessed 9 December 2008).

Sarah, P. 1989. 'Introduction'. In *A Year in the Arts: Australia's Bicentennial Arts Program 1988*, edited by Sarah Overton, 6–7. Sydney: Australian Bicentennial Authority.

Schmidt, Chrischona. 2011. 'The Development of the Utopia Art Movement through the Lens of Relationships between Artists and the Art World.' In *Global Studies. Mapping Contemporary Art and Culture*, edited by Hans Belting, Jacob Birken, Andrea Buddensieg and Peter Weibel. Hatje Cantz Verlag, Ostfildern: Global Art and the Museum. Online: http://www.globalartmuseum.de/site/guest_author/299 (accessed 20 March 2013).

Schwartz, L. 1989. 'Dots for Dollars'. *The Age*, 26 November.

Senate Standing Committee on Environment, Communications, Information Technology and the Arts. 2007. 'Indigenous Art – Securing the Future: Australia's Indigenous Visual Arts and Crafts Sector'. Government Report. Canberra: Standing Committee on Environment, Communications, Information Technology and the Arts.

Shalom College. 2012. 'Shalom Gamarada Ngiyani Yana'. Online: https://www.shalomgamarada.org/ (accessed 25 November 2013).

Shelley, Percy Bysshe and Mary Wollstonecraft Shelley. 1904. *A Defence of Poetry*. Indianapolis: The Bobbs-Merrill company.

Shiner, Larry. 1994. '"Primitive Fakes", "Tourist Art" and the Ideology of Authenticity'. *The Journal of Aesthetics and Art Criticism* 52, no. 2: 225–34.

————. 2001. *The Invention of Art*. Chicago: University of Chicago.

Short, Damien. 2008. *Reconciliation and Colonial Power: Indigenous Rights in Australia*. Aldershot: Ashgate.

Sisley, Alan. 1988. Foreword to *Metaphysical Graffiti – A Bicentennial Project 1983–1987: Works by Charles Cooper*. Hamilton, VIC: City of Hamilton Art Gallery.

Skerritt, Henry F. 2010. Geographic Cosmology: The Art of Lucy Ward. Craft Arts International, 78: 34–39. Online: http://henryfskerritt.com/2012/08/16/geographic-cosmology-the-art-of-lucy-ward/ (accessed 28 March 2015).

———. 2014a. 'No Boundaries: Aboriginal Australian Contemporary Art'. In *No Boundaries: Aboriginal Australian Contemporary Abstract Painting from the Debra and Dennis Scholl Collection*, edited by Henry F. with contributions by John Carty Skerritt, Edwina Circuitt, William L. Fox, Stephen Gilchrist, Jens Hoffmann, Darren Jorgensen, Emily McDaniel, Ian McLean, Fred R. Myers, Una Rey, Luke Scholes, Henry F. Skerritt, Quentin Spraque, 11–17. New York: DelMonico Books/Prestel.

———. 2014b. 'Is Art History Any Use to Aboriginal Artists? Gabriel Maralngurra's Contact Paintings'. In *Double Desire: Transculturation and Indigenous Contemporary Art*, edited by Ian McLean, 223–41. Newcastle upon Tyne: Cambridge Scholars Publishing.

Smee, Sebastian. 2006. 'Culture Shift'. *The Weekend Australian*, 11–12 March.

Smith, Bernard. 1971 [1962]. *Australian Painting 1788–1970*. Oxford University Press: London.

———. 1979 [1945]. *Place, Taste and Tradition*. Melbourne: Oxford University Press.

———. 1980. *The Spectre of Truganini*. Sydney: Australian Broadcasting Commission.

———. 1988 [1985]. 'On Cultural Convergence'. In *The Death of the Artist as Hero: Essays in History and Culture*, edited by Bernard Smith, 289–302, 310–11. Melbourne: Oxford University Press.

———. 2006. 'Creators and Catalysts: The Modernisation of Australian Indigenous Art'. *Australian Cultural History: Antipodean Modern* 25:11–25.

Smith, Marian W., ed. 1961. *The Artist in Tribal Society: Proceedings of a Symposium Held at the Royal Anthropological Institute*. London: Routledge & Kegan Paul.

Smith, Terry. 1969. 'First Thoughts on a "Style of the Sixties" in Recent Sydney Painting'. *Uphill* 1:n.p.

———. 1974. 'The Provincialism Problem'. *Art Forum* 13, no. 1: 54–59.

———. 1988. 'Provincialism Refigured'. *Art Monthly*, no. 13: 4–6.

———. 2001. 'Public Art between Cultures: The "Aboriginal Memorial", Aboriginality, and Nationality in Australia'. *Critical Inquiry* 27, no. 4: 629–61.

———. 2002. *Transformations in Australian Art, Vol. 2: The Twentieth Century – Modernism and Aboriginality*. Sydney: Craftsman House.

Sorensen, Rosemary. 2006. 'Tell 'em They're Dreaming'. *The Courier-Mail*, 8 April.

Spencer, Baldwin, and Francis J. Gillen. 1899. *The Native Tribes of Central Australia*. London: Macmillan.

Spens, Michael. 1983. 'On the Beach, Beyond the Cringe'. *Studio International* 196, no. 1002: 6.

Spillman, Lyn. 1994. 'Imagining Community and Hoping for Recognition: Bicentennial Celebrations in 1976 and 1988'. *Qualitative Sociology* 17, no. 1: 3–28.

Spinifex Arts Project. 1999. *Pila Nguru: Art and Song from the Spinifex People*. Semaphore, South Australia: Spinifex Arts Project.

Spraque, Quentin. 2014. *The World Is Not a Foreign Land*. Melbourne, VIC: Ian Potter Museum of Art.

Stacey, Wesley. 1983. 'Wesley Stacey'. In *D'un Autre Continent: l'Australie la Rêve et le Réel*, 151–54. Paris: Association Francaise d'Action Artistique & Ministere des Relations Extérieures.

Stallabrass, Julian. 1999. *High Art Lite: British Art in the 1990s*. London: Verso.

Stanner, William E. H. 1968. *After the Dreaming*. Sydney: The Australian Broadcasting Commission.

——— Stanner, William E. H. 2009. *The Dreaming and other essays* [introduced by Robert Manne]. Melbourne: Black Inc. Agenda.

Stephen, Ann. 1984. 'A 'Roo Begging for funds?'. *Art Network*, no. 12: 28–29.

———. 2006. 'Early Inroads: MoMA and Australia'. *Art and Australia* 43, no. 4: 582–85.

Stevenson, Deborah. 2000. *Art and Organisation*. St Lucia: University of Queensland Press.

Sullivan, Nancy. 1995. 'Inside Trading: Postmodernism and the Social Drama of *Sunflowers* in the 1980s Art World'. In *The Traffic in Culture: Refiguring Art and Anthropology*, edited by George E. Marcus and Fred R. Myers, 256–301. Berkeley: University of California Press.

Sutton, Peter, ed. 1988. *Dreamings: The Art of Aboriginal Australia*. Ringwood, VIC: Viking in association with Asia Society Galleries, New York.

Sutton, Peter. 1989. 'Anchorites on the Loose? Anthropology in the Australian Art World'. *Agenda*, December: 20–21.

———. 1990. 'Dreamings: The Story Thus Far'. *Bulletin of the Conference of Museum Anthropologists* 123: 176–78.

———. 1992a. 'Reading "Aboriginal Art"'. *Australian Cultural History*, no. 11: 28–38.

———. 1992b. 'Aboriginal Art, the Nation State, Suburbia. *Artlink* 12, no. 3: 6–9.

———. 2005. 'Rage, Reason and the Honourable Cause: A Reply to Cowlishaw'. *Australian Aboriginal Studies* 2005, no. 2: 35–43.

———. 2009. *The Politics of Suffering: Indigenous Australia and the End of the Liberal Consensus*. Melbourne: Melbourne University Press.

Symonds, Michael. 1997. 'Beyond Exile: Theodor Adorno and the Question of Home'. *Communal/Plural* 5:131–44.

———. 2015. *Max Weber's Theory of Modernity*. Farnham: Ashgate Publishing.

Sykes, Bobbi. 1984. 'Introduction'. In *Koori Art '84*, edited by Vivien Johnson, n.p. Surry Hills, NSW: Artspace.

Taçon, Paul S. C., and Susan M. Davies. 2004. 'Transitional Traditions: "Port Essington" Bark-Paintings and the European Discovery of Aboriginal Aesthetics'. *Australian Aboriginal Studies*, no. 2: 72–86.

Tasmanian School of Art Gallery. 1981. *Landscapes (Some interpretations)*. Exhibition text. Hobart: Tasmanian School of Art.

Taylor, Luke. 1996a. 'Making Painting Pay'. *Meanjin* 55, no. 4: 744–53.

———. 1996b. *Seeing the Inside: Bark Painting in Western Arnhem Land*. Oxford: Clarendon Press.

———. 2005. 'John Mawurndjul – "I've got a different idea"'. In *Rarrk John Mawurndjul: Journey Through Time in Northern Australia*, edited by Christian Kaufmann, and Museum Tinguely, 42–48. Belair, South Australia: Crawford House Publishing.

Taylor, Paul. 1982. 'Special Section: Antipodality'. *Art & Text*, no. 6: 49–50.

———. 1983. 'Popism: The Art of White Aborigines'. *On the Beach* 1: 30–32.

Taylor, Paul, ed. 1984a. *Anything Goes: Art in Australia 1970–1980*. Melbourne, VIC: Art & Text.

Taylor, Paul. 1984b [1981]. 'Australian New Wave and the "Second Degree"'. In *Anything Goes: Art in Australia 1970–1980*, edited by Paul Taylor, 158–67. Melbourne, VIC: Art & Text.

———. 1989. 'Primitive Dreams are Hitting the Big Time'. *The New York Times*, 21 May. Online: http://www.nytimes.com/1989/05/21/arts/art-primitive-dreams-are-hitting-the-big-time.html (accessed 25 October 2011).

The Advertiser. 1989 'Hayden Sparks Mock Horror at Gallery'. *The Advertiser*, May 23.

Thomas, Daniel. 1976. 'Aboriginal Art as Art'. *Art and Australia* 13, no. 3: 281–82.

———. 1988. 'The Margins Strike Back: Australian Art since the Sixties'. *Art and Australia* 26, no. 1: 60–71.

———. 1992. 'The Hermannsburg Watercolourists: The View from the Art Museum'. In *The Heritage of Namatjira*, edited by Jane Hardy, John V. S. Megaw and M. Ruth Megaw, 201–15. Port Melbourne, VIC: William Heinemann Australia.

———. 2011. 'Aboriginal Art: Who Was Interested?' *Journal of Art Historiography*, no. 4: 1–10. Online: http://arthistoriography.files.wordpress.com/2011/05/daniel-thomas-document.pdf (accessed 4 January 2013).

Thomas, H., and J. Baily. 1973. 'The Role of Exhibitions in the Development of Arts'. Paper presented at the National Seminar on Aboriginal Arts in Australia, Canberra, ACT, 21–25 May.

Thomas, Nicholas. 1995. 'Art against Primitivism: Richard Bell's Post-Aryanism'. *Anthropology Today* 11, no. 5: 15–17.

———. 1999. *Possessions: Indigenous Art/Colonial Culture*. London: Thames & Hudson.

Thompson, Liz, comp. 1990. *Aboriginal Voices: Contemporary Aboriginal Artists, Writers and Performers*. Brookvale, NSW: Simon & Schuster Australia.

Thompson, Patricia. 1972. 'The Northern Territory Story: A New Direction for Aboriginal Craftsmen'. *Craft Australia* 2, no. 1: 4–7.

Throsby, David. 1997. 'But Is It Art?' *Art Monthly*, no. 2: 32.

———. 2010. *The Economics of Cultural Policy*. Cambridge: Cambridge University Press.

Tickner, Robert. 2001. *Taking a Stand: Land Rights to Reconciliation*. Crows Nest, NSW: Allen & Unwin.

Tillers, Imants. 1982. 'Locality Fails'. *Art & Text*, no. 6: 51–60.

———. 1983. 'Fear of Texture'. *Art & Text*, no. 10: 8–18.

———. 1986. 'Imants Tillers'. In *Origins Originality + Beyond – the Sixth Biennale of Sydney*, edited by Biennale of Sydney, 270. Sydney: The Biennale of Sydney Limited.

Toohey, Paul. 2008. *Last Drinks: The Impact of the Northern Territory Intervention*. Quarterly Essay, Melbourne: Black Inc.

Torgovnick, Marianna. 1990. *Gone Primitive: Savage Intellects, Modern Lives*. Chicago: University of Chicago Press.

Tranby Aboriginal College. 1984. 'Letter to the Editor'. *Art Network* 13:6.

Tuckson, Tony. 1964. 'Aboriginal Art and the Western World'. In *Australian Aboriginal Art*, edited by Ronald Berndt, 60–68. Sydney: Ure Smith.

Turner, Graeme. 2001. 'Reshaping Australian Institutions: Popular Culture, the Market and the Public Sphere'. In *Reshaping Australian Institutions: Popular Culture, the Market and the Public Sphere*, edited by Tony Bennett, and David Carter, 161–75. Cambridge: Cambridge University Press.

Van den Bosch, Annette. 1985. 'Ten Years on: The Provincialism Problem'. *Art Monthly (London)* 1, no. 86: 9–13.

Van den Bosch, Annette. 2005. *The Australian Art World: Aesthetics in a Global Market*. Crows Nest, Sydney: Allen & Unwin.

Velthuis, Olav. 2005. *Talking Prices*. Princeton, NJ: Princeton University Press.

Von Sturmer, John v. 1989. 'Aborigines, Representation, Necrophilia'. *Art & Text*, no. 32: 127–39.

———. 2006. 'A Set of Exchanges'. *Machine* 2, no. 4: 6–8.

Warakurna Artists. 2006. *Submission to Senate Committee Inquiry into Australia's Indigenous Visual Arts and Craft Sector*. Canberra: Parliament of Australia. Online: Online: http://www.aph.gov.au/senate/committee/ecita_ctte/completed_inquiries/2004–07/indigenous_arts/submissions/sub73.pdf.

Ward, P. 1987. 'The Michelangelo of Arnhem Land'. *The Weekend Australian*, 12–13 September.

Waterlow, Nick. 1983. 'A Tale of Two Cities Rewritten'. *Studio International* 196, no. 1002: 8–11.

———. 1986. 'Director's Introduction: Origins Originality + Beyond.' In *Origins Originality + Beyond: 16 May–6 July 1986, Art Gallery of New South Wales, Art Gallery Road, Sydney, PIER 2/3 Walsh Bay, Sydney*, edited by Biennale of Sydney, 11–15. Sydney: Sixth Biennale of Sydney, 1986.

———. 1988. 'A View of World Art c. 1940–88.' In *1988 Australian Biennale: From the Southern Cross: A View of World Art c. 1940–88*, edited by Biennale of Sydney, 9–17. Sydney: The Biennale of Sydney and Australian Broadcasting Corporation.

Webb, Jen. 2002. 'Negotiating Alterity: Indigenous and "Outsider" Art'. *Third Text* 16, no. 2: 137–52.

Wells, Kathryn. 1996. 'The Cosmic Irony of Intellectual Property and Indigenous Authenticity'. *Culture and Policy* 7, no. 3: 45–68.

Whitlam, Gough. 1972. 'It's Time for Leadership: Australian Labor Party Policy Speech' Delivered at Blacktown Civic Centre, 13 November 1972. *Treasures from the Collection*, Whitlam Institute (online), http://whitlam.org/gough_whitlam/Treasures_from_the_Collection (accessed 8 June 2015).

———. 1973. 'Speech by the Prime Minister Mr E. G. Whitlam at the Opening of a National Seminar on Aboriginal Arts'. Canberra: Conference Papers, edited by Aboriginal Arts Board, Australian Council for the Arts.

Williams, Raymond. 1958. *Culture and Society 1780–1950*. London: Chatto & Windus.

———. 1977. *Marxism and Literature*. Oxford: Oxford University Press.

———. 1988 [1983] *Keywords*. 2nd ed. London: Fontana Press.

Williamson, Clare, and Hetti Perkins, curators. 1994. *Blakness: Blak City Culture*. South Yarra, VIC: Australian Centre for Contemporary Art.

Williamson, Clare, and Tracey Moffatt. 1992. 'Exchange of Faxes'. *Eyeline*, no. 20: 6–8.

Willis, Ann-Marie, and Tony Fry. 1988. 'Ethnocentricism, Art and the Culture of Domination'. *Praxis M,* no. 20: 16–22.

———. 1989a. 'Art as Ethnocide: The Case of Australia'. *Third Text*, no. 5: 3–20.

———. 1989b. 'Aboriginal Art: Symptom or Success?' *Art in America* 77, no. 7: 108–116, 159–160, 163.

———. 1989c. 'Not What You'd Call a Good Paint Job'. *Artlink* 9, no. 3: 48–49.

———. 2011. 'Looking Back'. In *How Aborigines Invented the Idea of Contemporary Art*, edited by Ian McLean, 286–87. Brisbane, Sydney: Institute of Modern Art & Power Publications.

Wilson, Ashleigh. 2011. 'Law Paints Indigenous Art into a Corner'. *The Australian*, 16 April. Online: http://www.theaustralian.com.au/national-affairs/law-paints-indigenous-art-into-a-corner/story-fn59niix-1226039970594

Wilson, Ashleigh, and Corrie Perkin. 2008. 'Boycotting of Indigenous Art Award Attacked'. *The Australian*, 16 July. Online: http://www.theaustralian.com.au/news/boycotting-of-art-award-attacked/story-e6frg6po-1111116925846 (accessed 29 June 2012).

Winter, Joan G. 2002. *Native Title Business: Contemporary Indigenous Art: A National Travelling Exhibition*. Southport, Qld: Keeaira Press.

Wise, Tigger. 1996. 'Elkin, Adolphus Peter (1891–1979)'. *Australian Dictionary of Biography*. National Centre of Biography, Australian National University. Online: http://adb.anu.edu.au/biography/elkin-adolphus-peter-10109/text17845 (accessed 7 November 2013).

Wolff, Janet. 1981. *The Social Production of Art*. New York: St. Martin's Press.

————. 1983. *Aesthetics and the Sociology of Art*. London: Allen & Unwin.

————. 2008. *The Aesthetics of Uncertainty*. New York: Columbia University Press.

Woodhead, Alice and Tim Acker. 2014. 'Sideways Story: Aboriginal and Torres Strait Islander Community Art Production and Markets [Special issue: Red dirt research in remote Australia]. *Journal of Australian Indigenous Issues* 17, no. 4: 108–30.

Wright, Felicity. 1999. *The Art and Craft Centre Story. Volume 1 Report: A Survey of Thirty-nine Aboriginal Community Art and Craft Centres in Remote Australia, Undertaken by Desart Inc.* Woden, ACT: Aboriginal & Torres Strait Islander Commission.

————. 2000a. *The Art & Craft Centre Story, Volume 3: Good Stories from out Bush: Examples of Best Practice from Aboriginal Art and Craft Centres in Remote Australia*. Canberra: Aboriginal and Torres Strait Islander Commission.

————. 2000b. 'Summary: Making Art, Being Strong'. In *The Art and Craft Centre Story: Vol II Summary and Recommendations*, edited by Felicity Wright and Frances Morphy, 15–44. Canberra: ATSIC.

————. 2006. *SICAD Project – Submission to Senate Committee Inquiry into Australia's Indigenous Visual Arts and Craft Sector*. Canberra: Parliament of Australia. Online: http://www.aph.gov.au/Senate/committee/ecita_ctte/completed_inquiries/2004–07/indigenous_arts/submissions/sub46.pdf. (accessed 29 November 2013).

————. 2011. 'A Complex Dance: Working in Indigenous Art Centres'. *Artlink* 31, no. 2: 134–37.

Wright, Felicity, Jon Altman and Frances Morphy. 2000. 'Recommendations'. In *The Art & Craft Centre Story, Volume 2: Summary and Recommendations*, edited by Felicity Wright and Frances Morphy, 103–116. Woden, ACT: Aboriginal and Torres Strait Islander Commission.

Yúdice, George. 2003. *The Expediency of Culture: Uses of Culture in the Global Era*. Durham, NC: Duke University Press.

Yunupingu, Galarrwuy. 1997. 'Indigenous Art in the Olympic Age'. *Art & Australia* 35, no: 1: 65–67.

Zeppel, Heather. 1998. 'Selling the Dreamtime: Aboriginal Cultural Tourism in Australia'. In *Tourism, Leisure, Sport: Critical Perspectives*, edited by David Rowe and Geoffrey Lawrence, 23–38. Sydney: Hodder Headline.

INDEX

Aboriginal agency/victimhood 10, 82,
  99–101, 136, 151–52, 171, 181, 193
  See also Aboriginal art market: ethical
    discourses, cultural trauma;
    exploitation of Aboriginal artists;
    inequality and disadvantage
Aboriginal and Torres Strait Islander
  Commission (ATSIC) 1, 41, 53, 61
  cultural policy 163, 182, 189, 198
  funding of art centres 42, 164, 198
Aboriginal art
  as conduit of understanding and respect
    64–66
  history of movement 5–8
  as vehicle for empowerment 67, 141,
    178–79, 183
  performative properties of 32, 39, 78, 83
Aboriginal Art Centres
  See Art Centres
Aboriginal art market 4, 50, 164
  altruism in 135–36, 174
  auction houses 133–34, 143, 146,
    195–97
  authenticity and provenance 142, 144,
    150, 159
  bifurcation of (fine art dealers/
    entrepreneurial dealers) 143–44,
    146–49
  charitable initiatives 136, 196
  ethical discourses 137, 141–43, 150–53,
    171
  growth of 47, 134, 140, 195–96
  moral values in 143, 149–50, 166, 169
  public sector acquisitions of Aboriginal
    art 50
  speculation and volatility 134–36, 150,
    170, 197
tourist market 95, 113, 133, 135, 144,
  148, 155, 158–60, 167, 169
  See also Art Centres; exploitation of
    Aboriginal artists
Aboriginal art practices 6–8, 20, 23, 37,
  53, 58, 118, 128–29, 132, 141, 153,
  160, 192, 196
  collective 32, 167, 196
  economic dimension of 41–46,
    147, 151, 159, 164, 167–68,
    171, 182
  in conflict with western art conventions
    146–47, 166–71, 181
  performance 32–33, 39, 78, 83
Aboriginal Arts Board 7, 20, 22–23, 35,
  38, 41–44, 61, 93–94, 100, 127, 141,
  157
Aboriginal culture
  art as positive formulation of, in public
    culture 64–68
  concept of cultural rights 61
  density of meaning in public culture
    63–64
  meaning of 57–58
  survival and recovery of 2, 23, 25, 55,
    63, 66, 131
  See also Aboriginal identity, heritage, land
Aboriginal difference 21–22, 58
  negotiated in Aboriginal art world
    98, 105–11, 122–124, 126–132,
    174
Aboriginal disadvantage
  See inequality and disadvantage
Aboriginal Enterprises (Melbourne) 158,
  188
Aboriginal heritage 20
Aboriginal identity

and historicity 19
and loss 60
collective or pan-Aboriginal sense of
     23–25, 31, 57, 95, 97, 100
explored by Aboriginal artists 38, 88,
     91, 159
formation 33, 195
heterogeneity of 23, 37, 106, 131
perceptions of 58, 67
representations of 29, 32, 34, 36–37,
     103, 107, 129, 151, 178, 193, 195
state recognition of 21, 47, 162
tensions around anthropological
     expertise about 127–28, 130, 195
See also self-determination, Aboriginal
     difference
Aboriginal material culture 65
     early collection and trade 6, 119
Aboriginal Memorial (artwork) 36, 96–97
Aboriginal Tent Embassy 24
Aboriginalia, market for 156, 167
Acker, Tim 45, 152
activism 2, 19, 23–24, 66, 94, 97–98, 188,
     193
     relationship of Aboriginal art to 33–35,
         38–39, 94–95, 128, 179
Adam, Leonard 195
aesthetic public sphere, Indigenous 38–39,
     108–09, 129, 131
aesthetics
     agonistic relationship between art and
         money 46, 145–46, 166
     ethnocentricism of western 10, 73,
         81–82, 94, 99, 125–26, 179
     fine arts principles 119, 128, 180
     fine arts principles, challenged by
         Aboriginal art 106, 110, 135, 137,
         143, 146, 149, 170
     formalism, brought to bear on
         Aboriginal art 131
     Kantian 123, 145–46, 170
     principle of autonomy 100, 121, 124,
         129, 145, 166, 171, 181
     universalist, brought to bear on
         Aboriginal art 122–24, 130
     See also Aboriginal art practices,
         primitivism, anthropology; art/
         anthropology binary

All Stock Must Go! (artwork) 133
Allas, Tess 34
Altman, Jon 3, 8, 42, 45, 47, 121, 141,
     159, 167
Andrew, Brook 193, 195
anthropology 4
     anthropologists promoting Aboriginal
         art 121
     anthropologists representing remote
         Aboriginal artists 110, 121, 130
     approach to art and material culture 118
     approach to meaning in Aboriginal art
         121–22
     'armchair' 194
     art/anthropology binary 117–18, 120,
         126–29, 181
     contestation of anthropological expertise
         on Aboriginal art 86, 109, 120, 127
     critique of, by Aboriginal artists 95,
         128–29
     disciplinary relationship between
         anthropology and art history 121–24
     emergence of ethical thought on
         Aboriginal social justice 65–66
     evolutionist perspective 65, 118–19, 194
     historic relationship with colonialism
         126–27
Apmira 88
appropriation of Aboriginal art
     by non-Indigenous artists and designers
         81, 83–85, 94, 159, 197
     commercial 157–58
     debates around 95, 99, 197
     symbolic, by the state 49, 52, 179
     'white aborigines' concept 87,
         100, 192
Aratjara, Art of the First Australians exhibition
     35, 127
Art Centres 13, 41–46, 61–62, 108–09,
     113–14, 132, 146–49, 168, 194, 197
     See also Aboriginal and Torres Strait
         Islander Commission (ATSIC)
     and community wellbeing 152, 178
     and cultural maintenance 61
     Art Centre vs. non-Art Centre
         Aboriginal art 142, 144, 151, 169
     emergence 7, 141
     funding 44–46

importance to Aboriginal fine arts
149–54
management of 8, 44
market strategies 43, 135
subject of 2007 Aboriginal Art sector
Inquiry discourses 139–44
vulnerability of 48, 139, 142, 148
Art from the Heart? (film) 150
Art of Place Awards 50–51
arts and cultural policy
and economic rationalism 161, 182
creative industries model 164, 182
Creative Nation (1994) 49, 161–62
cultural industries model 160–64
cultural industries model, impact on
Aboriginal art movement 137, 164,
181
cultural planning policies 47, 54, 163,
190
focus on Aboriginal culture 26
history and objectives of Aboriginal art
subsidy 41–46, 62, 66, 105, 162
in settler and post-conflict societies 16
purpose in western democratic societies
15
See also Aboriginal art: economic
dimensions of, Aboriginal Arts Board,
Aboriginal and Torres Strait Islander
Commission (ATSIC), Community
Development Employment Projects
(CDEP), art centres, Government
Company, labour, Reconciliation,
tourism
assimilation 4, 5, 6, 65, 71
decline of 18–22, 57, 108
post-assimilation era 6, 15, 80, 177, 185
resistance against 24, 81
restoration of Aboriginal culture after
59, 64
ATSIC *see* Aboriginal and Torres Strait
Islander Commission
Australia Council for the Arts 7, 20, 42, 53,
66, 75, 191
Australian art journals 75, 79, 85
Australian art world
transformation in 1970s and 1980s 4,
72–73, 75–76, 85, 97–101,
117, 191

Australian Bicentenary (1988) 23, 25–26,
34, 36, 49, 51, 83, 88, 96–97, 128,
158
Australian Broadcasting Corporation
(ABC) 150, 186–87
Australian Heritage Commission 50–51
Australian Institute of Aboriginal and Torres
Strait Islander Studies (AIATSIS) 19, 50
Australian Perspecta 75, 78, 94
authenticity 86, 105–06, 111–12, 120, 131,
167
in Aboriginal art market 113–16, 142

Balarinji Design Studio 52, 158, 198
Bardon, Geoffrey 6, 9, 113, 169, 198
bark painting 7
Bark Petition 31
Barunga Statement 32
Basel Contemporary Art Fair 119
Batterbee, Rex 6
Baume, Nicholas 87, 175
Bell, Richard 9, 38–39, 128, 158, 178, 193
Benjamin, Roger 82
Bennett, Gordon 95, 193, 195
Berndt, Catherine 121–24, 195
Berndt, Ronald 121–24, 195
Bennett, Tony 125
Biddle, Jennifer 33, 121, 132, 167
Boas, Franz 65
Boomalli Aboriginal Artists Co-operative
7, 34, 38
Bourdieu, Pierre 108–09, 111, 131, 146
Brophy, Philip 93
Browning, Daniel 38
Bueys, Joseph 78
Burn, Ian 71–72, 76, 85, 88, 96, 191
Butler, Rex 106, 176

Campfire Group 7, 38, 133
Carnegie, Margaret 173, 190
carpetbagger
See exploitation of Aboriginal artists,
Aboriginal art market
Carter, Paul 66
Carty, John 44, 46, 168
Chatwin, Bruce 96
children, removal of 1, 5, 18, 26, 59–60,
80, 187

civil society, Australian 2, 4, 15–16, 25, 27, 36, 52, 63–64, 68, 129, 165, 170, 187
Clifford, James 2, 64, 94
Closing the Gap policy 185, 189
colonisation 181
    as an incomplete project 55
    history of 5, 126–27, 129
Community Development Employment Projects (CDEP) 45–47
conceptual art 86–88, 120
Continuum exhibition 89
Coombs, H. C. ('Nugget' 20–21, 32, 64, 157, 186
Cooper, Charles 83
Cosic, Miriam 118
Council for Aboriginal Affairs 20–23, 32, 186
Council for Aboriginal Reconciliation *see* Reconciliation
Coutts-Smith, Kenneth 81, 94
Cowlishaw, Gillian 34, 58, 110, 193
Craik, Jennifer 161–62, 191
Croft, Brenda L. 34, 37, 110, 185, 195
cross-cultural exchange 64, 86, 96, 100, 103, 106, 115, 119, 131–32, 159, 168
    see also interculturality
cultural colonialism 81–83, 178, 192
cultural convergence 79–80, 191–92
cultural cringe 76–77, 90, 161, 191
cultural property rights, Aboriginal 157
cultural trauma 17–18, 57, 68
    and Aboriginal art 36
    and Aboriginal art discourses 33, 37, 80–81
    and Aboriginal culture 63
    and Aboriginal disadvantage 178
    and the stolen generations 60
    in Australian culture 18, 28, 49, 80
culture industry critique 181–82
Culture Warriors exhibition 62

D'un autre continent exhibition 89–93, 96, 98–99
Davila, Juan 93
deaths in custody 23, 25–26, 34, 59, 88, 186, 189
Derham, Frances 194
Desart 142
Dexter, Barrie 20, 22, 32
difference

see Aboriginal difference
disenchantment *see hope and disenchantment, discourses of*
Dixon, Chika 35, 44
Dodson, Mick 24, 177, 186
Dreamings exhibition (1988) 127, 192
Dreamings/the Dreaming 5, 7, 9, 44, 64, 87, 113–15, 132, 167, 185, 196
Dunn, Richard 92

Eccles, Jeremy 150, 193
Edwards, Bob (Robert) 23, 43, 190
Edwards, Deborah 124
Elkin, A. P. 65–66, 123, 194
ethical intent
    Aboriginal art movement as site of 10, 98, 100, 103, 180
    See also Aboriginal art market:altruism in ethical discourses, non-Indigenous citizens:goodwill, sympathy and remorse, inequality and disadvantage
ethnocide, concept of 81–83, 94, 178
exploitation of Aboriginal artists 83, 141, 143, 148, 150, 152, 166, 178

Fisher, Andrea 38
Foley, Fiona 34, 53, 95, 188, 195
Foley, Gary 35, 44, 94, 127
Foster, Hal 94
Frazer, James 119, 194
Freeman, Cathy 54
Freud, Sigmund 119, 194
frontier *see* colonial relations
Fry, Tony 82

Gell, Alfred 3, 109, 112, 120, 156, 165
Gibson, Lorraine 58–59, 62, 159
Gilbert, Kevin 97, 100
Gilchrist, Stephen 109
Gillen, Francis 126, 194
Gough Whitlam
    See also self-determination
Gough, Julie 20
Government Company (Aboriginal Arts and Crafts Pty Ltd) 42–44, 50, 66, 78, 119, 159, 188, 198
government welfare 7, 108, 136, 186
Grishin, Shasha 98

Hage, Ghassan 25, 55
Hall, Fiona 174
Hall, Ruth 175
Hansen, David 181
Hawke, Bob 161
Hayden, Bill 52, 62
Healy, Chris 25
Herder, Johann Gottfried 11
heritage
   Aboriginal 20, 61
   Aboriginal art symbolic of Aboriginal
      165
   Aboriginal people's rights to their 61,
      81, 95
   Aboriginal, in public culture 27, 49,
      53–54, 107
   Aboriginal, in relation to contemporary
      Indigenous identity and rights 19, 23
   amalgam of Aboriginal and
      Australian 19–20, 52–53, 62–63,
      66–67, 80, 187
   antiquity of Aboriginal 66, 114, 157,
      162
   Australian, problematised by Aboriginal
      71, 197
   in cultural policy 161
   management of Aboriginal land and 51,
      54, 59
   See also Art of Place Awards
Hesmondhalgh, David 161–62
high/low culture 156, 169 *see also* mass
   culture
Hinkson, Melinda 21, 107
History Wars 1, 27, 187
Hodges, Christopher 144
Hogarth Galleries 78
Holding, Clyde 66
Hookey, Gordon 37
hope and disenchantment, discourses of
   9–10, 100, 134, 141, 177–80
Howard, John
   government's dilution of Native Title
      141, 187
   government's repudiation of
      self-determination 185
   refusal to say 'sorry' to stolen
      generations 26
Hughes, Robert 126, 195

human rights *see* inequality and
   disadvantage; activism; land, land
   rights; United Nations Declaration of
   the Rights of Indigenous Peoples
Human Rights and Equal Opportunity
   Commission 61, 187

Indigenous affairs governance *see*
   Aboriginal and Torres Strait Islander
   Commission; Aboriginal Arts Board;
   Art Centres; arts and cultural policy;
   assimilation; Australian Heritage
   Commission; Closing the Gap
   policy; Community Development
   Employment Projects; Council for
   Aboriginal Affairs; Government
   Company; government welfare;
   Hawke, Bob; Human Rights and
   Equal Opportunity Commission;
   Keating, Paul; labour; land; Northern
   Territory National Emergency
   Response; protection policies;
   Reconciliation, self-determination;
   Whitlam, Gough
Indigenous/non-Indigenous relations 15,
   18, 29, 49
   See also Aboriginal identity; civil society;
   non-Indigenous citizens; racism
   and racial discrimination;
   Reconciliation
Inglis, David 125
inequality and disadvantage 2, 21, 68, 88,
   98, 105, 134, 136, 140–41, 152, 163,
   178–79, 189
Inquiry into Australia's Indigenous Visual
   Arts and Craft Sector (2007) 3, 137,
   139–42, 148–49, 152
interculturality 55, 59, 103 *see also*
   cross-cultural exchange
Iseger-Pilkington, Glenn 176

Jagamarra, Michael Nelson 84–85, 94, 97,
   100, 175
Johnson, Tim 35, 84, 95, 192
Johnson, Vivien 33, 78, 81, 88, 97, 119,
   159, 192
Jones, Lyndal 89
Jones, Paul 12

Jones, Philip 131, 159, 167
Jorgensen, Darren 175
Jules-Rosette, Bennetta 111

Kame Kngwarreye, Emily 8, 43, 106, 115, 135
Kantian aesthetics *see* aesthetics
Keating, Paul 26, 59, 61, 64, 66
    and cultural policy 161
    and Reconciliation 27–29
    Redfern address 50, 59, 187
Kennedy, Peter 89
Kleinert, Sylvia 96–97, 159
Knight, Beverly 114, 124
Koomatrie, Yvonne 8
Koori Art '84 (exhibition) 33, 192
Kowal, Emma 28
Kupka, Karel 195

labour, Aboriginal artistic 137, 166–68
    configured as Aboriginal employment
        44–45, 159, 170
    cultural specificity of 167
    described as slave labour 10, 136, 147,
        166, 178
land
    *Aboriginal Land Rights (Northern Territory)
        Act* 1976 32, 37, 186
    Aboriginal meanings brought into
        Australian cultural imagination 6, 54,
        64, 80–81, 98, 141
    Aboriginal custodianship, expressed in
        art 5, 9, 31–33, 51, 113, 115, 132,
        141, 153, 167
    Aboriginal people's relationship with 6,
        26, 60, 185
    custodianship, Aboriginal art as means
        to assert 7, 32–33, 113
    dispossession 1, 18, 27, 34, 37, 59,
        79–80, 97, 197
    homelands movement 186
    land rights 1, 20–21, 23, 25, 39, 71, 82,
        88, 97–98, 107, 121
    Mabo 26, 187
    native title 1, 26, 32, 108, 121, 141,
        187–88
    Native Title Act 1993 187
    Native Title Amendment Act 1998 187

non-Indigenous artists responding to
    Aboriginal meanings 83, 174
Wik 26, 187
landscape, in Australian art 83, 85, 98
Langton, Marcia 88, 131, 140, 178
Laverty, Colin 65, 115
Lévi Strauss, Claude 126, 195
Lovitt, Carolyn 65
Lyndon, Jane 19, 68, 156, 174
Lynn, Victoria 34

MacCannell, Dean 105, 111–12
Macha, Mary 44
Mackay, Machmud 66
Maddock, Bea 78
Magicians de la terre exhibition 192
Malangi, David 20, 157
Maloon, Terence 124
Marawili, Djambawa 174
Marika, Mawalan 157
Marika, Wandjuk 157
mass culture 161, 182
    See also appropriation; high/low culture;
        visual culture
mass culture, Aboriginal
    concept of 155–56
    history of 156–60, 163
    problematising Aboriginal fine arts
        164–66
Mawurndjul, John 118
Maza, Bob 35, 188
McCarthy, Frederick 65, 123, 194
McEvilley, Thomas 94
McLean, Ian 3, 35, 79, 100, 178
meaning
    conceptual interpretation of Aboriginal
        art 87
    fluidity of Aboriginal art's meanings
        2–3, 15, 113–15, 129, 173
    in Aboriginal art 33, 54, 87, 121, 126
    in Aboriginal art, influenced by public
        representations of Aboriginality 107,
        109, 131, 165, 182
    of Aboriginal art's "success" 47
    symbolic meanings of Aboriginal art
        in public culture 17, 22, 52–53, 103,
        109, 156, 164–65, 176, 179

See also Aboriginal art practices;
    appropriation of Aboriginal art; land;
    primitivism ; visual culture; utopian
    thought
Melbourne Olympic Games (1956) 157
Mellor, Danie 195
Mercer, Colin 189, 198
Merlan, Francesca 28, 97, 167
Michaels, Eric 86, 121, 167, 192
Miller, Daniel 12
mining interests 31, 107
    funding Aboriginal art 108
Missingham, Hal 190
missions 5–6, 19, 31
Mitchell, W. J. T. 156
modernity 12, 105–6, 125, 127
    disenchantment with 99, 125
    disenchantment with, Aboriginal art as
        reference point 13, 123, 174–76 *see
        also* primitivism
Moffatt, Tracey 193
Mollison, James 78
money *see* Aboriginal art market, inequality
    and disadvantage, labour
Moore, Richard 150
Moran, Anthony 28, 62
Morphy, Howard 3, 120–21, 168, 171
Morris, Meaghan 90
Morrissey, Phillip 136
Mountford, Charles 23, 123, 190, 194
multiculturalism, Australian 25, 72, 187
Mundine, Djon 36, 128, 193
Murphy, Bernice 78, 87, 94, 96, 119, 131
Myers, Fred 3, 17, 32, 43, 100, 113,
    120–22, 132, 171, 189

Namatjira, Albert 6, 96, 167–69
nationalism, Australian 19, 25, 52, 64, 68,
    72, 96, 165, 187
    and multiculturalism 187
    indigenised settler nationalism 28, 62
    of interwar years 157
    See also Australian Bicentenary
        redemption; Sydney Olympic Games;
        settler state; Whitlam, Gough:
        government's 'new nationalism'
Neale, Margo 34, 50, 127, 133
Ngurrara Canvas 33

Nicholls, Christine 121
Nicholls, Trevor 188
non-Indigenous citizens
    goodwill 57, 63, 180
    partial embrace of Aboriginal culture
        177
    questioning urban Aboriginal identity
        128, 130
    support of Indigenous social justice
        movements 23, 25, 88–89, 98
    sympathy and remorse 25, 27–28, 59,
        64, 67, 80, 103
    views on settler state condition 2, 10, 68,
        80, 100
    visiting outback 157
Noonkanbah 107
Noonuccal, Oodgeroo (Kath Walker) 35,
    188
Northern Territory National Emergency
    Response ('Intervention') 191

Onus, Bill 188
Onus, Lin 35, 101, 158, 188
optimism
    See utopian though; hope and
        disenchantment

Pagé, Suzanne 90
Papunya 6, 85, 169, 192
    boards, early 195–96
    painting movement 3, 43–44, 52, 84,
        146, 198
    painting movement, founding narrative
        of 169
    painting, auction house treatment 143,
        195–96
    painting, emergence as fine art 78
    painting, initially viewed as inauthentic
        120
    paintings, public and private collections
        78, 190
    viewed as dangerous place 110
Papunya Tjupi Art Centre 194
Papunya Tula Artists 6, 8, 194
Papunya Tula: Genesis and Genius exhibition
    169
Perkins, Hetti 7–8, 34, 37, 152
Peterson, Nicholas 91, 168

Petitjean, Georges 113
Pilger, John 36
Pizzi, Gabrielle 118–19
Povinelli, Elizabeth 58, 59, 177, 187
post-colonial critique 82, 93–96, 127–28, 131, 174–75
postmodernism 11, 72, 75, 86–88, 90, 163, 193
Preston, Margaret 71, 117, 123, 190, 194–95
primitivism 105, 118–19, 122, 129, 175
    and colonialism 12
    and the folkloric 12
    and the repudiation of Enlightenment thought 11
    as critique of western industrial capitalism 12–13
    critical debates about 93, 106
    historic relationship with western secularisation 125–26
    informing reception of Aboriginal art 82, 89, 92, 96, 99, 112–13, 123, 131
    popular forms 96
    Romantic perspective 11–13
    See also authenticity; modernity: disenchantment with
    settler, of interwar years 157
Primitivism in 20th Century Art: Affinity of the Tribal and the Modern exhibition 93
proppaNOW 38, 176
protection policies 5, 19, 59, 65
provincialism in Australian art 76–77, 85, 98, 191

Qantas, Aboriginal art commissions and branding 52, 158, 197

racism and racial discrimination 1, 18, 24, 37, 129, 141, 152
    addressed by Aboriginal artists 95
    Racial Discrimination Act 1975 186
Radford, Ron 117
Ramingining 36, 78
rapprochement 81, 100, 103
Read, Herbert 123, 190, 195, 198
recognition, politics of 1, 15–16, 37–39, 57–58, 97, 129–31, 177, 182, 187
    See also Aboriginal identity; civil society; cultural trauma; heritage; redemption: settler state; Reconciliation

Reconciliation 1, 18, 27–29, 49, 52, 57–59, 62, 67–68, 158, 163, 165, 174, 189
    and national cultural policy 161–64
    and national public culture 54, 162
    Council for Aboriginal Reconciliation 26–27, 29, 61, 189
    discourses 60–61
redemption
    settler state 15, 52, 55, 57, 62, 64, 67, 129, 164, 174, 177
Referendum (1967) 18–20
remote Aboriginal art 9, 103, 106, 108, 110, 129, 174
    See also Aboriginal art practices; Art Centres; urban/remote Aboriginal art
Rennie, Reko 39, 53
resale royalty legislation 136
Resale Royalty legislation 47
Reynolds, Henry 187
Richter, Gerard 78
Rinke, Klaus 91
Romanticism 10–11, 106, 125, 145
Rothwell, Nicolas 118, 124, 140–41
Roughsey, Dick 23
Rousseau, Jean-Jacques 11
Rowse, Tim 21, 47, 107–8, 189
Ryan, Judith 118

Said, Edward 94
Scarce, Yhonnie 195
Schmidt, Chrischona 168
self-determination 19, 32, 47, 185
    Aboriginal art's connection to 22, 43
    and Aboriginal identity 59, 177
    policy 6, 19, 22
Shelley, Percy 11
Shiner, Larry 119, 145, 170
Skeritt, Henry F. 132
Smith, Benjamin 107
Smith, Bernard 76, 79–80, 85, 88, 191, 195
Smith, Terry 76, 85, 96, 170
social justice
    See activism, inequality and disadvantage, land, racism, recognition
sociology 2, 137
Sotheby's
    See Aboriginal art market: auction houses

Spencer, Baldwin 126, 194
Spinifex Art Projects 32
Stacey, Wesley 88
Stallabrass, Julian 153, 163
Stanner, W. E. H. ("Bill") 20, 32, 185, 194
State of the Art publication and TV series (UK) 94
Stefanoff, Lisa 132
Stephen, Ann 96, 197
Stevenson, Deborah 161
Stubbs, Will 140
Sutton, Peter 22, 63, 121, 178, 182
Sydney Biennale 35, 75, 78, 84, 89, 92, 192
Sydney Olympic Games 54, 163
Sykes, Bobbi 34
symbolism
    See meaning

Taylor, Luke 121, 132
Taylor, Paul 86–87, 90, 94, 99, 192–93
The Secret Country (film) 25, 36
The Storylines Project 53
Thomas, Daniel 117
Thomas, Nicholas 3, 218, 220
Thomas, Rover 44
Throsby, David 119, 161
Tickner, Robert 52
Tillers, Imants 78, 80–81, 84–87, 89, 94–95, 99, 175, 178, 191–92
Tjampitjinpa, Kaapa Mbitjana 169
Tjapaltjarri, Clifford Possum 78, 169
Tjapaltjarri, Tim Leura 78, 169
tourism 6, 113, 157–58, 163, 165
    Aboriginal cultural tourism 53, 162–63, 182
    analogy of tourist/cosmopolitan to art consumer 111–13, 116, 130
    and modernity 105
    See also Aboriginal art market: tourist market
Truganini 191
Tuckson, Tony 122–23

Uluru 157
UNESCO 63, 190

United Nations Declaration of the Rights of Indigenous Peoples 190
urban Aboriginal art 9, 33–35
    warrior metaphors in 34
urban/remote Aboriginal art, contrast and tension between 9, 36–37, 97, 101, 106–9, 127–30, 158–59, 176–77, 182, 188, 193
Utopia Art Sydney (gallery) 197
Utopia community (art created in) 8, 43, 146
utopian thought
    expressed through art 180
    regarding Aboriginal art movement 10, 43, 141, 171, 179
    regarding condition of modernity 12–13
    See also hope and disenchantment

Venice Biennale 7
Vico, Giambattista 11
visual culture 156
    Aboriginal art and imagery in 68, 83, 103, 156–60, 165–66, 170, 178, 181, 192
    See also mass culture
Von Sturmer, John 95

Waterlow, Nick 78, 97
Watson, Judy 8, 53, 195
Watson, Tommy 196
welcome to country 190
Whitlam, Gough 52, 59, 61, 64, 141, 185–86
    government's 'new nationalism' 62
    government's arts initiatives 75, 191
    government's introduction of heritage legislation 51, 186
    government's 'new nationalism' 19, 62, 197
    launch of Aboriginal Arts Board 22
    on Aboriginal social justice 22, 190
Williams, Raymond 11, 58
Willis, Ann-Marie 82
Wolff, Janet 11, 72
Woodhead, Alice 45
Wordsworth, William 11

Yirrkala 31, 107, 140